T0375349

Managing Corporate Impacts

Managing Corporate Impacts draws on the insights and experiences of managers from around the world to examine how companies can manage corporate impacts to co-create enduring value for business and society. Corporate impacts—the points at which businesses create or destroy value with others—extend well beyond financial impacts to include the workplace, procurement and delivery of goods and services, and shaping perceptions held about corporate behavior. This book uses simple frameworks to demonstrate why and how today's corporations co-create enduring value with multiple stakeholders simultaneously. By introducing multiplier effects and spillover effects, the frameworks move the attention of management beyond direct impacts to examine indirect impacts that create or destroy value connected to the core of the business. By purposely connecting with stakeholders through information-sharing, and effectively managing myriad impacts along supply and distribution chains, companies are poised to provide solutions and co-create value.

JENNIFER J. GRIFFIN is Professor of Strategic Management and Public Policy at the George Washington University School of Business, and Director of the Global Strategies Program at the George Washington University's Institute for Corporate Responsibility. She teaches courses on business strategy and public policy, issues management, social impact, and strategic stakeholder management.

Business, Value Creation, and Society

Series editors

R. Edward Freeman, *University of Virginia*
Jeremy Moon, *Copenhagen Business School*
Mette Morsing, *Copenhagen Business School*

The purpose of this innovative series is to examine, from an international standpoint, the interaction of business and capitalism with society. In the twenty-first century it is more important than ever that business and capitalism come to be seen as social institutions that have a great impact on the welfare of human society around the world. Issues such as globalization, environmentalism, information technology, the triumph of liberalism, corporate governance, and business ethics all have the potential to have major effects on our current models of the corporation and the methods by which value is created, distributed and sustained among all stakeholders—customers, suppliers, employees, communities, and financiers.

Published titles:

Fort *Business, Integrity, and Peace*
Gomez and Korine *Entrepreneurs and Democracy*
Crane, Matten, and Moon *Corporations and Citizenship*
Painter-Morland *Business Ethics as Practice*
Yaziji and Doh *NGOs and Corporations*
Rivera *Business and Public Policy*
Sachs and Rühli *Stakeholders Matter*
Mansell *Capitalism, Corporations and the Social Contract*
Hemingway *Corporate Social Entrepreneurship*
Hartman *Virtue in Business*
De Bruin *Ethics and the Global Financial Crisis*

Forthcoming titles:

de Bakker and den Hond *Organizing for Corporate Social Responsibility*
Knudsen and Moon *Visible Hands* Slager *Responsible Investment*

Managing Corporate Impacts

Co-Creating Value

JENNIFER J. GRIFFIN
The George Washington University
School of Business

CAMBRIDGE
UNIVERSITY PRESS

CAMBRIDGE
UNIVERSITY PRESS

University Printing House, Cambridge CB2 8BS, United Kingdom

Cambridge University Press is part of the University of Cambridge.

It furthers the University's mission by disseminating knowledge in the pursuit of education, learning and research at the highest international levels of excellence.

www.cambridge.org
Information on this title: www.cambridge.org/9781107058675

© Jennifer J. Griffin 2016

First published 2016

A catalogue record for this publication is available from the British Library

Library of Congress Cataloguing in Publication data
Names: Griffin, Jennifer J., 1964–
Title: Managing corporate impacts : co-creating value / Jennifer J. Griffin.
Description: New York : Cambridge University Press, 2016. I
Series: Business, value creation, and society I
Includes bibliographical references and index.
Identifiers: LCCN 2015028158 I ISBN 9781107058675 (hardback)
Subjects: LCSH: Social responsibility of business. I Corporate governance. I Multiplier (Economics) I Value.
Classification: LCC HD60.G743 2016 I DDC 658.4/08–dc23
LC record available at http://lccn.loc.gov/2015028158

ISBN 978-1-107-05867-5 Hardback

Contents

Contents ix

Figures

Tables

Foreword

Professor Jennifer Griffin has written a very important book. She has put meat on the bones of the idea that businesses co-create value for and with their stakeholders. She has done this by paying detailed attention to the impacts of corporate and stakeholder actions, and has given us a roadmap for how to do research in the area that has come to be known as stakeholder theory.

Of particular note is her attention to how the interests of stakeholders cannot be considered one by one, since there is a jointness to their interests and their actions. Create value for employees and you will also affect customers, suppliers, etc. Finding the sweet spot of where the intersection of interests lie is the task for those executives who want to build a great company. By examining spillover and multiplier effects, Griffin makes such an 'interdependence principle' part of the basic apparatus of stakeholder theory. Future research simply cannot ignore these arguments.

Professor Griffin also addresses the idea that firms sometimes actually destroy value. She believes that if executives can become more cognizant and conscious of their actual impacts on stakeholders, then value destruction is more easily avoidable.

Griffin envisions a world where business is clearly seen as embedded in society, where business and other societal institutions can cooperate to accelerate the process of value co-creation. In such a world, we will need to go beyond looking at impacts, but we will need a pragmatic conception of ethics that takes the nuances of Griffin's approach into account.

With this book, Griffin establishes herself as one of the co-authors of a new narrative about business, seeing business as a set of value co-creating relationships among stakeholders. This new narrative is beginning to replace the old story of business as just about the physics of money and competition.

Indeed, setting forth this new narrative is one of the main purposes of this book series, *Business, Value Creation, and Society*, and Griffin's contribution advances our understanding of how business operates and must operate in the twenty-first century.

R. Edward Freeman
University Professor
University of Virginia
Charlottesville, Virginia, USA

Acknowledgments

To Bob, Nathan, Ed, and Lauren, each of whom in their own way always believed in this long-term project regardless of the multitudes of barriers, blockades, and excuses I perpetually constructed. To Peter and Roberto, both of you are, forever, my hope, inspiration, and travel buddies. The book is done—on to the next one! To all y'all: Vanessa, John, Andrew, Stephen, Stephen, Bruce, Donna, and Virginia who created the village and kept the ideas, the laughter, as well as the libations flowing with a special thanks to the Stakeholder Theory Working Group including Tom and Heather, Michael, Shawn, Kathy and Rob. To my dear friends from around the world especially Ffiona, Lauren, Cara, Jessi, Aseem, Chuck, Yoona, Smita, Johanne, Paul, Krista, Wendy, Guler, Dima, Shallini, Michael, Michelle, Andi, Oana, Patricia, Juan, Jason, Shmuel, Rich, Rich, Duane, Jeanne, Phil, Sandra, Dawn, Mike, Harry, Jaime, Jill, Kirsten, Sanjay, Howard, Joel, Gaston, Jason, Eugenia, Kerry, Sarah, Jaoa Mauricio, David, Jennifer, Lissa, Wayne, Geoff, Jim, Fruzsina, Ray, Mary, Bart, Matt, Maggie, Clayton, Ibrahim, Perihan, Magdy, Mary, Mara, Char, Twilight, and the many students/colleagues/friends/executives from around the world that didn't get a shout-out by name: with gratitude for your extreme patience, great conversations, and good humor over the years—you have taught me far more than you will ever know! To Rochelle and Prabudh, you may never know how much your ever-present smiles contributed. All errors remain mine. With the unavoidable axiom in mind: to fly—to soar—you must leave the ground, I thank you all.

1 | *Corporate impacts: focusing on relationships and outcomes*

All of us need to accept responsibility for the damage done to the free-market system ...

You have to focus on all the stakeholders. It's a new thing for us. Long-term value is only achieved if growth benefits all stakeholders in a company, from owners to employees, communities and even governments.

Henry Kravis, CEO, KKR

If my bank is to get involved with its neighborhoods, what should it do? What can it do?

Senior banking executive

Corporations, the most powerful wealth-creation engines in the world, create value with their stakeholders on a daily basis (Freeman, 1984; Freeman et al., 2007) or—quite simply—they don't survive. Co-creating value delivers safe products and needed services for many stakeholders, encourages clients to come back time and again, creates jobs for employees in safe workplaces, and provides adequate returns to investors for mutual benefits (Wood, 1991). Positive impacts satisfy consumers and improve employees' welfare with spillover effects that increase the quality of life of communities through increased investments, sustained commerce, and tax receipts. In short, businesses co-create value with—and for—a multitude of stakeholders, including shareholders. A rising tide of thriving business districts builds a broader tax base, retains and attracts even more businesses, enhances a qualified workforce and contributes, in a virtuous cycle, to defraying the collective costs of community infrastructure.

Co-creating value seems like a simple concept: work with stakeholders, make a net positive difference for them and for you, improve lives, and repeat. Yet, if co-creating enduring value were simple to achieve, even more firms would match actions with intent. However, the daily news headlines suggest that co-creating value with multiple

1

stakeholders simultaneously—however important—is neither straight-forward nor easy to implement.

Implementing a process that mindfully co-creates value requires re-examining many, often implicit, aspects of the value-creation process. We start by focusing on the *interactions* of a firm's relationships with its stakeholders and with the not-so-startling observation that firms have both financial and non-financial impacts (Freeman, 1984; Baron, 1995). Financial and non-financial impacts are often intertwined and indistinguishable from one another, making assessing a firm's impacts messier than a simple accounting rubric such as share price. Purposely expanding impacts to include financial and non-financial impacts has a silver lining: more problems due to the sheer volume of impacts to consider also expands the possible solution sets available for figuring out how to continuously create value.

Lumping together all financial and non-financial impacts, how-ever, suggests a false choice between financial and so-called 'difficult to measure' non-financial impacts that can't always be monetized. Yet, financial impacts frequently have non-financial, intangible dimensions such as reputation, trust, or ability to attract top tal-ent that are equally difficult to monetize and are ignored at the business's peril. A one-size-fits-all rubric to assess all financial or non-financial impacts does not exist. Pride, loyalty, trustworthiness, safety, and effectiveness, for example, might be perceived, assessed, and measured in very different ways by employees, consumers, neighbors, and regulators. This book suggests a more nuanced perspective is needed based on the impacts that firms have with investors, employees, through the production chain, with consum-ers, as well as a broader set of thought leaders that are listening to, watching and influencing the firm. Influencing the influencers is increasingly an important aspect of managing corporate impacts to co-create value.

Effectively co-creating value that endures suggests, at a minimum, undertaking mutually beneficial activities while preventing bad things from happening. Mitigating harm by installing sprinkler systems and fire escapes in case of a factory fire that can kill employees is simply in the firm's best interests. When a fire occurs, the increased scrutiny of preventable deaths might irreparably harm a firm's reputation—better to prevent the fire in the first place. Creating an unfortunate legacy, these value-destroying events hamper growth and damage a firm's ability to expand. It's simply in the firm's best interests to consider its financial and non-financial impacts: businesses are in the business of creating mutual benefits that positively impact stakeholders and the firm.

Co-creating value often targets stakeholders directly impacted by a firm's actions. This book suggests that direct effects, as well as spillover and multiplier effects, of a firm's actions (or inactions) are where value is created or destroyed with stakeholders. When growing firms hire 100 new employees, for example, they often emphasize only the net positive benefits without a concomitant understanding of the spillover effects of hiring on the local neighborhood through traffic congestion or increased demand for local housing affecting local neighborhoods through increased property values or undue pressure on municipal services for trash, sewage, water, fire services, and police protection. Over time, a narrow, firm-centric understanding of the positive and negative spillover effects of growth can affect the firm's ability to continuously attract top talent in the future.

Capitalism is under siege, in part, as the stakeholders impacted are not always accounted for; nor are a firm's impacts always positive, as value may be destroyed and lives irrevocably harmed. Nor are benefits to stakeholders proportional to their contributions or achieved simultaneously: poverty and disease endure and persist within a firm's sphere of influence (and those of business communities), while shareholder returns are near record highs. When the brunt of the burden is borne by stakeholders not reaping benefits, capitalism causes lopsided risks and tenuous rewards that may not endure over time. Lopsided equations of who contributes to value creation as well as who realizes the burdens when value is destroyed requires thinking beyond a firm's direct impacts to incorporate the value-creation process and potential for value destruction.

Value, easily destroyed, makes the headlines with extensive reviews of what happened, who is to blame, and often with outcries for new public policies to be put into place. Rather than an after-the-fact blame game, some businesses are getting ahead of the curve by understanding their direct and indirect impacts on stakeholders by managing for the positive and unintended negative impacts. Staunching value destruction is preferable to standing idly by. Yet managing the true impacts of a business can, in turn, improve competitiveness, making it better—and less costly—for a firm than doing nothing.

In short, firms co-create *and* destroy value with stakeholders. Firms impact, directly and indirectly, a series of stakeholders, including shareholders, having financial and non-financial affects. This book explores a corporation's multifaceted impacts expanding the conversation about mutual benefits by including the value created and destroyed by the firm. In doing so, we explore two questions about stakeholder engagement: *who* shares in the value-creation process (and is the firm's story about value creation inclusive of these stakeholders)? And in the process of creating value, *how* are benefits and risks borne through multiplier effects?

By focusing on four types of impact where value is created or destroyed, this book identifies managerial blind spots and opportunities for innovation. Examining financial impacts alongside employees, products, and information impacts suggests there is more to creating value than returns to investors. Confidence in leadership, trust, prestige, recognition, or loyal customers might be impacts valued more than returns. Focused on impacts, an inclusive stakeholder approach offers a holistic perspective of the value-creation process by: (a) examining material impacts, financial and non-financial, that might directly, or indirectly, affect a firm's relationships; (b) identifying spillover and multiplier effects; and (c) intertwining impacts to enhance competitiveness.

With an emphasis on impacts—the points of intersection between a business and its stakeholders through employment, finances, production, and information—this book explicitly includes employees, creditors, suppliers, and communities (e.g., thought leaders, the media, or government) in the value-creation process. At points of impact, where the firm and stakeholders intersect, opportunities exist for value to be created or destroyed. It is simply in a firm's best interest to choose to optimize its positive impacts while mitigating harmful impacts. If designing business interactions with stakeholders creates enduring value without destroying value, aren't we all better off?

Interestingly, in the tangle of firm–stakeholder impacts lies the 'sweet spot' of value being co-created, as well as the 'messy middle' of value being destroyed. Increasingly considered a messy middle, addressing corporate impacts is not going to get easier, yet they are exceedingly important. The sheer number and variety of impacts due to the volume of stakeholders impinging upon a business with opportunities to create (or destroy) value is accelerating. The interests of stakeholder groups expand and morph on a seemingly daily basis. Therein lies the opportunity to create, destroy, or dissipate value if myriad relationships are not understood in the light of their true impacts on the firm.

While corporate impacts can seem a bit like chasing a moving target, resulting in an explosion of relevant relationships, the key is tying the impacts to the process of creating enduring value.

Let's start by examining the direct and indirect stakeholders impacted by the 2010 BP oil spill in the Gulf of Mexico.

BP CASE STUDY: CORPORATE IMPACTS

On April 20, 2010, BP's *Deepwater Horizon* exploded and caught fire in the Gulf of Mexico, killing 11 workers and injuring 17 others (Hoffman and Jennings, 2011). Two days later the rig sank, causing the worst oil spill in US history. BP eventually capped the well on July 15, 2010 after almost five billion barrels of oil—19 times more than leakage from the 1989 *Exxon Valdez* oil spill—contaminated the Gulf (Fahrenthold and Kindy, 2010).

The BP oil spill directly affected a variety of stakeholders, including the neighborhoods and households living near the 16,000 miles of coastline composed of Alabama, Florida, Louisiana, Mississippi, and Texas (Mackey, 2010). Thousands of animal species were killed or injured in the six months following the spill. The spill also had far-reaching consequences for the industry, including stricter regulation for deep-sea drilling with the potential for more regulations in the future (Goldenberg, 2010a; Webb, 2010c).

BP faced massive financial consequences: 2010 was BP's first financial loss in 19 years, with $4.9 billion charged against earnings due to containing and cleaning up the oil spill in the Gulf (Webb and Bawden, 2011). BP's share price fell by more than 115 percent. Once Britain's most valuable company, by June 2010 BP's shares had fallen to less than half of their pre-spill value (Bryant, 2011). One day in early June 2010, BP shares plummeted by 13 percent, immediately wiping £12 billion off the company's value as news was released that oil well was not likely to be capped for two months or more. In 2015, five years after the oil spill, BP's share price still had not returned to the pre-spill value of more than $57. Pensioners dependent upon BP's dividend payout were acutely affected as the dividend was cut to 7 cents, less than half the level before the April 2010 Gulf of Mexico oil spill (Webb and Bawden, 2011). BP lost $103 billion in market value and says it faced more than $40 billion in spill related costs with civil charges and numerous lawsuits still pending (Larino, 2015).

BP's loss of $103 billion in market value is equivalent to wiping out (in 2010 dollars) Intel, McDonald's, Visa, or Disney. The loss in shareholder value was acutely felt by both the American and British governments as both wanted BP to survive, and not only for financial reasons (Webb, 2010a). BP accounted for more than 10 percent of dividends paid by UK companies, with numerous British pensioners relying on its dividend income. The company is headquartered in London and is a well-known British firm formerly known as British Petroleum; its privatization from state-ownership began in the late 1970s (Webb, 2010a). The United States government was concerned that if BP went bankrupt then it would not be able to pay the potentially billions of dollars in compensation to victims, leaving the US government footing the bill *and* being responsible for implementing the cleanup activities (Webb, 2010a).

BP's operations were directly affected, with production dropping to 10 percent less oil and gas being pumped compared with the year before (Webb, 2011). And presumably operating procedures, rig operations and oversight, and deep-sea drilling protocols, as well as the reporting relationships—including the very public sacking of BP chairman Tony Hayward in June 2010—were significantly changed, with BP taking on a laser-like focus towards safety after the oil spill. What is unknown to outsiders is the effect of the oil spill on employees. Did BP have to lay off employees due to the drop in production or were layoffs and loss of contracts outsourced, borne by suppliers of BP and their contract workers? Or did BP have to pay a premium to attract engineers or geologists to work for them? And were there negative spillover effects onto franchise owners that lost money or were unable to expand?

Expectations of future production were also lowered as BP sold assets worth $25 billion to create a cushion of cash to pay for spill-related costs (Webb, 2011) and BP dropped plans to drill in the Arctic owing to its tarnished reputation after the Gulf of Mexico spill (Macalaster, 2010). The reputation losses were only in part captured by the market value loss of $103 billion, as the company's brand value was also diminished due to the way BP had promoted its Beyond Petroleum program in the years before the spill, but failed to execute when a disaster arose (Healy and Griffin, 2004; Sweney, 2010). With a damaged reputation, BP may find it harder to enter new markets or bid for new contracts (Sweney, 2010).

Other spillover effects included a cut in BP's credit rating—after US politicians demanded the company deposit $20 billion in an escrow account to cover the cost of the *Deepwater Horizon* disaster, making it more expensive for BP to borrow money (Wearden, 2010). Within a week, Moody's, a credit rating company, followed with a cut to BP's credit rating (Gutierrez, 2010).

Months after the largest oil spill in US history, speculation remained rampant in business news outlets that BP might become a takeover target, go bankrupt, or need to be significantly downsized and reorganized as the share price collapsed and was expected to drop even further (Webb and Pilkington, 2010; Tseng, 2010). What about BP's competitors? Are BP's rivals such as

ExxonMobil breathing a sigh of relief as the *Exxon Valdez* oil spill in Prince William Sound in 1989, previously the most notorious US oil spill, became yesterday's news with the BP oil spill (Hoffman, 1999; Hoffman and Ocasio, 2001; Hoffman and Jennings, 2011)?

Multiplier effects from the oil spill extended to the entire petrochemical industry, with new regulatory, political, and legal challenges. The Obama administration reversed an earlier decision and stopped offshore drilling until 2017, saying it had learned a lesson from the BP oil disaster. The cost and time delays in opening up new areas of the Gulf of Mexico to drilling affected the entire industry as more stringent safety measures were now required (Goldenberg, 2010a; Webb, 2011). Royal Dutch Shell, a competitor with an approved yet controversial drilling project in the Arctic, was required to upgrade its oil spill response plan, which delayed the planned start of the drilling until 2012 and then faced additional delays even after spending $4.5 billion on leases, equipment, and a campaign to persuade government officials (Broder, 2013). Shell initially refused to rule out pursuing damages against BP and other companies involved in the Gulf of Mexico disaster (Webb, 2010b).

The Obama administration sued BP and its partners in the *Deepwater Horizon* oil well disaster in the Gulf of Mexico, Trans-Ocean and Anadarko Petroleum. BP eventually settled with the Department of Justice in November 2012 for $4.5 billion in damages and pleaded guilty to 14 criminal charges while agreeing to pay fines to the Securities and Exchange Commission (Krauss and Schwartz, 2012). In later trials, BP was found grossly negligent, with the penalties and the appeal process still ongoing nearly five years after the oil spill (Larino, 2015; Stempel, 2014). BP faced hundreds of lawsuits filed by fishing interests, hotel chains, restaurateurs, even condo owners who say the spill ruined their holidays. The state of Alabama is also suing BP and other firms connected to the disaster (Goldenberg, 2010b; Larino, 2015).

In short, BP's financial loss of $103 billion in market value is only one aspect of the story regarding how BP co-created and destroyed value in the Gulf of Mexico oil spill. Only evaluating BP's financial impacts of the oil spill in the Gulf would miss the many financial and non-financial impacts on pensioners, financial analysts, partners, employees, suppliers, governmental contracts, local shrimp businesses and tourism companies, and neighborhoods, as well as consumers. Further, BP's prospects for co-creating value in the future are likely to be deeply intertwined with its responses to the 2010 *Deepwater Horizon* oil spill.

This book suggests it is simply in a business's best interest to understand how it impacts its stakeholders to enhance its value-creation process and mitigate risks that destroy value. We start by briefly identifying corporate impacts extending beyond financial impacts to include non-financial impacts, personnel and workplace, products/ services, and information (Evan, 1965). Briefly discussing each of the four impacts (financial, personnel, products, and information) in isolation allows us to deeply dissect each type of impact in the next three chapters while alluding to how they work in combination with one another in Chapters 5 and 6. It's not that one specific impact is more important than the other, nor that they all must be evaluated in sequence, nor that all impacts must be accounted for; rather the intent of having a deep description of each impact allows for different narratives to emerge of how a business co-creates value *with its many stakeholders*.

Financial impacts

Financial impacts are often the most readily described and easily measured impact for publicly traded companies as share price and accounting returns are required to be published on a periodic basis. Financial impacts are most easily monetized, reflecting an accounting of risks, costs, and benefits to assess performance. Performance incorporates more than just financial metrics as it reflects past investments, new ideas that are generating sales, how efficient operations are producing goods and services, serendipity, and avoiding the crises affecting a firm's financial war chest. Various constituencies are directly affected by the financial value created by firms, including shareholders and financial investment industries created to assess, compare, and share information on a firm's financial prowess relative to rivals, industries, or most admired firms. Comparisons to rivals, contributions to national growth, and growth projections for investors assessing publicly traded companies deciding on whether to buy, hold, or sell company stock are commonplace. Often the shorthand for commercial success, financial impacts assess the impact on the owners, those providing capital, as access to financial capital is a requirement for all firms.

Yet, a single-minded narrative of profit maximization is not serving the interests of the business community or its stakeholders (Stout,

2012). The ostensible pursuit of short-term profits at all costs, as we saw in the BP oil spill case, can stymie businesses' growth potential; multiplying risks and ignoring new opportunities. Attention to human health and safety, risk mitigation, forestalling lawsuits, sharing information, trust, and the ability to work with stakeholders may be valued more than current cash flows for BP, for example. With even more stakeholders asking 'what's in it for me?' a financial payoff may not be the best answer, nor in the best interests of the firm.

Further, different firms are targeting different types of investors—particularly those investors that are focused on the long term. CEOs from Microsoft and Facebook are defending long-term investment strategies that don't provide immediate returns by asking investors to either be patient or to find another firm for their investment portfolio (Goldman, 2015). These firms are looking beyond short-term financial impacts to invest in future business growth. Investments in R&D, for example, can immediately benefit employees while in turn benefitting customers and investors in the long term. Without an adequate response to questions about how business co-creates enduring value with its many stakeholders, naysayers will continually undermine the financial value created by businesses.

Employees in the workplace impacts

Corporations directly impact—and are impacted by—employees and through workplace facilities. How a company engages its employees, builds its internal feedback systems (hiring, firing, training, and development processes), and facilities in which employees work (safety, security) increasingly helps to tip the balance in the competition for top talent (Turban and Greening, 1997). Employees and contract workers are often the first stakeholders to see gaps between the policies of a company or aspirations of its leadership and the way in which people are actually treated. Employee pride, retention, diversity, and loyalty as well as programs appropriately tailored to education, volunteering based on building skills and expertise, matching contributions, or internal training and development can contribute to employee effectiveness (Mackey and Sisodia, 2013).

Workplace impacts can be numerically accounted for as: workplace safety (accidents or deaths of employees and contract workers); number of regulatory violations (e.g., child labor and human trafficking policies); number of lost workdays per year; carbon, water, or energy consumption; waste and efficiency; as well as LEED certification of facilities. These workplace impacts often spill over to contract workers, partners, and suppliers as we saw in the fallout from the BP oil spill.

Overall, personnel and workplace impacts are a combination of both actual and perceived value. Being perceived as a trusted employer, an employer of choice, or winning 'best place to work' awards, alongside appropriate consumption of water, carbon, and energy or LEED certification of offices are not substitutes for headline-raising issues such as child labor, human trafficking, or unsafe workplace conditions, yet can often help when workplace conditions make headline news. A steady paycheck at living wages, for example, may be valued differently than safe working conditions or policies on human trafficking by employees or non-governmental organizations (NGOs) specializing in human trafficking. Adopting a co-creating value mindset suggests that both types of value, actual and perceived, need to be satisfied as risks can threaten the survival of the company and its ability to continuously create value as it seeks to retain its employees or expand facilities into new markets.

Product-based impacts

A third way that firms directly impact and are impacted by stakeholders are through day-to-day production and procurement decisions. In short, how a product is sourced, produced and delivered. Decisions that encourage (discourage) the use (misuse) of goods and services impact many stakeholders along the value chain: suppliers, suppliers of suppliers, distribution networks, clients (product purchasers), and consumers (product users). Whether it is a local barbershop offering free haircuts or a multinational company with production facilities and kiosks in numerous communities around the world, every organization impacts stakeholders through sourcing and delivery of its products or services.

Assessing the economic aspects of product/service impacts are quite common as they can be readily measured through, for example: pricing; loyalty of consumers; carbon, water, and energy consumption per unit of product; recycling programs or lifecycle analysis; traceability and accountability in the sourcing of pesticide-free or organic goods in grocery stores; or donations of in-kind products. Consumer behavior research about perceived value, especially the use of branded products, is of particular interest in assessing product/service impacts as allegations of exploitation or misleading disclosures in nutritional labels, cigarette packaging, and mortgage loan disclosures are well documented (Perry and Blumenthal, 2012).

Branded products have unique risks, as a brand promise might allude to specific aspirations, lifestyle choices, status, or prestige. If a brand promises eco-friendly manufacturing yet research uncovers unethical suppliers promoting unsafe workplace conditions, the brand can come under attack, such as when Greenpeace attacked Timberland (Swartz, 2010).

Increasingly, transparency regarding the sourcing and distribution of commodity products such as coffee, soya, rubber, water, and forestry products is demanded by consumers, investors, non-profits, and governments. Decisions about sourcing, packaging, advertising, social media, return policies or end-of-life recycling of products directly and indirectly impact other decisions, and thus have the potential to create or destroy value. Effectively addressing multiplier effects of products/services beyond economic impacts to include social and environmental impacts throughout the value chain is increasingly important for modern businesses.

Information-sharing impacts

Another, perhaps more subtle mechanism by which corporations directly and indirectly impact stakeholders is through sharing information. This is information that influences influencers, shapes opinions, or educates thought leaders and other critical stakeholders. Transparency and disclosure creates (new) value by connecting consumers with producers via location-based cell apps that review hotels, restaurants, or gas stations, for example. Information connects financiers through crowdsourcing with local independent musicians wanting to produce another album. It has never been easier to find a specific store, search for people with common food interests, or deal with food allergies, with friends, tips, blogs, and tweets to share ratings, rankings, preferences, and 'how to' videos. The value created through information-sharing communities is often overlooked and underappreciated, yet when value is destroyed and stories go viral, information-based risks multiply rapidly.

When recognized as a trusted partner, corporations can become convening forums that exchange information, enabling even more value to be created. By providing thought leadership or critical expertise, businesses exert influence far beyond individual products, services, or their physical locations to help others (local communities, potential consumers, regulatory agencies asking advice on promulgating new regulations) with skills, expertise, know-how, training, and outreach.

On the flip-side, a business can also irritate the media, regulators, industry bodies, opinion leaders, potential investors, or local communities and destroy value. As seen in the BP oil spill case, once a creditor publicly downgraded its evaluation of BP, other credit agencies followed suit, leading to cascading effects and ongoing speculation that can distract management while multiplying the risks of future growth.

Impacts of corporations' information-sharing are often highlighted in the wake of natural disasters or world sporting events (e.g., FIFA World Cup, the Olympics). During the 2011 Fukushima tsunami, the world's worst nuclear disaster since Chernobyl, for example, when information was scarce regarding safe shelters, electricity availability/ outages, and safe drinking water, many companies made donations ranging from road-clearing equipment and logistical support to technology and satellites to coordinate information, gain access to water, medicines, and support to rebuild critical infrastructure. One silver lining of the tsunami is Japan's boom of green technologies, which resulted in the highest rates of renewable energy in the world in 2014 (Kageyama, 2014).

Information impacts—an oft-overlooked and underappreciated area of corporate impacts—affect many constituencies and, in turn, affect the value-creation process. Positive and negative information impacts can be direct or indirect, as well as perceived or actual. For example, financial analysts, potential customers, Facebook friends, regulators, the general public, and pundits opining about an organization, its products, and promotions is blurring the boundaries of 'relevant' communities; social media has enabled communities of users, thought leaders, consumers, beta testers, Facebook friends, and partners to be critical communities, extending traditional communities beyond local neighborhoods. Appropriately defining communities is becoming critical to creating—and mitigating risks of destroying—value.

Information shapes future expectations requiring communications that goes well beyond traditional newsletters, intranets, technical reports, lobbying, grassroots advocacy, and political contributions. The broadening and deepening of opportunities stemming from information impacts is both a challenge (misinformation) as well as an incentive for businesses to create new business models (crowdfunding, crowdsourcing) with many overlooked communities.

Table 1.1 provides an abbreviated view of just two types of impacts—financial and workplace—on various stakeholder groups, which is explored in more detail in Chapter 5. These few examples highlight the direct impacts that many firms already take into consideration. Yet, many firms undermine what they are already doing by limiting managerial focus on just these few, direct impacts and by attributing their corporate impacts, narrowly, to solely financial impacts.

BP, for example, operating for many decades as a company with the British government as a majority owner, had carefully created relationships with investors, employees, customers, government regulators, and communities, as well as its suppliers/distributors. Yet the conversations from BP prior to the oil spill were seemingly focused upon its financial impacts on investors, even though BP proclaimed itself as 'beyond petroleum' (Healy and Griffin, 2004; Sweney, 2010). The oil spill crisis broadened and deepened BP's focus to meaningfully engage and articulate the contributions from multiple stakeholders. BP has acknowledged its multiple impacts beyond financial considerations to include legal and political risks stemming from employee, product, and reputation impacts. Lessons from the oil spill suggest myriad stakeholders, with financial and non-financial impacts—often not included in a storyline businesses tell about themselves—increasingly important in how value is created and destroyed in an interconnected world. By leaving value-creating stakeholders out of the conversations and narrowly focusing on isolated impacts rather than multiple impacts, opportunities for co-creating value are missed. When value is destroyed, stemming the negative tide is often very difficult if a deeper understanding of how value is created and destroyed is overlooked.

Table 1.1 *Examples of financial and workplace impacts on stakeholder groups*

		STAKEHOLDERS				
IMPACTS		Investors	Employees	Customers	Government	Communities	Suppliers/distributors
	Financial	Share price; dividends; returns	Employee stock ownership programs; wages	Price; cost	Taxes; oversight	Sponsorships; economic disparities	Costs; price
	Workplace	Lawsuits; safety record	Safety; training; human trafficking; hours worked; benefits	Child labor; recalls	Oversight; jobs created; local content	Child labor; human rights; safety; jobs	Skills transfer

Multiplier effects

While direct effects of financial, employee, product or information impacts are frequently straightforward, corporations often don't consider their multiplier effects. BP, for example, was blindsided by numerous lawsuits and claimants allegedly impacted through the oil spill. Multiplier effects stem from everyday decisions but are often highlighted during headline-making events, such as a fire, a rogue trader, or an oil spill. Multiplier effects exacerbate a corporation's ability to continuously co-create value with consumers, governments, and neighborhoods.

Multiplier effects extend a firm's reach beyond its direct impacts to include impacts along the entire value chain, across geographies, and over time. Multiplier effects may directly or, more importantly, indirectly spill over to the value-creation process. Firms with global supply chains are particularly vulnerable to spillover risks. Focusing on the employment policies to eliminate human trafficking, for example, in factories owned and operated by a large multinational retailer is fairly straightforward. Yet if a factory operating under contract with a supplier-of-a-supplier has a fire, the multinational retailer might be heavily scrutinized about employment policies or workplace conditions in a factory they do not own or operate. The retailer, merely through the daisy chain of contracts with suppliers, is complicit by a supplier-of-a-supplier's employment policies.

After the oil spill in the Gulf of Mexico, for example, BP faced many claims from local tourism, shrimp, and fishing businesses physically affected by the oil spill. Communities further down the coast *without* oil slicks covering their beaches, however, also made claims without bearing *direct* physical impacts of the oil spill. They claimed the oil spill harmed or halted tourism in the neighboring region and in doing so had an impact— financially and non-financially—on their businesses, communities, and way of life. In this way, the impacts of BP were extended beyond the direct, physical impacts upon neighboring communities even if these further afield neighborhoods were not marred by the physical impacts of the oil spill.

Well-intentioned businesses might narrowly focus on financial returns, fulfilling contracts for clients, or creating safe workplaces, but a narrow focus on direct—and predominantly financial—impacts is simply not sufficient for twenty-first-century firms. Corporations' impacts extend and multiply beyond direct impacts with investors, employees, and consumers through the value chain, across geographies, and over time.

Multiplier effects along the value chain

Multiplier effects along the value chain extend a firm's interests to suppliers and the suppliers of suppliers, clients who buy the product, consumers who use the products, and governmental agencies or others that monitor, rate, or review products. Multiplier effects extend the reach of an enterprise to both ends of the value chain, across multiple geographies, and over time in a 24/7 social media frenzied world. Multiplier effects are important because they can significantly enhance mutual benefits or rapidly accelerate the costs/externalities borne by stakeholders and in doing so expand the risks for the firm.

Focusing on a firm's extended value chain explicitly links consumers' interests with suppliers' designs by creating feedback loops, for example. Tying consumers' recommendations for safety features for children with product designers reimagining the next generation of products creates mutual benefits for consumers, suppliers, and the firm. In this way, consumers help dictate changes in design, manufacturing, or sourcing of raw materials.

In a related fashion, multiplier effects stemming from one firm often ripple throughout an industry sector affecting many other firms. For example, BP's *Deepwater Horizon* spill affected the entire deep sea-drilling industry through regulations and increased scrutiny. Industry-level multiplier effects during the global financial crisis contributed to the demise or detriment of numerous investment banking and real estate firms. 'Too big to fail' firms such as JP Morgan and Countrywide failed, while global giants Goldman Sachs and Citigroup had their operations significantly affected. Multiplier effects can indiscriminately affect swaths of firms within an industry.

After the BP *Deepwater Horizon* oil rig exploded killing 11 people, for example, the ensuing oil spill created a crisis for the company *and* the petrochemical industry. While BP had already established a 'beyond petroleum' presence with deep relationships throughout many Gulf of Mexico communities, extensive partnerships, alliances with international NGOs such as the Nature Conservancy, university experts available in drilling and capping wells, as well as a robust legal, media, public policy, investor relations and operations team, missteps still occurred (Healy and Griffin, 2004; Healy, 2014), which lead to the sacking of BP CEO Tony Hayward (Macalaster, 2010).

Despite being the US's largest-ever oil spill, more than two months passed for BP's stock price to drop by more than 50 percent after the oil rig exploded (Stout, 2012). BP was able to recover far more rapidly because it had developed—and was able to *leverage and learn* from—an extensive stakeholder network developed prior to the crisis and upon whom BP relied upon as soon as the spill occurred. Leveraging myriad relationships to spearhead a multifaceted recovery effort, in the end, was applauded. The relationships forged and relatively rapid responses throughout BP's extended stakeholder network, created from an extensive stakeholder network developed prior to the crisis and upon whom BP relied upon as soon as the spill occurred, helped its recovery.

Exxon's stock price, on the other hand, dropped far more rapidly just a few days after the *Exxon Valdez* oil spill in 1989. ExxonMobil spent days, and some would argue months or years, denying the spill and then was hamstrung with its defensive stance throughout the oil recovery process, hampering its stock price and casting doubt on its ability to generate future earnings.

Yet, positive multiplier effects from the BP spill also occurred. Can you name any of them? Likely not as many (newly created) innovations, interestingly, received much less national or international media coverage. Operational changes and an enhanced focus on safety would be a positive multiplier effect for BP's operations in the Gulf that likely extended to all the firm's operations worldwide. The drilling industry, more generally, benefited if collaborative partnerships and new businesses specializing in cap and contain technologies were created.

Net impacts and combining impacts

To assess net impacts, defined as mutual benefits net of costs, the indirect and multiplier effects of corporations' relationships need to be considered. Imagine for a moment that your firm has just one supplier, one consumer, one regulator, and one employee. How many relationships might, theoretically, affect your ability to create value? Focusing solely on the four direct relationships would sub-optimize your effectiveness, as there are 24 possible relationships (4-factorial or in mathematical notation, 4!, which is $4 \times 3 \times 2 \times 1$). Now think about a real-world organization. Does the firm focus solely on its direct relationships? Or does it look beyond the urgent, direct relationships to examine the risks, rewards, and perceptions of other, indirect or seemingly dormant yet influential, stakeholders?

Understanding the multitude of direct, indirect, and net impacts is helpful when examining what is important to a wider set of constituencies such as governments, service providers, advocacy groups, or non-profits. As more stakeholders become more involved in shaping a firm's value-creation process—in developing countries with foreign direct investment; during urban renewal projects when permits for growing business are required; or when governmental oversight is required for manufacturing controversial products—what is of value may change, and change rapidly, for relevant constituencies. If a firm's survival is at risk, if growth is desired, if a crisis occurs with employee layoffs, or the facility is shuttered, governments, service providers, and advocacy groups can enhance or tarnish a firm's reputation with spill-over effects. The BP example discusses the downside risks and multiplier effects in more detail.

Quite often, unfortunately, stakeholder impacts are simply reduced down to financial contributions to a firm's bottom line for its shareholders. A more inclusive narrative of creating jobs, however, discusses benefits for the town, the employees, the firm, and the consumers. A holistic, integrative narrative of business acknowledges the many and varied impacts of business and hiring employees, capitalism and the value-creation process is increasingly under siege (Porter and Kramer, 2011; Crane et al., 2014a, 2014b).

Seemingly simple everyday decisions about employing local talent, for example, have potentially far-reaching impacts that can undermine (or reinforce) other stakeholder relationships. Figure 1.1 depicts how multiple stakeholders might be inextricably intertwined in the value-creation process as discussed in more detail in Chapter 5. Hiring local talent, for example, can set the stage for a company in tune with the way the (local) world works, attracting a larger pool of talented applicants, encouraging more consumers to buy from a 'well-respected' company that treats its employees well in a virtuous cycle. Alternatively, being perceived as a company that seemingly does what it wants regardless of the community in which it resides and being culturally *insensitive* to local preferences may unwittingly stir up

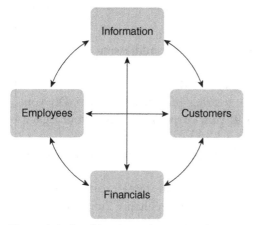

Figure 1.1 Combinations of corporate impacts

animosity that extends far beyond the local community, the physical products, and the ability of the firm to compete effectively.

If a hotel, for example, deepens its relations with its employees by creating training and development programs benefitting all employers in the hospitality business, value can be co-created with ripple effects on consumers, investors, and through a reputation (information effects) for being a good employer. These improved employee relations create value, which spills over to other stakeholders, as shown in Figure 1.1; thus the firm creates a mutually reinforcing means to continuously create value.

In other words, a firm is helping others help themselves while also helping itself in the process. Will other communities look upon the hotel as a trusted partner and welcome it as it expands into new communities or will it just examine its potential for a tax contribution? Similarly, if the hotel obeys local laws yet voluntarily goes beyond compliance on human rights, for example, when the law is silent, does it make it a trusted partner differentiated from its rivals? Or, do the financials trump all considerations? Small contributions, in their own way, over time, make a difference. And when multiplied by a million (products, customers, employees, lives touched in the product process), the impacts can be quite astonishing! Many firms are multiplying their legacy of good (or harmful) impacts.

Aggregating financial and non-financial impacts assesses how value is co-created (or destroyed) by the firm. That is, thinking about how

Box 1.1 Food for thought

Is the firm aware of and appropriately addressing its multiple impacts?

What value is being co-created (or destroyed)?

What direct impacts are creating (destroying) value? Do you know the multiplier effects of your corporation? How your legacy of good is being expanded?

How can a firm best align, leverage, and learn to create positive multiplier effects?

What issues, industries, and nation-states create exponentially helpful (or harmful) impacts that enhance (mitigate) your competitiveness?

stakeholders work together in different combinations makes for a more versatile, flexible, and resilient value-creation process. Rather than a static, hub-and-spoke, one-dimensional view of a firm as a wealth creator, by envisioning the firm as a network of stakeholders, with multiple interactions that ultimately create value, many different types of value are created. An impact perspective creates new questions to consider, identified in Box 1.1, which are explored throughout the book.

Why now? And why bother?

What's different today? First, a crisis can put at risk a firm's survival (Heineman, 2008). With a firm's survival threatened by individuals' rogue initiatives such as JP Morgan's London Whale, one employee may bring down a multibillion-dollar, century-old company in less than a year. Seemingly epiphenomenal events are occurring with far more frequency as businesses previously considered 'too big to fail' are failing.

It's not just once-in-a-century crises affecting firm's survival an operational decision can, if not properly managed, affect survival (Griffin, 2008; Heineman, 2008). Routine decision processes without an adequate understanding of the true impacts on the firm can quickly become a head-turning, top-of-the-fold newspaper story that goes viral on YouTube, blogs, and social media sites, causing employees to be fired or firms such as BP to be heavily scrutinized. It's not a matter of *if* a crisis is going to occur, it's a matter of *when* it will occur.

Survival can be at stake due to multiplier effects rippling through an industry. Some beef processors went bankrupt after reports about the use of 'pink slime,' a meat-based additive to ground beef composed of fatty scraps treated with citric acid to kill bacteria. As public outcry grew, pink slime was banned by the US Department of Agriculture from school lunches for children in primary and secondary schools (Korn, 2014). Retail companies such as McDonald's and Kroger, a grocery store, said they would no longer use pink slime. As demand waned, two of the largest beef producers of pink slime closed plants and fired employees. Yet two years later, pink slime was making a comeback as beef prices climbed (Korn, 2014). So, cascading impacts might ebb and flow over time as public attention moves on to new topics.

Systematically assessing impacts as a result of a crisis is not new, but the stakes are now higher if learning from crises doesn't occur. What is new is the need for rapid learning about how direct impacts and multiplier effects affect survival and ability to co-create value. Not all organizations flirt with dismissal after a crisis threatens survival. Siemens emerged more fortified after allegations of corruption. Timberland changed its sourcing requirements to focus on tracing sustainable inputs once Greenpeace ran an expose (Swartz, 2010).

Similarly, when the Australian government proposed a super-tax for resource-based companies during the global financial crises, the resource sector—including Rio Tinto—took out full-page advertisements to actively, and successfully, advocate for public sentiment to drop the tax (Henisz, 2014). In this book, we explore how firms co-create value by learning to incorporate their economic, socio-political, legal, and ethical impacts into the narratives about the business.

Further, conceptualizing a business as merely a wealth creator for investors is often not sufficient in today's 24/7 global information-rich world. Companies are far more than mere money-makers as they engage many stakeholders in the value-creation process. Sure, companies make money or else go out of business. Yet companies create jobs, make customers happy, build opportunities where there weren't any before, and provide information that might not otherwise be available even if the talk is only about value created for shareholders. By expanding the economic pie, building a more robust narrative about co-creating value with stakeholders, firms are creating enduring value.

Corporations are uniquely qualified

Making positive impacts, mitigating harm, and satisfying multiple stakeholders continually over time is simply in the best interests of firms. Corporations are uniquely qualified to co-create value with multiple stakeholders due to their scale, scope, and unique resources.

Corporations have scale. Some corporations are larger than some governments in the post-World War II economy while governments—the traditional source for foreign direct investments as underwriters for the earliest explorers, and designers of the Marshall Plan and Bretton Woods Organizations after World War II—are no longer the primary source of foreign direct investment. Foreign direct investment by private enterprise now surpasses government aid and public-sector donations (Zoellick, 2011). Multinational corporations, unlike many governments, have a global scale and scope whereas governments focus more directly on national, regional, or local populations.

Corporations, unlike many governments, often choose the products they produce, how to produce them, and in what quantity. Corporations can choose to be thought leaders as well as business leaders. Corporations are uniquely qualified to create value since they are in the business of satisfying people's needs. Providing products, goods, and services (e.g., a Tata Group commitment to build the low-cost Tata Nano automobile) that respect consumer desires, government restrictions and are mindful of their environmental impact can create value continually over time.

Corporations have scope. Firms are financially and culturally exposed across continents and numerous neighborhoods. They have the ability to align, leverage, and learn from their multiple vantage points. Certainly, operating across multiple countries is more complex; it creates more information and more noise while creating an opportunity for information arbitrage. As more companies have global supply or distribution chains, the proportion of firms operating in more than one country has increased since the 1950s. Growing at an increasing rate, the acceleration of globalization has made the problems (and the actors contributing to the problem set) more complex, but the solution set has also expanded. New expectations call for learning about new ways to create value. As value is co-created (or destroyed) across a broader landscape, many more actors are involved: multilaterals, international NGOs, religious elders, and community groups, for example, with both financial and non-financial motivations requiring more than financial justifications for business decisions.

Corporations are unique. Staffed with uniquely qualified personnel, corporations have technical experts, management expertise, and convening power. Corporations have the ability to plan, prioritize, and create performance targets (e.g., key performance indicators, KPIs) to piece together multifaceted supply chains with sophisticated distribution logistics. Corporations create jobs and employ people. Multinational corporations address challenges affecting multiple communities, with multiple points of interaction with federal, state, and local regulators and administrators, and can convene multi-stakeholder discussions.

Private enterprise is innovative in its governance systems by embracing a wide variety of mechanisms for ownership (family, publicly traded, private, social enterprise, benefit-corps, institutional pension funds, religious affiliated organizations, etc.), allowing it to adapt across generations and geographies, reflecting the changing mores, needs, and aspirations of the owners. The chameleon-like qualities of corporations allow them to adapt to different conditions across the globe across issues, industries, and nation-states to create distribution, transportation, and pricing solutions (Griffin, 2010).

Firms striving to be self-sufficient are points of national pride due to their outreach efforts in satisfying stakeholders. International companies such as Tata Group in India; Toyota in Japan; LVMH (Louis Vuitton Moët Hennessy) in France; and Banco do Brasil in Brazil frequently adjust to changing requirements around the world.

Corporations are often able to rapidly respond to trends by shifting allocations and drawing on their networks for needed expertise. Corporations' responses to crises are often faster, broader, and more effective than those of many local governments directly affected by a crisis. Organizational reach (scale and scope), leadership, distribution, logistics, and rapid response (e.g., ability to respond to hazardous material spills) while having an extended enterprise unaffected by the immediate local crisis are all qualities that enable a corporation to respond more effectively to crises than some governments.

Branded businesses have unique risks. Branded, consumer-driven companies such as Cadbury, Nike, Unilever, or Matsushita must meet changing global expectations while maintaining their competitiveness to thrive. Companies whose branded products have government restrictions preventing them from selling directly to consumers (e.g., British American Tobacco or Diageo's premium drinks) have an added hurdle to meet regulatory approvals that differ country-by-country due to custom, taste, and traditions. Pharmaceutical companies—whose direct-to-consumer branded products such as Cialis, Vioxx, or Viagra rely on insurance or government reimbursements—face unique risks as they rely heavily on government and public approval to remain in business. Despite these risks, consumer-driven companies are likely to be first movers in addressing myriad financial and non-financial impacts.

Sparking new conversations

This book aims to spark new conversations about the impacts of firms by incorporating direct and indirect impacts as well as multiplier effects. Addressing the positive and negative impacts of firms identifies ways in which value is co-created or destroyed—along the entire value chain, across geographies, and over time. We expand value creation beyond solely financial value (Harrison and Wicks, 2012) as the multiplicity of ways in which a firm creates values helps the firm be resilient in times of turbulent change. By expanding our understanding of how a firm impacts stakeholders, a firm can better withstand the material risks, crises in confidence, strong regulatory headwinds, new economic realities, salient social issues, or hiccups in operations that inevitably emerge in modern businesses.

Articulating and demonstrating the multiple beneficiaries in the value-creation process is a hallmark of successful businesses. By understanding the impacts on local governments, the natural environment, neighborhoods and civil society groups, as well as beta testers and traditional stakeholder groups—employees, investors, and clients—the firm anticipates the inevitable questions 'what's in it for me?' and 'what's in it for others?' The relevant question now becomes: do you have your narratives of impact and value creation ready?

A traditional view of the firm-focused predominantly on financial impacts-leaves many other, important, constituencies of the firm unaddressed and isolated. Financial impacts, important in and of themselves, are even more powerful when in combination with employees' wages and the ability to retain loyal consumers, for example, is when value is shared, grown, and expanded.

Adding in employee impacts incorporates contract workers and workplace conditions. A focus on products and the production process with the delivery of services connects the firm to many stakeholders in the value-creation process. And finally, flows of information tie the firm together with more distant stakeholders. The media, public policy, special interest groups such as environmentalists, financial institutions, business associations, and numerous non-governmental groups affect the value created by the business. Information sharing shapes the real and perceived impacts of a firm which, in turn, shapes how stakeholders perceive the firm.

The Starbucks agreement with the Colombian government, described in the following text, highlights the importance of multiple stakeholders working collaboratively over a period of time with mutually beneficial impacts—financial, employee, product, and information—that enhance the reputation of both Starbucks and Colombia.

STARBUCKS' PUBLIC–PRIVATE PARTNERSHIP WITH COLOMBIA

In cooperation with USAID, Starbucks announced in 2014 a public–private partnership to support coffee growers in Colombia (USAID, 2014). The Colombian coffee market is traditionally difficult to penetrate due to cultural barriers to entry, such as local pride, the cultural relevance of coffee, and the economic importance of the industry (Economia, 2010). By cooperating with the Colombia Coffee Growers Federation (FNC), implementing the 'Centro de Apoyo al Caficultor,' providing research on coffee beans, and supporting small coffee farmers and the coffee sector as a whole to increase coffee quality, quantity, and pricing is leading to positive multiplier effects for Colombians, USAID, the FNC, and Starbucks, with measured development and prosperity. On the same day as the Starbucks–USAID partnership in Colombia, news was released of another Starbucks partnership with a restaurant and distributors, Alsea SAB (ALSEA*) and Grupo Nutresa SA (NUTRESA), to expand the Starbucks brand in Colombia.

Purposefully working with governmental agencies, civil society organizations, and communities to build capacity and provide market-based solutions to societal problems such as employment and education requires new narratives about businesses that extend beyond profit maximization. These problems (and the opportunities embedded in the challenges) are too large for any one organization to tackle in the short term. Yet we as citizens, business leaders, or government officials all stand to lose or gain in the long term if the focus is merely on financial impacts. Seizing these opportunities requires a different kind of approach by private-sector leaders and will require them to, at the very least, attempt to understand public-sector priorities and work with civil-sector leaders (Edelman, 2014).

For Starbucks in Colombia, creating positive corporate impacts is part of a larger conversation about managing risk, leading organizations, and co-creating value. Actively addressing corporate impacts before policy requires a mandated change in behavior and can result in greater autonomy, a wider range of options to address issues, while enhancing trust. Focusing on direct impacts—such as financial indicators, employee satisfaction, product safety, or public perceptions of the firm—is not new for many firms, yet the impacts are often assessed separately, in isolation from one another. Focusing predominantly on share price or profitability before other considerations, for instance, reduces a firm's internal conversation to financial affects and prohibits a deeper understanding of the firm's wider-reaching impacts on employees, products, and perceptions.

How the book is organized

In this book, we explore how firms co-create value by focusing on four impacts and three multiplier effects that create (or destroy) value. We take a close look at a firm's impacts to better understand the processes, resources, and mindsets driving (or stalling) the co-creating value process. The first part of the book examines four direct impacts: financial, employees, products, and information. Elaborating on each of these direct impacts, we look at impacts in various combinations to assess net impacts and understand indirect, multiplier and spillover effects.

In the second part of the book, we look at underlying myths about value creation, destruction, and redistribution. Once value is created, perceptions of loss are felt more deeply than gains (Kahneman and Tversky, 1979) so we examine shifting pressures stemming from competition, public policy, and civil society affecting a firm's value-creation process. In the third and final part of the book, we explore how impacts and the processes of co-creating value change across different issues, industries, and nation-states. The book concludes by looking at the art and science of creating value amid shifting expectations going forward.

Chapters 1–6 lay the analytic groundwork regarding the corporate impacts of a firm by focusing on the points at which firm co-create or destroy value with their stakeholders. This first chapter introduced key concepts underlying the book: how all of a corporation's impacts—both financial and non-financial—are often given short shrift, with a focus predominantly on financial impacts or direct impacts. Yet corporations create value with profound effects well beyond the boundaries of a firm through multiplier effects influencing products, the value chain, and employees in the workplace, as well as shaping information and perceptions. Multiplier effects are changing expectations of what is valued and how value can be continuously created, across geographies, for multiple stakeholders. In the next chapter (Chapter 2), we start with the tradition view of a firm and its financial impacts. We elaborate on a firm's non-financial impacts by discussing employees in the workplace and products and services in Chapter 3. The impacts of information-sharing and how information blurs the boundaries of communities is examined in Chapter 4. Chapters 5 and 6 expand our focus to combine impacts and include net impacts, spillover effects, and multiplier effects. Each chapter is detailed in the following text.

Chapter 2 examines financial impacts by exploring four different mindsets about how creating (destroying) value is related to creating (destroying) value for shareholders. These four mindsets about financial impacts uncover different assumptions, processes, and expectations about creating mutual benefits: who benefits? Do others benefit and, if so, how? The first mindset focuses on win–win mutual benefit scenarios promoting efficiencies and sparking innovation. These win–win scenarios may improve product yields, increase throughput rates, or decrease the amount of carbon, water, and energy required to make and transport a product. The second mindset focuses on headline-grabbing 'parade of horribles' crises wherein nearly everyone loses. In the wake of crises there is an opportunity to reconfigure resources and priorities to examine future financial, workplace, product, and information impacts. The third mindset examines what happens when other stakeholders benefit but a return is not evident for shareholders. Shareholders may expect a return, in time, creating an investment opportunity or if no return is expected, a cost center may be created. And finally, the fourth mindset about financial impacts examines scenarios when shareholders receive benefits but other stakeholders are harmed. That is, if mutual benefits for multiple constituencies are claimed but some stakeholders may be harmed, these activities can be perceived as pernicious behaviors.

Chapter 3 examines two additional corporate impacts beyond financial impacts: employees in the workplace (including conditions and personnel) and products (sourcing and distribution networks, including customer impacts). By more broadly conceptualizing corporate impacts to simultaneously include workplace and product impacts alongside financial impacts, a broader set of opportunities for co-creating value is explored. This in turn creates new opportunities for co-creating (new) value.

Chapter 4 examines a fourth, often overlooked yet increasingly important impact: the impact of information. By examining if, when, and how a corporation can be a convener of information, a trusted partner, or an enabler of others by sharing appropriate information about how it operates it is creating (new) value. Disclosing who it supplies from, the intended and unintended consequences of its products, as well as the externalities it passes off to other stakeholders, information is another means by which an organization impacts and is impacted by others.

Chapters 5 and 6 explores net impacts, spillovers and the ripple effects of impacts by examining multiplier effects of corporations—the impacts of stakeholders on still other stakeholders, which in turn are often attributed back, rightly or wrongly, to the focal firm. Multiplier effects come in different forms and guises but have one trait in common: they can upend who benefits and for how long the benefits last by destroying value. We focus on one multiplier effect by tracing the traditional product-related multiplier effects throughout the entire value chain. We then layer on social and environmental multipliers impacting different components of the entire value chain. By adding in feedback loops we illustrate how suppliers of suppliers in the value chain, often examined in isolation from one another, are increasingly interconnected.

In Chapters 7 and 8 we unpack some long-held myths about corporate impacts as well as looking at how expectations are changing a firm's value creation process. In Chapter 7 we examine five long-standing myths stemming from age-old beliefs about a corporation's impacts during the value-creation process. In Chapter 8 we focus on the future by examining how expectations of businesses are changing at an accelerating pace. Our focus shifts to networks of businesses and examining businesses as embedded within public policy and civil society. We explore how the Venn diagram of private, public, and civil society sectors is changing expectations of businesses and changing the prioritization of financial and non-financial corporate impacts.

More specifically, Chapter 7 examines five longstanding myths about a corporation's traditional responsibilities. Addressing impacts by giving away time, talent, or money to charities and good causes is explored in detail. When framed as a philanthropic giveaway, corporate impacts can become unnecessarily limited to foundations, employee volunteer hours, or donations of in-kind products, most often with a cost center mindset. Rather than giving away money, this book suggests that corporate impacts are about creating value by creating net positive mutual benefits. A second longstanding myth is that corporate impacts are important only for large, generally multinational firms with excess resources. Large, multinational firms with seemingly abundant resources can be unsuccessful without clarity of focus regarding their desired (and actual) corporate impacts. Alternatively, organizations with relatively few resources can be extremely successful in deploying targeted resources to achieve a desired impact. A third myth about corporate impacts is the overwhelming number and variety of requests received due to market failures, government failures, or gaps in coverage. Firms might feel unprepared to add yet another responsibility to their own plate because government, multilaterals, neighborhoods, parents, or others failed to do their job or to do it properly. Fourth, we examine the tension between managing local impacts while struggling with their role as a member of a larger company. And finally, the fifth myth: managing corporate impacts is equivalent to being in compliance with local, extant law. As industries and firms routinely shape regulations, being in compliance may be merely an initial ante rather than a stretch goal that creates value.

Chapter 8 takes a step back from focusing on day-to-day decisions to examine how shifting expectations in the private sector, as well as in governments and civil society, affecting a firm's ability to create enduring value. Shifting expectations of who shares in the value-creation process are explored, as well as changing expectations of value and how value might be defined by competitors, governments, or neighbors. We examine changes in competitiveness, regulations, and cultural beliefs, which are permanently shifting the demands on corporations. The implication for co-creating value is straightforward: a firm can either choose to adapt to changed expectations of what is valued and how value is shared or face continued threats, slowdowns, and resistance from various constituencies. As expectations for businesses stemming from competitive markets, regulatory environments, and attitudes/beliefs are increasing ever-faster, businesses are expected to keep up. Converging interests makes thriving in this complex milieu even more interesting as the opportunities for creating value and providing solutions expand exponentially.

Creating mutual benefits with global competitors, parochial public policy, or engaged civil society organizations requires going beyond traditional descriptions based solely on a corporation's financial impacts. Workplace conditions, wages, benefits, products, services value chain, and information impacts are part of a new narrative, widening the solution set of ways in which the firm can co-create value with others. Simply put, as the problems facing firms become more entrenched and more complex, broadening the solution sets to be more inclusive of multiple impacts expands the ability of the firm to co-create value. Value is created by interweaving in innovative ways the financial, personnel, product, and information impacts that satisfy stakeholders.

Chapters 9–11 explore how contextual factors affect the value-creation process. Exploring how variation in issues (Chapter 9), industries (Chapter 10), and nation-states (Chapter 11) significantly alter the ability of a firm to co-create value, we consider how information flows and information-sharing affects value creation. We begin by examining how complex, thorny issues thwart managerial autonomy by stymieing the ability of firms to exert influence and share information (Chapter 9). In Chapter 10, we explore how some firms within specific industries are well-positioned to address different impacts by effectively aligning initiatives (what they choose to do) and mechanisms (how they achieve an impact). And finally we explore the implications of corporate impacts in a global context when operating in multiple nation-states with varying levels of compliance and governance, civil society participation, and varying comparative advantages in Chapter 11.

More specifically, Chapter 9 focuses on creating value by converging information, interests, and issues to create influence in the value-creation process. In this chapter, we address the limitations of a narrow narrative about an issue-by-issue approach or a stakeholder-by-stakeholder approach. Rather than traditional issue-by-issue or stakeholder-by-stakeholder approaches, thinking about corporate impacts means considering employees, for example, as citizens, consumers, and voters, as part of the value-creation process. When introducing a new product, for example, considering how employees as neighbors, bloggers, or consumers might react favorably or unfavorably broadens the potential for understanding how value is created or destroyed by creating disparities. Convergence means examining a portfolio of activities that benefits multiple groups by integrating policy, production, and employee impacts, for example. That is, simultaneously lobbying regulators, engineering changes to products, and educating employees and their families on the importance of preventing water-borne diseases for pharmaceutical companies or beverage companies dependent upon fresh water converges, with mutually reinforcing benefits, with employee, product, and information impacts.

Chapter 10 examines the value-creation processes by separating initiatives (*what* firms are doing) from mechanisms (*how* they achieve desired outcomes). Initiatives might be deployed within specific functions (e.g., employee relations, advertising, procurement) or cut across the entire organization (e.g., governance, development, climate change). Similarly, mechanisms deployed may be narrowly construed as solo activities directly controlled by the firm to more collaborative (e.g., cross-sector or public–private) partnerships. Aligning initiatives and mechanisms highlights new outcomes, new mindsets, and new opportunities for addressing old problems. Firms acting unilaterally via foundations and employee volunteer time or cooperatively with other businesses can be uniquely qualified to address literacy issues or crime in local neighborhoods. Corporations with access to specific resources or convening power might be uniquely positioned to exert leadership, enabling others to address thorny issues traditionally resistant to solutions, such as access to medicines, poverty alleviation, or promoting peace through commerce.

Chapter 11 focuses on how multinationals create or destroy value when operating across multiple nation-states. We highlight a key tension within multinationals: the desire for uniform responses while also being locally responsive (Bartlett and Ghoshal, 1989). By expanding Bartlett and Ghoshal's focus on a firm's product-market to explicitly include a firm's socio-political/cultural context, being locally responsive might require customizing workplace conditions to local neighborhoods while also being in compliance with global standards on human trafficking, wages, or hiring child labor. In light of the growth of global accountability standards such as the United Nations Global Compact (UNGC) or the Global Reporting Index (GRI), pressures are mounting for unifying, overarching, comparable practices that are also locally sensitive. Creating value with customized approaches adapted to the particular customs, beliefs, and traditions community-by-community while harmonizing policies across the globe with limited resources can lead to opportunities to leverage and learn from one location to the next. The chapter concludes with a discussion for firms 'stuck in the middle' without credible community involvement and without unifying global themes on corporate impacts.

We conclude in Chapter 12 by examining the art and science of the value-creation process by highlighting how corporations are co-creating value in innovative ways and identifying new areas on how enduring value is co-created. For example, with information and trust as centerpieces of their business models, Google, Airbnb, and Uber are turning business models upside-down and innovating by sharing information. With a central focus on sharing and searching for information, disclosure and trust become paramount as information drives financial returns (rather than financial returns driving disclosure); attracting specific employees while remaining compliant and ensuring the safety of their consumers are challenging the ways in which products and services are delivered and value is created (or destroyed).

Drawing upon lessons from leaders, we offer new research questions about co-creating value in light of managing a firm's true impacts. We explore the implications of identifying and appropriately addressing a firm's true impacts. Multiplier effects, creating opportunities for being doubly productive (or doubly harmful) in creating value are changing how firms compete. Firms not creating mutual benefits—or that are unwilling to articulate mutual benefits—are at risk, with growth, survival, and competitiveness on the line. When trust is lost and a crisis strikes, the way in which firms are able to create value going forward amid the myriad expectations, motivations, constraints, and resources is non-trivial, as BP is finding out. This book suggests co-creating value means focusing on the myriad ways in which corporations impact others: how a firm co-creates (destroys) value in mutually beneficial (or unbalanced, harmful) ways that endure over time.

Looking ahead

The next chapter, Chapter 2, examines four mindsets about the financial impacts of a firm, revisiting Friedman's (1970) mantra that a firm's first and foremost responsibility is making profits without fraud or deception. By expanding Friedman's shareholder-only perspective and testing its underlying assumptions, we explore what happens when co-creating value with others is explicitly included in the process of value creation. Expanding relevant impacts to include financial and non-financial impacts on shareholders and other constituencies, we identify four mindsets underpinning the value creation (destruction) process. These four mindsets create a foundation to help us explore how monetary impacts are related to personnel, product, and information impacts in Chapters 3 and 4.

2 | *Four mindsets on financial impacts*

Discussing how businesses co-create value has traditionally centered on the value created for shareholders (Griffin and Mahon, 1997; Margolis and Walsh, 2003). Co-creating value for the owners of the firm—the shareholders—assumes all other stakeholders have been appropriately compensated. Contracts are fulfilled, expectations met and appropriately satisfied, wages paid and accounts payable settled. The value left over for shareholders, recipients of the residual value created by the firm, are often measured as accounting returns (e.g., net income) or market-based metrics (e.g., return on equity, price to earnings ratio, share price). Yet financial metrics paint an incomplete picture of who benefits, who bears the costs, and the true impacts of the process of co-creating value as it focuses solely on one stakeholder: the shareholder.

As explored in Chapter 1, the value-creation process is inextricably intertwined with many stakeholders. Each stakeholder, with varying interests and, not so surprisingly, different types of contributions, differentially affect the value-creation process. Exploring the many relationships involved uncovers a plethora of exchanges based, in part, on finances. This chapter looks predominantly at financial impacts, which—while admittedly a myopic view—is nonetheless an important starting point to examine how value is created and destroyed.

Shareholders, as owners of the company, often value a portfolio of material impacts based on multiple financial metrics such as share price, returns, long-term growth, or free cash flow. Some shareholders may prefer higher risk with the potential for high returns sometime in the future and invest with zero expectation of a positive financial return in the short term, while still others may choose steady growth with a continual stream of dividends. All in all, there is no singular depiction of firms' financial impact and there is no singular view of a shareholder. Rather a firm's financial impact is multidimensional. The value created and the risks of value creation are likely borne by different groups.

Different firms attract different groups of investors by setting expectations of high risk, steady growth, or dividend growth, for example. Highlighting aspirations, restating the firm's purpose as a rationale for investments, or explaining missed targets solely in costs/benefits to the bottom line reinforces a financial mindset with shareholders only wanting one thing: a return. Yet, different investors consider different types of impacts as important to the business; not just today's return. A myopic view focused solely on today's financial impacts ignores critical aspects affecting how value is created.

A firm's financial mindset often becomes explicitly reinforced when myriad financial and non-financial impacts, signaling conflicting outcomes, are included in evaluating investments. Given noisy signals, long-held heuristics about financial impacts are often relied upon even in the face of contrary evidence (Stout, 2012). Dismissing unexpected results, for example, rather than paying attention to surprising findings, can lead to minimizing hard-to-quantify impacts such as convenience, predicting success in development opportunities, forecasting consumption practices, reputational impacts, or the ability to quickly scale up production. Rather than dismissing non-financial impacts out of hand or minimizing hard-to-quantify impacts, we systematically address them in the next two chapters.

A business's financial relationships with shareholders are a place to start when examining how financial value is co-created. This chapter identifies multiple mindsets regarding financial impacts to achieve net positive outcomes. When it comes to creating value, one size does *not* fit all; there are many paths to consider, each reflecting different mindsets towards shareholders.

We begin by examining direct and indirect financial impacts then introduce a matrix that highlights four different mindsets towards financial impacts: win–win; investments; 'parade of horribles'; and pernicious mindsets.

Financial impacts: direct and indirect effects

Evaluating financial impacts stemming from a firm's process of co-creating value is complex, as financial impacts may be direct or indirect, acute or chronic, and may be assessed based on perceived, expected, or actual effects. As such evaluating financial impacts must address expectations and effects on stakeholders (Wood and Jones, 1995).

Hiring a business school graduate, for example, has a direct impact on the new employee's financial situation: she is earning more money and the income taxes she pays will benefit the local and federal governments. Indirect effects on the local economy will increase as she is able to hire a housekeeper, a laundry service, daycare providers, or a landscaper, while local grocers and restaurants may benefit from her increased consumption. Her ability to maintain a high-paying and steady job while others are unemployed or underemployed, as well as the young woman's newfound independence from parental financial support, may empower additional intangible rewards beyond the weekly wages earned, such as feelings of self-confidence, self-worth, and self-reliance. Yet the expectations of wages earned, hours occupied with work-related activities, and impacts on attending annual family reunions in a distant country, for example, may render the job unsatisfactory in the eyes of the business school graduate.

In this example, assessing the financial net impacts must somehow effectively combine the immediate and direct effects of wages earned by a business school graduate with multiplier effects that might evolve over time or affect others, such as reduced levels of unemployed people, increased demand for dry cleaning and landscape services, and changes in transportation and perhaps community composition as over time the woman gets married, buys a house, perhaps adopts two kids and uses the local school.

Quantifying the direct financial impacts of today's wages paid to the newly employed business school graduate, her expected productivity, or the aggregate change in share price based on all of the new hires and their productivity for a quarter, is arguably easier than appraising other types of impacts. Yet, understanding other impacts: the total wages paid to the local government in the form of taxes (net of the costs of employing an educated, single, healthy woman without children enrolled in the local school system) might be a considerable advantage to the firm as it seeks to attract and retain a young educated workforce. The firm often claims credit for positive financial impacts such as the wages paid and perhaps the number of employees continuously employed for, say, three years. Yet the expected net contributions to community stability and demand for local services while acknowledging the potential for increased traffic congestion might be in the firm's best interests when applying for a municipal permit to expand the business. Multiplier effects are explored in greater depth in Chapter 6, while in this chapter we stay focused on the direct effects and financial impacts.

In this example, justifying the hiring of this woman based solely on wages paid (the out-of-pocket costs weighed alongside the expected productivity benefits) paints a fairly narrow—but easy to measure—picture of the benefits of the hiring decision. Similarly, firing employees, shutting down factories, or closing retail stores in a region are often attributed to financial justifications as an easy to grasp, easy to compare measuring stick across different decisions. Yet, the benefits and costs, in light of the true impacts of the decision on the firm and the community, affects numerous stakeholders.

Similarly, using financial metrics such as stock price, dividends, or quarterly accounting profitability to measure value created by a business with its stakeholders is an easy metric to compare different firms. Yet using only financial indicators relies on several assumptions.

First, stock prices reflect net present value of future profits with value created for and measured by a single stakeholder: the shareholder. If creating value continually over time is a goal, returning money to investors in the short term is one indicator of management success (Freeman, 1984; Mackey and Sisodia, 2013; Freeman et al., 2007; Wood and Jones, 1995). Profits or paying dividends, however, provides only a partial picture of the health of the firm's relationships with investors, suppliers, employees, governments, and others that have a stake in the sustained growth and development of the company.

Second, in a stock market-centric model, all risks, efficiencies, innovations, and perceptions are assumed to be appropriately identified and monetized without delay. The 1990s Asian financial crisis, the 2008 global financial crisis, and the BP oil spill example from Chapter 1 all suggest that identifying—and appropriately monetizing—risks is nearly impossible in today's increasingly complex and interconnected market (Baron, 1995; Husted and de Jesus Salazar, 2006; Windsor, 2006; Krugman, 2009). Appropriate risks include, but are not limited to, an assortment of indictors: whether survival is threatened if the project quickly goes pear-shaped (i.e., fails to meet expectations); any expected delays due to additional regulatory oversight; or the

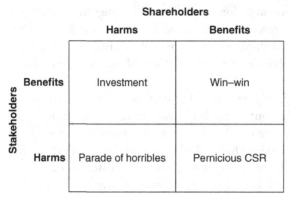

Figure 2.1 Integrating shareholders and stakeholders

likelihood of community uprisings or Twitter feeds resulting in reputational risks and delays (McKinsey, 2014).

Third, stock market or accounting profits reduce managerial decisions to a singular outcome. While this enables investors to avoid cognitive overload, a singular, universal, widely available rubric can have unintended consequences. Taken in isolation, a single financial metric may not necessarily highlight *how* the desired financial outcome is achieved. That is, the process of co-creating value addresses, in part, with *whom* value is created or destroyed.

To overcome the limitations of focusing solely on financial impacts, we juxtapose shareholder impacts with impacts on other stakeholders (Freeman, 1984; Mackey and Sisodia, 2013). By evaluating shareholder and stakeholder impacts simultaneously, business decisions can be assessed for benefits and harms beyond purely financial metrics (see Figure 2.1).

By weighing gains and losses for shareholders as well as other stakeholders, a matrix of four different mindsets about co-creating value emerges: creating win–wins; preventing a parade of horribles; making investments; and avoiding pernicious behaviors (Griffin and Mahon, 1997; Mahon and Griffin, 1999; *The Economist*, 2005, 2008). The four mindsets represent differing perspectives on how business decisions are judged based on their financial and non-financial impacts on other stakeholders. The four financial mindsets are explored in the following text. We also address the underlying assumptions regarding relevant risks and the relative importance of shareholders and other stakeholders in the value-creation process (Margolis and Walsh, 2003; Orlitzky et al., 2003; de Bakker et al., 2005, 2006; Godfrey, 2005).

Win–win situations

When companies create profits for owners while providing positive benefits for multiple stakeholders, it's a win–win situation. This is the desired outcome: shareholders receive a return on their investment, and other stakeholders share in the benefits too. Mutual benefits occurring through increased efficiency and innovation can sustain the benefits. Efficiencies reduce costs and improve profits while effective deployment of resources (e.g., hiring talented employees) increases yields and enhances productivity.

Decreasing water, energy, or carbon consumption, for example, creates a win for owners by reducing expenses while also conserving these scarce natural resources, a win for the environment. In drought conditions, reducing water consumption benefits many others including the local users of water and the local municipality if it provides water and wastewater treatment. Similarly, when carbon costs are high, reducing unnecessary plastic packaging saves on disposal costs.

Securing favorable credit ratings or 'most admired' rankings can lead to an increase in trust and a decrease in transaction costs with lowered interest rates, reduced costs of capital, or fewer oversight costs, thus saving or freeing up money for other investments (Jones, 1995). By building trust between contracting partners, corporations decrease costs and increase efficiencies (Jones, 1995; Kish-Gephart et al., 2010). Efficiencies and productivity that create mutual benefits are explored in more detail in the following text.

Efficiency

Efficiency of inputs and increasing productivity are critical aspects of the financial mindset represented in this quadrant. Efficiently using *inputs* can decrease noxious gas emissions in manufacturing plants or reduce food waste in restaurants, for instance. Increasing the concentration of laundry detergents, engineering a new formula of detergent,

or changing the demand for detergents, for example, can create efficiencies with benefits for shareholders and other stakeholders.

When a large greengrocer partners with a manufacturer of heating,
ventilation, and air conditioning (HVAC) equipment, to create new,
efficient compressors, blowers, and heating/cooling units, this saves
the retailer money on refrigeration of frozen and perishable goods.
Working together they can create efficiencies with a new design and
claim a win–win partnership. The grocery store reduces its electricity
costs as it replaces its aging HVAC equipment in existing stores and
can pass the cost savings on to customers in its everyday low costs.
The HVAC equipment manufacturer, meanwhile, can expand its product line and sell the new HVAC equipment to grocery stores, restaurants, and industrial plants needing energy-efficient refrigeration and
cooling.

Efficiencies in reducing carbon, water, energy, and waste streams can
be achieved by many organizations, not just corporations. A public
library achieved a 38 percent reduction in energy costs over nine years
with new light bulbs, light sensors, and other innovations to reduce
electricity use when a room is not occupied. Similarly, universities are
finding budget savings of 1–2 percent on electricity bills of $25 million
by installing light sensors, creating competitions within dorm rooms,
and carefully examining all facilities. These savings can be passed on
directly to citizens in lower tax bills or directly to students through
limited increases in tuition bills.

'Win–wins' result from improving *productivity*. Initial technological investments in computers, Skype, video conferencing, or distance
learning can pay off in improved employee connectivity and productivity. Simplifying global supply chains with exclusivity contracts can
improve productivity by building deep relations with selective worldwide suppliers for enhanced delivery, quality, and on-time standards.
Building relationships based on more than just pricing can help both
the firm and the supplier mutually benefit and withstand issues such as
wage arbitrage and transportation costs as both organizations evolve
over the lifetime of the relationship.

Fast-moving consumer goods companies can reduce the volume of
packaging by concentrating products in smaller containers, removing cardboard rolls within toilet paper, or redesigning products to use
less material (e.g., less plastic in water bottles). Installing low-flow
toilets or reducing energy costs can also result in significant savings.

Replacing Styrofoam cups with ceramic mugs may, over their lifetime of use, reduce the water, carbon, and energy costs associated with the production and disposal of these items. Recycled cardboard reduces costs, reduces demand for non-renewable resources, and extends the lives of landfills by eliminating excess waste.

Innovation

Technological innovations co-create value by adapting products, processes, or management practices that in turn create wins for multiple stakeholders. When shareholder value increases and others benefit, a mutually beneficial 'win–win' outcome is created.

Product innovations co-create value by satisfying clients (those that buy) and consumers (those that use), resulting in increased revenues to the firm. Fast-moving consumer goods firms, for example, are creating smaller, individualized sachets using less material and/or recycled material to reach new markets (Vachani and Smith, 2008). Creating more individualized sachets is not without controversy, as the net impact of this innovation is often borne by the local community with an increased volume of materials sent to landfill. The innovations in reducing the size of disposable diapers by creating 'thin' diapers resulted in even more disposable diapers that ended up in the landfill.

Product innovations targeting new customers create win–win scenarios for both the firm and its consumers. Tweaking existing products to attract a new segment of consumers or dedicating a proportion of the proceeds from a product to a specific cause builds the brand, satisfies customers, and helps others at the same time. For example, numerous organizations and products target breast cancer survivors and their supporters by promoting pink products or prominently displaying a pink ribbon. The National Football League (NFL) partners with the American Cancer Society to increase breast cancer awareness, particularly in underserved communities, by publicly displaying (and selling) shoes, socks, sweatshirts, and uniforms adorned with cancer survivor symbols. This partnership has enabled the NFL to expand its product offering and incorporate women or people that have been touched by breast cancer into its customer base, while cynics would claim this attempt at impression management obscures other issues, such as domestic abuse of women by NFL players.

Technological innovations have fundamentally changed how value is created by people in remote locations to access information and communicate from nearly anywhere there is a satellite signal. A handheld cell phone is no longer a simple telephone. Rather a cell phone is a mini-computer that can send and receive emails, surf the web, provide directions via geo-positioning satellites (GPS), and serve as a handheld library complete with books, magazines, and a dictionary. A smartphone enables fishermen in faraway villages to record the precise coordinates of where their fishing nets are dropped each morning, increasing the yield for a single fisherman in a given day. Rather than spending time trying to find where the nets were dropped in the morning, village fishermen go directly in their boats to the GPS coordinates. Using phones or internet access, the fishermen can then easily compare prices offered by different fish wholesalers, which in turn increases the village fishermen's wages, keeps prices stable, and passes savings on to consumers.

The increased demand for smartphones is, interestingly, a continuously evolving story in the potential to create or destroy value. Increased demand for smartphones has also increased demand for rare earth metals, which in turn exacerbates the demands on extractive companies, which can worsen the working conditions of child laborers with the potential increased incidence of human trafficking and claims of poor treatment by employees. Recycling handsets, or offering rebates on old phones when a new generation of smartphones is released, however, is quickly becoming a new norm in how smartphone manufacturers are competing for new customers while limiting the demand for the rare earth metals.

Increases in cell phone usage has been linked to increased spillover effects such as the rate of new businesses being created in Africa (Lane, 2012), which in turn can help perpetuate a growing African economy, thereby enabling even more people to purchase cell phones. A self-reinforcing positive feedback loop of innovation and economic gains in turn can perpetuate spillover impacts and innovations. In the case of cell phones, developing solar-powered phones at an economically feasible price can help perpetuate access to a growing economy while limiting costs and demands on electricity. Or designing cell phone devices that shut down, eliminating the demand for electricity, after fully charging the device's battery, for example, would save money while reducing the demand for electricity.

Process innovations focus on how the product is created; from the procurement of raw materials to delivery of the product to the end users. Process innovations occur along the entire value chain and may focus on specific activities, such as using water rather than chemical solvents to clean or degrease products. Using high-pressured water has the added benefits of decreasing greenhouse gas emissions and reducing the toxic effluents that need to be treated.

Creating alternative fuel sources (e.g., solar power, wind turbines) to power a business often creates win–win scenarios after the initial investment has been recuperated. Toyota has been able to develop its leadership position in hybrid (gas–electric) cars and has expanded its product line beyond the bestselling Prius, passing the six million mark of cumulative hybrid vehicles sold in 2013 (www.toyota.com). With increased worldwide competition in the hybrid vehicle market, the Toyota Prius has been able to continuously innovate, maintain its lead, and penetrate new markets around the world. Similarly, Tata redesigned a lighter automobile with less material and high fuel efficiency as an alternative to a family riding on a small scooter. While the Tata Nano vehicle didn't become the bestseller that was expected, the innovations in lighter weight materials to be used in automobile construction has led to numerous spin-off innovations used in other product lines (www.tata.com).

Management innovations create opportunities for win-win situations centered on employees or using information more effectively. Analyzing large volumes of data for consumption patterns and new service opportunities is emerging as a growth business (Kiron et al., 2011). Directly linking consumer demands for seasonal goods, for example, with manufacturers that supply highly desirable seasonal goods (e.g., Halloween costumes in October in the US) has enabled more rapid restocking of stores, which in turn generates more sales and is tied to actual supply and demand rather than forecasts. Just-in-time delivery of products removes inefficiencies and decreases the costs of storing inventory. The increased demands for next-day delivery of products allows online merchants to effectively compete with bricks-and-mortar stores on convenience and delivery.

Two relatively new restaurants in the Washington, DC area, Founding Farmers and Farmers Fishers Bakers, have created a niche business by serving quality food grown from local, sustainable sources. By meeting a demand for sustainable sourcing, farm-to-fork logistics has grown since the turn of the century. Successful restaurants are working directly with a variety of local farmers to ensure reliable delivery of quality food during all four seasons. By supporting farmers with fertilizer, education, and seeds, these restaurants are actively investigating if disposing of today's food scraps can be used as compost for next year's garden—with the potential to eliminate waste and increase productivity while building the relationship between restaurant and farmer.

These restaurants are removing food scraps from landfill, which saves the restaurant disposal fees and potentially decreases transportation costs, while a revenue stream might be created from farmers willing to pay restaurants for waste food that can be used in compost. Net benefits, of course, will need to be assessed against the need to offset the costs involved in separating organic food scraps from non-organic restaurant waste.

At the same time both restaurants have continually reconsidered many business relationships, enabling them to successfully thrive during a recession when competition is tight. The restaurants employ chefs willing to continually adjust the menu for seasonally available ingredients and a cadre of staff culled from students studying at a local university. Also featured is a green garden on the rooftop, complete with bees as pollinators whose honey is used in the restaurant. The restaurants have identified local farmers, rather than wholesalers, which in turn required new skills in restaurant management. These innovations elevate some decisions as strategically important to the organization that might have been previously been delegated to a low-level subordinate to decide: the supply of fresh food, the menu, and the design of the restaurant itself including the tables, chairs, lighting, and recyclability of the swizzle sticks.

In another example of management innovation, a large telecommunications firm worked with Underwriters Laboratory (UL) to expand the safe operating specifications for heating and cooling units, thus saving energy. By allowing transmission units to operate at a higher temperature in the summer and a lower temperature in the winter, the telecommunications firm saves money on cooling its data storage facilities in the summer and heating in the winter, while not compromising the integrity of the heating and cooling units and ensuring continuous transmission for its consumers.

New innovations with win–win situations might be spun-off as new organizations in their own right. Pharmaceutical giants GlaxoSmithKline and Pfizer, for example, combined their efforts to combat HIV/AIDS. ViiV Healthcare, an organization dedicated to addressing HIV/AIDs in Africa in 2009 (www.viivhealthcare.com) co-locates medicines, policy and distribution expertise. Hiring a well-trained and highly focused staff, ViiV Healthcare has been able to continuously prioritize HIV/AIDS in a way that was not possible as a product line in either of the two large multinational corporations. As an independent entity, ViiV Healthcare is able to garner the support of foundations, non-profit organizations, and human health organizations to holistically address the prevention, treatment, and implications of the HIV/AIDS disease for the patient and his/her family.

A financial mindset focused on win–win opportunities is often the focus of social entrepreneurs: creating a positive financial impact while also solving a problem. Timberland, for example, was created to increase shareholder value while simultaneously benefiting others (Swartz, 2010). Customers gain new products or services, damage to the natural environment is minimized with carbon-neutral management, and positive benefits to communities are integrated into the founding norms, beliefs, and traditions of the firm. Value is created for the shareholders, the firm, and many other stakeholders.

A win–win financial mindset that continuously creates win–win situations is certainly optimal. Following Milton Friedman's (1970) mantra that the social responsibility of a firm is to increase profits without fraud or deception this is the only quadrant in which a business should operate. If a clear-cut profit cannot be immediately identified, an activity should be eliminated as part of the firm's portfolio of activities. Regardless of the activity's contribution to the firm's mission or how the activity contributes to the firm differentiating itself from competitors, if the activity can't be monetized and attributed to profiting shareholders, it should be eliminated.

A win–win financial mindset creates a narrative about businesses that shareholders benefit while other stakeholders (proud employees, satisfied consumers, healthy and happy neighbors, fairly compensated suppliers) also benefit. While a win–win mindset clearly benefits many stakeholders simultaneously, it is only one narrative about how firms co-create value. We explore a second mindset, 'preventing a parade of horribles,' in the next section.

Parade of horribles

A business crisis creates downward financial pressures while negatively affecting many constituents. Neither shareholders nor other constituents benefit, and many stakeholders are negatively harmed. A crisis is often depicted as a 'parade of horribles,' as newspapers and social media outlets can exacerbate the importance of an event and the firm's risks with constant worldwide media coverage. Clearly, preventing crises is in management's best interest, as mitigating harm and avoiding the headlines justifies investments in reputational risk management (Fombrun, 1996; Flanigan, 1990).

A 'parade of horribles' mindset is often a defensive stance resulting from efforts to mitigating future crises, curtailing the spread of a current crisis, or actively preventing sensitive issues from becoming full-blown crises (Mahon, 1989; Wartick and Mahon, 1994). Preventative strategies are often depicted as insurance policies (Godfrey, 2005), one aspect of a risk-management mindset aimed at preserving capital or avoiding the loss of value by not becoming further implicated in a public 'parade of horribles.' Product recalls, for example, often result in decreased stock valuation and if the recall follows a product failure that caused harm, inconvenience, even death, the recall can start a downward spiral of a 'parade of horribles' (Wood and Jones, 1995; Frooman, 1999).

A parade of horribles may be initiated by internally or externally generated events. Internally oriented crises often stem from technical or management mishaps that halt production, interrupt service delivery, or result in significant loss of top talent. Often under the direct control of management, internally generated crises can often be contained with seemingly little change in the outward appearances of the firm. Internally generated crises, with the flexibility containment within the boundaries of the firm, are managed quite differently from externally oriented crises that involve multiple organizations, sectors, or communities and include natural disasters (Mitroff et al., 1987).

Crises such as natural disasters are often more widespread, out of the direct control of a single organization, and frequently become headlines news as a story among a continued stream of bad news, thus perpetuating the moniker 'a parade of horribles.' These crises can rapidly spread across firms, industries, and geographies, making crises more difficult to manage, contain, and recover from (Mitroff et al.,

1987). Identifying, prioritizing, and creating communication systems to anticipate crises, as well as legal support to protect or staunch the flow of value, is essential (Wartick and Mahon, 1994; Mitroff, 1994). Being implicated in a parade of horribles as collateral damage can test even the strongest relationships, as the Ford and Firestone families found when the Bridgestone/Firestone tires were found to be at the center of the Ford Explorer roll-overs resulting in a massive recall of Ford Explorers and a nationwide effort to replace Firestone tires on Ford vehicles in the early 2000s (Moll, 2003).

A parade of horribles mindset requires a company to focus on risk management and communications. As the firm works through the crisis—gathering information, communicating with constituencies, empowering employees to be ambassadors, benchmarking what others are doing to avoid crises, creating industry- or country-level norms, and being compliant with local and national laws—shaping stakeholders' expectations is a large part of management's job.

The crises of others can serve as an investment opportunity for unaffected businesses watching from the sidelines. In times of oil spill disasters, for example, competitors can be assessing their own environmental containment efforts by refreshing their safety plans, rehearsing oil containment drills, or researching technologies to skim the oil from the surface of the water, while the focal organization is forced to react to the oil spill. Far from the spotlight, preparations can be fine-tuned, containment techniques refined, press releases readied for the moment when they might be needed, and websites developed that can immediately be deployed in the event of a widespread crisis.

The largest management challenge often starts after the public crisis ends. Once the spotlight is off and social media has moved onto a new story, fatigue can set in within the company. The energy to make long-lasting changes may dissipate, which increases the risk that the post-crisis opportunity to institutionalize changes might be lost until the next crisis occurs. Quite often when the spotlight is turned off, the firm moves on to address the latest new challenge and the moment passes with a lost opportunity to rethink the design and delivery of products, or more closely examine logistical and manufacturing processes (Mitroff, 1994).

Once the crisis has passed, the company can develop the habits of keeping abreast of legal changes, using competitive information to predict future trends, and monitoring changing consumer sentiment.

Apologizing, repairing relationships, and rebuilding confidence with stakeholders requires a commitment from top management to move out of a crisis-oriented mindset and deeply embed the learnings from the crisis. Quite often an early warning system is installed to anticipate future crises by collecting and filtering vast quantities of information to mitigate surprises (Ansoff, 1975, 1980) or develop management responses to adapt and build resilience when (not if) a crisis occurs next.

A win–win mindset is surely optimal, and a focus on crises with a 'parade of horribles' mindset is to be avoided when possible. Yet two additional mindsets are more prevalent in today's modern businesses: making investments and avoiding pernicious behavior.

Investments and cost centers

An investment mindset reflects a narrative about other stakeholders benefitting immediately while the payoff for shareholders is sometime in the future. Being able to articulate the positive benefits of an activity for employees, consumers, or communities while encouraging investors to patiently wait for their return on investment is a hallmark of this 'making investments' mindset. Interestingly, this same scenario: positive benefits to other constituents while not increasing profits is also, by definition, a cost center. That is, spending money without an expectation of a return is a cost to the business. Sorting out if a decision is an investment or a cost center is at the heart of this narrative about financial impacts.

When a decision creates benefits for others without immediately generating profits for shareholders, will you proceed with this necessary investment or see it as an unnecessary cost? Investment decisions tied to a firm's strategy, even if profits are currently not being generated, are never redundant (Immelt, 2005). The financial narrative surrounding these decisions will determine whether the mindset is more closely aligned with an investment decision or a cost center.

A cost center mindset focuses on issues as unfunded mandates: another issue to manage on an already full plate of responsibilities or as a bolted-on activity (Grayson and Hodges, 2004). Cost center-oriented activities are particularly vulnerable to being axed during economic downturns. Without a positive return to shareholders or a narrative of how value is co-created over time, these activities are readily axed or significantly curtailed during economic downturns as they are considered discretionary activities, without a clear narrative of the potential value to shareholders. Philanthropic give-aways of products, money, time, or endorsements are often (erroneously) depicted as cost center decisions not tied to the value-creation process of the business. Philanthropic giveaways are explored in greater depth in Chapter 8.

The difference between bolted-on activities and investments often becomes clear when leadership changes, economic hardship strikes, or political instability occurs. Without an explanation of how others share in the value created, bolted-on activities—however noble yet without a clear alignment with the business's value-creation process—are often difficult to justify when pressed for a rationale. Management's challenge is to understand how an activity creates value for employees, suppliers, retailers, and the community and why it to be maintained as an investment (Freeman et al., 2007; Mackey and Sisodia, 2013).

Toyota, in the late 1980s, started investing in new hybrid technologies beyond a fossil-fuel engine, with significant support and encouragement by the Japanese government. Numerous attempts were considered before the Prius, a hybrid gas-electric vehicle, was introduced as a commercially viable, mass-produced hybrid passenger vehicle in 1997 (www.toyota.com). As a stand-alone project supported solely by the private sector, the Prius and its commercially viable hybrid gas–electric technology might have only been considered a cost center.

During the same time period in Detroit, Michigan, home of the Big Three American automobile manufacturers, the technology for a mass-produced hybrid passenger vehicle was underway but seemingly without the same vigor until the beleaguered General Motors (GM) faced an unprecedented bailout from the American government in the 2000s. Shortly after the US government became a majority owner in General Motors, the Chevy Volt, GM's first hybrid vehicle and the first of the Big Three hybrid passenger vehicles, became available. And with tax credits available to purchasers of hybrid vehicles, sales increased.

Investments that co-create value can help a firm become an employer of choice by attracting, retaining, and developing top talent. In tight labor markets the ability to attract and retain employees, especially skilled employees in some countries (e.g., China, India, areas of the Australian outback), can boost pride and loyalty while reducing recruitment and retraining costs within the workplace. Competition for top talent is changing the employer–employee relationship by altering expectations of hours worked and benefits such as pensions and signing bonuses, which in turn improves potential candidates' perceptions of a company (Greening and Turban, 2000).

The investment quadrant is often composed of investments expected to eventually pay off financially, shifting the activity to the win–win quadrant. Yet, investments might be justified for ethical reasons without a specific monetized return or 'that's just how we do things around here' when additional safety precautions not required by law are instilled across all plants of some petrochemical refineries.

Investments in co-creating value might include property, plant, and equipment purchases of solar panels, wind turbines, geothermal heat sources, or low-flow toilets as experiments in reducing consumption of carbon, water, or energy. Investing in projects to reduce water consumption signals the willingness of the firm to reduce its environmental impact by using fewer scarce natural resources.

Investments can also focus on improving the firm's reputation (Rindova et al., 2005) as a preferred partner to build trust and decrease costs (Jones, 1995). Securing the proverbial seat at the table with regulatory officials and community representatives during business panels or government reviews is especially important for companies in the controversial alcohol, tobacco, or casino industries (Mahon and McGowan, 1996). There's a saying in Washington, DC that 'if you're not at the table, you're on the menu.'

Overall, business decisions yielding positive benefits without providing short-term profits for investors are investments that can be considered cost centers. The last financial mindset we explore occurs when shareholders benefit but other stakeholders are harmed: pernicious behaviors.

Pernicious behaviors

Pernicious behaviors create harm (real or perceived) while shareholders receive profits, perhaps unaware of the externalities created by the profit-making activities. Pernicious from a stakeholder's perspective, these actions are often heralded by shareholders as necessary evils or the cost of doing business. As businesses are increasingly exposed to more and varied expectations from diverse stakeholders, internalizing others' interests is important, yet new, for many businesses.

Pernicious behaviors create externalities that others must bear the brunt, pay for, or manage. Externalities of businesses often considered in environmental terms include: an increase in traffic, noise pollution, and congestion as well as new job opportunities affecting local households when new businesses relocate within their community. One typical response to perceived pernicious behavior is an increase in regulations to mandate safeguards and protect individuals from undue harm.

The externalities in modern businesses are often borne by dispersed communities, making pernicious behavior difficult to manage via a regulatory response (i.e., we'll just increase sanctions). For example, online retailers in the US do not have to pay state taxes unless the online retailer has a significant presence in a particular state, the rationale being that it's too cumbersome to force an online retailer to collect taxes across multiple municipalities. Certainly, a tax exemption gives online retailers and their affiliates a competitive advantage that benefits shareholders. State treasuries and their citizens, however, bear the burden of additional costs, including opportunity costs of missed taxes, and are increasingly interested in leveling the playing field for their own local businesses. In response, states have passed legislation requiring online retailers to pay state taxes. These laws have caused online retailers to close warehouses in states that pass tax legislation, causing significant hardship for local employees. Overall, online retailers claim that online delivery benefits shareholders by keeping costs low, yet this practice is exacting a toll on state treasuries. Furthermore, the spillover effects of laid-off employees from affiliated business increases unemployment benefits paid by the state and national governments.

Similarly, food trucks are becoming a popular sight in downtown urban areas for quick lunches. From downtown Washington, DC to Los Angeles, CA and including communities in the heartland such as Ames, Iowa, food trucks are experimenting with new routes, menus, and advertising to increase their following. Able to offer lower prices with lower overhead costs while also not being subject to the local food tax (at the ire of many local lunch restaurants), food trucks are able to adapt quickly to seasonal trends, allow loyal customers to track their location online, and provide more food options than what is available in traditional restaurants.

Pernicious behaviors highlight how benefits and costs stemming from businesses can be unequally distributed: stakeholders sharing in

the benefits of commerce are often quite different from the stakeholders bearing the brunt of the business's externalities (Wood and Jones,
1995). Pernicious behaviors create disparities. The disparities between
who receives the benefits and who bears the costs can lead to unequal
opportunities in jobs, education, and healthcare services provided by
the firm with unequal access to capital, computer skills, or telephony.

Whether an intended or unintended consequence of business, pernicious behaviors are often at the center of conversations about value
destruction rather than creation. Many stakeholders are implicated
when value is destroyed, including suppliers, employees, consumers,
clients, regulators, and neighbors. That is, a supplier-of-a-supplier
might be hiring child labor or engaged in human trafficking behaviors
to save money and generates better returns for shareholders yet vio-
lates international laws. While the firm itself is not engaged in these
illegal behaviors, by sourcing materials from a company that engages
in human trafficking, the firm becomes complicit as its profits are
ill-gotten.

As the disparities of benefits received by some stakeholders with
costs borne by other stakeholders are made more visible via social
media, vitriolic situations occur. Retribution and retaliation acceler-
ated by anger is often targeted, rightly or wrongly, at neighborhood
franchises. Pernicious behaviors, even without pernicious intentions,
can also be exacerbated by differences in attitude, religion, gender,
or race.

Allegations of pernicious behavior, real or perceived, might include
taking advantage of local, indigenous employees; expropriating disproportionate profits to home countries or to investors domiciled elsewhere; creating disparities in wages, information, skills or expertise;
transfer payments or contributions that support corruption or repres-
sive regimes.

Attempts to ameliorate pernicious behaviors often target specific issues or corporate practices: child or forced labor; human
trafficking; unhealthy workforce conditions; corruption; unethical
sourcing practices; expropriation of profits; or national security
(Kedia and Kuntz, 1981; Cochran and Wood, 1984; Marcus and
Goodman, 1986; McGuire et al., 1988). National legislation and
international regulatory frameworks to address these issues are rapidly increasing in numbers but with inconsistent results (Prakash
and Potoski, 2014).

Often mandated by government rather than motivated by the market, these demands on businesses stretch already scarce time and limited energy. Mandates become additional costs that must be absorbed or passed on as higher prices to consumers if they are not an opportunity for innovation (Porter and van der Linde, 1995). By flipping pernicious impacts into opportunities the firm (or a new firm) can fulfill unmet needs. Fulfilling unmet needs creates value by converging new demands with new responses. Creating new business models, however, quite often requires rearranging relationships with shareholders, employees, consumers, the government, local communities, and/or thought leaders. In short, an incremental change won't do. Rather, a radical readjustment of how a firm creates value is needed.

Implications for co-creating value

The four financial mindsets suggest financial decisions are neither clear-cut nor easy decisions as they are inextricably intertwined with more than just shareholders. Multiple stakeholders co-create financial value, share in the value created, and multiple stakeholders bear the costs when value is destroyed. A focus solely on shareholder benefits paints an incomplete picture of modern management and how value is co-created or destroyed.

Co-creating value with owners must also include concomitant narratives regarding impacts on suppliers, employees, consumers, and many others. Narrowing the scope of success to target shareholders with discussions centered solely on financial impacts: (a) is not in the best interests of modern managers; (b) unnecessarily limits the opportunities to co-create value; and (c) creates myopia when managers are faced with challenges that can't be solved by giving more money (Godfrey, 2014).

Clearly, understanding a firm's financial impacts is important, since without economic well-being the corporation would fail and many stakeholders would be negatively impacted including shareholders and employees. At the same time, corporations affect more than just shareholders. And corporations have more than just financial impacts. As new narratives are being developed and new questions are being asked, the heuristic of a shareholder-only mindset is showing its age and its limitations of how value is created and destroyed by firms with their interactions across stakeholders.

New questions are being asked: who, beyond the owners, shares in the benefits created by businesses? Is value created by efficiencies only, or is value also being created through innovations? What investments are being made with what expected returns? Are these expenses merely sunk costs perceived as the minimal threshold of doing business? Can value be created that fuels future growth or are these activities merely an 'insurance policy' to offset future (or past) crises? Listening carefully to the answers to these questions creates new opportunities for co-creating value, building more robust justifications beyond merely financial considerations while also expanding the expected outcomes of the value that businesses create.

Businesses, for example, voluntarily engage in beyond-compliance activities in order to benefit shareholders and other stakeholders—including but not limited to governments, employees, or rivals—to signal priorities, gain advantage, or pre-empt future actions (Russo, 2009; Russo and Fouts, 1997). Identifying and prioritizing appropriate activities might be done by an entrepreneurial manager, driven by employees in the manufacturing process or correspond to demands of customers, suppliers, investors, or governmental agencies. Alternatively, activities might arise from the firm's desire to address a social issue while simultaneously ensuring its economic growth: hunger, homelessness, pollution, climate change, poverty alleviation, disease prevention, etc. Rather than considering social and economic goals as trade-offs, linking customers, neighborhoods, and employees through volunteerism, transfer of skills and expertise, etc. creates a win for the business, which develops more productive employees, and for employees, who willingly contribute to their local community (Harrison and Freeman, 1999).

Corporate impacts, when considered as profit depletion or a cost center rather than as an outcome of the value-creation process, are often narrowly contrived as financial impacts. The challenge is in part broadening the mindset of businesses as purely profit creators and away from appeasing stakeholders through a giveaway mindset. Rather, a focus on the process of how value is created is required. And second, what is of value that is created by the firm and being sought by different stakeholders? In the meshing of common interests among stakeholders innovation is often sparked. That is, co-creating value with stakeholders becomes a process of seeing challenges as opportunities to configure new products; identify new activities or new markets that require new attributes; prioritize different impacts such as thinking about employee as ambassadors to the communities; or address employee impacts alongside product, financial, and information impacts. A focus on corporate impacts shifts to investment opportunities tied to the value-creation process.

Every business can co-create value when faced with seemingly insurmountable, intractable social problems if the scale of the problem is redefined (Weick, 1984). That is, numerous small-scale activities that cumulatively co-create value enable all businesses, regardless of size, to make a positive difference. Rather than focusing on national goals such as GDP growth or malnutrition rates, concentrating on job creation creates opportunities for the business, the newly employed, and the community. We explore the tension between addressing local customs and traditions while being mindful of the desire for global efficiencies in Chapter 11.

Focusing on the many direct *and* indirect effects stemming from a firm co-creating value, we expand attention outward from the firm to the stakeholders involved in the process. Co-creating value involves suppliers of a raw material as well as the suppliers of the supplier as well as the distributor and the retailing. In the same way, by focusing on indirect effects, a firm's focus expands from just the employee to include their family and entire household to address issues affecting absenteeism, productivity, and retention. Focusing on direct and indirect effects emphasizes the employee and his/her extended family to continuously co-create value. These multiplier effects of the value-creation process are expanded upon in Chapters 5 and 6.

By adopting a portfolio approach of impacts across the entire organization, one question becomes how each business unit makes the company more vulnerable to becoming a parade of horribles. Have the expectations of the businesses changed? Overall, when looking across the entire set of businesses in a firm, is the firm in investment mode, operating as a cost center, or hovering just beyond the parade of horribles in its approach to co-creating value?

From a competitive perspective, positioning an organization within an industry for competitive or comparative advantage has been researched for decades (Porter, 1985). Adding in a dynamic perspective: when times change, expectations alter, and regulations are promulgated or consumers change preferences, are you positioned to move from a crisis or pernicious quadrant to an investment area or the win–win quadrant? For example, tobacco-related issues have been important on and off for US shareholders and regulators for more than five decades (Mahon and McGowan, 1996).

In sum, co-creating value is the goal, and creating net positive impacts is a choice. But how does a manager choose, and choose wisely? Which impacts are relevant, and how can companies achieve the desired impact? If only one yardstick assesses financial performance against shareholder expectations or yesterday's returns, then a corporation is unnecessarily reduced to narrowly focusing on financial metrics that can be monetized, such as cost-cutting efficiencies and new product innovations. This win–lose financial narrative of a company co-creating for shareholders at the expense of employees, customers, communities, governments, or suppliers needlessly narrows the solution set of a modern company. Addressing multiple impacts simultaneously, and holistically, is in the firm's best interests and has unexpected payoffs (Jones, 1991; Fort and Schipani, 2004; Freeman et al., 2007; Porter and Kramer, 2011; Crane et al., 2014a) that we will explore in the following chapters.

Thinking broadly, corporate impacts beyond financial flows include personnel, product, and information impacts. Employees and facilities are often directly affected by corporate decisions. Through products, supply chains, and distribution networks, corporations make significant impacts. Corporations affect others via information through informing, educating, and enabling others. Taken individually each impact (financial, employee, products, information) is an isolated opportunity for creating value. Taken altogether, in the aggregate, corporate impacts demonstrates how a firm co-creates value (or not) in a global economy.

Thought experiment: can the firm articulate the value that is co-created and with whom it is created? Key questions from this chapter include: is the expected outcome an economic engine for future growth or an insurance policy to offset past practices? Is it an investment with an expectation of a future return to stakeholders or a cost without an expected return for shareholders?

Looking ahead

The next two chapters focus on broadening the narrative of a corporation's impacts beyond its financial impacts to explicitly include employees, products, and information, providing a more nuanced understanding of how value is co-created or destroyed. We first examine impacts in the workplace with employees and then impacts from firm's products in Chapter 3. Chapter 4 examines the impacts created through information-sharing that educates and enables others to create value.

While employee, product, and information impacts are often collectively called 'non-financial impacts' or 'human impacts,' there are considerable financial implications intertwined with employees, products, and information-sharing. By purposely drawing attention to a multiplicity of impacts created by a firm, and recognizing the inextricably intertwined financial and human impacts of corporations, we also expand the possible solution sets for addressing entrenched problems faced by modern managers. An expanded perspective of a corporation's impacts towards the value-creation process involves many stakeholders in the workplace, the production process, and when sharing information.

3 | *Employee and product impacts*

Businesses depend upon their interactions with many stakeholders to co-create value. Embedded within a network of relationships, it is in a business's best interests—and for that matter in the best interest of others involved in the process—to co-create value rather than destroy it. Yet, creating and sustaining value requires a company to think about its multiple impacts. That is, how a firm's process of creating value is mediated, enhanced, or destroyed by employees, products, and sharing of information as well as through its finances (Evan, 1965).

In this chapter we focus on two additional impacts in the process of value creation, starting with two observations. First, a business impacts stakeholders, and is impacted by its relationships with stakeholders, in more ways than merely through financial impacts. Expanding a firm's network of impacts to include financial considerations alongside personnel, product, and information impacts creates a more holistic and realistic picture of modern businesses. And second, it is in a business's best interest to make a net positive impact since the cumulative effects of a business enhances its ability to survive, adapt, and thrive (Henisz et al., 2014; Cheng et al., 2014; Henisz, 2014). Focusing solely on a firm's financial impacts unnecessarily narrows management's attention and—as depicted in the BP oil spill example in the first chapter—misses opportunities to co-create value while losing out on the chance to mitigate the destruction of value.

Imagine an organization that considers value created is for the benefit of shareholders, with everyday decisions continuously reinforcing a 'shareholder is king' heuristic. When a hiccup occurs and shareholder value is destroyed, the underlying drivers of how value is created might be obscured, poorly interpreted, or entirely misunderstood, making the path to regaining value cloudy or muddled at best. Getting to the underlying levers that co-create value for the firm and its stakeholders is the focus of this chapter.

Imagine a different organization that continuously reinforces the heuristic: the 'customer is king.' This firm would have vastly different priorities from a shareholder-focused firm, with different norms, values, and heuristics—even though both organizations can be very successful. Success for both companies is likely measured by their ability to satisfy shareholders and customers—it's just different mindsets that, in turn, create different management systems undergirding how each organization develops relationships with shareholders, customers, employees, suppliers, retailers, and stakeholders in the value-creation process.

In this chapter and the next chapter we add to the financial impacts from Chapter 2 by exploring ways in which firms interact with and are impacted by their stakeholders: (a) with employees and in the workplace; (b) with customers through product production process; and (c) with communities and the broader public by sharing information. At these points of interaction, an impact occurs, and the potential for value is created or destroyed. Impacts, often quantified into solely financial costs and benefits, can also be perceptual assessments with non-financial and human implications affecting the effectiveness of stakeholders *and* the firm.

By exploring employees, products, and information impacts of firms, we connect the why, what, and how of co-creating value. We examine *why* certain firms may be well suited for addressing one, or more, impacts simultaneously. *What* impacts different firms are addressing based on their specific contexts, and *how* unequal value creation (disparities or inequalities arising from what stakeholders receive from a business, as well as what they contribute to the value creations process), is leading to new questions regarding the viability of capitalism (McKinsey, 2014).

We build upon Freeman's (1984, p. 23) insights to examine stakeholders of a business: groups that affect or are affected by the achievement of a business's objectives—including employees, financiers, governments, and communities—to understand the value-creation process. By discerning if, when, and under what conditions the interests of various groups are met. Quite simply, if stakeholders and the firm do not create mutual benefits net of costs in light of the true impacts, the relationship will likely wither away. Without articulating the mutual benefits, the relationship will lose the attention of value-creating managers.

Combining Freeman's (1984) insights to focus on stakeholder groups, and Evan's (1965) insights that finances, employees, products, and information mediate organizational relationships, we broaden our focus to the relationships involved in co-creating value: a firm's relationships with employees, consumers, and suppliers involved with products, as well as the firm's broader communities through information-sharing.

It is neither simple nor straightforward to focus on relationships as a multitude of stakeholders are involved in the value-creation process. If you are a manager of a very small firm, for instance, with only one supplier, one customer, one financier, and an employee alongside you, the manager, there are already 24 possible combinations of relationships (i.e., four factorial relationships) to consider.[1]

Now imagine if you are a manager of a slightly larger firm expanding its network through globalization or technology. Both the volume and variety of expectations grows. An exclusivity contract with your supplier might have originally been based on low costs with price, volume, and product quality considerations. Yet as growth exposes your firm to increased global competition, new considerations are added to your vendor's contract: sourcing requirements, codes of conduct, financing support for future growth, variety of packaging sizes (e.g., single-use sachets and family-sized bottles), coordination with other suppliers, or labeling details in a variety of languages to satisfy an array of clients in the region.

No longer are price, volume, and product quality the only overriding factors within the contract. The volume and variety of expectations has increased, perpetuating a more complex relationship to include sourcing, codes, financing for growth, variety of packaging, coordination with others, etc. that include financial and non-financial considerations.

---

[1] Theoretically, there are 24 possible one-, two-, or three-way combinations. Calculating the number of possible combinations is different than calculating the maximum number of (dyadic) ties in the network. The maximum number of ties is achieved when everyone knows everyone else. This is the maximum density of a structural network. In our simple network of five actors, maximum density would be calculated via $[N * (N-1)]/2$ or ten two-way (dyadic) relationships. Certainly, ten dyadic relationships is perhaps easier to manage than the 24 possible combinations, yet a narrow dyadic perspective on ten relationships precludes more than half of the possible combinations, limiting the manager to myopic thinking about problems, and possible solutions, to just a few dyadic relationships.

Focusing solely on financial impacts, as explored in Chapter 2, can unnecessarily narrow the attention of managers to shareholders and obfuscate opportunities with stakeholders for co-creating value.

In this chapter we build out two additional impacts stemming from the value-creation process: employees in the workplace, and through the production process from suppliers to consumers. In Chapter 4 we examine impacts through information-sharing that informs, influences, and enables others (Evan, 1965; Granovetter, 1985; Freeman et al., 2007; Selznick, 1957).

As impacts often quickly expand the number and variety of stakeholders involved, for managers an impacts perspective quickly becomes a complicated puzzle to assess the value created in a rather tangled web of relations. So let's take it in small steps.

In the next section we examine ways in which corporations impact stakeholders by first looking at impacts with employees and facilities, including workplace conditions, buildings, infrastructure, offices, manufacturing plants, and fleets. Then, we explore the impacts of products and services within the value chain of suppliers, suppliers of suppliers, distributors, wholesalers, and retailers, including lifecycle and products-in-use.

Personnel and the workplace

Without credible commitments to employees, commitments to other stakeholders may ring hollow. Employees as wage-earners, heads of households, neighbors, consumers, and/or ambassadors for the company have unique stories to tell about the company. An employee-focused narrative on co-creating value might focus on treating employees with dignity and respect. More broadly, impacts on personnel in the workplace includes whether or not respect is extended to all workers—including contingent workers, part-time employees, work–study students and interns, temporary workers, and/or illegal immigrants. Further, it explores the conditions under which minimum legal thresholds are upheld or exceeded. Even with lower wage rates, a collegial workplace that works together to eliminate unnecessary costs can improve a firm's ecological and economic footprint, build loyalty, and increase retention, differentiating the firm from rivals in the competition for top talent (Greening and Turban, 2000; Jones et al., 2014b; Griffin et al., 2015).

Co-creating value with employees does *not* imply a 'no layoffs' or a 'no furlough' policy. Rather, it is during financial downturns when layoffs are warranted that the relationships with employees are tested and the true spirit of the relationship emerges. Activities reinforcing respect rather than undermining trust between the employees and the firm can turn a termination of employment into a new beginning.

In gaining workplace efficiencies, companies may shutter old manufacturing factories or replace aging equipment with computerized, high-speed product lines. In the process of closing buildings, just like the earlier example of firing employees, the way in which downsizing takes place matters as the treatment of employees sends signals to the remaining employees, future communities, and many others. Perhaps a firm could partner with the local community to put facilities into productive use, or convene forums to discuss employee impacts with new equipment, or provide computer training to its employees. While the factory may need to be shuttered, *how* the firm goes about making necessary changes is important (Smith, 2003; Waddock, 2008a). Here's one thought experiment: when you close a manufacturing site, does the local mayor come to closing day activities and thank the company for being part of the community?

It might be counterintuitive, but engaging employees during downturns can often reap future rewards such as improved morale among employees that survived layoffs. Cross-training employees can offer a low-cost alternative during turnarounds or asking employees to identify cost-saving ideas such as purchasing lower cost materials, changing processes to increase yield, or creating new features on existing products; these employees may help the company survive a downturn (Clay, 2005). Employee engagement that builds loyalty, enhances retention, and creates prestige with employees is a long-standing hallmark of being an 'employer of choice' in the competition for top talent (KPMG, 2005). By combining the hiring (or firing) policies with supportive management systems (Wood, 1991; Mitnick, 1995), a systematic approach to engaging employees reinforces—or can undermine—the rhetoric of employee relations.

Consider Nokia. Since the turn of the century, Nokia, the largest employer in Finland, has laid off thousands of employees as the company's share of the cell phone market evaporated with increased phone competition from smartphones. As part of Nokia's redundancy packages, some former employees were given grants to create new businesses. In doing so, the net impact of the layoffs has been in part to create a new set of entrepreneurs in Finland (Bosworth, 2014).

The way in which layoffs are managed often provides evidence as to whether employees are valued members of the organization or just cogs in a product production process meant to create value only for shareholders. Are retraining policies or relocation benefits being offered to the affected employees? Is the company working with local municipalities or non-profits that offer job training courses? If the company was acquired, were accommodations for employees provided beyond what is required by law? Some countries have stringent policies (in this case, regarding hiring and firing employees), creating a considerable minimal threshold that becomes difficult to exceed while retaining competitiveness (Prakash and Potoski, 2014). Yet, some firms, often those highly dependent on their employees, see opportunities for being distinctive and innovative by voluntarily expanding activities that are beyond compliance with the legal minimums (Porter and van der Linde, 1995). Some fast-food restaurants are voluntarily increasing the minimum wages to attract and retain employees.

Measures of positive personnel impacts often focus on jobs created, productivity, morale, loyalty, pride, and retention, with similar metrics for contractual workers. Diversity and inclusion efforts are increasingly required metrics in annual reports. In addition, intangible impacts affecting morale includes attending training and development programs, being nominated for awards, being mentioned in newsletters, being selected for special or international assignments, choosing assignments or team members, and other accolades are often intrinsic motivators for employees.

On the other hand, metrics about the risks and concerns of personnel in the workplace might focus on retention or retraining costs as well as fees from lost-time accidents, lawsuits filed by employees, employees laid-off for more than 90 days, or fines from a lack of compliance. In some industry sectors, the number of employees (or contractors) killed or injured on the job are relevant metrics. These metrics often involve financial and non-financial considerations such as safety, security, well-being, or productivity that can't always be easily monetized.

Traditional employee-focused financial inducements remain popular including: matching employee contributions in retirement funds; matching alumni donations; making financial contributions to the employee's charity of choice; employee stock ownership programs for small businesses; or tying bonuses to specific social or environmental objectives, such as reduced carbon consumption or zero-waste goals.

Retaining employees by engaging them in creative ways while leveraging their talents and expertise is increasingly being emphasized as competition for top talent grows. Companies such as FedEx, for example, are fusing employee volunteering with leadership development by sending rising leaders on month-long international corporate volunteer programs in emerging markets with new companies being created to support the win–win–win value-creation process (e.g., Ashoka or Pyxera). Companies see a return on this investment in their employees in the form of enhanced loyalty, increased innovation, additional market information and an improved corporate reputation; employees gain professional development well beyond typical volunteer experiences, while gaining insights from international assignments; and community organizations in emerging markets receive technical assistance and expertise. It's a win–win–win that co-creates value for the firm, the employees, and the community organizations. By working with selected partners, FedEx has spread the risks and created a self-sustaining, highly selective, ongoing program for executive development.

Non-financial employee-centric inducements often highlight employees in decision-making, team-building, or transferring skills and expertise beyond volunteer programs to paint houses or build new fences (Alperson, 1995; Smith, 1994, 2003; Allen, 2007). Employee-chosen programs form the core of many firms' neighborhood outreach activities, with volunteering hours directed towards employee-designated charities. Interestingly, financial inducements such as cash and in-kind donations are boosted once employees begin assisting in deciding where the money would be donated (Allen, 2007; Armstrong and Boseley, 2003; Smith, 2003).

Rather than directly engaging employees, some companies co-locate services that save time with built-in conveniences for the employees. For example, thinking about employees as parents, sons or daughters, partners or caregivers, intangible benefit could be made by creating special arrangements with a local daycare or elderly care centers, building cafeterias to provide takeaway meals for dinner, encouraging dry-cleaning kiosks, or providing extended-stay hotels for relocated employees. Benefits subsidizing parking, transportation, creating flexible hours, reimbursing the higher education costs of employees or membership fees for gyms in close proximity to the office all build on the narrative of an employee being valued as more than just a wage-earner and viewing employees as ambassadors.

Expanding benefits beyond wage-paying employees, many firms now report benefits accruing to interns, temporary workers, and other workers co-located in the same workplace as an indicator of inclusivity. Inclusivity is a motivation in extending benefits to consultants or subcontractors such as paid religious holidays as a signal of mutual respect, regardless of who employs the worker. Employees from Environmental Defense, for example, might have team members working alongside a large retailers' employees in a remote rural town to improve the retailer's environmental, social, and economic bottom lines. Alternatively, a large company may form an internal competition to focus on sustainability initiatives and encourage part-time employees such as interns to work alongside full-time employees to build morale while exploring viable sustainability ideas that increase the retailer's competitiveness.

Ensuring a minimal level of respect for employees is so important that it is often standardized in local, national, or international laws with monitoring and enforcement to ensure compliance. In regions with strong regulatory regimes, extant laws regarding unionization with collective bargaining, wrongful termination, good faith and fair dealing, fair labor standards, civil rights and civil liberties, affirmative action, diversity requirements for boards, disabilities, and whistleblower protections are often codified into legal statutes.

Not all decisions about workplace conditions, however, are voluntary. Minimal levels of appropriate workplace conditions are codified into laws for especially sensitive topics such as human trafficking, child labor, and corruption from the International Labour Organization's (ILO) ILO 26000 Guidelines on Corporate Responsibility, the Millennium Development Goals (MDGs), the Global Reporting Initiative (GRI), or SA 8000 on labor conditions.

For better or worse, not all employee and workplace expectations are codified into laws; there may be policies or norms within a business, an industry, or a region that remain as expectations of businesses while specific hot-button issues such as child labor or human trafficking are codified (Leipziger, 2009). Policies regarding executive pay policies, or golden parachutes and recruitment, promotion,

and advancement are often enshrined in codes of conduct or governance policies. Culturally sensitive issues regarding employees and
employment such as diversity, gender equality, stigma reduction,
skills development, minority representation on boards, religious tolerance, or other quotas are increasingly becoming explicit in governance policies or norms in how a business operates (Dalheim et al.,
2010). Some companies have voluntarily created ethical ombuds-
men or incorporated grievance processes and other forms of outreach to address employee concerns. These voluntary activities are
often more cost-effective than incurring additional oversight and
governance charges if the norms are codified into laws (Prakash and
Potoski, 2006).

Focusing on workplace conditions is a corollary to examining how
businesses affect employees and are affected by employees. Facilities
and employee offices often speak volumes about the importance of
employees in the value-creation process. The upsides are win–win–win
benefits: employees are motivated and productive in a safe work
environment with fewer disruptions—such as turnover, boycotts, or
unionization with local media coverage—perpetuating a positive buzz
beyond the walls of the workplace.

In many facilities, efficiencies are realized by reducing carbon, water,
and energy consumption. Cutting unnecessary waste saves money
and is often a source of pride for employees—another win–win–win.
Reducing waste, decreasing electricity demand for overhead lights,
computers, or chillers creates many mutual benefits for the firm, the
employees, and the natural environment.

Some firms, due to their dependence on personnel, risks inherent in
their workplace conditions, or their context are uniquely positioned to
effectively address employee and workplace impacts. These firms have
found it is simply in their best interest to innovate by creating mutual
benefits with employees in the workplace as the company's interests
are aligned with those of employees. Four leadership opportunities are
identified in the following text.

Leadership opportunities

Focusing on employee impacts can be a differentiating strategy
for companies unable to be low-cost providers or unable to pay
premium wages. Relatively inexpensive personnel policies such as

creating flexible work schedules customized to family commitments (e.g., doctor appointments, soccer coaching, or ill health of parents) or telecommuting options create a win-win. Firms often provide cell phones, computers, printers, or other electronic goods to facilitate working 24/7 with virtual meetings or teleconferencing with productivity improvements in mind.

In tight labor markets, effectively addressing employee impacts is a business imperative. This is especially true with highly trained skilled workers such as software engineers, scientists or geologists, who are in high demand (e.g., Siemens, Microsoft, Toshiba, Sony, and Novo Nordisk). Retaining and encouraging a skilled workforce improves the attractiveness of the firm, which in turn improves the applicant pool and the loyalty of employees in a virtuous cycle (Greening and Turban, 2000; Orlitzky et al., 2003). Training and development opportunities for employees are especially prized among highly skilled knowledge workers.

Knowledge-based businesses such as consultancies, banks, lobbying firms, or financial services companies requiring specific skillsets and relying on employees for tacit knowledge and professional networks are more likely to focus on producing positive employee impacts. The continuing shift toward data analytics to build maps, search engines, or location-based services requires specific skillsets. Keeping employees challenged and motivated—especially employees working in engineering or the hard sciences—while also enhancing productivity is a critical concern for large and small businesses such as Infosys or Wipro in India, or high-tech firms in the California area such as Google or Apple.

Firms operating in some regions within labor-intensive sectors—such as mining, pulp and paper, or other natural resource-dependent sectors—rely heavily upon employees. These companies, often large, centralized, and vertically integrated to achieve a sustained source of inputs, might be logging on remote mountainsides; extracting minerals in sub-Saharan Africa and Chile; or operating in Australia's remote outback with operations adjacent to indigenous sacred dreamlands. To attract the best talent to these isolated locales, a broad range of services are provided: commuting (fly-in and fly-out arrangement), transportation options, housing choices, and severance packages including placement services. At the same time, specific trades such as carpenters, doctors, engineers, builders, shopkeepers, and plumbers might be important in these geographically remote or sensitive locales—trades that *indirectly* affect the quality of life, satisfaction, or productivity of a business's employees.

An employee's workplace also affects satisfaction and productivity both directly and indirectly. Focusing on workplace efficiencies through heating, ventilation and air conditioning units, electrical infrastructure, or reducing operating costs by reducing consumption of electricity demands or paper for zero-waste is another means to address personnel in the workplace impacts. Ambiance-producing amenities such as music, wall decorations, display cases, flooring, cash registers, utensils, and furniture may require the same level of thoughtfulness. If, for example, creating a unique customer experience is at the core of the brand promise, these seemingly 'extra amenities' might create a new business opportunity (selling CDs or promoting local musicians). Or procuring low-cost commodities might be in the firm's best interest, as not all aspects of the customer experience require the same level of attention (Donaldson, 1996).

In addition, when thinking about impacts on employees in the workplace, many firms struggle with three additional considerations taken up in later chapters. First, net impacts inclusive of benefits and true costs with spillover effects and multiplier effects are explored in Chapters 5 and 6. That is, ensuring a net positive impact in the process of co-creating value is in the best interests of the firm. Second, attracting skilled employees in tight labor markets or attracting non-skilled employees when labor is plentiful creates different conditions and might lead to different policies, behaviors, and incentives in the same company. Chapter 11 explores in more detail the global context by examining the influence of nation-states.

Product impacts

Many firms are inherently focused on co-creating value with their customers by offering safe, useful products and services. Simply put: businesses stay in business by selling products and delivering services that keep customers satisfied. By building loyalty, the customer repeats purchases time and again to create a mutually beneficial win–win–win: the business thrives, the customer is happy, employees are paid wages, and shareholders get a return for their investment. Thriving and growing by increasing the number of customers or expanding product lines keeps the business competitive and customers satisfied.

Creating value through the production process starts with creating safe, durable, good quality products that work as promised. Making convenient, user-friendly products right-sized and right-priced with on-time delivery is important. Continuously adapting products to customers' demands by creating concentrated products, small single-use sachets, changing the shape or color as well as creating complementary services are all intended to extend the consumer's satisfaction.

Firms create product-related impacts by personalizing products and customizing them to local tastes. Examples include Mars's M&M chocolate candies available in packets of all green for environmentalist groups or Dove soap bars being colored pink for breast cancer survivors, demonstrating how firms continuously adapt their products to satisfy local customers while aligning themselves with specific groups (Allen, 2007; Griffin, 2008). Restaurants and branded food manufacturers often customize global products to local tastes. For example, soy-based ketchup rather than tomato-based ketchup can be readily found in Indonesia. Chocolate manufacturers have adjusted their recipe for milk chocolate due to the flavor profile preferred in New Zealand. Veggie burgers can now be found in fast-food hamburger restaurants in India and the hot-wing sauce available in China contains different spices than found elsewhere in a global fast-food restaurants.

Examples of firms co-creating value with customers are not new narratives. Staying in tune with customer desires—even if fickle customer preferences change daily—is how consumer-oriented firms create ongoing win–wins. Yet, continuously satisfying consumer preferences is often not enough to address product impacts. Just as creating jobs is only a start in addressing employee impacts, satisfying customers with a safe, reliable product alone is just not enough. Questions regarding the impacts incurred as a product is marketed and used are explored in the following text.

Product marketing

Impacts of products extend beyond delivery of the product itself to focus on the relationship between the firm and its clients. That is, the focus is on clients who buy the product, such as wholesalers or retailers, and consumers who use the products or services. Setting expectations with client or consumer relationships includes implicit and explicit promises. Implicit brand promises of a product, as portrayed through advertising, labeling, delivery, or customer service extend the impacts of the product and can be an integral part of the process of co-creating value.

It's simply not enough to manufacture a low-cost product, since questions are being asked about how it was produced, where the key components are sourced, and the product's brand promises. The locally grown food movement—branded as farm-to-fork—is promising accountability across the entire food chain. Labeling products increases transparency with assurances of safe, fair trade, pesticide-free, or GMO-free (genetically modified organisms-free) growing conditions. As customers demand more socially responsible, gluten-free, reduced calorie, or organically grown foods, product labeling is increasingly important. Product labeling and creating brand promises such as pesticide-free products extends the value created to include intangible value.

Voluntarily labeling products enhances the product in the eyes of consumers, potentially leading to higher margins (Griffin et al., 2005). Labeling products are often focused on one of two outcomes. Labeling either establishes minimum production standards—such as conflict-free diamonds for De Beers or child-labor-free textiles by Rugmark—or signals new production standards, such as is found with Fair Trade labels or eco-friendly carpets. Labeling innovations differentiate firms initially but over time these products (gluten-free, cage-free, pesticide-free) become more readily available. Fair Trade labels on coffee, tea, and cocoa require additional oversight with guarantees of specific requirements before the Fair Trade label can be affixed to the products, with the expected promise of a premium price and higher margin for the farmers, aggregators, and retailers. In the same way, Interface created a new line of carpets that were environmentally friendly, creating a higher margin niche market for a commodity product (Anderson and White, 2009).

Product use

How clients and consumers use, reuse, recycle, or repurpose products is increasingly important to manufacturers and designers of products.

A products-in-use mindset expands the ways in which firms are being held accountable for how others (mis)use a product. It is now commonplace in some hotels to urge customers to reuse towels or replace sheets after a few days to reduce water consumption, leading to lower operating costs for the hotel that can be transformed into lower prices for the consumer.

Companies, rightly or wrongly, are being linked to issues related to the use, misuse, consumption, or disposal of their products. For example, obesity is exacerbated by many contributing factors including poverty, food scarcity, food choices, exercise, education, etc. Yet large beverage companies, rightly or wrongly, selling sugar-based drinks consumed by youths in elementary schools are being held directly accountable for obesity concerns that might be largely out of their direct control. Rather than addressing questions regarding whether large beverage companies are directly, indirectly, or complicity involved in these issues, some large branded manufacturers with significant marketing power are now actively creating programs and partnerships to be accountable and considered part of the solution of a healthy, active lifestyle rather than being tarnished as a company that is either apathetic or is contributing to an ongoing obesity problem.

Accountability may be considered as 'not my job', mission creep or an innovative business opportunity to differentiate product, expand to new markets, or gain market share. Mission creep might occur when branded firms become involved but may not be the most competent or have the most appropriate skills and resources to address an issue. Large global beverage companies with the scale and resources to forward integrate into recycling plastic bottles or aluminum cans may engage, while smaller bottlers or beverage companies may not have the necessary expertise. On the other hand, local beverage companies or bottlers might be able to leverage their relationships, political acumen, access, celebrity, brand, etc. to effectively engage local communities.

For example, it is in a company's best interest to ensure that bottles prominently displayed with their brand contain what the label says. Illegal filling and refilling of branded bottles compromises the brand, so a company with strong brands may be very interested in supporting recycling programs to remove the empty, recyclable bottles off the streets and preserving the brand.

For example, some communities on the outskirts of Cairo have refined the collection and separation of recycling materials in the city. Using recycling as a means to learn math skills (bundling shampoo bottles into packets of 100) and business acumen (negotiating prices to get volume discounts) has improved the community's education and management skills. This is an example of deepening a positive impact by focusing on how recycling creates multiple types of value for this community, the branded shampoo company, and the individuals learning math and negotiation skills.

Impacts stemming from product use often raise questions about disparities arising from using and misusing products. Understanding how cell phone coverage enables start-up businesses yet exacerbates the digital divide, for example, is important for rolling out countrywide cell phone programs. Other sectors face continual scrutiny for negative externalities associated with their products (e.g., automobiles, tobacco, drinks, etc.).

Cause-related marketing campaigns are another means by which value is transferred, and at times created, through product impacts. Cause-related campaigns encourage consumers to purchase a product, while the company passes a portion of the proceeds from the sales to a third party such as a charitable organization (Kotler, 2007; Porter and Kramer, 2011). Alternatively, many firms make in-kind product donations by distributing surplus products such as canned goods to food shelters. Combining in-kind products with employee donations of volunteering and skills can leverage the commitment and impact of an organization creating engaged employees while making a positive impact by supporting local charities (Muirhead and Tillman, 2000; Murphy, 2001).

A downside of in-kind product contributions is creating sporadic, unpredictable flows to beneficiaries. A holiday food drive with perishable items or providing hot meals, for example, helps the food shelters and families in need for a day, a week, or perhaps an entire month. Yet finding a predictable, sustainable supply of nutritious food to feed families during the other 11 months of the year is important too. With enduring supplies in mind, many food pantries are building a cadre of corporate donors and farmers, complemented by education on sustainable agriculture, and building food storage areas enabling families to be more self-sufficient. That is, rather than relying on sporadic donations of food from corporate donors, companies are partnering with food pantries to create self-sustaining feedback loops to deliver nutritious food as needed, when needed. Building in self-reliance by partnering with others having expertise in food handling, farming, or logistics creates a new business model of win–win–wins rather than simply a giveaway of surplus foods. The outcome has changed from distributing surplus to a self-sustaining food supply.

Complementary products or services

Offering client-based activities free of charge or at a reduced price can enhance, enlarge, or better equip current consumers and attract future customers. For example, financial services firms help small and medium-sized clients understand insurance requirements and gain access to capital through financial literacy programs and individualized support in filling out loan applications.

Oftentimes the government mandates acceptable levels of product impacts. The US government mandates, for example, nutrition and allergen contents be clearly labeled on some products. New York City requires calorie content be posted in certain restaurants while laws restricting advertisements to youth or mandating blank packaging on tobacco products restrict negative product impacts.

New laws and regulations emerge following recalls regarding consumer safety. While loose enforcement might be a contributing factor to product recalls many companies find it in their best interest to gather information and voluntarily recall products to ensure the safety of their products, well beyond the requirements of the legal statutes to reduce risks, decrease long-term costs, and pre-empt regulatory mandates (Raufflet and Mills, 2009).

Foxconn, a supplier to the Apple iPhone, made worldwide headlines with workplace irregularities including workers committing suicide, as well as underage and/or undocumented employees in 2010 (Apple, 2011, 2012; Barboza, 2010; *Bloomberg*, 2012; *China Daily*, 2012). Even two years after the Foxconn incident, Apple was continually adjusting its policies with suppliers regarding worker training and product quality while also leading the industry to change policies and disclosures with respect to suppliers' workplace conditions (*China Daily*, 2012; *Bloomberg*, 2012). The policy changes were not without controversy as allegations of workers strikes in suppliers' factories were still being reported (*China Daily*, 2012).

Some firms are predisposed to creating new, innovative processes to increase mutual benefits from their products and services. Highlighted in the following text are examples of businesses well-positioned to address shifting consumer expectations by focusing on product impacts.

Leadership opportunities

Fast-moving consumer goods (FMCG) companies and retail-oriented business are often leaders in creating value by addressing product impacts. As leaders in product and process innovations, with global supply chains and vast distribution networks, they sell products consumers use frequently, even daily, with many products adapted to local tastes and needs. Adapting to local customs might be required by government legislation specifying eco-friendly sourcing or the amount of local content in production. Or, the harsh reality of the marketplace might encourage adaptation to local preferences if consumers refuse to purchase your product. All in all, FMCG firms are often front-runners in focusing on net positive impacts of their products while mitigating harm with rapid customer feedback.

Companies offering premium, prestige-laden, and status products are predisposed to being aware of value created (destroyed) via product impacts. As purveyors of prestige-laden products, they have created a brand promise. In the competitive international beverage market, Starbucks responded to consumer demands by sourcing from Fair Trade organic farms and adapting its product offerings. Similarly, the grocery store Whole Foods has created a lucrative niche in the grocery business by offering a wide range of organic products in its stores. The diamond extraction industry has created blood-free diamonds at a premium price point, while the textile industry has differentiated its products by offering sustainable cotton or Fair Trade textiles.

Vertically integrated global firms are particularly vulnerable to negative impacts stemming from their products. Vertically integrated firms owning all operations along the value chain presumably have access to all information, with direct control to change negative impacts. Yet the assumption that vertically integrated global firms have appropriate, timely information about critical impacts occurring across all areas of their global supply chains and distribution networks is being tested. Sourcing mishaps (as occur in the extraction industry) can directly impact end users. Trust and credibility can be tested, as demonstrated by the BP 2010 oil spill in the Gulf of Mexico (see the BP case study in Chapter 1). Given the challenges of centralized information, companies must demonstrate credibility through local actions.

Some vertically integrated businesses are state-owned (SOE) or nationalized (e.g., tobacco, telephone, petrochemical, and transportation), and so are doubly blessed. It's easy to assume a vertically integrated, government-controlled organization will have more control, more information, and the power to dictate how its product impacts will be perceived, thus ensuring that its impact will be reflected in a positive light. Yet, there are limitations to the ability of state-owned enterprises to set expectations of their impacts. Government ownership may or may not be the most effective means of addressing product impacts. The product itself may have externalities related to its consumption whether or not it is a SOE or publicly traded manufacturer. Being owned and operated by an SOE doesn't mitigate its product impact. Yet the perception of negative product impacts, such as in the case of tobacco, might be (erroneously) toned down if a government relies on tobacco production for positive cash flows, for instance. In a similar way, vertically integrated SOEs have an opportunity for creating either a double positive—as they are centrally owned and coordinated—or a double negative, with accusations of obfuscation and limited transparency and accountability.

Implications for co-creating value

In the previous chapter we highlighted four different financial mindsets involving owners and others: 'win–wins'; avoiding a 'parade of horribles'; making investments; and avoiding pernicious behavior. We expanded upon these financial impacts by considering additional impacts on stakeholders alongside owners when assessing the value created by the firm. Investments, for example, are not always obvious successes (a win–win) for both owners and stakeholders, rather, investments might eventually turn into a win–win, or they might be perceived as necessary expenses acting as an insurance policy that mitigates harm (Godfrey, 2005).

In this chapter we explored *how* a corporation co-creates (destroys) value with others as a business impacts—and is impacted by—a multitude of stakeholders extending well beyond solely financial interests. In doing so, we expand the narrative of a business and its impacts beyond solely financial considerations. By highlighting impacts: on employees in the workplace; through access to products and the production process from sourcing of materials to consumers; new opportunities for co-creating value come to light.

By being purposefully inclusive of financial and non-financial impacts (Freeman, 1984), we broadened our perspective and focused on risks, relationships, and co-creating value. More specifically, we examined how a firm impacts different stakeholders so as to better understand the conditions under which value is co-created or co-destroyed. As impacts increase, opportunities for co-destroying value also increase. By focusing on relationships the types of value and with whom value is co-created becomes far more tricky than creating merely financial value. Yet, at the same time, the opportunities for co-creating value are exponential. A more holistic understanding of the risks and consequences from everyday decisions to co-create value becomes important for managers to choose and choose wisely how to co-create value.

Value creation is neither myopic—focused solely on financial impacts—nor rhetorical—based on symbolic communications. Rather, value creation narratives allow for expression of the company to distinguish itself in the eyes of an increasingly crowded field of top talent, discordant voices, and material goods. When the narratives of the firm's impacts are tied to the core of the business, rather than mere rhetoric, the activities and aspirations of the business becomes something employees, owners, consumers, and communities can count on reinforcing a win-win-win.

Looking ahead

In the next chapter, Chapter 4, we examine a fourth type of impact that can create or destroy value: value creation through information. Information-sharing, and how information shapes (or is perceived to shape) attitudes, beliefs, and customs is all too often an afterthought in a company's impact strategies. As the internet expands the quantity of information available and dispersed around the world, a firm's relationships with its many communities are becoming more important for survival.

Focusing solely on local, geographically defined communities is likely too restrictive when thinking about a corporation's information impacts. Corporate impacts on communities of users, virtual communities, thought leaders, financial analysts, public policy officials, and the media are important yet often overlooked or misunderstood. Similarly, mechanisms addressing community concerns via philanthropy, while noble with lofty goals, is often not enough and more often than not misses the mark entirely. Successful firms are redefining community while engaging and partnering with myriad organizations to co-create value with stakeholders.

4 | Information-sharing impacts: redefining 'community'

To be the best in the world you've got to be the best for the world.

Senior executive, *Fortune* 100 company

[T]o preserve for the corporation the greatest degree of autonomy from constraint by other social actors.

Epstein (1969, p. 115)

As businesses create jobs, generate returns for shareholders, develop and train employees, procure raw materials from suppliers, and build safe products in accident-free workplaces while meeting government standards and satisfying loyal customers, does this appropriately address their impacts? Often the answer is, unfortunately, no! Building upon Freeman's insights to focus on value-creating stakeholders, one stakeholder group is often overlooked or taken for granted—communities. Interestingly, communities are overlooked precisely because they are always present, ubiquitous, yet without well-understood ways in which they contribute to co-creating value. When bearing the brunt of negative externalities, communities are often in the headlines decrying when firms destroy value. Virtual community groups, for example, affect and are affected by businesses—an opportunity for alumni to display college pride or increasing sales of university T-shirts—yet are often overlooked as they are not 'local.'

Just as finances connect the firm with investors; the workplace connects the firm with employees; products connect the firm with customers, suppliers, and distributors; information-sharing connects the firm with its communities—geographically close and virtual communities affecting the ability of a firm to co-create value now and in the future. The consequence of today's business decisions co-creating or destroying value is felt by communities that, in turn, affect the firm's ability to create value tomorrow.

Several narratives persist regarding communities' involvement in value creation with the private sector. Friedman (1970) famously supported the idea of a firm focusing on the business of its business by making profits, which in turn supports suppliers, consumers, employees, and owners, etc., the community will also be taken care of through strong democratically elected governments fulfilling the needs of its citizens through taxes paid or roads paved. Another narrative suggests that government agents, as elected representatives of community interests, ensure that community needs are met and codified into law, so direct representation of community interests in the private sector is unnecessary or redundant, thus community groups are considered a secondary stakeholder indirectly involved in value creation (Clarkson, 1995; Waddock and Graves, 1997). A third narrative views communities as a repository category of latent stakeholder groups or a pool of potentials: potential employees, potential consumers, potential suppliers, or potential shareholders (Phillips and Freeman, 2008).

Each of these community narratives defines, explicitly or implicitly, community as pertaining to the local community (for an exception see Dunham et al., 2006). Yet online businesses are flourishing by connecting virtual communities (Social Media, 2014). Virtual groups congregating in chatrooms, writing blogs, finding jobs through LinkedIn, using Facebook to network with friends, or tweeting complaints and getting immediate customer care are thriving, growing, and affecting businesses. The internet is offering consumers an opportunity to voice concerns and have their voices heard: when tracking lost luggage, when employees get fired over racist remarks posted on Twitter, or when tourists need help finding local restaurants. The internet is offering a sense of place wherein being a friendly neighborhood place can drive more customers to your business rather than location (Lane, 2012). Newer businesses such as Uber are challenging traditional taxi-cab business models while Airbnb, valued at more than $10 billion in just a short span of years, is challenging the traditional business model of hotel accommodation (Ferenstein, 2014; MacMillan et al., 2014) by creating business models based on trust-building among communities. An updated view towards community, geography, and a sense of place is changing how communities co-create or co-destroy value with businesses.

In this chapter, we explore how the ability of firms to create value is impacted by a variety of communities through information-sharing. By examining firms as embedded with a set of relationships, we explore how information-sharing is changing the composition and location of communities. That is, geography-based 'local' communities are being augmented by communities of individuals having common interests (e.g., cancer survivors, marathon runners, community gardeners), which might meet in person or virtually, and have stable or ever-evolving memberships. We then examine how types of information are changing the connections between a firm and its communities. Communicating fact-based and perception-changing information, for example, is shaping relationships between a firm and its communities. And finally, we examine the sheer volume of a firm's connections and communities thanks to globalization and technology.

Information impacts: connecting communities

Corporations often create opportunities for others where none previously existed. By creating jobs and providing products that consumers want to purchase, many spillover effects with employees' families, neighborhoods, and local businesses are often taken for granted. Entire neighborhoods flourish when clusters of suppliers, distributors, universities, and government or civil-society services help one another continuously improve as mutually dependent clusters (Porter and Kramer, 2011; Crane et al., 2014a, 2014b). By supporting and being supported by the local community, a firm and its local community can reap reciprocal benefits: safe, productive wage-earners and a tax base to support public safety, education, parks, and other municipal priorities. Perpetuating positive net impacts with win–win–wins via better roads, better infrastructure, better schools, and well-paying jobs can be mutually reinforcing for the firm, the community, and the citizens.

And yet, disparities persist and value can be inadvertently destroyed with this traditional thinking of community as solely local communities, prompting a reconsideration of three long-held beliefs about community relations. First, traditional community relations focus predominantly on the local community of the firm's headquarters that can, unintentionally, create disparities: local communities prosper while outlying communities languish. While quieter communities in 'languishing' neighborhoods have their own appeal, when local shops are unable to meet payroll or the community members have to drive long distances for hospitals, locational disparities are often acutely felt. Locational disparities are one of the advantages, as well as disadvantages, of company towns with hospitals, access, opportunity, and education concentrated in specific locales where commerce flourishes. Other communities are left to fend for themselves without the support of a large tax base or the largess of businesses.

Second, connecting communities through information-sharing creates new business opportunities. In the 1970s and 1980s, for example, non-profit US public broadcasting service (PBS) television stations produced food shows as a public service to local communities. Starring chefs such as the French-trained Julia Child and Jeff Smith from *The Frugal Gourmet*, these shows targeted the home cook with 'safe' entertainment and commentary appropriate for viewers of all ages. Often of limited duration, these food shows had a steady audience by tapping into a subculture of homemakers with few options to watch on TV. These food shows created a foodies subculture, a community of foodies (Salkin, 2013). When TV options in the United States expanded from three standard channels to hundreds of channels, new stations dedicated entirely to food, such as the Food Network, emerged. The Food Network used digital technology (e.g., taping shows) to spark a new generation of specialty shows available on cable TV. Cooking shows emerged as a form of entertainment—informative, relaxing, family-friendly (usually filmed without profanity)—that could be enjoyed by a wide range of viewers (Salkin, 2013). In doing so, multiple businesses and even more foodie communities emerged, creating new restaurants, fusion foods, and reality-based shows with a worldwide audience such as *Iron Chef* hosted by Takeshi Kaga. Expansion from three channels to hundreds of channels allowed for an expansion of shows dedicated to communities with specific interests (Salkin, 2013).

Third, the internet significantly expands the number of communities with common interests. Many high-tech or cyber security companies have communities of beta testers or chatrooms sharing ideas, improvements, and criticisms (Price, 2000, 2002). Yahoo's Alibaba helps exporters find importers with common interests through its search engines. Facebook encourages friends to connect and share their latest activities and information aggregators such as StumbleUpon.com specialize in content delivery according to users' pre-set preferences. Information-sharing has created communities with common interests such as beta testers, chatrooms, matching exporters with importers, or reconnecting high school friends for retirees.

Communities of common interests come in all shapes, sizes (large or small), duration (exist for an hour's Snapchat or persist over years). As technology connects people with common interests, the duration, type, and relationship of the members to the group and members to other members may shift over time. Members may join, leave, and then rejoin groups. Members may be latent purveyors of information or be active participants with other members and create spin-off communities or sub-communities such as the Manchester City football sub-community on Reddit. Communities may also have a limited time span. Membership in communities may be episodic, such as fans watching US college basketball games may see group membership peak during March of each year. While communities within communities are likely to emerge, knowing all other members is neither needed nor desired.

Traditional mindsets about community have two important implications for value creation. Traditionally, community groups are often thought of as either local neighbors or more broadly as the general public or 'society.' Yet thinking about community in these traditional ways is too restrictive and at the same time too general. Defining community as geographically adjacent neighbors unnecessarily restricts a firm's thinking about its community impact to physical boundaries. As such, community impacts are often considered as giveaways with local neighborhoods who are, rightly or wrongly, perceived as undeserving beneficiaries of products or monies created by others. Thus, a firm with a giveaway mentality towards community investments might miss opportunities for partnering with a community to achieve mutual benefit (e.g., enhancing the firm's ability to attract even more top talent while building a desirable, affordable community). With the internet enabling information to be shared instantaneously without boundaries, thinking about the broader impacts of a business as restricted to the local community is simply not in a business's best interests.

Further, thinking about community, society, and societal issues from a 30,000-meter perspective can stymie managers into inaction. When pondering complex societal issues such as hunger, homeless, or poverty, managers in the firm may reasonably throw up their hands and ask what difference an individual manager can make or what difference a single company can make. Managers might be frustrated into inaction by the firm's inability to tackle the problem alone, and this sense of helplessness might even exacerbate problems (Daft and Weick, 1984; Weick, 1984) leading to a firm being perceived as part of the problem rather than part of the solution.

In the next section, we examine three ways that relationships between businesses and their communities are creating value through information-sharing. First, information-sharing is blurring—and in some cases shattering—the boundaries of traditional community groups. The common bonds and composition holding community groups together are changing without restricting community to geographical boundaries. Second, the variety of information connects communities of stakeholders in different ways. As information about shopping preferences and delivery needs, for example, are aggregated, expectations of service and the ability to rely on real-time supply and demand rather than forecasts are heightened. Third, the sheer volume of information being shared is creating opportunities to customize information, and use crowdsourcing or flash mobs to test products, or use online reviews to guide tourists to your new restaurant.

Blurring the composition of community

The boundaries and composition of communities are changing. Traditionally communities were defined geographically, based on locations adjacent to headquarters, retail outlets, or manufacturing facilities. Yet communities based on common interests, for example, including virtual communities are increasingly relevant. Communities can be affinity-based: employment and training, such as professionalization associations; workplace issues, such as benefits, compensation, or unions; hobbies, such as woodworking, duck-hunting, or military aficionados; shared events, such as veterans' or travel groups; movies, games or entertainment, such as World of Warcraft, Game of Thrones; or specific issues, such as cancer survivors, Alcoholics Anonymous, or halting the expansion of a manufacturing plant; former affiliations, such as alumni of universities; or other combinations, as this list is neither exhaustive nor mutually exclusive, it is merely illustrative.

Thinking about communities in the same way we think about private-sector organizations—being chartered with legal standing, formal governance and oversight—needs to be reconsidered. Communities of common interests are far more fluid. Communities might form and then reform, with members overlapping with other communities and having choices about how active or passive their participation is, including latent members. They might exist as a chatroom with an ad hoc hierarchy, or be more formal as a non-profit, internationally accredited association or as a local provider of services.

When broadening the concept of community focused on individuals with a common interest, a great number of communities exist. A network of consumers can be a community since communities may be a self-appointed voluntary group of beta users or a dispersed network of a firm's clients. That is, communities may be voluntary or involuntarily formed; they may be active advocates or passive observers; they may be well-connected with everyone and know everyone else in the group, or they may be unconnected and even anonymous. The common interests might be specifically defined (such as stopping a new building from getting a permit) or be broadly construed (e.g., climate change).

Communities composed of individuals with common interests relaxes many traditional assumptions about the boundaries of communities. Communities of common interests may be virtual communities or may exist only in physical space. Members may join, leave, and disband the community altogether or create competing groups even though everyone has similar interests. The important distinction between a community and a stakeholder is in the ability of a community of similar interests to affect or be affected by the business and its value-creation process. That is, a community is a critical stakeholder if it affects value creation.

An individual in a remote community in Western Australia might be surfing the web to find other individuals with the same complaint against a large multinational firm operating in the extraction sector. By sharing information (facts, perceptions, and opinions), these individuals form a community (virtual, self-defined, without boundaries) trading insights, sharing stories, providing advice, and supporting one another. As the community of interested individuals grows, it can continually reach out to other interested groups to build a bigger and potentially more powerful network spanning the globe (Lucea and Doh, 2012) affecting a firm's process of creating value.

Networks of suppliers, employees, consumers, and financiers can be considered specialized communities affecting a firm's value-creation process. Suppliers, employees, and financiers have a common interest in supplying materials, contracting for wages, or providing capital, respectively. Their interest in the business defines, in part, their relationship with the business. Just like we explored in the employee impacts section in Chapter 3, employees certainly have a common interest in being employed. Yet, employment might be only one of multiple shared interests. Further, some members of the group may prioritize job security over wages, or benefits over hours worked, or other activities depending on their specific situation.

Communities based on common issues include: disease alleviation, promoting peace, eliminating corruption, greening a neighborhood, or reducing human trafficking. These communities might overlap with communities of consumers, scientists, analysts, beta testers, or shareholder activists, for instance. In doing so, communities often have overlapping members with numerous or potentially conflicting needs. That is, a community might share an interest in a common issue, but with different perspectives, priorities, desired outcomes, and levels of participation.

Closely related to communities with common interests are communities of experts. Communities of experts might have knowledge that is unique (local community groups), access to influential individuals (thought leaders, opinion leaders, the media), or develop overlapping relationships with other expert groups. Experts might form formal associations (e.g., trade or professional associations), or they might share the same type of expertise yet be loosely coupled, such as all financial analysts included on a conference call being updated on earnings projections by the CEO. Similarly, institutional investors, service providers, the media, journalists, universities, multilaterals, thought leaders, raters, professional athletes that endorse products, and philanthropic recipients that promote (or acknowledge support of) the company might be considered relevant communities as they are able to shape opinions, provide endorsements, influence opinions, and thereby enable the business to co-create value.

Communities of experts might include public policy communities or lobbyists that link the business community with government agencies and the public policy community. Lobbyists, for example, might be involved in creating standards, sharing information on best practices, or educating legislators about the impacts of proposed rules on the business community. Interestingly, since governments help shape expectations and are directly affected by businesses, while also evaluating, in part or in whole, businesses, they are a unique community with multiple roles (Wood and Jones, 1995): communities of overseers and enforcers yet rarely as enablers. Governments, unfortunately, are all too often portrayed as a community that redistributes value, composed of elected politicians with an ax to grind, or motivated by special interests with a singular focus (Freeman et al., 2007). These stereotypical depictions of governments unnecessarily narrow its role in the value-creation processes to overseer or gadfly without acknowledging the government's ability to set expectations, affect businesses directly, or evaluate the impacts of businesses (Wood and Jones, 1995). The role of government and its changing expectations on commerce is explored further in Chapter 8.

Communities can also be composed of latent groups. Latent groups are inactive (hence the term latent), yet have the potential to affect firms. Latent groups include potential employees or potential clients that might have an unarticulated or an unformed opinion about a firm. For example, the potential pool of applicants for a job might be widened due to the way in which employees are treated or perceived to be treated by the firm (Greening and Turban, 2000). Potential employees are particularly keen to understand how they might be treated if they become employed in the firm (Cheng et al., 2014).

Expanding the notion of community to include the general public focuses on how citizens affect the value-creation process by setting norms, expectations, and reinforcing cultural mores. That is, the general public as members of a society expect certain levels of acceptable behavior from businesses and may punish practices or behaviors that violate cultural mores (Margolis and Walsh, 2003). Expectations generalized from society are often taken for granted and assumed to be homogeneous. Yet public opinion polls and generalized surveys such as the Generalize Social Survey (GSS) conducted periodically over the past three decades suggest shifts over time but also differences among different, seemingly homogeneous groups.

All in all: thinking about communities as they affect the value-creation process requires understanding the changing composition of communities and the types of information shared. As community groups change, businesses are also changing: connecting with new communities and co-creating value where none existed. In the next section we explore ways in which the type and variety of information-sharing is a catalyst for learning and creating value across communities.

Variety of information shared

Information-sharing—directly and indirectly—connects different communities to a firm's value-creation process in different ways. Community–business connections might be tangible and direct, or consist of psychological connections (e.g., we expect the railcars carrying toxic chemicals through our community to not derail and release dangerous vapors), or be a mixture of both. Online dating sites, for example, are a business model premised on the idea of sharing information about common interests creating a psychological connection before a lunch date is arranged.

Connections between firms and communities might stem from sharing factual or perceptual information. Fact-based information might describe the technical adequacy of the products and services offered, how they might be returned or recycled, or compatibility with other products. Alternatively, perceptual information might be recommendations from friends, reviews by others, endorsements or certifications by accredited agencies. Perceptual information builds trust, reinforcing the firm's status or reputation. Higher status or reputation might in turn create loyal customers, reinforce a brand promise, and lead to the firm's goods and services chosen among many alternatives.

Outreach to communities traditionally occurs through direct investments such as community investments in physical infrastructure including water, electricity, roads, and hospitals, for example. These have traditionally been built by private contractors on behalf of local governments (Grimsey and Lewis, 2007). Yet private sector outreach is changing as demand for information-based infrastructure complementing physical infrastructure accelerates. Information-based infrastructure, such as education, data-sharing, or health-service provisions, requires access to knowledge and tacit resources that are becoming increasingly important (Grimsey and Lewis, 2007; Vachani and Smith, 2008).

Most importantly, sharing information is reciprocal and mutually reinforcing. A utilities firm, for example, might generate warnings about an impending typhoon cutting electricity to the surrounding areas, affecting customers, families and entire neighborhoods. Alternatively, a community member might send notices about downed telephone poles or electricity inadvertently shut off providing important real-time information to the utility.

Commercial applications of firm-centric and community-centric information-sharing are still to be explored. From a commercial perspective, a popular jeans store might send notices to the cell phone of a customer that has just withdrawn money at an ATM around the corner from their favorite jeans store. Combining the timely notice with a coupon might add an extra incentive to purchase the jeans in the next hour. By converging different types of information that might be useful to the consumer, an impulse buy might happen.

Information—shared as parcels of facts, statistics, and data or as commentaries, expert or popular opinions, and editorials—can be displayed in images or in print media ranging from blogs, tweets, and newspapers transmitted around the world. Information sharing builds awareness as well as engagement opportunities for the firm across its networks. Powerful search engines sift and sort through data, statistics, responses, and images with mapping tools to put information into a geographical or historical context. Tying together the firm with its network through information sharing affects how firms co-create (or co-destroy) value.

Pollution plumes, for example, can be scientifically modeled for risk mitigation during worst-case scenarios to understand community risks and potential health hazards for at-risk populations. By working with local hospitals and nursing homes, as well as police, fire, and safety officials, a heavily polluting firm can inform the community about potential leaks or adjust its activity during 'code red' days when there is a high probability of fire, smoke, or smog that might aggravate the health hazards of an elderly population of asthma sufferers.

The geographical reach of a firm's footprint is rapidly expanding through information sharing. Informing local populations (as part of the Emergency Planning and Community Right-to-Know Act in the US) through blogs, Twitter, or YouTube is increasing expectations of convenience and timeliness. But competition among media channels is accelerating expectations about the timeliness and customization of information. In today's world, the consumer expects information sent out by a firm to be customized to the individual consumer. By making information readily available, easy to access, and nearly ubiquitous, traditional forms of knowledge (e.g., encyclopedias) are being challenged. Rather than using encyclopedias, Google and CNN are used to verify and aggregate data.

Businesses are using videos to engage their critics and vice versa. Film and the performing arts are used to disseminate information or promote a specific cause. Several movies, including *The Corporation*, *Thank You for Smoking*, and *Super Size Me*, have all been released since the turn of the century promoting specific points of view. Flash mobs enabled by Facebook and Twitter continually upend the ways information is leveraged for commercial value, affect change and social betterment. Overall, the variety of information has increased exponentially, which means that company-generated information may be drowned out by information from others with a far more critical view of the firm. The implication is straightforward: what others are saying about a company, rather than what the company is saying about the company, is increasingly important.

Volume of information shared

Systematically examining volumes of new information generated daily can be daunting yet create new business opportunities to co-create value (Kiron et al., 2011). A local arborist, for example, overlays community maps available through a geographic information system (GIS) with horticultural information on climate, growing conditions, temperatures, frost dates, and trees prevalent to anticipate when trees will be dropping their leaves. Based on the probability of peak times for raking, collecting, and composting leaves, the arborist's firm is hiring students to help with leaf-raking, tree-pruning, and spreading mulch. It is also selling information to local hardware stores regarding when to have sales of rakes, leaf-blowers, spring bulbs, and other seasonal products.

The challenge of integrating data across multiple sources—private-sector, public-sector, and civil-society organizations, for example—is creating new competitive advantages for some businesses. Some hotel chains, for example, are offering eco-friendly tourist programs—reducing carbon and water consumption, guaranteeing purchases of locally grown food for their kitchens, providing local crafts for sale in the gift stores, or providing exclusive tours of restricted sites that have strict visitation limitations imposed by local authorities—or working with local community groups to develop workplace-ready skills programs at hotels around the world. Providing culturally sensitive customized services shows business savvy by building relationships between the hotel and its local community. The hotel chain is now a preferred partner in developing countries around the world that might otherwise be reluctant to have a subsidiary of a multinational company in their community.

The sheer volume of stakeholder connections is expanding with globalization and technology. Facebook, Twitter, blogs, websites, and chatrooms are replacing warranty cards as methods of gathering customer feedback. Rapid responses to problems are now expected. Consumer preferences gathered from customer call centers and stock-keeping unit (SKU) data help firms examine shifts in purchasing behaviors by tracking deliveries between suppliers, manufacturing plants, and retail stores. Rather than disregarding amorphous, vague, or conflicting pieces of information, businesses are investigating anomalies to see if there are new business opportunities by customizing services.

With the variety of channels sharing information, time is becoming an intangible factor underlying competitiveness. Time is being used as a means to proactively inform communities but is also being used as a competitive advantage to keep stakeholders abreast of concerns or to send out warnings in case of a potential brownout.

A shifting mindset that expands the boundaries of communities and treats information as central to creating (new) value encourages firms to think differently about *their* responsibilities as shared responsibilities (Mahon, 1989). Firms have unique capabilities to be part of the solution to some community challenges rather than the tradition perception of firms being part of the problem. Insurance companies, for example, sponsor community centers dedicated to teaching teens a trade—keeping at risk youth off the streets, decreasing vandalism, which in turn reduces clients' insurance premiums, thus providing an example of a mutually beneficial win–win–win. By helping teenagers build a trade, insurance companies are reducing teenage crime in specific neighborhoods and reducing costs.

Beverage companies, for example, are voluntarily limiting access to alcoholic products and spirits to reduce alcohol-related problems in remote or vulnerable areas (e.g., domestic violence, abuse, poor nutrition, limited education opportunities, and limited economic opportunities in isolated villages). These voluntary restrictions might hurt alcohol sales for bottling distributors, yet by offering alternative beverages such as water or nutrient drinks, a net increase in sales is occurring while local norms to restrict access to alcohol are supported.

Two-way information sharing builds a cache of unique information enhancing a firm's competitiveness. McDonald's in China offers spicy chicken fingers and in India it offers veggie burgers. It is only a matter of time until McDonald's begins offering these country specialties in even more cities: veggie burgers might sell well in communities with a large population of vegans, while spicy chicken fingers might be a welcomed addition to universities with niche enclaves of ex-pat Chinese students.

A commitment to systematically collecting, collating, and combining information in new ways allows the creation of innovative opportunities with positive multiplier effects for multiple sectors. We explore leadership opportunities for enabling and educating others via information in the next section.

Information impacts: leadership opportunities

Enabling community members to become more self-sufficient, building skillsets, sharing information that creates financial literacy or language literacy has often been delegated to NGOs and not considered the business of businesses. Local NGOs with specialized knowledge of the local context and ties to the local community leaders might be better positioned to help community members. The logic goes something like this: by engaging with local NGOs, the firm builds trust and reaffirms its long-term commitment to the community. The firm voluntarily uses its skills, expertise or connections to help the community in some way, thus creating a halo effect that buffers the firm during times of uncertainty and crisis (Brown and Perry, 1994). When a crisis eventually hits, the crisis is perceived as 'a bad event for a good company' rather than 'just another bad event for a bad company.'

Balancing a visible local presence with economies of scale and efficient supply chains to remain competitive is a challenge. The desire of Kroger to be a national grocery chain while also being attuned to local communities by offering everyday low prices requires coordination of suppliers and consumer preferences to keep costs low. Similarly, Whole Foods, a national grocery chain that features locally produced organic foods, requires a complex network connecting many local farmers within each region it operates in (Mackey and Sisodia, 2013).

Many global businesses are increasingly finding it in their own best interests to be considered a local company. Toyota and Honda, for example, are keen not to be considered just another Japanese company and assiduously built trusted relationships with the US government that included a voluntary recall by Toyota in 2007 (Thomas and Foster, 2010). When Japanese cars arrived in the US in the 1970s they were perceived as 'cheaply made and unsafe' (Ahrens, 2010). Over the ensuring decades, both companies built reputations for high-quality, prestige cars. Honda has positioned itself as a local company carefully choosing to build its plants within neighborhoods that share similar concerns regarding taxes and employment, and sourcing from local suppliers. Toyota systematically built a loyal US customer base and support network over two decades that was stretched thin during the recalls in 2010 (Ahrens, 2010). Toyota's stock price and reputation were dented while loyal relationships were tested with testimony before Congress, public statements, and restatements, yet the company weathered the public relations storm and rebounded stronger than ever (Healy, 2014).

Being perceived as a good neighbor insulates a firm from downturns, avoiding some negative publicity from local news outlets. Community members often defend their neighborhood businesses—especially those businesses that are actively engaged in the local community over businesses that are not as well-known, either favorably or unfavorably. Imagine three different scenarios. First, the US Environmental Protection Agency (EPA) investigates a neighborhood manufacturing plant and levies fines against the company. Once published, few in the community speak up for or against the company. Imagine a different scenario wherein violations are discovered, fines are levied, and many neighbors join the chorus of complainers, the issues deepen and broaden, undermining the company's survival. And the third scenario is when numerous community leaders and municipal officials advocate strongly for the business, its jobs, and share in the responsibility to actively monitor and enforce federal laws. Having neighbors advocate on a company's behalf is quite a coup when the headlines are questioning the business's future viability. Which scenario is likely to occur in your hometown?

In a similar vein, the need for a deeply local presence is addressed by many corporate giving programs through private foundations or corporate foundations. A foundation in a rural community can help local farms become more productive, which in turn builds a stable community for local businesses and local households. No job is too small: educating farmers on tilling the soil to minimize erosion, helping farmers gain access to and fertilizing seeds, or supporting farmers clear the land in sustainable ways. Local foundations can provide needed information and infrastructure that local governments can't or won't provide.

Community outreach programs are often centrally coordinated from headquarters yet increasingly allow local customers to designate donations and volunteer time to local schools or non-profit groups of their choice. Coordination by headquarters aligns the business and the community while allowing for economies of scale, learning across projects, and consistency helps create win–win–wins. The business wins with tangible impact that can be sustained in the region or across communities. And the community can win if there is adequate flexibility for customizing programs according to the needs and interests of individual communities.

Trade associations or professional associations are increasingly important mechanisms for sharing information. With common concerns, these groups often advocate resolutions before an issue enters the public policy arena and risks becoming politicized (Prakash and Griffin, 2012; Griffin and Prakash, 2014). In this way, trade associations, professional associations, and business associations are rapidly evolving in their role, stature, and purpose to be important information navigators and as legitimate information mediators prior to issues being decided in public forums through formal public policy process. As information arbiters, some associations and NGOs are becoming trusted intermediaries between private-sector organizations, civil-society organizations, and the public sector.

The Environmental Defense Fund (EDF), for example, a well-respected international NGO, works alongside large multinationals and private equity firms to reduce pollution, save money, and lower consumption by gathering information on the energy footprints of firms. By mapping where energy is being used and strategizing to lower energy costs, the multinational firm and the EDF are creating a win–win–win even without the threat of mandates. Similarly, when faced with pending legislation on carbon consumption, for example, some companies have saved significant sums due to coordinated efforts to voluntarily reduce carbon, water, energy, and waste.

Decentralized multinational firms are faced with similar challenges yet dispersed among countries. Global financial institutions, for example, must hire a quota of local talent in order to remain within a country. As a global service provider, these financial institutions often rely upon economies of scale to be competitive, yet many governments require local employment in check-clearing or transaction-clearing activities, making the bank's services more expensive. Rather than closing branches in small, often rural countries, some banks are using the local content requirement as an opportunity to transform unbanked rural communities into customers by hiring community leaders. By listening to community leaders, the banks are customizing financial literacy programs to build economic stability.

Community banks are responding to changes in local content to deepen relationships with local government officials and local retail customers by expanding financial literacy programs. Rather than a traditional financial literacy program focused on individualized budgets, financial literacy is being expanded to understanding mortgages and housing, personal and household finances, and strategies for applying for and repaying loans. These expanded programs are designed to create a win–win–win for employees, potential clients, local officials, and community members. By listening to community groups, using employees' pro bono efforts to transfer skills, building trust and capacity among local communities, these service-based companies are effectively targeting niche populations and at-risk groups. Increasing the community's financial stability one household at a time while educating potential applicants on loan requirements and assisting vendors in completing loan applications deepens and broadens the impact of community banks.

Knowledge-based multinational firms in high-tech, consultancy, and engineering sectors often need to attract and retain highly skilled employees to remain competitive. Building internal communities of employees with mentor–mentee relationships are creating an innovative atmosphere, retaining employees, and building loyalty. Building communities requires understanding the needs and interests of employees and how the company is—or is not—meeting their expectations.

And finally, firms are addressing complex community issues such as HIV/AIDS, poverty, unemployment, homelessness, or youth crime rates by sharing information. Aggregating information from various sources, companies are able to turn data into useable knowledge to address pressing social issues. McDonald's is actively addressing childhood obesity by disseminating nutrition and local sourcing information while encouraging healthy lifestyles with exercise and a balanced diet. McDonald's is also pre-emptively addressing issues within its supply chain by requesting reports from suppliers such as the privately held McCain Foods to identify opportunities for cutting costs, reducing waste, using less packaging, and including post-consumer waste packaging (McCain Foods Limited, 2009).

Companies facing community issues can turn their images around by selective partnerships. Walmart, for example, came under heavy scrutiny for its hiring and labor practices in 2005 after numerous complaints that unfair competitive practices were forcing small 'mom and pop' stores out of business by introducing their megastore concept (Gumbel, 2005). A few years later, Walmart was being heralded for its potential to decrease the relatively high local unemployment of skilled and unskilled workers while agreeing to purchase more local produce in all US stores (Clifford, 2010; Connell, 2011).

As a convening forum, some organizations are increasingly coordinating dispersed, fragmented community information; allowing the community to make their own decisions and set their own destiny. Rather than telling communities how to run their water or sewage counsels, for example, companies are convening multi-stakeholder forums to understand underlying issues, possible solutions, and identify ways in which the community can begin to address the problems it sees as salient. Perceived as a lightning rod for controversy or as a catalyst for new dialog, some companies have cultivated the ability to pull together government agencies, community leaders, NGOs, university specialists and technical experts for a multi-stakeholder forum. A trusted company, especially a large company with ties to local communities and national governments, may have access to resources, capital, or networks that a local community leader may not be able to tap into.

Whereas discussions about financial, employee, and product impacts are often motivated, at least initially, by compliance with extant laws, the starting point for identifying information impacts is different. The starting point is often based on perceptions and adhering to norms and customs. By focusing on perceptions *and* what others say about the company (and what the company thinks about itself), gaps in expectations arise. Information-sharing can widen the gap or close it.

Gathering information from others, and understanding the demands of many and varied communities, has many companies scrambling for feedback. While sharing information with local officials and employees' families if a factory is closed might seem critical, a narrow view of community as the local neighborhood is often too myopic. Alerting local, state, or federal politicians about closing factories might also be important. The process of how information disclosure is managed is important: when is notification given? If an explosion occurs in a manufacturing plant, how is notice communicated throughout the community? Are scenarios practiced bringing together local police and fire services with the company's health and safety services? Is anyone in the company partnering with local officials or other employers to attract other types of businesses to town?

Implications for co-creating value

Quite often community is considered a 'residual' group of stakeholders (Dunham et al., 2006; Phillips and Freeman, 2008) tangentially affecting a business but not neatly classified as, or perceived to be, the 'true' value creators such as suppliers, consumers, and employees. Further, governments are presumably the official voice of communities in a democratically elected country (Friedman, 1970). Both of these assumptions are often wrong or ill-conceived. The way in which businesses think about community and community issues (and vice versa: how communities think about businesses) needs to change by focusing on smaller-scale problems and concrete actions. Redefining the scale of problems and concrete actions are discussed in the following text.

Thinking about community or societal issues (Margolis and Walsh, 2003) by focusing on smaller-scale problems connected both directly and indirectly to the business: its ethos, finances, employees, workplace, products, value chain, and reputation. Focusing on smaller-scale, doable, viable projects a firm can 'control' encourages action. Choosing a relevant small-scale community problem that can be addressed is important.

Choosing issues is doubly difficult since the number of communities affected is significantly expanding. Being inclusive of virtual communities and interest groups as well as immediate neighborhoods can triple or quadruple the number of viable communities. As the number of communities expands, the variety of issues also grows. Choosing, and choosing wisely, means converging the issues, interests, and desired impacts. Convergence occurs when impacts are connected (directly and indirectly) to the business via employees, products, consumer preferences, supplier demands, reputational effects, expertise, or locational needs.

Managing impacts means managing the business's impacts on communities or broader societies by managing smaller-scale problems *as* the firm makes its money rather than after the money is made or after the fact, when the firm wants to give back. That is, successfully addressing smaller aspects of larger society issues—with a bona fide contribution that 'moves the needle'—often requires addressing needs as part of the value-creation process rather than by giving money away afterwards to 'fix' the value destroyed.

Concrete activities demonstrating visible, credible, doable win–win initiatives can make a difference to the firm and its many varied communities. Building a pattern of coherent actions, a firm builds internal capabilities, can coordinate resources, engage stakeholders, commit to making an impact, and attract like-minded organizations that build momentum (Weick, 1984). A series of small wins allows for a cumulative, sustainable path to address social issues as part of business issues.

Win–win–wins are the goal: a win for the company to take pride in, a win for the community as a problem is being addressed, and a win for employees engaged in the community. In doing so, the win–win–win distinguishes the firm with the potential for escalation: by asking others what they have done (in a competitiveness sense by expanding the criterion upon which firms compete) or by combining efforts with other organizations to make a deeper, broader, or more sustained impact together. Small wins are a beachhead with demonstrated success that may spur further action. As more resources (e.g., technology, human capital, equipment, and products) are dedicated to the community with credible results tracked, new ways of thinking about how the business serves its communities and is served by the community emerge, perpetuating positive impacts that co-create value.

From a practical perspective, appropriately addressing exponentially expanding impacts and expectations of a business requires clarity of focus: clarity in what is valued by the business and its stakeholders; clarity in the types of impacts desired, clarity regarding impacts that create or destroy value; clarity in how scarce resources are allocated to achieve desired impacts; clarity in how value is created continually over time; and clarity in explaining a corporation's mutual benefits and why the firm—in conjunction with individuals, private foundations, professional associations, coalitions or governments—is championing a particular initiative.

Clarity is needed in ascribing why and how the firm can address this initiative, in this location, and at this time. Clarity is often enhanced when initiatives are explicitly tied to the business's core impacts: its financial prowess, transferring unique skills and expertise, consistently providing safe products, or convening power that enables others through information-sharing.

In striving for clarity, three critical managerial gaps often appear regarding thinking, doing, and explaining corporate impacts. The first gap looks at the alignment between the extolled mission, vision, and values of the company with its behaviors. If the rhetoric of the top management isn't matched with the reality of the everyday business behavior, credibility is at stake. The second gap examines whether the actual behavior of the firm (not just the perceptions) is window-dressing as it is focused on one stakeholder (e.g., consumers) or reflects a fad or a personal preference by the current top management team. As isolated, one-off initiatives centered on a single department/function (e.g., human relations, compliance, marketing, or operations) these band-aids are often forgotten when the next crisis or the next top manager comes along. The third gap looks at explaining a firm's actions through its communication strategies: how the firm portrays its activities, if employees are ambassadors supporting the firm and taking pride, and how other stakeholders portray the firm. As a point of differentiation, the firm can distinguish itself from rivals and enhance its competitiveness. Alternatively, the attributions motivating the firm's actions are important—the firm may act appropriately when under the spotlight, but will it be back to 'business as usual' once scrutiny is diluted? Each gap identifies a critical aspect of managing impacts: consistency for credibility, implementation along the value chain, and being connected to the firm's competitiveness.

Consistency in rhetoric and reality

Policy-focused rhetoric can be window-dressing decoupled from the firm's actual behaviors (Weaver et al., 1999). Businesses may include influential community members on company boards, engage in community outreach activities, and make significant philanthropic contributions, yet the actual practices at the local community level to affect critical community issues that align with the business remains paltry (Koerber, 2011). Decoupling policy from on-the-ground actions can foster cynicism if there are no tangible differences in the field after new policies and boardroom initiatives are set in place (Griffin and Dunn, 2004; Dalheim et al., 2010). Alternatively, decoupling can be an opportunity to isolate a small group of researchers dedicated to experimenting and innovating. These researchers might develop new products such as hybrid car technologies developed by Japanese automobile manufacturers with the support of the government, or develop new processes such as lowering greenhouse gas emissions or improving logistics for faster delivery of products (Mahon, 1989).

Consumer-driven and supplier-facing investments

Corporate impacts are, in part, about anticipating shifts in stakeholder expectations in the value-creation process. Often consumer-facing companies are more socially astute, as they respond to changing demands by consumers to create more eco-friendly products, support a national cause (e.g., voting, women's empowerment, cancer research, etc.), recycle products, or source from ethical suppliers. Entertainment, hospitality, logistics, travel, and tourism industries were among the first-movers in adopting environmentally friendly practices. And yet, consumer-facing demands requiring relatively easy adjustments for manufacturers can be just gimmicks to attract or retain consumers.

If firms' interest in impacts penetrates only so far as the consumers see or only so far as the consumers demand, than corporate impacts might be just another marketing tool. On the other hand, if corporate impacts are a part of a larger conversation about how firms co-create value, then viewing the entire value chain process (forward and backward linkages) becomes important.

As scrutiny of a firm's extended enterprise increases, more questions from increasingly more vociferous groups are asked about procurement processes of raw material to disposal in landfills of the finished product. Firms are being asked to examine and manage the impacts of the product as it is being created, used, repurposed, or thrown away (Phillips and Caldwell, 2005; Freeman et al., 2007).

So consumer-facing firms without codes of conduct for their own employees or for suppliers of suppliers may be investing in marketing campaigns targeting consumers while mistreating employees or squeezing suppliers. Being considerate of consumers' preferences while considering the needs of other stakeholders is essential in our 24/7/365 news cycle world.

Competitiveness, rivalry, and differentiation

Multinational companies blend into their host culture by being culturally salient, and being treated as one of the local companies is an opportunity to enhance the trustworthiness of the firm and its products. Cultivating the image of a culturally sensitive firm (the firm has adapted to our culture, norms, traditions, and beliefs, and is part of our community) allows the firm to build trust and create confidence in its activities. Corporations with the ability to learn rapidly, adjust fluidly, and be resilient while also knowing what is non-negotiable (ethics) are likely to thrive and survive ever-present change. Ratings and rankings proliferate, allowing comparisons across industries; yet impacts are not about relative success (Freeman and Gilbert, 1988). Being better than a rival may mean you survive to see another day but you do nothing to create tomorrow's success. The goal is to offer products that are needed, as they are needed, and in the manner in which they are needed, and to deliver products in a way in which impacts are recognized and understood.

Looking ahead

In the next chapter, Chapter 5, we combine the four corporate impacts identified in earlier chapters (financial, employees in the workplace, through products, and information-sharing) to examine a firm's net impacts and spillover effects. As financial and non-financial impacts are inextricably yet intricately linked to co-creating value, a focus on one impact necessitates looking at multiple interactions. By viewing the process of value creation more holistically, Chapter 5 combines and integrates the interactions a firm has with multiple stakeholders simultaneously. Examining net impacts with spillover effects on groups less directly involved, yet still able to impact the ability of the firm to create value, unlocks untapped potential across to create new value.

5 | Combining impacts, net impacts, and spillover effects

If the business of business is just business, why is it that ...

– a bank offers expanded services in rural villages including housing, education, job fairs and financial literacy; and

– a mining company expands its HIV/AIDs education to community households.

Rather than looking at corporate impacts in isolation, combining impacts creates opportunities for value creation. For it is the intersection, that point of impact, when a firm affects others that impressions are made, money is exchanged, goods are bartered, employment occurs, and trust is created or shattered. Being mindful of the many points of impact between a firm and its stakeholders creates opportunities to learn more, favorably impress, or plant a seed of doubt with stakeholders.

One starting point for examining multiple impacts simultaneously is where a firm focuses its attention. If, for example, a firm predominantly emphasizes financial impacts when making routine decisions and reporting progress to stakeholders, this suggests an investor-oriented firm with management's objectives geared toward all impacts being attributed to financial outcomes. This shareholder-oriented focus is typical of many publicly traded firms and is often reinforced by vision statements focusing on continually maximizing wealth for the shareholders. Alternatively, a legal, compliance-oriented focus would examine the number of lawsuits and legal claims. Yet survival might be at stake and if survival is at stake, a firm can't comply its way to greatness. Without a crisis to heighten the firm's sensitivity towards impacting others, do you know your company's multiplier effects? And are you appropriately addressing direct and indirect impacts?

If a firm predominantly focuses on customer satisfaction, management's attention is focused on meeting and beating customers' expectations. Firms *derive* financial benefits from exceeding customer's expectations, rebuilding loyalty when dissatisfied, changing product lines to adapt to new needs, hiring customer-friendly employees, and building thriving client relationships that endure. That is, a customer-focused firm emphasizes customer relations yet simultaneously satisfies shareholders, and attunes its hiring practices, procurement policies, and services to the customer. Building a successful consumer-based relationship continually satisfies the consumer, the owners, the employees, and the suppliers. That is, the interactions and ripple effects of an effective consumer-focused firm create a win-win-win.

Taking the sequential interaction between consumers, employees, and financial impacts one step further might be a laser-like focus on employees (Conley, 2007). In supporting, training, and developing a satisfied employee base, employees are well equipped to satisfy consumers. Creating a virtuous circle, satisfied employees meet and exceed the expectations of consumers, which in turn will reap additional benefits for investors and so on. A thriving business model is created with a focus on customers, employees, and investors. Interestingly, the triplet of employee–customer–investor impacts strengthens and supports employee and consumer engagement to create returns for owners (Conley, 2007).

Focusing on employee engagement to improve customer experiences is important for service-based businesses and increasingly for brand protection of global companies. Books about employee-centric businesses focus acute attention on improving customer service with front-line employees exceeding expectations in cleaning houses, trimming trees, booking hotel rooms, preparing meals, or accepting payment for a consumer's purchases. Empowering employees to exceed consumers' expectations has direct, tangible effects on the consumer experience. With motivated and engaged employees routinely recognized for positively affecting consumers, a self-reinforcing triplet is created among employees–customers–investors with mutual benefits intricately interwoven. Social media only serves to perpetuate the mutual benefits. If a customer has a bad experience with an employee, it becomes easy to post complaints on Facebook, Twitter, etc., tarnishing the reputation of the brand.

Overall, when combining financial, employee, product, and information impacts, one of the first questions becomes: which relationships receive attention? Closely related to that is another question: what are the desired objectives or net impacts of the business? The first question about focusing attention suggests the starting point to start examining corporate impacts and the second question regarding objectives suggests an end game of what is ultimately desired.

Examining a virtuous cycle of positively reinforcing relationships that creates net positive impacts (win-win-wins rather than increasing negative risks) is the focus of this chapter. The flip-side is equally important: understanding the risks and potential for a destructive cycle that creates harmful impacts. Viewing multiple impacts simultaneously, in tandem, or in various combinations emphasizes a more holistic view of firms. A holistic view is both a boon and a bane for managers. A holistic view increases the number of variables considered when diagnosing problems, yet it also increases the variety of solutions addressing underlying sources of the issue as more useful information is readily available.

During the global financial downturn in 2008, many companies lacked internal information on *how* the financial targets were achieved yet the emphasis (and bonuses) was tied to *whether* the targets were met. After the financial crisis, many American firms stopped community outreach activities as the value added by community connections was underdeveloped or misunderstood. When community (or employee, or customer) relationships are tied to the core of the business, they are never redundant. New narratives are being created around the engagement of employees as the core aspect of a hotel that satisfies customers and consequently satisfies investors (Conley, 2007), and creates customer loyalty with competitively priced products (Mackey and Sisodia, 2013). Let's look a little more closely at combinations of impacts to better understand diagnosis of issues and new innovations.

Value creation

Figure 5.1 shows ways in which the corporate impacts examined in Chapters 2, 3, and 4 can be connected in different combinations. Along the horizontal axis, employee and customer impacts are directly related, as would be expected in service-based organizations. Empowering employees to offer exemplary service that satisfies customers' needs often results in net positive relationships among the firm, its employees, and customers. When employees listen to consumer demands and

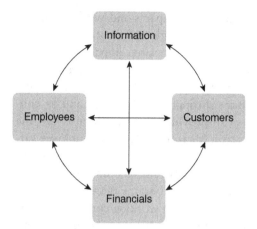

Figure 5.1 Combinations of corporate impacts

fulfil those new or changing expectations, the reciprocal relationship between employees and customers is further strengthened with benefits accruing to the firm: enhanced customer loyalty and retention of valued employees that take pride in satisfying customers.

Along the vertical axis, financial impacts are directly related to information impacts and vice versa. Relying upon both qualitative and quantitative information about a firm's performance allows financial analysts and investors to assess the net present value of the firm and determine whether, in their assessment, the firm is a worthy investment at the current price point. Information includes what the firm says about itself as well as what others say about the firm. The reciprocal relationship between information and financial impact is, in part, tied to what the firm says about its own financial prowess: the profitability, the growth, meeting or exceeding quarterly expectations. Equally important is what financial analysts, investment houses, rating agencies, and individual investors are saying about the stock and whether they are buying, selling, or holding the stock.

In addition to dyadic (two-way) relationships between stakeholders, three-way and four-way combinations among stakeholders can arise. Examining multi-stakeholder combinations uncovers new opportunities as dyadic relations can unnecessarily narrow a firm's attention sub-optimizing the overall value created by the firm with its many stakeholders.

For example, starting with employee impacts and work clockwise around the circle in Figure 5.1 to include information, customer impacts, and finally financial impacts. The positive impacts of employees being proud of their work in a safe workplace produces multiple ripple effects on retention, motivation, and loyalty. Employees willing to talk with potential customers through blogs, tweets, and as consumers of the firm's products can provide a unique glimpse into the firm from an insider's perspective. Measures related to employee satisfaction, if this firm is admired by others, the number of new workplace violations, or if this a place you would recommend to others to work for or to purchase products from become relevant. Referrals from employees give invaluable insights on working conditions in the firm, the happiness of employees, and the consistency of management's rhetoric with the experience of employees.

When employees act as ambassadors for the organization, the firm is able to attract additional customers through word of mouth, employee referrals, and online reviews by former employees. In building a loyal employee base and keeping costs low due to more trust and less oversight, the firm can, in turn, build a loyal set of customers that are motivated by lower costs and/or employees that tout the product. A virtuous cycle starting with a focus on employees extends to employees being ambassadors with positive spillover effects when sharing their experiences with the customer. With the customer being satisfied and the firm rewarded financially, a renewed focus on employees can continue to generate more positive win–win–wins (Conley, 2007).

Now, think of the same cycle (employees to consumers to investors) in reverse. If the primary focus of the firm starts with financial impacts this creates a different narrative about the firm. With a focus on profits, growth, and investments, the firm is likely to seek to expand its product offerings or market. Looking for new customers of existing products and/or customers for new products generates the desired growth trajectory, which in turn requires hiring new employees. Market expansion is likely to generate headlines as the firm moves into new communities to sell new products, open up retail stores, build factories, and work with governments to secure the necessary permits to operate. As awareness increases with successful expansion, a full cycle of impacts from financial to customer to hiring more employees emerges.

Creating virtuous cycles of impacts from employees to customers to investors or, in reverse, from financials to products to employees—highlights where attention is focused, who gets credit for a job well done (the investors through profits or are employees singled out as key contributors?), and how different stories about how a firm creates value motivates different stakeholders. Different combinations of stakeholders create new opportunities co-creating value with employees, customers, communities, and investors.

In three-way or four-way interactions, employee and consumers impacts are tied, in turn, to financial and information impacts. Creating a mutually reinforcing feedback loop, fed by information touting the firm's reputation of treating employees well creates, in turn, a larger applicant pool, with more customers or more satisfied customers, leading to higher margins (increasing revenues or increasing margins) that reinforce the perception of the firm among analysts, the community, and attracting even more new hires. The buzz grows and the momentum surrounding the firm has positive multiplier effects. Of course, a downward spiral can also occur as we saw with the BP oil spill in Chapter 1. Paying too much attention to financials and time delays can lead employees to overlook important operational activities, such as safety, leading to implications for consumers, regulators, and neighborhoods.

Table 5.1 provides examples of one-way interactions between key stakeholders as they affect and are affected by a firm. This list suggests, rather than exhausts, the many relevant interactions among stakeholders. As specific relations are strengthened and deepened, new ways to co-create value are explored. As new value is created, the relationship accumulates trust. Trust in turn reinforces the relationship that is tested when a firm faces uncertainty.

Value destruction

Often the 'virtuousness' of mutually reinforcing, value-creating relationships is tested during moments of significant upheaval for the firm. As BP faced a major crisis in the Gulf Oil spill in 2010, survival was not guaranteed. Losing $103 billion in market value would bankrupt most companies. Upheavals germinating from external events outside the control of management, such as the global financial crises, test the

Table 5.1 *Impacts across stakeholder groups*

STAKEHOLDERS

IMPACTS	Investors	Employees	Customers	Government	Communities	Suppliers/ Distributors
Financial	Share price; dividends; returns	Employee stock ownership programs; wages	Price; cost	Taxes; oversight	Sponsorships; economic disparities	Costs; price
Workplace	Lawsuits; safety record	Safety; training; human trafficking; hours worked; benefits	Child labor; recalls	Oversight; jobs created; local content	Child labor; human rights; safety; jobs	Skills transfer
Products	Volume; price; margin	Potential customers; customer service; customer feedback	Safety; sourcing; price	Procurement; oversight	Waste; skills transfer; noise; pollution	Water; energy; carbon; sustainability
Information/ Data	Trends; momentum; disclosure; transparency	Newsletters; ambassadors; awards; updates	Availability; recalls; customer service	Macro-economic contribution; violations; stock market trading rules; logistics; local payments	Growth; jobs; skills; access to equity and institutions	Market access

ability of the firm to create value. When value is destroyed, layoffs often occur. When value is created, do employees get special attention?

When moments of change occur, do employees flee for the exit or do they stand up and support the firm? If the firm's response to frequent downturns is laying off employees, then paying a premium for hiring employees, knowing that layoffs might occur at any time, might be part of the price of doing business.

By examining combinations of impacts, a firm's net impact is (implicitly) assessed. Aggregating the various ills, harms, and benefits with relevant stakeholders is a tough yet important job. Comparing one firm's net impacts to another firm's impacts is trickier still. Part of net impacts is assessing if a firm is aware of and appropriately addressing its critical business impacts. Let's turn to assessing a firm's net impact now.

Net impact

The net impact is the summation of benefits and harms of a firm on its stakeholders. Summing up the effects of firms on its stakeholders involves subjective and objective facts and can vary according to the interpretation of such facts. Net impacts, due to their subjective nature based on widely held opinions, might weigh some events or activities more prominently than others. Rather than a predetermined, fixed calculus for assessing a firm's net impact, a firm's net impact is likely to vary widely within and across stakeholder groups. And yet we routinely assess firms, through rankings and surveys and form an opinion about their net impacts.

Favorable or unfavorable opinions of the net impacts of a firm, the intensity of the opinion, and the potential for harm to the firm's reputation likely vary across stakeholders, yet they are an important part of the net impact calculation. Each stakeholder is likely to have a different idea of what is important and how important it is (Harrison and Wicks, 2012). Now we will explore how to assess and aggregate impacts as they vary in types, intensity, and potential for harm. Aggregating net impacts often starts with understanding whether a minimal threshold of acceptable behavior is met or exceeded. Minimal levels of acceptable behavior, if widely held, are often codified into law. Adherence to legal standards while remaining profitable becomes a minimal yardstick by which a firm's net impacts are measured (Carroll,

1979, 1999). If a firm is in compliance with the legal requirements, this sets a necessary but not sufficient condition for net positive impacts. Yet the stringency of regulatory enforcement differs widely (Prakash and Potoski, 2014).

Laws may be codified in a country, yet without monitoring or enforcement a weak regulatory regime exists. Many multinational companies facing disparate legal thresholds and varying enforcement patterns decide to set universal internal standards for decision-making. With uniform standards throughout the company, including in developing countries where regulatory regimes are more likely to be weak, the company explicitly decides what it considers acceptable behavior. Reinforcing a strong culture that aligns mission, vision, and values reinforces the ethical norms of the business. Are all activities allowed so long as they generate a profit? Or is there a core set of values guiding a firm's everyday decision-making, such as 'do no harm'? The existence of a common, agreed-upon threshold of norms for conducting business (workplace conditions, sourcing products, relationships with governments, etc.), even if extant law remains silent, sets the baseline for acceptable behavior.

Just as there is diversity across investment funds that screen out firms engaging in tobacco manufacturing or nuclear power activities, the minimal level of acceptable behavior can vary across issues, industries, and nation-states. Thresholds for acceptable behavior might vary: privately held firms often adhere to a different standard than state-owned enterprises.

In sum, net impacts include indirect effects not directly controlled by the firm yet associated with the firm's value-creation process. Spillover effects are externalities affecting those that are not directly involved. The problem of assessing net impacts is, in part, assessing who bears the benefits and who bears the costs of the firm's activities. In many cases, the net positive financial impacts of a firm are often concentrated on a very few owners, founders, or top managers. On the other hand, net negative impacts are often dissipated indirectly among many stakeholders (employees, financiers, governments, suppliers, and communities).

Understanding a firm's net impacts helps in understanding how the company is perceived by others. Indirect effects often accumulate over time and ultimately create scenarios where, seemingly out of the blue, tempers escalate. Angry landowners in the outback of Australia, for example, won't sell their property without concessions on alleviating congestion, building primary schools, or sharing electricity with the town, which, in turn, limits the ability of a firm to grow.

In the next section, spillover effects from financial, employee, product, and information impacts are explored. The focus is purposely on indirect spillover effects to illustrate the wide variety of ways in which a firm's net impact can be assessed by stakeholders. Rather than making prescriptive judgments about how a firm's net impact should be assessed, the goal is raising awareness of the many, varied, and often indirect impacts that are borne by stakeholders other than the owners. That is, looking from the outside in, we examine from a stakeholder's perspective a firm's impacts. Doing so illustrates the multidimensional impacts of a firm on its many stakeholders, which in turn affects the value-creation process.

Financial spillover effects

Direct financial effects are relatively easy to trace as payments to different constituents. Tracing economic value created from owners' investments and shared as returns back to creditors is often aggregated, recorded, and tracked year after year as part of annual reporting guidelines and stock listings for financiers to make informed decisions. With the wealth of financial reporting information available, examining the magnitude and direction of direct financial effects is relatively easy and increasingly popular with the spread of business analytics.

Parsing data on the profiles and interests of financial investors is common among firms. As a starting point, examining the sheer volume of financial payments provides insights into where and with whom the firm shares value. Understanding which investors have a long-term perspective, which ones depend upon quarterly dividends, which analysts move the market, and their threshold for risk are questions often posed to investor relations departments.

Rather than examining shareholders as a monolithic entity, these analyses suggest equity owners have different preferences and interests as they are individual investors, pensioners, union funds, private sovereign funds, or private equity holders. Understanding the composition of equity holders and creditors and their motivation for dividends, growth, or long-term returns on investments provides a wealth of information useful in crafting messages to each investor class.

Sharing financial information as per unit of production, employee, shareholder, project, or unit helps stakeholders better understand how and where value is created and shared and allows for easier comparison across business units.

Reporting direct financial impacts along the value chain as payments to employees, suppliers, distributors, and governments, in addition to shareholders, is increasingly important to include alongside the returns provided to financiers (Porter and Kramer, 2011; Crane et al., 2014a; Rothaermel, 2015). These direct financial impacts along the value chain include but are not limited to wages to employees, payments to suppliers, taxes and fees paid to governments, and dividends or returns to shareholders. Sharing information on taxes, tariffs, and transfers paid in each municipality aggregated to a country level, for example, identifies how financial spillovers are distributed to governments that, in turn, can redistribute the proceeds and enable others (Clay, 2005).

As more financial information is reported, spillover effects involve even more stakeholders. Shareholder activists championing hot-button issues such as CEO pay or living wages extends the financial impact of a firm beyond mere expenses found in a balance sheet or income statement to social issues. Some stock markets are requiring governance oversight with regards to specific issues such as water in Bovespa, the Brazilian stock exchange. Some shareholders and institutions increasingly ask for new thresholds of acceptable business behaviors, or disclosure of benchmarking levels that address employee treatment, workplace conditions, and water consumption, spillover effects are occurring.

Financial multipliers are often highlighted after crises. During a crisis many stakeholders, not just investors, are financially affected by the misfortune of a firm. Employees might be laid off, customers are inconvenienced by returning recalled products, reputations are tarnished, partners might question future projects, and suppliers might have to rush orders with new features. Risks associated with profit loss, downturns in morale, and product availability can be quite significant. As we saw in the BP case study in Chapter 1, their loss of $103 billion in market value was equivalent to wiping out Intel, McDonald's, Disney, or Visa. Recovering from a major crisis tests many stakeholder relations. Not many organizations can survive significant financial tragedy, so preventing crises is justified as insurance against future incidents (Godfrey, 2005).

And yet, as the saying goes: never waste a good financial crisis. A significant crisis for one firm can create abundant new (spillover) opportunities for rivals offering similar products without the taint of being 'a bad company.' The Michelin tire company, for example, did quite well in expanding its customer base during and after the Ford/ Firestone crisis in the early 2000s, when underinflated Firestone tires were blamed for rollovers in Ford vehicles (Moll, 2003).

Financial spillovers extend to specific interest groups, charities, philanthropic activities, foundations, and sponsorships. These financial contributions may directly or indirectly support key issues (e.g., the arts or disease prevention), connect directly with the firm's activities (e.g., supporting education for a book publisher), or address urgent needs of the local community (e.g., hospitals, urgent care and wellness centers). While financial donations might be treasured by the local recipient, long-term impacts can be magnified by combining financial contributions with employee volunteer time and/or product donations to support qualified doctors and nurses, for example, with appropriate medicines and diagnostic equipment. The next section examines employee-based spillover effects and how powerful impacts can be created when employee-based spillover effects are combined with financial contributions.

Employee and workplace spillover effects

Unilever has created resiliency during a century of political and economic instability in Indonesia, ensuring continuity of operations, steady payments for employees and suppliers, and providing products and services for consumers (Clay, 2005). Interestingly, it was Unilever Indonesia's employees and their families that protected local manufacturing plants from random acts of violence during the Asian currency crisis of the late 1990s. When riots occurred, threatening supply lines and disrupting distribution, employees and management worked together to secure local supplies, create new recipes, and sustain operations with minimal disruptions—positive employee spillover effects that helped keep jobs and the production plants operating.

One of the most prominent direct contributions of a company is job creation. Yet, the creation of employment opportunities throughout the value chain is an oft overlooked spillover effect of a business. Unilever Indonesia (UI) with Oxfam International, for example, identified the number of full-time employees directly employed by UI as well as the spillover employment effects throughout its value chain. UI discovered that more than two-thirds of the workers are outside of its direct control. In other words, more full-time people are employed through UI's distribution networks and its suppliers of suppliers than as direct hires. Unilever's indirect, dispersed impacts on Indonesians are at least as important as its own hiring, firing, promotion, training, and wage policies.

In order to respond to government requests and nationalistic challenges, some firms are increasingly reporting their success in hiring local (indigenous) employees, minorities, and veterans, as well as the wages paid to local employees or the types of skillsets developed within the country verses expatriated. Similarly, income taxes paid and profits dispersed locally versus expatriated returns to shareholders or governments overseas are often tabulated to address allegations of exploitation and expropriation of rents. And access to healthcare, education, and training opportunities for employees, their households, and local communities can create positive externalities: an employable, productive workforce with decreasing turnover or missed days (Annan, 2001).

Driven by competition for top talent and employee retention goals, employer-sponsored volunteer activities create spillover effects. Firms with employee engagement programs often attract more motivated employees, as well as positive spillover effects on the company's bottom line, revenue, and reputation by building trust, pride, and respect among employees while communities benefit from the programs (Allen, 2007; Griffin, 2008). Spillover effects of employer-sponsored volunteerism, however, are poorly understood, as few organizations voluntarily collect information on the number of projects completed and the expected outcomes. The number of volunteer hours or number of projects completed are often reported, yet the stories of the lives altered two years later and other long-term impacts are often less well-understood and are not reported.

While business leaders may be tempted to throw up their hands and wonder what, if anything, can be done to quell employees' myriad and accelerating expectations. Surveys indicate that selecting initiatives that employees are passionate about and that the employer is willing to sponsor can create win–win–wins for the employer, employees, and the recipients. Co-creating value through employee volunteerism strengthens, deepens, and broadens the investments of a firm, yet the specific employee-related activities might vary widely by firm and by sector (Dunham et al., 2006; Griffin and Weber, 2006).

Spillover effects are often felt most acutely when the business suddenly grows or when the business shrinks. When a factory must be closed, sharing projections of the total number of jobs lost with government officials, for example, helps keep surprises to a minimum. If government officials have helped secure favorable tax breaks for the firm or if the firm is a primary constituent in the government officials' district, securing the support of government agencies to help retrain or relocate employees mitigates negative effects of withdrawing from a community. Spillover effects on local (un)employment rates are often important considerations to be shared as the intended (unintended) spillover effects may affect future relationships with municipal leaders or pending approval processes.

Employee-related spillover effects are often exacerbated in small, rural communities. When multiple firms lay off significant numbers of employees in a concentrated area, the burden is often borne predominantly by the local community (Stern, 1976). In urban, transient communities, employee layoffs are more easily absorbed, especially if there are universities or job training centers encouraging community members to change careers. Downsizing by multiple companies, such as manufacturers, investment banks, insurance companies, and law firms in a small community without many opportunities for high-skilled firms, can create employment deserts. Employees able to relocate leave the community bereft of talent and management skills. Without retraining laid off workers, poverty, homelessness, and bank-owned foreclosures can exacerbate a community's unemployment problems, making it less attractive for other employers to invest in.

Investments that purposefully leverage spillovers to connect a firm with its stakeholders deepen relationships, making the investments never redundant (Bies et al., 2007). Aligning investments directly with the firm's core competencies such as employee-driven engagement may open the door for many spillover win–win–win scenarios.

Employee-based investments using their skills and expertise with spillover effects on local neighbors, local municipalities, and state and national governments are identified in the following text.

Transferring skills and expertise

Service-oriented business such as retail banks might offer investor education, increased access, or financial literacy programs for potential customers including vulnerable populations such as indigenous cultures while promoting awareness of these populations among bank employees. Financial literacy, numeracy, and personal finance programs, for example, often benefit underserved populations, outlaying communities where branches are not located, or areas that are traditionally unbanked. Building a new customer base may not be the target outcome of extending these financial services. Instead, the company may aim to gain the trust of new communities and build trust with regulators that grant permits for growth and oversee compliance and re-chartering requirements for local branches.

Transferring skills and expertise such as project management, fundraising, advertising, prioritization, and management can help enable high levels of self-governance of the local community. Prioritizing meaningful community development leads to private investments in community activities such as: quality education for employees' children and those in the neighborhood; neighborhood police patrols to create a safe community; or building railroad spurs to improve distribution networks and access to markets for all businesses.

Moving investments in employee engagement from the periphery— as an afterthought—of a business decision to a central and integral strategic component of employee engagement requires a commitment to sharing value with employees. Rather than considering employee engagement a specialized pet project of a senior executive that can be cut when management changes, thoughtful investments can further the combined interests of the business, employees, and communities. These selective investments multiply the effects of the value-creation process.

One-time giveaways or longer-term in-kind contributions often combine the interests of employees and customers by providing products, skills, or expertise towards good causes of interest to employees. External pressures and the desire of firms to be transparent in their employee engagement activities enables a closer scrutiny of workplace conditions. In a Hawthorne effect, whereby firms improve an aspect of their behavior in response to being aware of being observed, company reports and disclosures through the Dow Jones Sustainability Index (DJSI) for voluntarily reporting the firm's environmental, social, and governance activities using the Global Reporting Initiative's (GRI) standards are gaining traction. These disclosure reports offer a comprehensive view of employee engagement and create a culture where firms are being observed and evaluated that in turn leads to employees feel valued with benchmarking progress against peers.

Building community infrastructure

Investments in building a community's infrastructure by using in-house expertise, skills, and resources is another wise spillover investment that addresses community-wide social issues (Allen, 2007; Griffin, 2008). Promoting healthy eating habits, for example, is a societal goal that can be supported by health food stores and fast-food restaurants, local gyms and premium drink providers. Each organization can bring different resources to address healthy eating: organic foods, providing healthy food options with calories prominently displayed, offering water alongside other drink options, as well as promoting wellness programs and exercise.

Similarly, firms offering hygiene and personal care products have some overlapping concerns with women who want to improve the lives of their children and their children's children. And telecommunications companies, public schools, and community centers can team up to tackle concerns regarding the safety of children that are home after school without supervision. All in all, aspects of complex social issues can be addressed by different firms by bringing together vastly different skills, resources, and capabilities with a shared desire to use core competencies to be part of the solution (Allen, 2007; Griffin, 2008).

Spillover effects occur when thinking about employees outside of work. For example, companies concerned about the pressures of commuting and the toll it takes on their employees might partner with local municipalities, taxis, or regional governments to improve transportation infrastructure. The focus on improving the lives of employees has positive spillover effects for the entire community. Building pedestrian walkways and bike-friendly roads into an integrated transportation plan incentivizes alternative means of transportation, such as motorcycles, mopeds, bicycles, walking, public transport, or carpooling, that alleviate congestion for the business, the business community, and the neighborhoods.

Employees as ambassadors

Companies creating the potential for future spillover effects purposely focus on indirect relationships between an employee and his/her network. By focusing on indirect effects such as employee's family, household, neighborhood, affinity groups, or neighborhood, the interests of more stakeholders are considered. An employee plus their partners, spouses, children, or parents become part of the value-creation process with spillover effects prioritized. As employees' attitudes towards their employers builds trust and shapes the attitudes of their families and neighborhoods toward the firm, so the ability to get permits to expand within the community might become more feasible. When a crisis occurs, the firm might be given the benefit of the doubt if it has taken the trouble to build goodwill among stakeholders when it didn't have to.

Informing employees is a form of engagement. By voluntarily distributing information on company donations not mandated by law or designed to solicit employee donations, the firm can tie internal corporate sustainability discussions to the core of operations while building respect and trust among employees. A firm can effectively engage employees by asking them about their favorite outreach projects instead of basing such decisions solely on input from management. Alternatively, asking the local community what they think are the needed skills or services can deepen ties to communities by converging employee and community interests.

Since employees are tied to the community as officials, volunteers, and neighbors, they are the stakeholders that can best contribute from understanding what the company is or is not doing in different communities, and the organization's position on different issues.

Employees might be a source of new product features or new ways of creating the product while saving costs. Charismatic CEOs frequently in the media may be quite helpful in aligning community needs with employee volunteers through their frequent interviews, blogs, and social media.

Product and service spillover effects

Firms regularly address negative spillover effects of their products by conducting detailed consumer research. Feedback about a product's spillover effects comes in many forms: consumer (dis)satisfaction, feedback on product enhancements, discounts on products and services for non-profits or underserved populations to better understand how the product is used or to improve penetration rates.

Clients and consumers contact corporate officials, attend board meetings, wage proxy fights, lodge complaints, and populate blogs, chatrooms, Twitter, and Facebook pages with content to have their voices heard. Customer satisfaction, feedback, and (un)favorability ratings are regularly employed to understand shifting consumer preferences as well as the social acceptability of products and corporate practices. Consumer-oriented firms with controversial products (e.g., tobacco, alcohol, firearms) are predisposed to analyzing negative spillover effects of their policies, practices that affect the willingness to pay and social acceptability of their products.

Similarly, many companies have created feedback processes to address the negative perceptions of their activities. Trending on social media sites, rapidly responding to blogs that detail complaints, and connecting beta testers with product development teams are ways in which firms are trying to mitigate negative spillover effects or turn complaints into good ideas about new product innovations. By listening to constructive criticism from customers—such as sharing ideas for lengthening the life of the product, extending the product to new uses, or bundling products—innovations are occurring.

Product-based spillover effects might be captured by a single firm, as in the case of the energy efficiency gains at Walmart. When faced with a challenge to reduce carbon, water, and energy waste in its own operations, the company began learning about process improvements that reduced costs, saved energy, reduced environmental impacts, and created new refrigeration and lighting schemes.

On the other hand, product-based spillover effects might have widespread community effects. Improvements suggested by customers or pressures from government to eliminate plastic bags in grocery stores, for example, have cut costs by eliminating unnecessary packaging on products and encouraged widespread use of reusable grocery bags in some locales. While costs may increase immediately as a store adjusts to paper bags, incentives to shift to reusable bags create benefits for the natural environment (reducing the number of animals suffocating from plastic bags) and for local communities by extending the life of local landfills. Additional multiplier effects of a firm's procurement and distribution channels are explored in greater detail in the next chapter.

Information spillover effects

Information effects are often thought of as directly affecting neighborhoods and local communities. That is, information effects often focus narrowly on local community groups that are geographically close to the firm's headquarters. Yet information, enabled by a globally connected internet, flows freely and widely, affecting many stakeholders. Examining information spillover effects creates new questions regarding: (a) if 'local' impacts might be shared among many communities and (b) how the free flow of (mis)information affects relationships with groups (communities) around the world.

First, local impacts might not be isolated to a single community—even if a community thinks its requests require customized responses. A large construction company contractually obligated to build electrical generation plants in every state of India, for example, addresses local community needs by voluntarily supporting local schools at each of its project sites. Supporting local schools while building needed power generation infrastructure is a win–win–win with numerous spillover effects. First, providing education at its remote locations is a point of pride among the workforce and the firm uses its education outreach as a recruitment tool and to help secure government-sponsored contracts over competitors. Second, workers that relocate onsite for the long-term construction projects are guaranteed adequate education for their children. Third, the local community gains the long-term benefit of electricity as well as continued education support (from employees that remain in the community or from state funding dedicated to education) that continues after the construction project is completed.

Thought experiment: if a retail business has many local branches in remote, rural areas of an emerging economy, are there local issues that can be addressed leveraging the company's logistical support from headquarters and the locational advantage of branches? Supporting local education classes, dysentery prevention, or overcoming malnutrition might be appropriate for a bank, a grocery store, or a beverage company. Local branches of a national bank, given its local presence, can disperse financial literacy information, deworming pills, or nutrition information alongside its normal banking activities to serve its customers, its employees with numerous spillover effects for the local communities.

Second, free-flowing dispersed information enabled by social media encourages relationships with groups around the world. The proliferation of social media can be a double-edged sword for firms. The availability of data has increased at an ever-accelerating pace, yet the ability to aggregate and interpret the data into useable knowledge remains underdeveloped. Firms embracing Facebook, Instagram, Yelp, Twitter, crowdsourcing, and other social media tools are learning the positive and negative spillover effects (targeting new markets, developing new products) on consumers, neighbors, opinion leaders, and the public policy community as 'friends,' 'reviewers,' or investors in future projects. Mindfully considering the spillover effects of information means understanding that the varied interests of stakeholders include: shopping habits, preferences, political ideology, religious affiliation, loyalty programs, university affinities, and even health issues (diabetes, depression, or cancer).

Rather than community impacts being an afterthought, treating community members as important constituencies that can vote, as potential consumers, or as potential employees involves community members directly in the value-creation process with the potential for positive information spillover effects.

The spillover effects of information are wide-ranging: friends 'liking' a company, which in turn leads to increased product loyalty and more coupons directed toward these loyal consumers; flash mobs supporting a specific company cause or executives sharing insights as board members of non-profit organizations, which in turn creates dialog that might lead to improvements. CEOs might be asked to provide expert testimony to help shape proposed legislation, while employees are empowered with more choices regarding community outreach, which in turn builds respect and the firm's reputation.

With a wide-ranging set of groups, and a cacophony of voices within any one group, firms are increasingly being tasked with understanding the interests of the groups but also the concerns and composition of its subgroups. Each firm may be physically present or virtually present, so the channels required to reach members of the same group are different.

Implications for co-creating value

Thus far—building upon the insights of Freeman (1984) regarding the significance of stakeholders, followed by a focus on managing for stakeholders (Freeman et al., 2010), to mindfully creating impacts with stakeholders—the progression from stakeholder awareness to stakeholder management to impact co-creating value suggests a long-term perspective generating mutual benefits.

The task for managers and researchers? Being able to articulate the mutual, multifaceted impacts (benefits net of true costs) for the firm and other stakeholders is increasingly important for creating long-term value.

Co-creating value is about optimizing value for the firm over the long term through networks of relationships (Rowley, 1997). Certainly not all relationships are going to work out. Nor should they. And certainly some relationships will deepen while other relationships will languish and be replaced. The mix of relationships is likely to change over time as a firm's product-market mix, geographical reach, and brand recognition status changes.

Purposefully combining impacts (financial, employee, product, and information) to multiply their positive effects can create significant value. This chapter explored how combining different impacts can create new opportunities for businesses. Conversely, when firms destroy value, mutually destructive combinations require interventions to mitigate harm by changing attitudes and expectations or eliminating destructive practices.

Overall, understanding spillover effects involves combining old data in new ways (e.g., examining how employee engagement is tied to customer satisfaction) as well as collecting new data (e.g., social trending). It requires thinking more broadly about the flows of financials, employees, products, and information between the firm and its stakeholders, which in turn focuses on the process of how value is created rather than destroyed.

A focus on spillover effects in the value-creation process underscores the need to rethink how effectiveness is measured and the data required to assess effectiveness. As intended and unintended impacts of organizations become highlighted in a 24/7 connected world, momentum and materiality are becoming important criterion in measuring effectiveness.

Momentum, materiality, and measurement

Momentum is one way in which effectiveness of value created or destroyed can be evaluated. Momentum focuses on the rate of change of interest in a given issue (e.g., if an issue or idea is trending) regardless of which stakeholders are interested. Analyzing momentum of multiplier effects on significant issues entails tracking the volume, variety, and volatility in blog postings, tweets, retweets, Facebook posts, or comments. These instantaneous responses are in addition to traditional metrics of share price or the number of regulations, shareholder resolutions, or lawsuits filed. Irate customers may indeed be important to protect the value of the brand so the rate of (positive) change in attitudes towards customer service, customer retention, and customer attitudes become important.

Similarly, tracking how (new) issues are being talked about in the community and reframed over time (e.g., attitudes towards expansion within the community) is likely to provide a glimpse of important expectations. Rather than tracking the sheer volume of respondents to an issue, the rate of change in respondents is especially important if the issue becomes a priority, for a community organizer can bring in (or block) a large amount of votes/voices. If an important stakeholder with a track record of success can garner lots of support for (or against) a particular issue, that is important to track, too.

A focus on momentum suggests that analyzing how an issue is attracting ever-more attention via trending in social media is more important than tracking the number of issues facing a company at any given time.

Materiality, on the other hand, suggests that stakeholder demands or issues brought by stakeholders must affect the business in ways that significantly alter the ability of the organization to meet its objectives. Materiality examines benefits in light of the true costs on the business and its stakeholders. Materiality may entail positive, negative, and neutral impacts on the business. That is, the impact may create a windfall of profits for shareholders, for example, creating a positive upside to the change. Alternatively, the impact may create additional noise pollution (a negative externality borne by the local community), creating an unfavorable impression of the company.

While the materiality of an impact changes over time, understanding the ebb and flow of some relationships can turn the tide, making a negative impact into a positive impact—such as not renewing a suppliers contract after numerous warnings due to the supplier's continued human trafficking violations. Materiality, as an assessment of risk, examines unintended consequences as much as the intended consequences of action. Negative spillover effects with 'hardcore,' entrenched opposition can spark retaliation when a hiccup occurs, as shown in the BP example in Chapter 1. Speculation of bankruptcy, being a takeover target, or significantly curtailing the operations of BP ran rampant for months after the oil spill. Such speculation was sparked and kept alive by mounting legal challenges and environmental groups opposed to drilling.

Pre-emptively building relationships to create favorable impressions of an organization can help ensure momentum in unfavorability doesn't accelerate to the point it blocks growth or threaten survival (Cheng et al., 2014; Henisz, 2014) when a crisis of material proportions affects the firm. The idea here is not to wish away opposition entirely, but to think about an optimal level of favorability *and* unfavorability regarding material issues that ensures continuity of operations and the ability of the business to continuously seek new growth areas.

And finally, momentum and materiality often trigger a rethinking of appropriate measurements for effectiveness. Rather than creating a scorecard measuring investors' satisfaction, accounting for multiple stakeholders requires understanding the interactions of impacts among many actors on continuity of operations, and vice versa. Measuring spillover effects necessitates different types of data gathered from a number of sources. For example, point-of-purchase usage is important to capture for retail stores, but so is climate (raining, sunshine, cloudy, temperature), seasonal and location-specific demands. Some of this data is housed in large quantifiable bytes while other data is perceptual or more qualitative in nature. Effectively combining quantitative and qualitative data from multiple sources will lead firms to optimize, and continually revisit, what they pursue as a benchmark for creating value.

All in all, spillover effects can create double positives or double negatives through momentum of material impacts. Measuring momentum suggests focusing on the ways in which positive and negative impacts can rapidly ripple through the process of co-creating value. Quite often getting to neutral (with equal and opposite forces that are in favor of and oppose the firm rendering both sides muted) might be the best a highly visible firm can manage.

Thought experiment: can a company ever be considered to have a net positive impact? And, if so, what would this entail? That is, how does a firm give evidence of net positive impacts? Overall, co-creating value focuses on the interactions inherent in the process of creating value so as to not destroy value. In turn, new ways of thinking about corporations and their multiple, varied, and at times conflicting relationships with stakeholders are needed.

Looking ahead

While direct effects of financial, employee, product, or information impacts are frequently straightforward, corporations often don't know their multiplier effects. As described in Chapter 1, BP's financial loss of $103 billion in market value is only one aspect of the story regarding how BP co-creates—and destroyed in the *Deepwater Horizon* oil spill—value with its stakeholders. Evaluating only BP's direct, financial impacts of the oil spill in the Gulf would miss the many—financial and non-financial—impacts on financial analysts, partners, suppliers, shrimp businesses, and tourism companies based in the Gulf. Communities further down the coast *without* oil slicks covering their beaches made claims without bearing *direct* physical impacts of the oil spill. Some businesses claimed the oil spill harmed or halted tourism in the neighboring region with the perception that the Gulf was contaminated. These claims, whether they hold up in a court of law or not, multiplied BP's perceived impacts beyond direct, physical impacts upon close-by neighborhoods to encompass communities further afield that, allegedly, bore the brunt of the spill but did not have their neighborhoods marred by its physical impacts.

In the next chapter we examine multiplier effects, as firms can have far-reaching impacts well beyond their direct, physical boundaries. We examine three types of impacts: impacts along the value chain; impacts that combine social, environmental, and economic (the so-called triple bottom line) effects; and impacts that extend across countries and over time. Chapter 6 suggests that co-creating enduring value depends upon a firm's ability to understand its financial and non-financial impacts, including its spillover and multiplier effects, in light of the true impacts of the company.

6 | *Multiplier effects*

Do you know your multiplier (network) effects?

Are you unwittingly contributing to multiplying disparities?

How are you being a catalyst that enables others?

During the global financial crisis, General Motors (GM) successfully made the argument for a government bailout by US citizens by enumerating the jobs that would be lost in the event of the company's bankruptcy, across all of GM's independent car dealerships, located throughout the 50 states of America. Calculating not only the potential for jobs lost at headquarters in Detroit, Michigan, but also the impacts on workers manufacturing ball bearings, chaises, or iron struts and working in car dealerships exponentially multiplied the employment impact of a GM bankruptcy. By citing its extended network of suppliers and distributors—the multiplier effects of one of the Big Three going out of business was calculated at 3 million lost jobs—the auto industry was able to successfully convince Congress how its operations extensively impact numerous other businesses, the constituencies in the Senators districts, and employment throughout the nation to gain financial backing from the US government. A bankruptcy would have increased unemployment rates and caused a commensurate increase in government provision of social services, such as child care, food stamps, as well as a rise in incidents of domestic abuse and bank foreclosure. When combined with a decrease in tax receipts for local charities and municipalities, the multiplier effects of a GM bankruptcy are not solely relegated to workers in Detroit.

Ikenson (2009)

Multiplier effects extend the borders of a business to include the indirect impacts of a firm on its stakeholders. The last three chapters explored impacts: financial impacts, employee impacts in the workplace, enhancing customer experiences, and information-sharing to create win–win–win situations. We also examined spillover effects, defined as externalities affecting stakeholders not directly involved in the business. In this chapter we expand upon indirect effects by focusing on multiplier effects: impacts viewed as ripple effects magnifying in intensity or dampening risks as business risks are dispersed across many relationships.

When viewed as a network of stakeholders (Rowley, 1997), typical business risks involving the firm's access to capital, information, and reputation are spread broadly across suppliers, manufacturers, and investors. While risk is shared across the network with no single organization being targeted, managing risks can be difficult as anticipating system-wide risks cannot be easily identified, as the global financial crisis demonstrated (Santoro and Strauss, 2012). With positive and negative contagion effects possible, the old adage of 'choose your friends and choose wisely' is loosely translated into 'choose your partners and choose wisely'!

In this chapter, we examine the multiplier effects of a business by expanding our focus from the firm to its network of relationships of stakeholders that co-create value. By focusing on a network of relationships in the process of creating value, we explore the intended and unintended multiplier effects as the potential risks or contagions that destroy or enhance the value among the stakeholders. Three multiplier effects are explored in this chapter: multipliers along the value chain; multipliers due to combining social, economic, and environmental effects; and multipliers across geographies.[1]

What are multiplier (network) effects?

Multiplier effects extend the interests of a firm beyond the direct hierarchical control of management to the multiple, and varied relationships that co-create value with the firm. That is, the business of business is not just within the boundaries of the business itself but extends outwards to encompass stakeholders residing in numerous organizations: suppliers, suppliers of suppliers, wholesalers, journalists, retailers, kiosk owners, thought leaders, or recyclers. The relationships between members of this network with the focal firm might be direct or indirect, while the intended and unintended affects might create, or destroy, value. Multiplier effects extend positive impacts such

---

[1] Multiplier effects over time are addressed in Chapter 9.

as employment and wealth creation to the families of employees while also having the potential to heighten negative effects through dislocation or pollution, affecting local communities and neighboring communities well beyond the traditional bricks-and-mortar boundaries of a business.

Multiplier effects reflect the ability of management to co-create value by influencing and being influenced by stakeholder networks. Managing multiplier effects becomes influencing the influencers. That is, direct effects via legally binding contracts, for example, are necessary but not sufficient in explaining how value is created. Indirect effects significantly expanded by a firm's multiplier effects are increasingly important but are often overlooked as a means by which a firm becomes a catalyst for good or harm. Measuring indirect effects of networks can be equated with fuzzy math as the identification, attribution, and measurement of indirect impacts of stakeholders on other stakeholders might be widely dispersed. The BP case study in Chapter 1 is a prime example, as households and businesses throughout the Gulf region made claims in court alleging that they were negatively impacted by the oil spill. From BP's perspective, many of these claimants prior to the oil spill would not have been considered relevant stakeholders, yet the courts decided differently.

Indirect effects are quite important in some industries. Consider for a moment how pharmaceutical medicines are sold in different countries. Some countries forbid pharmaceutical companies from providing medicines directly to consumers (DTC). Instead, these countries create tiers of legislation allowing manufacturers to sell to pharmacies and hospitals yet not directly to consumers. Individual physicians prescribe medicines while a dispensary fills the prescription and sells the medicines directly to consumers. During each transaction, the government is involved as an overseer, regulator, and reimbursement mechanism for approved medicines. These countries create layers of oversight and approvals, discouraging abuse of medicinal drugs, limiting access to prescribed medicines, and avoiding misinformation that could lead to suboptimal decisions by individual citizens. Forbidding advertising direct to consumers is one way in which a government tries to forestall the possibility that a consumer might be persuaded by effective advertising campaigns of a single product for private company benefit without consultation or diagnosis with a certified professional.

Gaining access to medicines is often considered one of the most urgent needs of communities in emerging countries. Providing access to medicines often means working collaboratively with national governments to ensure reimbursements, local service providers or NGOs to provide ongoing support for long-term chronic illness, and individual medical doctors to provide preventative treatments and appropriate medicines for patients rather than directly working with patients themselves.

Using the pharmaceutical example, the indirect effects of access to medicines is complicated by the overlapping network of stakeholders. A single pharmaceutical manufacturer cannot claim credit for directly demonstrating an uptick in access to medicines nor an increase in a healthy population. Yet it can help. Pharmaceutical manufacturers can be part of the long-term solution of access to medicines.

As a pharmaceutical company expands its focus to a network of stakeholders, the daisy-chain of direct responsibility becomes rather complicated. Thinking about positive impacts of products two or three tiers down the distribution chain, and thinking about sharing responsibility through partnerships with governments or NGOs makes for a complicated problem.

Quite often, a pharmaceutical manufacturer's response to access to medicines is reducing the prices of pharmaceuticals for vulnerable populations. Yet lowering prices for a medicine is just the start of the process of ensuring healthy communities, as multiplier effects need to be considered to ensure healthy communities over time. To ensure repeat purchases, it is in the pharmaceutical company's best interest to ensure that the appropriate product in the appropriate dosage gets to the patient and that the patient is sufficiently supported to take the medicines as prescribed. To demonstrate effectiveness in combating the disease, it is in the pharmaceutical company's best interest to demonstrate the effectiveness of the government's purchase of its medicine and how it has alleviated disease or prevented recurrences.

Pushing out the boundaries of a firm exposes the organization to even more points of criticism as more stakeholders are likely to have an opinion of what the firm is (not) doing and how well (poorly) it is doing whatever it does. Criticism may stem from not so friendly reviewers, retweeters, and bloggers as social media exponentially expands the comments about a firm.

Indirect, multiplier impacts present many pragmatic challenges for managers. If firm A creates a safe product, product A, and sells it to firm B then firm A has ostensibly fulfilled its responsibility as contracted. When firm B in turn sells product A to the next stakeholder, firm B becomes responsible for selling product A to their end user and for making a net positive impact. So, once firm A has fulfilled its responsibility and sold its product, firm A might be indifferent as to how the product is subsequently used, recycled, and disposed of at the end of its useful life, or the consequences of product A being misused. Once firm A has sold the product, as sequential coordination thinking goes, it is someone else's responsibility to worry about.

In reality, sequentially addressing issues and ascribing responsibility can exacerbate problems as issues raised by stakeholders of stakeholders are often conceptualized as someone else's problem. Yet managing the issues may pragmatically be in the best interest of the originating firm, especially if the firm is a branded company with a significant consumer interest.

Alternatively, the coordination required might be better suited to radial (hub and spoke) relationships, with a firm centrally involved during design, as well as during sourcing and distribution decisions. Radial coordination is often centered on contracts a firm might have with a number of independent groups.

A third means of coordination is a federated style involving networks. Federated coordination allows for a set of smaller, loosely coupled entities rather than a focus on a single large monolithic firm (Evan, 1965). Federated coordination requires timely information (daily, monthly, or quarterly rather than annually) with substantive data on the true impacts of the firm and its network.

Whereas internal control systems are often designed for sharing robust financial information, financial controls alone are inadequate for addressing multiplier effects. Financial controls alone do not provide the necessary information about all of the firms' impacts and its multiplier effects. Adapting financial control systems to convey non-financial information is imperfect at best as financial metrics have numerous shortcomings—as explored in Chapter 2—that are often not attuned to measuring the nuances of employee, product, or information multiplier effects.

The process of creating value is complicated as the costs, energy, and timing required for sequential, radial (hub and spoke), or federated coordination is non-trivial. Take, for example, a hypothetical firm that has a series of contracts with a variety of different suppliers, each relationship is likely designed to meet specific goals—on-time delivery, budget targets, etc. A focus on optimizing individual goals/contracts might obscure the overall project goals. By focusing on specific, internal goals without coordinating with others about the overall project goals, the overall objective of satisfying the end user may not be met. Even though every single internal deadline was met on time and on budget, the outcome was unsatisfactory. A focus on aligning internal goals with the overall outcome is required.

Another example would be choosing between equivalent suppliers offering the same price and on-time delivery guarantees. If supplier A has a record of unsafe work conditions, making it susceptible to warehouse fires or work stoppages, the unsafe workplace conditions might ultimately undermine the ability of supplier A to get a contract. Alternatively, if information about supplier A's unsafe work conditions are not questioned, not available, or not verified, the contracting firm might be taking on undue risks without appropriate information to make a decision.

Multiplier effects require a mindset focused on big-picture objectives. While individual deadlines might be missed (e.g., a zoning permit might require more time and money than expected, delaying the start of construction), the ability to adjust timetables with second- and third-tier suppliers might enable the firm to make up time through the construction phase. Tying overall project goals to the incentives of second- and third-tier suppliers, for example, requires continuous education and including the suppliers in periodic progress reports.

Indirect impacts also include a company's contribution (or lack thereof) to prevailing commentary on social and environmental issues. Fast-food companies, for example, supply a needed source of readily available cheap food to a willing public often in underserved communities; however, large volumes of fast food can contribute to obesity. Obesity is a complex issue with many interwoven dimensions—activity, nutrition, psychological, physiological, and cultural to name just a few—that is of concern to many organizations, including fast-food firms. While a fast-food company might argue that its food does not, by itself, make an individual obese, the public is increasingly asking what firms are doing or not doing about obesity (or other social externalities) that can be linked to using its products. Even if consumers misuse the product, the questions are still being asked regarding what the firms have done and what they can do.

Questions of how clients use or misuse a firm's products are also often asked of alcoholic beverage or tobacco companies. While the proportion of clients that are binge drinkers might be small relative to all who imbibe alcohol, it is increasingly in firms' best interests to address the potential misuse of products. The company and the public share a common goal: addressing impacts by examining how the product is used or misused.

Addressing multiplier effects enmeshed in complex social and environmental issues, such as obesity, binge drinking, or disease alleviation, often requires collaboration among multiple organizations (e.g., charities, non-profit, for-profit, governmental, and quasi-governmental organizations) for a sustained solution. Partnerships are explored in more detail in Chapters 10 and 11 as a means to address complex issues and global challenges, respectively. With different governance structures, goals, and resources, tri-sector partnerships face the challenge of finding ways to work together to maintain relationships through good times and bad when addressing deeply entrenched persistent issues.

In this chapter we explore positive and negative multiplier effects by examining three ways in which organizations extend and blur their traditional organizational boundaries. First we examine the entire economic value chain from acquisition of raw materials to the end of the product lifecycle. Second, we expand a triple bottom line perspective *across the entire value chain* by combining financial, social, and environmental impacts of products and services regardless of who owns, captures, or creates value. And third, as firms grow their operations in different geographical markets, we explore multiplier effects when expanding sourcing and distribution across geographies.

Multiplier effects: along the value chain

Extending the focus of a firm's economic value chain to include forward and backward linkages, such as suppliers of suppliers, subcontractors, franchisees, and retailers of retailers, creates multiplier effects. The next step is overlaying social, environmental, and economic impacts *along the entire value chain* (the so-called triple bottom line) to identify new opportunities and challenges for the firm. Starting with the

Figure 6.1 Traditional product-based value chain

traditional product-based value chain, as shown in Figure 6.1, a firm might control all of the entire process, or just a piece of it.

The traditional product-based value chain depicts the relationships of the focal firm with suppliers of suppliers and distributors through to retailers. Viewing a firm as a network of relationships encompassing raw material providers through to clients is akin to thinking about an extended enterprise (Freeman et al., 2007, 2010). This network of relationships includes stakeholders supplying raw materials for assembly, including capital and labor to help the firm produce products, deliver its services, and satisfy customers. Contractually specifying expectations throughout the network might involve detailed obligations specifying financial remuneration, longevity of contract, workmanship quality, quantity of material, oversight or accountability (Stout, 2012; Harrison and Wicks, 2012).

Contracts are important, yet limiting, as a firm expands its control via vertical integration (e.g., petrochemical firms with long-term leases on the land for drilling, mining, or extracting minerals and fossil fuels with upstream and downstream businesses). Making explicit the value expected in contracts binds companies together by detailing the nature of the product, personnel, and information within the business. A common focus with an agreed-upon objective helps reinforce the value that is expected with details regarding for whom the value is created and what type of value it is.

And yet, contracts are imperfect in detailing what value is shared. Not all expectations are codified into contracts, as mutual trust decreases the need for oversight (Jones, 1995; Wicks et al., 1999). Some expectations will remain unspecified in the contract or unmet by the terms of the contract (Stout, 2012). Intentionally specifying a wide variety of expectations along the economic value chain makes for long documents but may not expand the ability to create (or mitigate destruction of) value for the company. Contracts are imperfect. And enforcing contracts takes time that may not be in the best interests of the firm.

In addition, proximity matters. The further out from the organization, the more varied the definition of value may be (Clay, 2005). That is, subcontractors may want job security and are willing to bargain with lower wages, or communities might want less pollution and more opportunities for education and are willing to bargain through tax breaks.

This multiplication of potential and real impacts makes clarity about co-creating value paramount. Clarity of what is of value to the different stakeholders, as well as to the firm, requires a focus on what is of value and how value can be co-created over time. Clarity does not mean expanding the exact same set of activities conducted in the exact same way in every community across the globe. Rather, clarity means having a consistent logic to answer the key questions about objectives, strategy, and tactics: what is meant by co-creating value? How does this strategy address the relevant impacts? And how will this process continually create value for all involved? Clarity of what is and what is not to be expected is necessary to build a foundation for authenticity, credibility, and goodwill for future relations (Rothaermel, 2015).

Clarity is often based upon the information that cascades from multiple business units, stakeholders, and geographies, is integrated with financial, social, and environmental insights, and filtered through the firm's objectives. Clarity can reassure stakeholders that the company will operate in a responsible manner when continuity of operations is uncertain. Clarity builds trust and allows the firm to ask others to take a leap of faith during times of crisis or uncertainty (Ansoff, 1975, 1980; Dess and Beard, 1984).

Stakeholders of stakeholders, without direct access to decision-makers, are likely to be concerned with downside economic risks, such as the firm's early withdrawal, failure to honor commitments, or changes in management causing changes in strategy. Creating a clear rationale involving multiple stakeholders based on common interests—such as a viable tax base, creating job opportunities for the local community, providing training and expertise—is one step towards co-creating value over time with projects that will continue beyond the current executive team. The ultimate goal, of course, might be enabling the stakeholders of stakeholders to continue to be financially independent after a project is completed, a product is no longer available, or the firm has left the community.

Multiplier effects of traditional product-based value chains focus on the impacts of the product itself, including the effects of its manufacture, distribution, and use. Disposal, reuse, and recycling loops are also part of an organization's extended enterprise. We look at multiplier effects at different stages of the product-based value chain; where the raw materials for the product are sourced and how the product is distributed and used or misused by consumers.

How the product is sourced—backward linkages. Suppliers often have contractual obligations to the firm, which set minimum levels of product quality or parameters for on-time delivery. As the number of suppliers grows vertically and horizontally, the ability of the supplier network to adjust to changing consumer demands is challenged. Coordinating becomes a challenge as a series of linear, sequential contracts may devolve into numerous independent contracts without a hierarchy to ensure governance and oversight. The overall project goals may be lost for all with all of the focus on individual contracts with losses multiplying as information is lost or dissipated through the network.

As higher yields are demanded, for example, farmers may need to learn how to apply fertilizers with the appropriate protective equipment to supply the volume and quality of produce contracted by the firm. Universities may become involved in teaching how to apply fertilizers, adapting seed to the local climate conditions (e.g., short growing season; drought conditions). And yet, rather than applying the fertilizer supplied at a discount by a conglomerate, a farmer may sell the fertilizer to a neighboring farmer at a better price and turn a quick profit. In this case the original farmer gains, but the conglomerate supplying the fertilizer has lost value. Companies must also invest in additional governance and monitoring systems to safeguard their investment with the farmers to ensure the fertilizers and the equipment are put to productive uses. Conducting regular visits to the farms (or factories to monitor workplace conditions, for example) to assess the critical impacts increases costs to the firm and must be weighed against other investments.

A focus on product sources often leads to triple bottom line conversations about economic, environmental, and social impacts. Organizations required to label their products—genetically modified organism (GMO) labeling, or GMO-free labeling, for instance—can lead to detailed procurement conversations about the environmental-friendliness of bamboo flooring versus hardwood flooring, the disposability of recycled or compostable swizzle sticks in cafés verses wooden sticks, or the viability of producing tea bags without metal staples.

The pressures on suppliers and suppliers of suppliers to comply with social and environmental expectations are increasing due to changing public opinions, industry practices, and incentives to consolidate supply chains. Firms might announce the names of suppliers whose contracts are not being renewed to publicly shame suppliers that aren't compliant with the firm's expectations; other suppliers might receive warnings for insufficient progress towards established social or environmental targets. Still other suppliers may be cautioned that they must work to improve practices or risk losing their contracts. The number of announced (and unannounced) supplier audits is increasing, along with the variety of deficiencies suppliers are being asked to address. As large manufacturers consolidate their supply chains, auditing suppliers helps focus attention on multiple goals—lower costs, quality products, and safe workplaces—if there is also a potential for higher volumes of goods purchased.

How the product is used—forward linkages. Distribution networks are often more complicated, with more stakeholder groups involved than backward linkages when purchasing raw materials. Forward linkages are often more complicated to trace, as many relations are not directly tied to the firm itself. Forward linkages between the firm and the ultimate end user might be separated by regulation, efficiency requirements, or the ability to provide complementary services.

Regulations often bar firms, particularly in the pharmaceutical, alcohol, or tobacco industries, from direct-to-consumer marketing of their products. In the case of pharmaceuticals, governments may purchase a large volume of pharmaceuticals at a discount rate and then distribute them throughout their hospitals, physician networks, and urgent care clinics.

As firms focus on efficiency, they might become separated from the demands of the end user. Many firms are intermediaries in that they supply industrial products to other industries, B2B, making the end users nearly impossible to identify. For example, suppliers of benzene to a plastic manufacturer might only be interested in the industrial market for benzene rather than the consumer market for all plastic goods or PET (polyethylene terephthalate) plastics. And yet, these intermediary companies may become squeezed with demands for high-quality, lower-cost products while ensuring safe workplaces.

In some cases, it might not make a difference if firms might be separated from end users, as the delivery of a service or product is commoditized or integrated with other services. A pulp and paper manufacturer producing cardboard shipping products may not know precisely the end user receiving their cardboard packaging, working instead through a shipping company or a distributor due to the sheer volume involved. Or a homeowner might employ a housecleaner who purchases numerous cleaning supplies or equipment. The shipping company may source from local cardboard manufacturers, or the housecleaner may buy CFC-free cleaning products, yet the end users may not care (Donaldson, 1996).

And finally, consumers often have many products to choose from. Even branded products (e.g., Apple iPhone or iPad) are often in competition with cheaper substitutes, complementary products, or locally produced products. In response, many firms differentiate their products based on voluntary certifications and labeling. Assurances that food products are free from genetically modified organisms (GMO-free), or rugs are manufactured without child labor, or diamonds are conflict-free proliferate as third-party certifiers audit the conditions under which these goods are produced, processed, and transported.

As manufacturers are separated or prohibited from contacting end users by fragmented distribution networks or regulatory statutes, it is difficult to trace products to their end users. Yet many firms, especially those with branded consumer products, are beginning to voluntarily trace their product to the ultimate end customers in anticipation of regulatory mandates or consumers' demands. Tracing the forward linkages of products through franchisees and numerous intermediaries with limited direct control is highly problematic—but is being demanded by consumers, governments, multilaterals, and rivals as a new norm or as a point of differentiation.

Thought experiment: does your organization know the number of employees involved in getting your product/service to the final consumer? That is, everyone involved in packing, shipping, and transporting, and placing your product on store shelves, for example? If you are a hospital or a university, how many people are employed (contracted) within the stakeholder network to serve a patient or educate a student?

And the next step: do you know the number of veterans, employees from the local area, minorities, protected classes, child laborers, small business owners in your supply and distribution network? And if so, is preferential treatment given to you by governmental contracts due to the composition of your workforce (e.g., veterans, local content, minorities, etc.)?

Vertically integrated sectors (e.g., petrochemical, energy) and logistics firms (e.g., DHL, FedEx, and United Parcel Service) are often predisposed to understanding multiplier effects up and down their value chain. As they often compete through cost leadership strategies, it is in their best interests to efficiently link suppliers with consumers. These vertically integrated firms are able to reduce costs (e.g., a focus on logistics while increasing yield and decreasing overhead costs) to be competitive. Through their scale and scope, investments to efficiently use raw materials (e.g., energy, carbon, and water) can pay off over time.

Multiplier effects: combining social, environmental, and economic impacts

While financial and product-based impacts of forward and backward linkages along the value chain are important, the multitudes of social and environmental impacts are often overlooked at a firm's peril. As firms expand their operations into different markets, navigating local norms, beliefs, and socio-cultural traditions is often non-trivial. When making foreign direct investments or selling products to global consumers, the range of social and environmental expectations often intensifies as the variety of countries and stakeholders it affects and is affected by expands and often coalesces on the larger, deeper pockets of the firm.

Social impacts along the value chain

Social impacts are often expressed as local, community-based issues or as widespread socio-cultural issues. Transportation across indigenous lands with its inherent religious implications, for example, must often be considered alongside traditional financial impacts of employment suitability, training, and wages. Community-based issues surrounding employment practices often include human trafficking, firing,

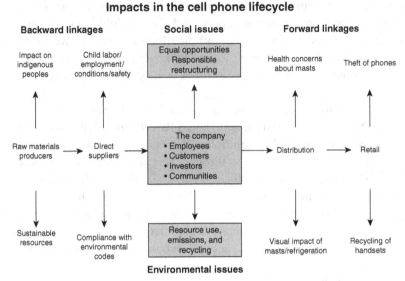

Impacts in the cell phone lifecycle

Backward linkages		Social issues	Forward linkages	
Impact on indigenous peoples	Child labor/ employment/ conditions/safety	Equal opportunities Responsible restructuring	Health concerns about masts	Theft of phones
Raw materials producers →	Direct suppliers →	The company • Employees • Customers • Investors • Communities →	Distribution →	Retail
Sustainable resources	Compliance with environmental codes	Resource use, emissions, and recycling	Visual impact of masts/refrigeration	Recycling of handsets

Environmental issues

Figure 6.2 Social, environmental, and economic impacts in cell phones

training, diversity, retention, loyalty, child labor, and/or assurance of human rights.

Cultural sensitivity might include explicit details of local employment and expected tax payments, or might be focused more broadly to address widespread social issues such as regional unemployment, education, healthcare, or transportation. Pressing social issues might be outside of the firm's direct impact, including promoting peace and prosperity, alleviating homeless, or addressing education and healthcare needs, as these requests may or may not be tied to the firm's resources, relationships, or capabilities (Delmas et al., 2011; Russo, 2009).

These impacts are often identified with negative connotations as an *issue* rather than as an *opportunity* to make a positive impact. Firms, rightly or wrongly, are also often asked to address complex social issues or to articulate their contributions to being a net positive contributor to the broader society. Given that these issues often outdate the firm's presence in the community, the expectation a firm can fix or combat the issue is not always realistic.

Examining the impacts along the extended value chain (see Figure 6.2), extends the footprint of the firm to a wide variety of stakeholders, each with its own expectations about co-creating value up and down the value chain. At a minimum, understanding the multiplier effects along the value chain requires counting the number of jobs created, tax payments, and wages paid to employees. Yet, these relatively simple measurements are just the beginning of the potential impacts of a firm.

The breadth and depth of sentiments about social issues often makes social impacts trickier to trace than product or financial impacts for two reasons. First, stakeholders that bear the (direct) negative impact of the firm's activity might be different than the (indirect) stakeholders that actively speak out about the social issue (Wood, 1991). For example, workplace safety conditions in Papua New Guinea might directly affect subcontractors of a petrochemical firm, yet it might be NGO bloggers in Sydney, Australia that are alerting other activist groups and investors about the impacts of the drilling activities. Both direct and indirect stakeholders are important when addressing social impacts along the value chain.

Second, the definition of social impact varies broadly among stakeholders, which in turn broadens the idea of what constitutes co-creating value, which in turn creates a plethora of requests of the firm to address impacts. That is, focusing on one issue, such as safety in the workplace, can quickly become entangled in additional workplace issues. Separating out safety in the workplace from child labor, human trafficking, wages, hours, or benefits can quickly escalate the types of issues and the responses required. The issue of poor workplace conditions, in this case, creates a network of stakeholders associated with workplace conditions. These stakeholder networks, in turn, create multiple ways in which the issue can be addressed (e.g., courts of law, blogs and public opinion, contracts with multilateral organizations, stock price adjustments).

At the heart of social impacts are impacts on people. In the case of corporate (social) impacts, it is the impacts of and on people in the value-creation process. Social impacts include impacts on employees, suppliers, or suppliers of suppliers as well as the families and neighbors of consumers. Positive impacts such as job creation, wealth creation, education, training, and development exist alongside negative impacts such as human trafficking, illegal or harmful effects of raw materials, or misleading labeling. How many people are employed when a hospital is constructed? Alternatively, how many individuals are unemployed (employed) when a car dealership is closed (opened)?

Or, how much child labor is employed to produce this T-shirt, cup of coffee, or pair of shoes (Rivoli, 2005)? Ongoing employee concerns such as training and development and alleviating human trafficking extend the firm's impacts over time as it continuously co-creates value.

While multipliers often focus on negative externalities and are frequently considered as part of the business or political risks of international development, firms also have numerous positive impacts along their value chains. Positive impacts, which are often overlooked, might include: minority-owned businesses, veteran-owned operations, and the depth and breadth of small and medium-sized enterprises as suppliers, and using the services of local content handlers or local content providers (United States, 2005).

Multiplier impacts can also be grouped into broad cause-related impacts. Broad social issues such as worker exploitation via child labor or encouraging working that precludes attending school require careful monitoring. Other activities that may need close monitoring including offshoring or outsourcing in industries where the low cost of labor is important, such as textiles and apparel (Blinder, 2006), and wage arbitrage by moving locale or avoiding taxes by incorporating businesses in Bermuda, for example. Narrowly targeted and broad social impacts are highlighted in the following text.

Narrowly targeted social impacts predominantly focus on mutual benefits with stakeholders closely tied to the firm's sponsorship, operations, or service activities (e.g., consumers, communities around mine sites and large factories, clients, potential consumers, employees, suppliers) and often have return on investment (ROI) justifications. The benefactors of these activities might receive resources, products, or services from the firm. For example, expanding everyday services to vulnerable or underrepresented populations is a targeted social impact such a bank offering discounts on financial products, consulting, and investment advising to non-profit organizations or local communities to improve their financial literacy (Griffin, 2008).

Broadly targeted social impacts, on the other hand, may benefit the firm's industry, businesses in general, not-for-profits, or capacity for addressing broad social causes such as community health and wellness, poverty, or homelessness. For example, supporting breast cancer research or breast cancer survivors via the National Breast Cancer Foundation (NBCF) may not be tied to specific consumers, yet supporting continued research is a common goal.

Similarly, many firms focus on an issue with cause-related marketing or product promotions that donate a certain percentage of profits to a specific issue. Often these companies making generous donations are not able to measure their direct impact. Think about efforts to address breast cancer by increasing research, expanding awareness Breast Cancer Awareness Month, and selling products with pink ribbons. Australian-based biscuit-maker Arnott's produces pink packaging for its Tim Tams; the US-based National Football League honors mothers, sisters, spouses, and female fans by encouraging players to wear pink and by selling special line of jerseys; Coca-Cola Amatil, a bottler in the Asia-Pacific region, has limited-edition pink-topped bottles; Unilever's Pink Dove campaign celebrates women surviving cancer; and GlaxoSmithKline donates directly to cancer research as a proportion of product purchases (Griffin, 2008). Each of these honorable, noble, and widespread efforts heightens sensitivity towards breast cancer.

Impacts of corporate breast cancer awareness campaigns might be more effectively tracked by measuring the number of mammograms directly related to these campaigns, the clinical trials conducted, or the scholarships provided to medical practitioners addressing oncology-related issues. This information would be helpful to close the loop and understand the impact of numerous efforts to address breast cancer. Yet none of these measures exactly explain what a specific corporation gains from these campaigns—making support for these initiatives more difficult (as it is a broad-based issue) that often requires partnering among private, public, and/or civil society organizations.

As worldwide efforts from multiple organizations increases awareness of breast cancer, treatment and prevention of breast cancer remains, however, often lagging. Thus, solutions for breast cancer remain elusive. Further, an individual firm's direct contribution or its ability to calculate a return on its own investment to create awareness, prevent or treat breast cancer, in a traditional accounting sense remains elusive. Without a definitive return nor a positive cost/benefit analysis, a traditional firm making investment decisions solely on short-term shareholder benefits would stop future contributions to breast cancer. Yet, intangible benefits and multiplier effects stemming from supporting breast cancer might be underemphasized or improperly monetized, if included at all. That is, the audience reached by supporting breast cancer might be wider than the firm's traditional consumers and clients, casting a positive halo effect on the firm, which in turn might help during economic downturns or periods of heightened scrutiny (*The Economist*, 2015).

Complicating a firm's desire to positively contribute to social issues such as breast cancer is the broad set of stakeholder involved in social issues. Extracting an individual firm's contribution and its specific benefit(s) is difficult at best, given the broad stakeholder network involved in certain social issues. Without direct attribution and specific, tangible benefits to their shareholders many firms decline to invest. Instead, issue networks emerge. Issue networks are composed of loosely coupled organizations engaged in a specific issue area that share information, convene conferences, act as panelists, and are recognized experts or thought leaders. Issue networks might crisscross firms, geographies, and political boundaries for any given issue such as environmental releases for petrochemical companies or cyber-espionage for information technology firms. These networks might be local or global in scope with the same actors (e.g., BP, Chevron, Greenpeace, Earth First, WHO) negotiating in different communities about different projects (e.g., Alaska pipeline, North Shore project off the coast of Australia), yet are concerned with similar issues (Lucea and Doh, 2012), making for complex relationships with intertwined interests that span the planet.

Other issue networks might focus on human trafficking or child labor in specific countries. When a crisis hits, social issues can rapidly become publicized around the world, such as a fire in a Bangladeshi garment factory that killed more than 1,000 workers. While a firm may be compliant with their home- or host-country regulations, it may be insufficiently prepared to respond to worldwide scrutiny, especially from developed countries. While local regulations and enforcement may vary, a 24/7 news cycle and increasingly powerful social media channels continuously inform the public on newsworthy activities that affect perceptions of the firm's success in meeting expectations.

To address global issues, standards of acceptable business practices are being created in discussion forums led by multi-stakeholder networks such as the Global Reporting Initiative (GRI) and others.[2] While organizations are increasingly expected to anticipate or rapidly

[2] Global standards are explored in Chapter 11.

respond to all stakeholders when these socio-cultural or environmental issues become newsworthy, a coordinated corporate response requires effort from many stakeholder networks around the world to address the issue along the entire value chain. Anticipating critical 'hot-button' social issues that might erupt at any point in time along the value chain might buy precious time before unwanted disclosures in the news media from watchdog organizations. In a sense, this is only avoiding a 'parade of horribles' (see Chapter 2).

Increasingly industry, trade, and professional associations are taking an active role in certifying or acting as independent standards boards for specific social and environmental impacts along the value chain. Creating a level playing field, outlining minimal thresholds of acceptable behavior, providing necessary sanctions for rogue behavior, and publishing membership lists is in the collective interests of many member-driven industry associations as it provides peer pressure. Labeling guidelines or certifications, common tools for trade associations to ensure consistency among members, serve to certify practices from independent overseers. Fair Trade labels, for example, certify the conditions of operations, farm size, and other conditions of the coffee, tea, and cocoa produced.

Environmental multipliers along the value chain

Environmental multiplier effects are consistent with a cradle-to-grave mindset that requires manufacturers to trace their production process from original equipment manufacturers (OEMs) through manufacturing and distribution to product use and disposal. This value chain perspective explores direct opportunities to reduce, reuse, and recycle materials without wasting energy, water, and effort. Indirect effects, such as the latent effects of construction, operating buildings, and products as they are being used (products-in-use) on biodiversity, ecosystems, access to water, effluents, waste, and climate change impacts are secondary and tertiary effects multiplying the footprint of the firm with the ability to co-create or destroy value.

Environmental multipliers consider how the product is sourced, made, and distributed and who benefits from its production, as well as its externalities. Externalities include the carbon, water, and energy required in each step of production and distribution; the wastes emitted to the air or sent to the landfill; greenhouse gas emissions; toxicity of materials used; the waste generated from packaging and transportation of the product; as well as recovery and reuse options once the product has met the end of its useful (first) life.

Environmental impacts are often easier to quantify as they include counting carbon, water, and energy usage to increase efficiencies with measureable impacts on the bottom line. Questions being asked include: how much carbon is in a glass of orange juice? How much water does it take to produce a unit of beer? How much energy is required to produce a pint of maple syrup? Environmental impacts across the extended enterprise encourage a cradle-to-grave-to-cradle mindset. That is, environmental externalities stemming from original equipment manufacturers, through suppliers of suppliers, including the production, distribution, consumption, and disposal of the product.

By working throughout the entire value chain, efforts to eliminate waste, water, or energy usage becomes a win–win–win rather than an issue transferred to another business unit, supplier, or product. Carbon trading, for example, can be deceiving. Reducing a manufacturer's carbon footprint by buying credits elsewhere might create efficiencies and awareness for the manufacturer but does not necessarily decrease the carbon footprint of the planet. By putting a price on carbon, something that is often considered free, carbon markets increase the awareness of carbon's significance and carbon becomes another resource to be managed alongside human, technical, financial, and other resources. In Europe, the EU emission trading system (EU ETS) drove energy costs down and forced innovation while preparing companies for a future that may or may not include a cap on carbon.

Similarly, if a trading system were created for water or water-based products such as beverages, trading credits might be a future option as severe drought in the southern hemisphere are being exacerbated by the lack of annual rainfall and unusually high temperatures. Water is often considered a free resource, yet access to potable water is still limited to many people in the world (World Bank, 2001).

Firms can choose to manage its social and environmental impacts by using a 'go-it-alone'[3] strategy, such as creating its own internal market for water or carbon. Large conglomerates such as the Tata Group or the Indian construction firm Larsen & Toubro might create an internal market and demonstrates to employees, stakeholders, and rivals the

[3] Go-it-alone and partnering strategies are discussed in Chapter 10.

importance the firm places on conserving water. Pricing water would allow firms to treat water as a valued asset, even with local abundance. By experimenting within the firm, and across the value chain with suppliers, new ways to recycle, reuse, or reduce water consumption are likely to emerge.

Multiplier effects across geographies

The dual tensions of global expansion—the desire for consistency across communities in order to increase efficiency and the need for flexibility to respond to local tastes and traditions—unleash opportunities for innovation. Companies able to respond locally while also providing consistency at a global level are best positioned to learn from each community while retaining a global identify.

As firms expand their operations or sales across neighborhoods, there are more and varied communities that affect and are affected by a firm. A German grocery chain with an international footprint, for example, works hard to be considered as a neighborhood grocery store despite operating in many different communities. By sharing back-office information on logistics, distribution, and prices, it can build an efficient, low-cost supply chain while allowing flexibility to choose the specific products that locals prefer.

Product disclosure can be complicated by the need for using multiple languages, requiring a firm to adapt product-use information to specific communities. In addition, regulations about package size, delivery, or other details might further complicate product disclosure. Labeling pharmaceutical products, for example, might require different languages, dosages, and reimbursements that comply with local and national laws.

An extended enterprise perspective across local, state, national/federal, or regional communities increases, the number, concentration, and variety of impacts of a firm. Geographic expansion requires firms to think about local content and/or customize products and processes in ways that are culturally appropriate.

Multiplier effects stemming from geographic expansion are discussed in Chapter 11, when we juxtapose the need for consistency and the need for local responsiveness. Firms are facing a 3D chess game at the local, country, and global levels: creating consistency in principles while allowing for flexibility in local responsiveness and yet enabling timely sharing of information on critical impacts across the value-creation process. Including financial impacts alongside employee, product, and information impacts builds credibility yet challenges managers to continuously think about how value is co-created.

Consistency is one of the goals of global standards. Global standards that are truly applicable worldwide have an additional hurdle of creating legitimate specifications that are relevant and enforceable across different countries (Gilbert and Rasche, 2008). Foreign subsidiary managers can be frustrated with requests from headquarters to implement 'yet another new program' (Kostova, 1999). Having different socio-political concerns and goals than headquarters (Ghoshal and Bartlett, 1990), subsidiaries may ceremonially adopt global social initiatives (Kostova and Roth, 2002). Ceremonial adoption is 'formal adoption of a practice on the part of a recipient unit's employees for legitimacy reasons without their believing in its real value for the organization' (Kostova and Roth, 2002, p. 220). Ceremonial adoption is likely when a subsidiary's managers and employees feel that the mandated practice is not valuable and face strong pressure from the multinational company (MNC) to adopt the practice.

Addressing the twin tension of global integration and local responsiveness requires coordination with clear lines of authority and accountability. Accountability is important when addressing who bears the brunt of unexpected, negative impacts. Significant impacts with risks that are high (or low), and the degree to which the effect is felt globally (or locally) creates different forms of coordination between headquarters and local communities. In Figure 6.3 we examine the different types of geographical multiplier effects based on risks and impacts.

Global coordination

When expected impacts are of significance to the overall corporation with implications for the firm globally, then global coordination to address the global multiplier effects is warranted. With headquarters staff leading the efforts to ensure consistency, a centralized team can selectively draw upon insights from local jurisdictions and rapidly coordinate a response. This team of senior decision-makers with access to the CEO, authority to spend resources, and a focused mission is likely to be drawn from multiple functions to address governmental, political, legal, ethical, financial, and social impacts, as well as the

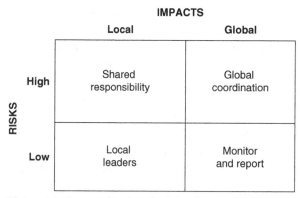

Figure 6.3 Geographical multiplier effects

needs of diverse stakeholder groups (e.g., governments, financial analysts, customers, neighborhoods).

One example of a coordinated global effort to address global multiplier effects was the Ford Explorer crisis in the early part of the century sparked by the explosion of underinflated Firestone tires on hot pavements that led to numerous deaths. Ford voluntarily recalled the vehicles, issued replacements, and coordinated its message with daily meetings with the CEO (Moll, 2003). Creating consistent messages and coordinating quick action across a network of stakeholders is often achieved by headquarters dictating the terms of information with selective local engagement. A downside of this centralized coordination is a singular focus on this issue and it may blindside the firm to other pressing issues in outlying jurisdictions.

One of the core objectives of global multiplier effects is risk mitigation, with a laser-like focus on the top priority of preventing additional negative risks from overwhelming the company due to international visibility. Companies headquartered in the European Union, for example, may want to focus on mitigating climate change, yet their subsidiaries in South America might see education, transportation, or healthcare as the most pressing issues in their region.

Shared responsibility

If expected impacts of multiplier effects are of high risk to the firm, with significant implications at the local level, active cooperation between headquarters and the local subsidiary is warranted. For example the BP case in Chapter 1 had significant risks to the entire corporation while also immediately harming the local communities. While head-quarters can provide additional resources and support, and liaise with groups that are affected at the corporate level to keep them informed of developments, the local employees can take the lead in responding in appropriate ways that are attuned to local needs.

Reciprocal coordination with active listening between headquarters, country managers, and community leaders allows for locally sensitive, nuanced community responses while keeping headquarters appraised of high-risk impacts that might escalate. A downside risk of a local leader is often the lack of resources to address a complex issue and/or the inability to anticipate issues that might escalate. For example, the 2014 EU court finding that EU citizens have expansive privacy rights requires Google and other technology companies to delete hyper-links with embarrassing information. Privacy issues are significant to Google, with multiplier effects on the entire high-tech industry, yet the jurisdiction of the EU courts and its ruling on protecting the pri-vacy of EU citizens is restricted to a specific geography (Timberg and Birnbaum, 2014).

Local leaders

If expected impacts are of low risk to the entire corporation, yet have significant local implications, then local country managers are likely to champion the activities. This is the traditional view of corporate responsibility in multinational companies: the country manager hav-ing the autonomy to make investments into local communities.

Creating autonomy for local country managers by giving them free-dom to identify pressing issues within the local community, region, or nation before the issues become crises is a win–win–win for all. Decentralizing leadership with local country managers rather than expatriates that are only temporarily in the local country, keeps the company attuned to the local aspirations of important stakeholders. For example, Infosys might transfer employee engagement initiatives from its headquarters in India to locations in China or England, yet the details of implementing the employee engagement programs are cus-tomized by local Chinese and UK employees of Infosys (Barnett and Sunyoung, 2012). Local adaptation of corporate goals creates a broad umbrella of engagement initiates ranging from securing employment to increasing management skills or healthcare provision for employees' families. With coordinated customization at the local level, the focus shifts from what social impacts are undertaken to a common objective and why the activities are undertaken.

Monitoring and reporting

If the current risks to the firm are low yet with global implications if an issue occurs, then monitoring progress, assessing new events against priorities, and reporting out to all stakeholders are important considerations. For example, subsidiaries in countries known for corruption or human trafficking might require additional monitoring and reporting specifically on these topics. If the corporation has made a public statement that does not allow corruption, for example, then regular appraisals with announced and unannounced visits dedicated to seeking out the potential for fraud is important. As are local communities and staff in case an issue escalates across regions or around the world.

The downside of monitoring and reporting is the imperfect transfer of practices. For example, transferring practices from the formal economy to the informal economy by encouraging financial literacy among the unbanked or under-banked might be inconsistent with the local norms and smack of imperialism. Persistence and training might yield long-term results that build the capacity of the country and develop financial literacy across many communities. Partnering with local universities to identify future leaders and to disseminate best practices about financial literacy or digital literacy, for example, creates a threshold of awareness that can create opportunities where none existed before.

Overall, when addressing multiplier effects in a global economy, a firm might want to coordinate from headquarters, yet it must address significant local, social, and environmental issues. So while the desire for consistency in products and processes might encourage the firm's managers to focus on rules-based consistency, as Figure 6.3 suggests some issues are better handled with a principles-based consistency. That is, addressing issues consistent with principles set out by headquarters yet deployed in a way appropriate to the local communities. Diversity, for example, is likely to mean something different to a firm operating in the Middle East than a firm operating in Australia.

Similarly, climate change may not be the pressing issue for communities in India, where job creation or access to clean water to prevent diseases may be of top concern.

Implications for co-creating value

Overall, this chapter examined multiplier effects that can blindside businesses and exacerbate losses or be leveraged to the firm's advantage creating a sweet spot. By addressing the direct effects of a business (Chapters 2, 3, and 4), as well as the indirect and spillover effects within the business (Chapters 5 and 6), this chapter examines the impacts of a firm extending through its network of stakeholders. Assessing the expanded value chain is important as value can be created or lost with attribution pinned to one, or a few, firms in the network.

This chapter examined indirect effects of creating value wherein a firm can be complicit in financial, social, and environmental issues across the globe, begging the broader question: is business a part of the problem or is it a part of the solution, since it has direct effects and indirect influence on many stakeholders? In this section, we identify four underlying assumptions when addressing multiplier effects in the value-creation process.

First, an underlying assumption of current global strategies is positioning products in new markets. Yet a firm's socio-environmental-political risks are underdeveloped. The result is often that getting products out to consumers is the top priority, while addressing compliance issues, for example, becomes secondary. In some cases, market mechanisms help drive efficiencies passed along to consumers. In other cases, like socially sensitive issues such as human trafficking or employing child labor for cost savings, market mechanisms create a perverse outcome. The intended outcome of children working rather than going to school creates significant risks.

A second assumption about multiplier effects is that practices transfer seamlessly round the world. That is, large MNCs with deep pockets and exposure to international trends of local sourcing, for example, can share these experiences and best practices with smaller companies in their supply chain who can, in turn, share them with even smaller supplier companies. As such, corporate impacts are sometimes assumed to be the primary responsibility of a foreign multinational to give back to the local communities in exchange for being allowed to operate in the neighborhood. The narrative goes something like this: large companies can (financially) afford to experiment, benchmark best practices, and then teach smaller companies (such as suppliers) what to do and how best to do it. Assumptions about size and scalability are explored in more detail in Chapter 7 as part of the myth that 'size matters' and in Chapter 11 when discussing the implications of impact-thinking for multinational corporations.

A third assumption about multiplier effects is the type of information needed. In the process of co-creating value, the firm requires information about direct, indirect, social, environmental, and economic pressures along the entire value chain. Specific types of information such as the amount of money paid in taxes to each country, the amount of money reinvested in each country, and the amount of full-time equivalent employees along the entire value chain might not be regularly collected, yet can become important when contribution questions are asked.

At the same time, social media tools force firms to consider information from a wider (and sometimes less reliable) variety of sources. Information comes not only from government agencies, multilaterals, and other firms but also from the public at large, which means firms must have the capabilities to communicate with and send information to this larger group of sources as well.

And the fourth underlying assumption is that learning will occur. Yet learning is optional! Large, branded firms operating global supply chains without clarity on how they create (destroy) value throughout stakeholder networks will increasingly be playing catch-up as they follow the leaders who lower costs and improve efficiencies. Focusing solely on efficiencies is a trap. Efficiencies *and* effectiveness are needed for addressing multiplier effects. Being able to demonstrate the value add—to create a narrative around value being created and not just redistributed in the network—is important to survive. Effectiveness extends beyond physical, easier-to-count, measurable, tangible items such as water usage and carbon consumption to intangible items such as human dignity, trust, goodwill, and legitimacy, global MNCs will be caught flat-footed.

Looking ahead

In Chapters 1–6 we identified four impacts of firms (financial, employees in the workplace, products, and through information-sharing).

While these impacts are often felt within the boundaries of a firm, we explored how these impacts interact, morph, and radiate out from the firm, crisscrossing financial, employee and workplace, product and information networks involving many stakeholders that are indirectly or complicit in the value creation/destruction process.

The next chapter, Chapter 7, examines different myths about corporate impacts, while providing a modern context that updates, eliminates, or transforms the myths into new, realistic considerations for modern managers.

Focusing on co-creating value by examining numerous stakeholder networks simultaneously is important for organizations. We suggest that examining (and unlocking the value inherent within) combinations of interactions are important for modern organizations. Rather than dealing with interactions on an ad hoc basis or via exception, this book suggests a purposeful examination of the myriad interactions that can unlock additional mutual benefits and create value.

7 | *Debunking persistent myths about co-creating value*

Long debates over multiple decades have spilled much ink perpetuating different beliefs and attitudes about corporations' responsibilities. Implicitly or explicitly, such debates often consider the redistribution of residual value rather the creation or co-creation of value. Friedman's mantra (1970) that 'the social responsibility of a firm is to increase profits' suggests a firm taking on any project other than activities that directly contribute to the profitability of the business does so at the expense of shareholders' rightful profit.

But what if creating value generated benefits for multiple stakeholders, including investors, employees, and even suppliers or communities, simultaneously? Would the narrative about how value is created include the contributions of shareholders, solely, and thus be in Friedman's (1970) worldview seen as profit-seeking? Alternatively, would employees or consumers consistently be part of the story about how value is co-created, just like shareholders? And finally, must there eventually always be trade-offs between stakeholders' interests instead of innovations to address mutual interests?

The attention and attribution given to shareholders, employees, and customers, for example, in the value-creation process becomes a de facto narrative of the firm's beliefs. If, for instance, employees talk about value creation as a means to create profits for investors or if the talk is about creating satisfied customers, the focus of management changes. Both narratives might create profits and satisfy customers, but the means and the ends differ in each narrative.

When a firm defends, describes, or explains its decisions, it identifies key stakeholders. Listen for it! The firm's narrative rightly or wrongly points to where management focuses its attention and elaborates its strategy to employees, investors, consumers, regulators, and neighbors.

Attributing strategic decisions to financial motives may mask many different, sometimes conflicting, considerations. Yet simple mantras ('the business of business is just business' or 'we seek to maximize shareholder profits') are likely to focus employees' attention on a single outcome: financial impacts. When a firm's narrative emphasizes investors, returns on investment, and financial values, it might unnecessarily narrow management's focus and implicitly undermine the contributions of employees, customers, and other stakeholders in the value-creation process.

In this chapter, we challenge five longstanding beliefs about a corporation's ability to co-create value for different stakeholders. We examine these assumptions in light of current realities facing modern managers and suggest that it is in a firm's best interest to broaden management's attention beyond a singular outcome (financial impacts) and adjust their narrative because of the narrative's self-fulfilling prophecy on all stakeholders.

The first belief we challenge is addressing corporate impacts is akin to philanthropy. That is, once money has been made, a corporation can manage its (negative) impacts by giving money back to the communities from which it has taken resources. In this shakedown mindset, one of the critical questions we address is: why are impacts an afterthought akin to charity rather than purposely designed into how a company makes its money?

Second, we challenge the notion that size matters: addressing corporate impacts is a luxury only accomplished by those firms having already secured needed financial resources. In other words, only those that have money can give. Underlying this assumption is a mindset that the business of business is business, and that only once a business is successful can it think about creating positive non-financial impacts. We suggest that being a first-mover to embed an impact mindset into how the business makes money, by design, has advantages.

Third, corporate impacts are often considered 'not my job.' When corporate impacts are defined as risk mitigation, compliance with extant law, or defending corporate actions where the law is silent, then setting limits of appropriate behavior is often considered to be the role of government. A privately held firm undertaking activities assumed to be the responsibility of government suggests mission-creep at best or imperialism at worst. Instead, it might be in the best interests of business, government, and citizens for businesses to pursue partnerships, or take unilateral action to create and maintain a railroad spur a government is unable to build in order to achieve mutually beneficial outcomes for multiple stakeholders.

A fourth assumption regarding corporate impacts is that impacts are a proxy for community relations. That is, the negative impacts of a business are most often felt by the local, geographically adjacent community that, in turn, warrants additional attention directed towards the concerns of that community. In short, it assumes that the impacts of the business are felt by the local community and, further, these impacts are net costs to the neighboring community and thus the business must give back and purposely build its local community relations.

Finally, we examine the assumption that corporate impacts are defined by extant law and thus mere compliance is in a firm's best interest even when the law is silent or poorly enforced. When defining impacts as equivalent to legal compliance, a business unnecessarily limits its attention to legally ordained activities. While compliance with extant laws might be necessary, it is often not sufficient for firms facing a crisis, under intense scrutiny, competing for top talent, or trying to enter new markets and build new partnerships. Beyond-compliance investments can lead to new innovations and new opportunities. We debunk these five persistent myths about co-creating value in the next section.

Corporate impacts are 'giveaways'

The assumption: co-creating value is tantamount to a philanthropic donation. Once money is made, then and only then can a firm entertain thoughts about its corporate impacts—and consider mitigating or rebalancing its negative impacts by making positive contributions through philanthropy. Philanthropy is often seen as a way of 'giving back,' as if something was taken during the process of co-creating value.

Corporate philanthropy has a long and healthy tradition and positively affects millions of people worldwide every day. Individual philanthropists have voluntarily contributed time, talent, and resources, and enabled others to give and receive (Buchholtz et al., 1999; Smith, 1994). Hospitals, universities, roads, and health clinics continue to be built in areas of desperate need because of generous donations. Education, wellness, housing, and hygiene have also improved in numerous households around the world thanks to individual and corporate philanthropy.

Philanthropic traditions in the West have historically been led by industrialists such as the Carnegie, Rockefeller, and Ford families, and in this century by billionaires Bill and Melinda Gates and Warren Buffett. Sir Cadbury and the Lever brothers built a legacy of giving philanthropically, creating Cadbury and Unilever, respectfully, upon an ethos of giving and giving back. (Smith et al., 1990; Bradley, 2008).

The well-developed ethos of individual corporate leaders giving back through philanthropic donations has been an important part of business leadership in the UK, Europe, and throughout the Middle East and Asia (Allen, 2007; Campbell et al., 2002; Brammer and Millington, 2003). In Turkey, for example, the Koç family has one of the largest foundations in the country. The Tata Foundations, established more than a century ago in India, have benefited many communities and families, as has the Tata Group (Lala, 1984, 2007).

Philanthropic giving by large and small companies through corporate and private foundations is significant and outpaces giving by private individuals (Brammer and Millington, 2004; Chang et al., 1996; Renz, 2001, 2002; Murphy, 2001). About $335 billion, an amount larger than Denmark's GDP, was donated by individuals, corporations, and foundations in the United States in 2013 (Daniels, 2014), which would be the 35th largest economy in the world (CIA, 2013).

Corporate philanthropy, managed through private foundations or the corporate treasury, often involves cash contributions, donations, sponsorships, bequests, or gifts. Interest-bearing donations allow for the principle to be reinvested, creating a stream of funding for future years. Some companies have longstanding policies on annual philanthropic giving while other companies also create private foundations to separate corporate ownership from philanthropic decisions. While often aligned, the corporation and the private foundation have separate legal decision-making authority to avoid conflicts of interest.

Philanthropy is certainly one way organizations often begin thinking about the externalities of the value-creation process (Brammer and Millington, 2003). Focusing solely on philanthropic giveaways, however, assumes that redistribution of wealth is the most efficient way for a corporation to manage its impacts. Philanthropic giving assumes: (a) gifts, either one-time or periodic, can provide tangible (and easily quantifiable) evidence of responsibly managing impacts; (b) profits must be made before non-financial impacts can be considered; and (c) excess profits should be the primary, and perhaps the only, source of funding for positive non-financial impacts.

With vigilance and transparency, companies can align outreach efforts with employee attraction and motivation goals or enhance their reputation in the eyes of customers (Turban and Greening, 1997; den Hond et al., 2014; Vock et al., 2014; McKinsey, 2014). Genuine displays of outreach, as opposed to a thin veneer of engaging employees for the sake of appearances, requires analyzing and addressing employees' needs and the community's desires. Asking employees where they would like to volunteer or involving employees in selecting the firm's community outreach efforts are often first steps in motivating employees to be genuinely engaged. Studies show that a more engaged employee is a more productive and satisfied employee (Greening and Turban, 2000; Vock et al., 2014).

Aligning community outreach with business objectives has many, perhaps unforeseen, benefits. While community outreach can motivate employees or enhance pride in the workforce, it can also directly help vulnerable populations. For example, assisting vulnerable populations by using the skills and expertise of newly hired engineers and project managers to build playgrounds or improve community centers is a win–win–win for team building, supporting the community, and attracting prospective employees. Similarly, staffing training centers and providing computer literacy or financial literacy classes with volunteers from the workforce can have multiple benefits. On the other hand, donating products is often invisible to employees and if they are perishable products then the impacts of donations may not be sustained for the community.

The unforeseen benefit is enhancing pride in the workforce, being an employer of choice, building capacity in small community clusters to create self-sufficiency, or developing a positive reputation so that the company is welcomed in other communities. Some multinational companies are increasingly insisting that their brand names not be prominently displayed so as to focus on the recipients rather than the company's largess and to avoid criticism that the company is only undertaking activities for its own gain.

When aligning community outreach with employee interests, there are potential pitfalls if employees with higher earnings disproportionately chose the charities. Organizations must ask whether organizations in certain neighborhoods receive more funding because of the homogenous profile of the firm's employees. For example, employees of a large, international investment fund based in Washington, DC might employ parents of children enrolled in a local private school in Georgetown. When employee donations and the matching employer donations are tallied, the primary recipient of funds is an exclusive primary school.

To avoid additional pitfalls, three additional questions help align community investment intentions with actions: how much is given, to whom the money is given, and why the company is giving to this particular organization. If funds are designed to support education for disadvantaged or vulnerable populations, are the funds being sent primarily to exclusive private schools?

Thinking about philanthropy from an impact perspective incorporates a narrative about why this activity and this organization are being funded. Is the funding designed to create self-sufficiency, to motivate employees, to give back, or as an example of giving because the company believes in giving? Depending on the reason, the metrics used to assess impact might start with the amount of funding or the number of employee matching donations. Yet new metrics are needed to assess the firm's overall impact year after year. More specifically, to whom, and to what degree is support warranted? That is, is the impact sustained year after year? Another way to think about the impact of philanthropic dollars is matching short-term donations (in-kind product donations) with short-term issues such as providing food for families this weekend or for a special holiday, and matching long-term donations (e.g., sustained donations of time and talent) for longer-term social issues such as alleviating hunger over a period of time in a local neighborhood is one example.

Being able to describe how multiple recipients are affected by the giving (e.g., neighbors, investors, employees and their extended families, partners, etc.) means that the firm succeeded in going beyond contributions that merely build its brand to make a meaningful difference. For example, when a healthcare company helps build a hospital, there is certainly an opportunity to promote the company's products, logo, and contribution, but the company must also track how it has enabled access to healthcare for more members of the community or how disease prevention has improved as a result. Similarly, when a school is built or computers are donated, the company should follow-up to determine the actual effects of its contribution on education and whether the project caused literacy rates to improve the digital divide to close.

A giveaway mindset also lacks a 'how a firm makes its money' perspective (Andriof and McIntosh, 2001; Allen, 2007; Griffin, 2008). That is, addressing corporate impacts by writing checks of 2 percent of corporate profits, for instance, is vastly different from a mindset focused on how the other 98 percent of the value the firm creates (Brammer and Pavelin, 2005). How a firm makes its money emphasizes how a firm co-creates value with its stakeholders to generate profits *and value* in the first place (Porter and Kramer, 2006; Freeman et al., 2007; Crane et al., 2014a, 2014b).

A solely philanthropic strategy for value creation fails to consider the corporation's non-financial contributions, such as employees' time, talent, and expertise; in-kind product donations; and sourcing and distribution networks. Many corporations make significant contributions (time, talent, clothes, IT services, rebuilding products) to struggling communities after a natural disaster, with employees taking pride in making a difference in the lives of others (Brammer and Millington, 2003).

A philanthropic giveaway mindset is too often a short-term strategy that suffers from dependency on the profitability of the firm. When profits are strong, philanthropic outreach is strong. When profits are weak, philanthropic outreach is often scaled back significantly. Yet, in times of economic downturn a community might be in dire need of support. From a community perspective, this fluctuating ebb and flow of resources can be problematic for planning purposes and ensuring continuity of services for vulnerable populations.

Fluctuations in philanthropic giving can be further exacerbated by reliance upon specific individuals in leadership positions. Once those individuals move on or are promoted out of the area, the philanthropic activities of the firm in a specific community may be curtailed or eliminated altogether. Furthermore, when the firm breeds community dependency through its financial contributions in lieu of developing capacity within the community project to eventually be self-sustaining, it becomes difficult for the firm to say 'no' when its funds might be better used elsewhere.

Relying on other non-financial resources, such as employee volunteer time, can help smooth the peaks and valleys that may exist with philanthropic giving. By expanding the firm's impact beyond monetary outlays to include employee involvement, product-based initiatives, or information-sharing, the relationships with stakeholders can deepen and expand, giving way to new means through which value can be co-created. For example, a firm that supports new ventures and provides limited start-up capital or know-how can help its employees create new companies or help other companies create a robust community.

Co-creating value via philanthropic giveaways is just one of multiple means to engage stakeholders. Let's examine another assumption about co-creating value: size matters.

Corporate impacts are only felt from large firms

The assumption: only large firms, and especially multinational firms, have the luxury of thinking about their impacts and creating value for stakeholders besides investors. In this line of thought, the struggle of small firms for resources justifies a narrow, short-term focus on survival. In addition, the impacts of small firms are smaller and less visible, affecting fewer constituencies (Miles, 1987), so a focus on their minimal impacts isn't warranted. In other words, size—measured as the number of employees, visibility, financial resources, or variety of technological and human resources—matters when co-creating value.

Certainly smaller firms have potentially smaller economic, socio-cultural, and environmental footprints than large firms. Yet being underestimated or overlooked can be an important asset. And impact is not always equivalent to profitability or stock price. Amazon.com, for example, favored growth over profits and has remained a favorable investment among investors while upending many traditional business models, especially for booksellers (Maxfield, 2014).

Small firms have the advantage of being nimble, so they are able to focus and rapidly respond to emerging issues yet are often resource-constrained so they must focus on specific issues (Martin and Osberg, 2007; Khavul, 2010). Being focused and committed, entrepreneurial firms often have an advantage since the genesis for their creations is often centered on a founder who reframes issues as opportunities as opposed to constraints (Martin and Osberg, 2007; Khavul, 2010). An opportunity-seeking mindset motivates an entrepreneur to persevere in their dream to create a new business that serves existing needs in new ways or addresses unfulfilled wants. Being small and entrepreneurial can be an asset, since the impact of a firm, especially its information networks and its reputation, can reach well beyond the borders of the firm, making the traditional definitions of size less important.

While a small firm can't address in their entirety fundamental societal issues such as poverty, homelessness, disease, or climate change, firms of all sizes can leverage their core competencies to make a difference. The question becomes: will a firm purposely choose to make a net positive impact? If so, how will the firm impact others?

Those who subscribe to the 'size matters' school of thought often equate corporate impacts with profits. They believe commitment to generating profits must precede commitments to anything or anyone else. Any additional non-financial activity is therefore deemed a cost center (an expense) rather than an investment as the shareholders are the sole purpose for the business rather than considered residual owners after others are satisfied.

That is, addressing non-financial impacts is optional; to be pursued only after the small firm has grown larger and achieved its financial goals. Opportunities to make investments that *indirectly* benefit the bottom line are often foregone. Investments into a new market segment (online financial payments for non-profits, sports teams, or community organizations) might seem like a waste of time, money, and effort. However, firms of all sizes that take the time to learn about the interests of seemingly indirect stakeholders and communities could reap future rewards if they are first movers in an untapped, previously overlooked market segment.

Friedman (1970) argued that any activities voluntarily undertaken by managers beyond those required for the firm's survival would constitute a redistribution of the owners' wealth—obtaining by undemocratic means that which could not be obtained through democratic means. In this mindset, managing impacts requires additional slack resources entirely removed from how the business makes its money or how the firm co-creates value, which is often reinforced in small businesses with fewer slack resources.

Large multinationals, with significant and visible global impacts, as this line of thinking plays out, are the ones that need to think about corporate impacts. Small entrepreneurs deserve a 'pass' because they are just starting out; they have so many more important concerns. This argument is akin to Granovetter's (1973) concept of the liability of newness. A new, small firm has so many liabilities that adding one more consideration to their plate, such as thinking about impacts, would put excessive strain on limited resources.

Beliefs that reinforce the 'size matters' myth include:

1 Those that have can give; profit as primary objective.
2 The more you have, the more you are expected to give; bigger is better/beautiful.
3 More visible, more vulnerable, and thus more venues.
4 Vertically integrated firms have more control, more information, and thus should be held to a higher standard when assessing impacts.

Certainly large firms, particularly publicly traded multinationals, have an added incentive to be transparent, create GRI reports, voluntarily engage in beyond-compliance activities, and adapt their policies to various rating and ranking scorecards in an effort to enhance reputation. Building trust with governments and communities is in their own self-interest, especially when trying to enter new consumer markets. Being a known and trusted, if not well-understood, organization is an advantage when expanding across borders (Fort and Schipani, 2004). Allaying fears and getting a literal license to operate in the government approval processes is often accomplished, in part, by demonstrating reliability, and credibility through managing impacts (den Hond et al., 2014).

Yet, corporate impacts are not solely the province of large firms. Small and medium-sized businesses often fill market niches by designing products and strategies explicitly focusing on exploiting employee, product/consumer or information-sharing impacts. Natura, Aveda, Timberland, and Wahaha are small firms created with specific principles regarding the corporate impacts of their products, sourcing, workplace conditions, or consumer relations. These companies have enjoyed considerable financial success (Swartz, 2010). These entrepreneurs created new opportunities by dovetailing societal interests with consumer interests to build new business models. As small and nimble organizations, they created demand and developed new markets explicitly aligning their business practices and desired impacts. Their very existence depends on serving their clientele well while simultaneously thinking about impacts.

In part, what is missing in a 'size matters' mentality is redefining social issues from large, esoteric, important issues for someone else

(Weick, 1984) to focusing on the difference a firm can make about a particular aspect of an important issue, regardless of its size (Easterly, 2006). While a single firm acting alone may make only a slight dent in reversing the trends in climate change or poverty or homeless, for example, all firms can do something, if they choose to do so and see it in their best interest to act. Regarding climate change, firms can reduce their energy bills by shutting off lights when a room is not in use, using energy-efficient light bulbs, or examining their fleet of cars to minimize energy use. Firms can encourage less electricity usage per computer per employee, be mindful of products' carbon content, and try to understand the carbon emissions made by employees in the daily commute, which can simultaneously save money and/or improve morale.

Although small firms, as well as small countries, might be more hard-pressed for resources and may focus on fewer activities (Miles, 1987), they often distinguish themselves as experts on specific issues. The Netherlands, for example, is an expert in water recovery, land reclamation, and water purification. Denmark is known for its prowess in wind energy and has set a goal of using only energy from renewable sources by 2050.

The 'size matters' myth also highlights a design flaw when choosing from among alternative investments. Often projects are chosen based on their expected return on investment. Yet a 'size matters' mindset suggests projects should also be evaluated based upon their ability to be scaled up. But designing for scalability from the onset is difficult, with the undesired side-effect of potentially overlooking numerous viable projects.

In theory, scalability shouldn't matter, but in practical ways it changes the mindset of what's possible. The search for the Holy Grail, the big idea, the scalable project can be all-consuming for a large, multifaceted business without a clear mission and with multiple stakeholders. Tensions between experimenting with many different localized projects and a *big* scalable project are very real. Coordinating, interweaving insights, sharing learning, and communicating the pride and impact stemming from many localized projects versus a few large projects are explored more in Chapter 11.

A 'size matters' mentality often does not consider that large businesses face unique challenges. Large businesses often owe their very size and existence to the fact that they are particularly good at efficiently satisfying their consumers' needs. Their consumers are happy buying the company's products, creating increased demand that per-petuates further growth. This success can breed a laser-like focus on efficiencies, as well as reliance on the path that created past successes. Attaining future success, however, is not likely to be achieved by the replicating the past. Competition is increasing. Others are learning. And entering new markets opens up the potential for even more new competitors.

Large multinational firms are often unique in that their success has been achieved by successfully satisfying multiple stakeholders with var-ied interests (governments from different countries, neighborhoods to locate manufacturing plants or to build retail stores and warehouses). While governmental and community relations are often critical when expanding into new markets, small, community-minded companies have an advantage.

Small businesses have numerous advantages. Small companies often, by design, incorporate business and community goals (e.g., social entrepreneurs), or create uniqueness by using sustainable sourcing (e.g., Patagonia). These firms co-create value with multiple stakehold-ers from the beginning and create a mindset geared towards address-ing multiple corporate impacts. For these firms it is just how business is conducted rather than something that is bolted-on after the business is established when it desires additional growth.

Small firms are often not as vulnerable as some large, visible, global firms. Large, fast-moving consumer goods firms, for example, are rationalizing factories, cutting employees, standardizing products, and streamlining back office activities to cut costs and stay competi-tive while improving the quality, consistency, and on-time delivery of products. Entering new consumer markets, many activities may need to be customized, including permits, distribution outlets, government approvals, product sizes, language requirements, labeling, advertising, and marketing, which small companies may be willing to do. While downstream the company is rationalizing and cutting costs, upstream the company is spending more money customizing its approach to the individual consumer and government protocols as well as creating dif-ferent niches for its various brands/products. Thus, in large businesses upstream and downstream businesses need to be managed differently, with different expectations and different impacts.

Vertically integrated, natural resource-based companies, such as those in the agricultural, pulp and paper, petrochemical, or mining sectors, can also be particularly vulnerable without an impact perspective. Without the ability to choose where to locate, these firms must overcome climate conditions and tight labor markets that are often less than optimal. Often one of few businesses in the area, they have the added burden of building a community to support the business and thus may engage in long term projects such as education in schools or disease prevention through improved hospitals. A long-term view focused on investment opportunities, with some divisions operating as loss-leaders while encouraging other portions of the business to focus on capacity-building might appropriately spread the risks across the businesses.

In sum, it is not easy for large companies to address the risks from their corporate impacts. While having more resources, large businesses may also be more recalcitrant or slower to implement than their smaller peers when it comes to identifying, prioritizing, and addressing corporate impacts. At the same time, large businesses have more exposure to more risks. With blogs, tweets, and intranets creating even more venues for discussion, dissent, and mobilization about acceptable business behavior, large companies are more visible, making them vulnerable to the opinions of others.

Large companies with few clients, such as business to business (B2B) industrial conglomerates or corporations with government contracts, are especially vulnerable to complacency. Operating out of the public eye and 'protected' from consumers, activists, and the media, these firms have less incentive to change bad habits. Yet once government contracts or sourcing supplies are questioned, they face intense scrutiny that they may be unprepared to handle. Transparency and accountability demands have increased for all companies. All in all, large companies are more exposed to risks from impacts yet may not be best positioned to respond to the risks. Small, innovative companies that experiment with combining social goals with business goals may have better responses.

Consumer-facing companies can also face intense media scrutiny, lose consumer confidence and see profits plunge when a panic sets in. In Shanghai, China, for instance many foreign-domiciled fast-food restaurants, such as McDonald's and Yum! Brands, the parent company of Burger King and KFC, were forced by tainted meat scares in 2014 to publicly display the suppliers of their ingredients and re-examine contracts to ensure adequate levels of food safety (Waldmeir, 2014).

Since large businesses operate in more and more varied environments, they do have significant impacts that are often publicly disclosed. Being large certainly has advantages but being small has numerous advantages, too. Small businesses operating underneath the intensity of media scrutiny may be best positioned to experiment as they can gain significantly more than they risk losing by emphasizing net positive impacts as they co-create value.

Corporate impacts are 'not my job'

The assumption: it's not my job; it's the government's job or it's the local municipality's job or it's the community service organization's job. The government's job is to provide transportation, education, hospitals, infrastructure, sewage, etc., while the business of my business is just business and wealth creation. It's not my job as a private-sector organization to provide infrastructure, even though it might be in the firm's best interest (e.g., faster and cheaper with timely completion of building a railroad spur with fewer capital costs and operating costs). The firm may have neither the expertise nor the skillset to appropriately address the stakeholder's expectations. Rather, governments are responsible for allocating resources towards training, development, and education. If skills need to be developed or additional expertise obtained, then education is best facilitated by government, non-profit, or community groups more attuned to the local needs of the community rather than a corporation or a foreign-domiciled multinational.

The 'it's not my job' mindset often assumes corporate impacts are strictly voluntary decisions to undertake discretionary activities used to shape public policy and public opinion. This mindset often views corporate impacts as externalities that should remain as externalities until laws are promulgated mandating the firm to take action. Once laws are created, reflecting the will of politicians and citizens, then a firm can act. Overall, this mindset believes being compliant with extant laws means a firm is appropriately addressing its impacts. When a crisis does occur and the firm's behavior is called into question, the firm immediately turns to its general counsel, who reaffirms compliance with local laws.

Implicitly this mindset suggests the task of defining corporations' impacts lies with each nation-state. Therefore, expectations about a firm's impacts may vary widely between jurisdictions. And to add to the complication, the expectations might be codified in formal regulations specifying what is and is not allowed. Or the impacts might be specified as general principles (e.g., do no harm) that can vary widely in their implementation.

This mindset relies on each country, regardless of its method of governance and regardless of its regulatory regime being stringent or weak, to set thresholds of acceptable behaviors. The nation-state must set expectations and sanctions if thresholds are not met. The burden of identifying and enforcing corporate impacts is borne by countries. It is the responsibility of the country to harmonize laws, monitor safeguards, and/or rely upon others to enforce appropriate behaviors while bringing outliers to justice in order to minimize egregious activities.

When a crisis occurs, an 'it's not my job' mindset is particularly vulnerable, as it is reliant upon others while the spotlight is squarely on the firm. Increased scrutiny with a barrage of negative media that might allege the firm is pursuing 'profits at the expense of people' leaves little time for the company to respond. With the company on the defensive, it is more likely to create even more problems for itself as described in the BP case in Chapter 1. In these high-stress situations, a company quite often begins talking about its voluntary (e.g., philanthropic) activities that go beyond the minimal requirements of local law in order to demonstrate how it has tried to prevent escalation of the crisis or to shift the focus onto a new issue.

An 'it's not my job' mindset often sees yet another obligation piled on top of all the other important (financial) considerations of a firm. By piling on one more obligation, overworked managers are continually asked to do more with less and are uncertain about what seem to be conflicting priorities (Abrams, 1951; Margolis, 2009). They see consideration of non-financial impacts as yet another task and tend toward an 'I'll get around to it later' attitude, creating a reactive response.

Being reactive or allowing issues to escalate into crises leaves precious little discretion for thinking beyond purely financial impacts. As soon as the crisis has passed and media attention has died down, management returns to 'normal' routines and disregards this corporate impacts 'nonsense.' Rather than viewing a crisis as a shift to a new normal, this mindset reinforces a crisis as a one-time event that amplifies a specific issue for a heightened time period and then dies down to allow business as usual to reign. Chapter 9 explores the differences among crises, issues, and impacts.

In addition, an 'it's not my job' mindset may underestimate the prerogative of individual local country managers. Local country managers rather than expatriates from headquarters are often attuned to local norms, customs, and beliefs, such as tithing, housing concerns, transportation, or local labor skills. While the local knowledge put into practice by native country managers often reflects the spirit of corporate impacts (e.g., 'let's focus on education or healthcare of employees and their families and maybe the local community'), the activities may not be tied back to the company's value-creation process. That is the ability to leverage the learning occurring in one local neighborhood is often lost rather than shared across the company as the local managers might think he/she is facing an unique situation no other manager has dealt with before as it 'is not my job.' Yet there may be similar situations in multiple countries around the world helped by the manager's insight.

Perhaps a local eco-tourism hotel creates a training center to build language proficiency or vocational courses within the hotel, extending opportunities to the local community. Yet this approach creates a very limited impact solely reliant on the local manager. Partnering with a local college or government may ensure better long-term outcomes, building resilience in the community and/or self-reliance within the workforce that in turn allows the local tourism industry to flourish.

Focusing narrowly on the business of business as solely profit generation for the owners unnecessarily restricts the attention of managers and in doing so misses profitable investment opportunities for the firm to create net positive impacts. Businesses are uniquely qualified to prioritize issues, move product from point A to point B, gain access to capital, convene a set of experts or transfer skills and expertise to successfully implement multifaceted projects involving numerous stakeholders. In doing so, managers are often at the front line identifying win-win-win opportunities. Does the business have the foresight, willpower, and motivation to be part of crafting a win-win solution?

The 'it's not my job' mindset fails to recognize limits to and the potential for ineffective government mandates. Waiting for government agencies to establish thresholds of acceptable private-sector behavior may result in mandates not necessarily suitable to a firm (such as increased taxes), with the end result being blunt hammers needlessly affecting an entire industry rather than selective scalpels addressing the individual firm as an egregious outlier.

Regulations mandating specific behaviors (e.g., rules-based regulations such as requiring specific scrubbers to remove noxious sulfur dioxide from smokestacks emitting fumes) limit the options for firms. In limiting options, the regulation often becomes a blunt hammer-like vehicle of compliance rather than innovation-oriented opportunity for the firm to differentiate its products or production processes (Porter and van der Linde, 1995). Rather than blunt, hammer-like rules-based regulation, responding to principle-based regulations (e.g., reduce the carbon footprint of the firm regardless of the means via product efficiencies, production changes, purchasing carbon offsets, or arranging for telecommuting) allows for innovation (Hull, 2012).

Crafting principle-based corporate responses based on the firm's unique location, capabilities or impacts allows for consideration of a wider range of options with the *potential* for a better net outcome. Combining market motivations to remain competitive with government mandates to behave appropriately (reduce noxious emissions in California's AB32 law to reduce carbon footprint via principle-based regulations) can create a sustained net positive impact more than a hands-off 'it's not my job' mentality (Hull, 2012).

An 'it's not my job' mindset at the headquarters level, when combined with an overreliance on the local executives' expertise in understanding local needs, can be problematic. Delegating authority locally, within a widely decentralized company, while not appropriately acknowledging how shifting socio-political and culture norms impact a business can cause big problems. Delegating local authority can lead to a mish-mash of locally desirable, imminently noble projects, initiatives, and investments that align with local needs. Yet without sharing best practices across countries, these individualized noble efforts can create dispersed impacts with little to show for the efforts after years of investments. Royal Dutch Shell, for example, consolidated its head offices to solely The Hague, Netherlands in the late 1990s as it realized a need to protect its global brand and addresses global socio-political issues that threatened its survival after accusations of political interference in the case of Saro-Wiwa in Nigeria, and the Brent Spar oil spill issue in the North Sea, among other highly publicized international issues (Lawrence, 2002).

Firms that see non-financial impacts as 'not my job' and are reactive rather than proactive face the challenge of addressing negative impacts in a crisis situation. Learning during a crisis is often non-linear, under considerable pressure, with a spotlight highlighting each misstep along the way. The company may eventually succeed in generating positive impacts, but the 'it's not my job' defensive stance means that a successful strategy is likely to cost more time and effort overall.

On the other hand, firms that actively get involved by taking responsibility when a crisis occurs can lead to new outcomes as explored in the following text in Walmart's reaction to the Rana Plaza fire in Bangladesh.

Walmart and the fire at Rana Plaza

Bangladesh, a poor country in Southeast Asia, is home to around 4,500 apparel factories and second only to China in apparel exports (Gayathri, 2013). Europe accounts for around 60 percent of the country's total garment exports, while the United States accounts for close to 25 percent (Greenhouse, 2013). The country is an attractive production destination for global clothing and textile firms because the minimum wage is only about '$37 a month, compared with $61 in Cambodia and $150 in coastal provinces of China' (Kapner et al., 2013). However, the millions of workers that sustain the industry suffer notoriously unsafe conditions, which posed reputational risks for the many multinational companies that produce their products in Bangladesh even before the tragic collapse of the multilevel Rana Plaza apparel production facility that killed more than 1,100 people (Associated Press, 2013; Gayathri, 2013).

After news of the tragedy broke, most global apparel companies 'denied they authorized work at factories in the building even when their labels were found in the rubble' (Associated Press, 2013). Others, such as British Primark and Canadian Loblaw, came forward and started a fund, chaired by the International Labour Organization (ILO), to compensate the victims. These industry leaders encouraged the firms responsible for the other 30 global brands found at the site of the disaster, as well as competitors and colleagues not implicated in the incident, to contribute to the fund (Associated Press, 2013). Unfortunately few brands donated, and some—including Walmart, Benetton, Gap, and several others—decided to give a pooled sum of around $5 million instead to BRAC, a Bangladesh development organization, which then gave half of this amount to the ILO fund. The ILO Fund's goal was $40 million, less than a fraction of

1 percent of the profits made by the 30 or so companies that worked with Rana Plaza, but the goal was never met (Rana Plaza, 2014). This outcome is hard for some critics to swallow, especially considering that Walmart's profits are $2 billion more than Bangladesh's gross domestic product (Strasser, 2014).

As a more long-term solution, more than 150 brands signed the Bangladesh Accord on Fire and Building Safety, a legally binding mechanism for signatories to thoroughly inspect all the factories they use in Bangladesh for fire dangers and structural instability (Strasser, 2014). Walmart did not sign the Accord, instead announcing a unilateral, voluntary inspection program of all its 279 factories in Bangladesh. The inspection allows the corporation to avoid legal liability but requires Walmart to pay for audits of all the factories. Meanwhile the Bangladesh Safety Accord signatories will pay up to $2.5 million over five years based on their production levels in Bangladesh.

By creating its own audit for the Bangladesh factories and funding a Bangladesh development organization that indirectly contributed to the ILO fund, Walmart is protecting its brand and assuming direct control of its brands. Presumably, Walmart will work directly with the factories in Bangladesh that supply its goods, or find new ones that will continue to protect Walmart's brand promise with workplace conditions that meet international standards. While the factory fire is important—the loss of life is irrefutable and very tragic—the factory is just one of many for Walmart. With specific expertise from factories around the world combined, a clear desire to protect their global brands at risk of being tarnished, Walmart is saying 'it's my job' and is taking direct and very visible action, regardless of the economic costs, as their preferred course of action. Time will tell if fatigue sets in or if the focused intensity changes lives for the better for all stakeholders.

Corporate impacts predominantly affect local communities

The assumption: a company's non-financial impacts are acutely felt by the local community in which the company produces its products or hires its employees. Thus a company focuses on impacts in the communities in close geographic proximity of headquarters or manufacturing facilities (Allen, 2007; Brammer and Pavelin, 2005; Jones, 1991). Being an employer and creating jobs with decent wages is often the start (or perhaps the end) of a firm's commitment to being a good community citizen. As this type of thinking might target the focus of management's impact to concentrate on local communities, the myth becomes: a focus on corporate impacts is equivalent to developing good community relations by providing appropriate community investments to affected neighbors.

On the one hand, initially focusing extensively on a few tangible (local) community activities can create immediate, measurable results. Providing visible benefits to the local community has spillover effects for employees, their families, and even potential employees by generating pride for those close to the firm. The company can use quick successes to differentiate itself from local competitors and challenge other neighborhood firms to create positive impacts. Working with or leading local business associations to think about collective impacts (e.g., congestion), for example, can broaden the impact started by one firm yet felt by the town and the local business community.

On the other hand, disproportionate focus on the community located closest to headquarters can lead to multiple unintended consequences. Here are two unintended consequences: first, the community might present a seemingly unending list of activities for the firm to undertake, turning the firm's interaction with the community or local government into a shakedown situation. This risk looms especially large for businesses that are the sole employer in a town or have chosen a location based on the natural resources available (e.g., shale gas, fossil fuels, or timber).

Second, focusing excessively on headquarters can alienate locations that employ more people, have a greater negative impact (pollution of manufacturing plants compared to headquarters office building), or offer more significant impact for the same level of investment (cost of vaccines in different parts of the world vary significantly). For decentralized companies or firms with a franchise model, focusing solely on neighborhoods near headquarters, where employees live, rather than where products are produced or consumed, misses the potential for material impacts. That is, considering financial, employee, product, and information impacts broaden the definition of affected communities beyond the local neighborhood.

And finally, community relations function is often designed as a cost center focused extensively on (a) spending the company's hard won profits and (b) expectations that the money spent is reflected somehow in intangible financial outcomes.

An unintended outcome is always thinking about communities as hubs of naysayers. That is, communities are considered a source of continued friction, fraught with conflicts, which might not ever be resolved. When thinking of communities as stakeholders who can 'bugger up the business' the focus is on loss, risk mitigation, insurance-like policies that contain or mitigate damage rather than a positive upside that looks for growth or mutual benefits. Communities, when conceived as naysaying stakeholders, unnecessarily constrain competitiveness, halt growth, and stymie the firm's innovation.

The corporate–community conversations take on an 'us versus them' quality rather than 'we're in it together.' That is, representatives from headquarters fly in and offer opinions then jet out the next day without really understanding the community's needs. Creating a superficial understanding of needs and addressing the needs by throwing more money at education or sponsorships often does not endear the firm to the community. Superficial understandings of needs might create community investments that are not necessarily nuanced (we invest a percentage of our pre-tax profits in our communities) and may not address real issues with tangible results. In short, employees, managers, and community members continue to talk past one another without resolving underlying issues.

Community outreach could be seen as an investment opportunity to build and reinforce the brand promise with ambassadors closest to the firm, the employees and their local communities. But often community investment becomes a one-way outpouring of money that is not returned in any fashion to the firm. Since community outreach is not mandated by government legislation nor motivated by a market, companies can choose the magnitude and direction of community investment. It becomes in a firm's best interest to choose and choose its community investments wisely based on the resources, capabilities, and strategy of the firm and its relationships.

A narrow conceptualization of communities as people living in neighborhoods adjacent to headquarters also overlooks the many communities being created daily on social networking sites, such as Facebook and Twitter or beta testers. People that endorse your product, recyclers or artisans that profit from your business, as well as journalists and academics that have an opinion about your business are oft-overlooked communities that can shape opinions about your business and its reputation.

In short, focusing solely on corporate impacts on neighborhoods adjacent to headquarters unnecessarily limits the conceptualization of the firm's impacts. Bounding a company's impacts to its community stakeholders does not align the true impacts with the key strengths of the business: employees, products, and as a thought leader.

Corporate impacts are equivalent to compliance

The assumption: addressing corporate impacts means being merely compliant with government-enforced standards of corporate behavior. In other words, the relevant impacts are those sanctioned by extant laws. Therefore, the motivation for identifying and addressing corporate impacts is compliance with laws and regulations (KPMG, 2011). Related to the 'it's not my job' approach to corporate impacts, compliance is a risk mitigation strategy based on legal departments, strength of law, and courts of law for resolution.

Addressing corporate impacts by being compliant with extant law may be misleading for a number of reasons. First, to be merely compliant in the branded pharmaceutical industry, for example, is likely to keep the firm behind the curve. Not being aware of what is being proposed and vetted by the various governments is likely to render the firm a reactive actor. Pharmaceutical companies, for example, maintain active and sophisticated government relations just to remain competitive without being able to differentiate themselves from rivals. Not being in compliance may be acceptable for firms producing generic pharmaceuticals but is untenable for branded pharmaceutical companies.

Second, some goods might be legally for sale, yet communities (or an entire country) may forbid the use of the products. For example, although alcohol, pornography, and tobacco are not illegal in Muslim countries, they are all forbidden. Deciding whether a firm should offer these products for sale might be a matter of consumer/client choice based on religious, cultural, community, and individual preferences. In these cases, corporate impacts are not questions of legality; they are questions of morality, as firms will be questioned as to whether they are abiding by widely held social norms, customs, and beliefs.

Adopting a compliance-based mindset makes a couple of assumptions: first, compliance reflects the highest level of what a firm can and perhaps should do. That is, compliance reflects an aspiration of acceptable behavior rather than a minimal threshold of acceptable behavior. Reimagining compliance as a minimal threshold (a floor) versus a ceiling of the best practices possible can reconfigure how firms think about government regulations and whether they aim for beyond-compliance objectives. When compliance with laws is viewed as a ceiling, beyond-compliance innovations are likely limited. Thinking about compliance as minimally acceptable thresholds of corporate behavior creates the freedom to consider beyond-compliance activities as a way to enhance competitiveness in a regulated industry.

For example, multinationals based in Europe or the United States might value employee diversity, yet what diversity or an inclusive workplace means may vary by country or sector. Diversity can mean a diverse set of male, female, gay, lesbian, transgender, ethnic minority, or religious minorities in their workforce. What represents compliance with anti-discrimination laws in one country might be a beyond-compliance innovation elsewhere.

Second, a compliance-based mindset often implicitly assumes that a 'strong' government with rule of law, monitoring, and enforcement resources is in place. Yet, there is not always a formal government presence to make and enforce explicit compliance expectations. Implicit norms and behaviors are likely to exist, but understanding the bright lines of compliance or the light lines of acceptable norms might be difficult for organizations based outside of the community.

The lack of formal governance models may not mean there are no expectations of acceptable behavior. Acceptable norms might be set or reinforced by elders within a village, worship houses, or longstanding cultural traditions that don't conform to outside expectations.

In addition, countries with newly emergent governments arising after civil wars, for example, might have priorities besides creating infrastructure, regulating markets, overseeing workplace conditions, or building a viable commerce sector. Creating a viable economy friendly to foreign investment might not be the top priority.

And third, a compliance-based mindset assumes risk is mitigated by merely disclosing environmental, social, and governance activities. Critics of corporate disclosure, however, claim firms are only providing minimal levels of information in order to meet the letter of the law. Risk mitigation by ensuring compliance with extant laws may be economically viable: because the cost of noncompliance, the costs of not participating, or the potential for mishap is too high and carries significant risk yet does not address the underlying sources of risk.

Implications for co-creating value

Multiple longstanding myths surround the mindset of corporate impacts. Often confused with corporate social responsibility, corporate impacts emphasize the value created by firms and the points of impact or contact with key stakeholders that co-create value with the firm. Rather than a focus on how a firm gives away its money corporate impacts emphasize the relationships and the processes by which value is co-created or co-destroyed. It is simply in the firm's best interest to design a value-creation process that endures. This, in turn, means thinking beyond the narrowly defined financial impacts of a firm, considering employees and the workplace, the products and their distribution, and other stakeholders affected through information-sharing. As thought leaders, it is not how the firm sees itself; it is often a question of how others view the firm.

Corporate impacts refer to the mutual benefits created by a firm with other stakeholders. Making money is one benefit, but firms must ask with whom financial and other benefits are shared. Articulating the mutually beneficial outcomes, the variety of organizations and actors that benefit, and how the firm meets or beats expectations are increasingly important in competitive, socially complex, and more active markets.

Addressing the various myths surrounding corporate impacts underscores three takeaway lessons: a need for clarity of focus, a comprehensive perspective, and consistency in addressing impacts. First, clarity regarding material impacts is needed as a corporation has numerous impacts affecting myriad stakeholders that money alone can't solve. A giveaway mindset that suggests money can resolve corporate conflicts is perhaps too simplistic. Once money is accepted, more money might be expected, leading to an escalation that is ultimately untenable, whereas time and talent might be a better means to create the desired impact. Thus, clarity of focus on the impacts desired and the strategies to achieve those impacts is needed. Managers must decide which strategies to use for different outcomes and stakeholder relationships. It's a 3D chess game: locations, stakeholders, and impacts.

Second, a comprehensive approach to impacts that holistically examines a company, and the opportunities presented by multiplier effects is in the business's best interest. Expanding impacts beyond a sole focus on finances or beyond a single issue or community makes the decisions more complex but allows for more nuanced, innovative, and effective solutions. In the 21st century of competitiveness, managers must simultaneously consider how employees are treated; how products are designed, built, and sourced; and how regulators, pundits, and community leaders are informed.

Companies aiming to create genuine impacts without wasting resources must think about how everyday decisions, tied to the core of the business, affect the ability of the firm to co-create value today and tomorrow. Yesterday's expectations are being inculcated into today's new norms with new requirements for a firm to distinguish itself or its products. Looking to governments to set the thresholds of acceptable business behavior might miss opportunities to identify new trends that change the competitive landscape.

Third, consistency is required to build authenticity and overcome cynicism directed at businesses. Businesses are losing the confidence of consumers and the trust of the general public (Edelman, 2014). As society's trust in businesses declines, people increasingly look to the public sector, for better or worse, to raise standards of acceptable business behavior, with the unfortunate result of blunt legislation that may negatively affect competitiveness without encouraging the requisite innovation (Porter and van der Linde, 1995). Internal consistency means consistency across thinking (strategy), doing (programs and activities), and explaining (impacts and communications). Employees will be the first to point out the gaps in expectations and rhetoric versus reality while consumers and investors won't be far behind.

Looking ahead

This chapter addressed five longstanding myths that have stymied thinking about corporate impacts while the next chapter, Chapter 8, looks to the future and expands the discussion by addressing some underlying changes in business, governments, and civil society. Chapter 8 digs deeper into the changing expectations about corporate impacts due to changes in competitiveness, regulations and communities' norms, beliefs, and attitudes.

Apart from a series of checks and balances, businesses, government, and civil society are often examined in isolation from one another since they are often motivated by different outcomes and have access to different sets of resources. In the next chapter we bring these three sectors together, examining how the boundaries are blurring, creating opportunities to address entrenched social issues, create business value, and rethink the role of businesses as they work solo or by partnering with others (governmental agencies, civil society organizations) to create value and build a better future for us all.

Interactions among all three sectors can become an important defining point for co-creating value. That is, some firms might choose to not engage with civil society organizations, as they perceive the government to be the legitimate voice of citizens in that country. Yet what happens when a government is overthrown, the ruling party changes, is fragile, operates with considerable fraud, or does not represent the people or its organizations? Is a firm to remain apart from interactions with all or most of the civil society organizations waiting for the/a legitimate government voice? What can a firm do and what is it likely to do by engaging with governments and civil society organizations?

Not content to examine each sector in isolation, Chapter 8 begins to address the convergence of public, civil society, and private-sector interests in different organizations and business models. It also identifies opportunities for crossover, such as government agencies breaking the traditional mold of being seen as a redistributor of wealth, or community organizations acting as if they are thought leaders and not just geographically adjacent neighbors. It also continues a theme in the book that encourages activities with multiple impacts, such as engaging employees in local or far-flung communities to build teams, transfer skills, and develop expertise while supporting the brand promise and enhancing morale. These mutual win–win–win opportunities are, after all, in the best interest of managers.

While other books address two-way interactions of public policy and private sector, examining three-way interactions and their various combinations multiplies the new opportunities to co-create value. Examining all three simultaneously also focuses on mitigating externalities that might be borne by the sector left out in the value-creation process.

We broaden the perspective of business by looking at the value-creation process as embedded within societies. That is, we examine firms and their stakeholder networks embedded within a web of relations involving civil society and governments. By broadening our perspective in this way, we find that businesses are just one voice among many in an increasingly crowded civil space. Tapping into civil society networks, issue networks, and governmental networks helps a firm to navigate the direct, indirect, spillover, and multiplier effects of its business activities. Articulating the mutual benefits for the firm and other stakeholders becomes increasingly important in an ever-crowded field of competing interests, misinformation, and social media.

8 | *Anticipating changes in expectations*

While previous chapters have examined aspects of the value-creation process often under the direct control of a business (e.g., setting profit expectations, deciding who is hired and fired, writing contracts to ensure appropriate sourcing and distribution of products, setting the tenor at the top, and sharing information about the company), in this chapter we look outside the business. We explore pressures such as competition, regulation, and civil society perceptions affecting how value is created, attenuated or destroyed.

We are particularly interested in examining under what conditions businesses shape and are shaped by external pressures (stakeholders acting alone or in various combinations with one another) in the value-creation process. While stakeholder research often, yet erroneously, assumes stakeholders are unitary actors with homogenous interests acting in isolation from one another (shareholders want returns, employees want employment, customers want safe products, governments want to redistribute value, etc.), we relax these assumptions and explore how individualized groups of businesses, governments, and civil society organizations are affecting the value-creation process.

As businesses continuously create value for numerous stakeholders, expectations of businesses continue to grow and grow. This happens in part because businesses are good at what they do: creating value. Stakeholders that did not traditionally benefit from the company's value creation may capture the value, while others may want to ensure value creation is sustained, equitable, or redistributed for others to benefit, too.

Another explanation for expanding expectations is that businesses, through their extended networks, possess the relationships, resources, and influence to address complex challenges that have eluded others. Lastly, society expects more and more of businesses because in the process of creating value, firms may also be unwittingly destroying value.

In this chapter we anticipate how expectations of businesses are likely to (a) continue to increase; (b) diversify with a wider range of requests of seemingly non-business-related requests; and (c) intensify as stakeholders become more adamant and as firms reluctantly or partially respond. In other words, going forward firms will need to respond to a broader range of increasingly adamant stakeholders in myriad ways to continuously create value. Engagement with a larger number and broader range of stakeholders is increasing firms' access to capital by enhancing transparency (Cheng et al., 2014), affecting a firm's reputations (Allen, 2007), helping to attract and retain employees (Greening and Turban, 2000; Turban and Greening, 1997), and enhancing firms' economic performance (Surroca et al., 2010). Some firms are effectively adjusting to expanded expectations and reaping rewards. Let's look at how they are successfully engaging a more diverse set of stakeholders.

First, we look at changes occurring within the business sector due to changing leadership techniques, new forms of legal governance such as B corporations, increasingly global competition, and shifting consumer preferences. As rivalry increases, tomorrow's consumers might reward instant access to data, or customized services that are 'liked' by virtual users. To anticipate these changes it is in businesses' best interests to listen, respond, and inform their stakeholders.

Second, we examine several ways that governments have changed expectations of businesses. New regulations have caused people to rethink how business is conducted while new forms of global governance, such as multilateral organizations, are changing how expectations of business behavior are shaped around the world.

Third, we examine civil society organizations and their role in setting expectations in an ever-changing society. As attitudes, norms, beliefs, and traditions change, expectations of businesses are changing. Acceptable levels of education, health, security, privacy, and self-sufficiency are shaping and being shaped by businesses. As attitudes change and civil society organizations become more prolific, their expectations may or may not overlap with business interests, creating the potential for increased friction or engaging early to understand shifting preferences.

Overall, this chapter examines changing expectations stemming from competition and rivalry, regulations and the public policy process as well as changes in attitudes towards commerce from civil society organizations. As businesses are embedded within a complex web of competition, managers must continually sift through attitudes, policies, and preferences to create value. Rather than being transfixed by the increased number of expectations, businesses are uniquely qualified to meet changing expectations—if indeed managing corporate impacts are taken as central to the business. Ignoring the numerous corporate impacts or steadfastly retaining a singular focus on just one impact (financial or product or employee safety) is risky. A firm's continuity of operations is likely at risk since survival may be at stake, but it need not be. Many businesses, adept at navigating unchartered waters, thrive when confronted by changing expectations and create new value via product lines, business units, and innovative services to meet the shifting expectations.

We are particularly keen on examining the relationships between commerce, regulations, and civil society by exploring the conditions under which one of these three groups supersedes another as the trusted source of information. In doing so, we take a more inclusive view of value creation of businesses. By explicitly including direct stakeholders (investors, suppliers, consumers, and employees in Chapters 2–5) as well as stakeholders indirectly or complicity affecting a business's ability to create value (e.g., regulators, local and virtual civil society organizations and communities, competitors, and the general public), we examine an inclusive, holistic value creation process.

Businesses: changing expectations through competition

Businesses are continuously innovating and responding to competitive expectations by changing their scope, structure, financing, and role within society. Business has survived over the centuries by changing. Businesses frequently respond to shifting expectations by creating: (a) faith-based, values-based missions, credos, and philosophies; (b) forms of ownership, including public, family-owned, or private; and (c) new business models.

For-profit organizations founded with specific religious beliefs often voluntarily impose faith-based guidelines central to *how* they conduct business. For example, many Muslim organizations tithe 10 percent of their profits to their communities, while fast-food chain Chick-fil-A's Seventh Day Adventist founder chooses not to open the restaurants on Sundays. Similarly, Sir Cadbury developed his chocolate company based on Quaker values and beliefs of taking chocolates to the public rather than having chocolate as a luxury item to be enjoyed by the richest members of the population (Smith et al., 1990; Bradley, 2008).

Other for-profit businesses without an explicit religious affiliation also have stated values-based missions that are integral to *how* they manage. CEO Marc Benioff's no-smoking policy cut insurance costs for his cloud computing company, Salesforce.com, while also improved the health of its employees. Food stores such as Marks & Spencer and Whole Foods cater to a broad demographic of consumers emphasizing organic, natural, and socially beneficial business practices and sustainable sourcing to bring organic, humanely treated grocery products to consumers (Mackey and Sisodia, 2013). By carefully sourcing their products, these firms can provide information about their sourcing practices that allows them to charge a premium creating satisfied customers while earning profits for their investors.

Other businesses, built upon the personal ethos of the founder/owner, are imprinted with their personal values from the start. Ben Cohen and Jerry Greenfield of Ben & Jerry's ice cream company, for example, produced unique premium ice cream products from fresh milk and cream, without added preservatives, from local farmers in Vermont. They successfully grew their bottom line and their brand, sold the company to the large conglomerate Grand Metropolitan and eventually rebuilt the brand when the company was bought by Unilever. Interestingly, Ben & Jerry's remains contractually obligated to offer organic products sourced from sustainable supplies (Edmondson, 2014).

Small and medium-sized enterprises (SMEs) from around the world have also built successful business models emphasizing specific workplace, employee, or product impacts (Corporate Responsibility Officer Association, 2011). Airbnb, valued in 2014 at more than $13 billion, a growth of more than 750 percent since 2009, has created a market for renting overnight accommodations in private homes, castles, yurts, or lighthouses around the world. Competing directly with the hotel industry, Airbnb has built a loyal customer base by providing online reviews of successful rentals as well as extensive insurance policies for landlords (Ferenstein, 2014; MacMillan et al., 2014).

Similarly, Grameen Bank, created in Bangladesh by Nobel Prize winner Muhammad Yunus, promoted peer lending and self-governance as key criteria in his for-profit bank (Yunus, 2007; Yunus and Weber, 2007). By lending small amounts of money to groups of women that share their successes, he has woven together a peer-lending group that supports one another financially and psychologically while building niche products profitable in niche markets.

Entrepreneurs build new businesses by responding to changing expectations to create new products and services that fulfill unmet needs (Martin and Osberg, 2007; Khavul, 2010). Entrepreneurs in health services, for example, are creating mobile or handheld devices that can quickly scan a body and provide health service professionals with critical information. These new products are crafting new opportunities in vision care, maternity care, and mobile health (Jones et al., 2014a).

Businesses responding to a changed competitive environment need not be entrepreneurs nor remain small. The Tata Group (www.tata.com), created more than a century ago, has grown from a small, local manufacturer into a multinational business that have adapted a central tenet of innovating over decades of growth and through two world wars to produce superior products (www.tata.com). Tata Motors reinvests two-thirds of its revenues in trusts to create hospitals and schools for employees, families, neighbors, and citizens of India. Tata's consistent commitment to the health and education of its communities remains a hallmark of this indigenously Indian multinational. Consistent with an ethos to innovating, Tata Motors pioneered the Tata Nano, an affordable car mass-produced at an affordable price for ordinary people (Lala, 1984, 2007; Elankumaran et al., 2005).

Privately owned or family-based businesses are uniquely positioned to address long-term impacts, in part, because family-owned businesses have an intrinsic interest in creating a business model that will survive and thrive across multiple generations. Privately owned businesses voluntarily report on critical non-financial business impacts, such as child labor and sustainable sourcing of inputs, without pressures from shareholders. Private equity companies, for example, are partnering with the NGO Environmental Defense Fund (EDF) to improve carbon, water, and energy efficiencies (Murray and Kapur, 2014).

All in all, businesses *are* responding to changing expectations through their missions, vision, and values. Establishing a clear mission or being a values-based business increases the attractiveness of a company as an employer in today's market for top talent, who now expects to work for an employer with aligned values and a positive working environment, of which they can be proud to work (Jones et al., 2014b). Research suggests stakeholder engagement to set expectations improves access to finances by enhancing transparency (Cheng et al., 2014). Firms are changing but not changing fast enough.

Formal and informal networks of firms, including trade and professional associations, are growing in membership and strength to respond more rapidly than individual firms. These networks of businesses reflect the desire of firms to share common practices, learn from one another, and cooperate to address common business issues. In many cases they also devise minimal thresholds of acceptable behavior and apply penalties in case of member non-compliance. Self-imposed codes of conduct can differentiate industries or competitors within the same industry, build credibility, prevent legally binding legislation, and secure the future of the profession. For example, the alcoholic beverage industry imposes a voluntary ban on advertising their products at certain times of the day.

Fair Trade certification, which takes a product's extended value chain into account, provides another example of the rise of self-regulation within certain industries. Coffee growers and some fruit and tea farmers work together under the Fair Trade certification to differentiate their products, ensure quality, and guarantee that products are produced without child labor, harsh working conditions, etc.

Such self-imposed standards are not new but are growing in number and adherence through professional associations. The medical community, for instance, has their Hippocratic Oath allowing surgeons to exclaim 'It's a matter of honor!' after being asked why they continue with specific practices that do not seem to make financial sense.

Yet, businesses do not always voluntarily comply with codes of conduct, follow local norms and expectations, or ascribe to industry norms without explicit consequences. Enforcement of voluntary behavior is often spotty (Rasche and Esser, 2006) as industry associations often rely upon honor codes, professionalism, and leadership rather than a process of regular oversight, monitoring, and reporting with verification (Raynolds et al., 2014). Yet voluntary standards and certification systems are proliferating around the world. Table 8.1 highlights a selective set of certifications drawn from Ecolabel Index (www.ecolabelindex.com).

Identifying guidelines for appropriate business behavior has been a growth industry among many multilateral organizations such as the United Nations, the Organisation for Economic Co-operation and Development, the International Monetary Fund, the International

Table 8.1 *Selective ecolabel certifications*

Food and Beverages
4C Association
Bird Friendly Coffee
CAFE Practices
Demeter Biodynamic
Ethical Tea Partnership
Fair Trade Certified
Fair Trade Organization Mark
Food Alliance Certified
Global Gap
Green Tick
Italian Association for Organic Agriculture
Rainforest Alliance Certified
Sustainable Agricultural Network
Utz Certified
World Fair Trade Organization

Meat, Dairy, and Aquaculture
American Grassfed
Aquaculture Stewardship Council
BIODAR
BIO Hellas
Bioland
Carrefour Eco-Planete
Certified Humane Raised and Handled
Chao Vivo
China Organic Food Certification
EU organic products label
Global Good Agricultural Practice
US Department of Agriculture Organic
Marine Aquarium Council
Marine Stewardship Council

Dining, Restaurants, and Hotels
Bio Hotels
Certified Green Restaurant
Green Key Eco-Rating Program
Leaders in Environmentally Accountable Foodservice (LEAF)
Ocean Wise
Seafood Safe

Table 8.1 (*cont.*)

Forest Products
Australian Forest Certification Scheme
Certflor: Brazil
Certfor: Chile
Forest Stewardship Council
Green Star NZ
Sustainable Forestry Initiative
Totally Chlorine Free

Flowers and Ornamentals
Fair Flowers Fair Plants
Florimark
Florverde Sustainable Flowers
Rainforest Alliance Certified
VeriFlora

Textiles and Footwear
Ecoproof
Fair for Life
Global Organic Textile Standard
IMO (Institute for Market Ecology)
Oeko-Tex Standard 100
Rugmark
World Fair Trade Organization

Chemicals
ECO product
Organic Content Standard
SCS Certified Biodegradable
Water Quality Association Gold Seal

Organization for Standardization, the Global Reporting Initiative, and the World Bank. And within civil society, voluntary regulations are now well-established in the non-profit sector as well (Prakash and Gugerty, 2010). The notion of corporate impacts pervades various organization types from for-profit firms to governments and non-profits, making it even more important for managers of for-profit organizations to better understand why and how to manage different types of impacts. Yet, a move towards a focus on impacts, in addition to discrete issues, is warranted as responses have been slow and spotty—inviting governments to mandate acceptable behavior through national regulations.

We now shift our attention to the government sector to examine how regulations are shifting expectations to redefine the responsibilities of businesses and governments in modern society.

Governments: changing expectations and responsibilities

Actively incorporating governments' expectations into corporate strategy is not a new idea (Preston and Post, 1975; Baron, 1995; Epstein, 1969). As corporate strategy shapes and is shaped by public policy, how expectations and responsibilities of governments are changing are important opportunities or potential pitfalls for the private sector. While governments traditionally provide infrastructure, set and enforce regulations, pursue national priorities, and redistribute wealth, some governments are unable or ill-prepared and thus must rely on private-sector support. Further, governments often specify thresholds of acceptable behavior.

Increasingly, more governments are explicitly specifying expectations of acceptable business behavior (Epstein et al., 2013) with thresholds changing over time (EU Commission, 2011). India, for example, has passed a corporate responsibility law stipulating that companies must dedicate 2 percent of after-tax money for community projects (Epstein et al., 2013). And the EU recognizes the spread of corporate responsibility to non-corporate organizations and is developing a series of research papers on corporate social impacts that include different types of organizations to explain or disclose material non-financial impacts (EU Commission, 2003, 2011).

The changing relationships among governments and the private sector still reflect the infrastructure-related traditions of public-private relationships. That is, governments have traditionally been responsible for maintaining a country's physical infrastructure such as water, power, public services, housing, waste disposal, hospitals, and transportation. Infrastructure projects often enable local economic zones to improve business districts and are increasingly financed by the private sector and multilateral institutions such as the World Bank Group, to share the risk and costs in infrastructure investments (Zoellick, 2011).

A government's ability to deliver on infrastructure projects is often related to the taxes collected. Governments, unlike publicly traded enterprises, collect revenues from individuals and organizations through mandatory fees and taxes. Fees are often assessed on a cost-recovery basis rather than a profit-making basis, while taxes can be used to affect demand for products by increasing prices through taxation. Infrastructure as a revenue-producing investment rather than a cost-recovery project requires considering new risks, new timelines, new roles, and new governance mechanisms.

For the private sector, paying taxes and making transparent all payments to governmental agencies can be viewed as one aspect of managing in a responsible manner (Griffin, 2000; Clay, 2005). Paying taxes is considered part of a firm's obligations to allow (democratic) governments to do what they were elected to do, without fraud or deception (Friedman, 1970). What if governments do not keep their (expected) end of the bargain? In extreme cases of failing states or limited statehood, corporations are often asked to voluntarily incur costs to supply and maintain public infrastructure (Börzel and Risse, 2009).

Increasingly, privatization and deregulation have increased the expectations of corporations even if there are not extreme cases of failing governments (Prakash and Griffin, 2012; Griffin and Prakash, 2014). For example, some services that traditionally fell under the purview of governments, such as the mail system, telecommunications and transportation infrastructure, hospitals, and education, are now more efficiently provided in some countries by private-sector companies.

By setting or signaling acceptable business behavior through oversight and enforcement, governments affect every aspect of commerce and exchange, including financial, employee and workplace, product, and information impacts.

Regulations often constrain the ways that companies can market their products and services. For instance, firms that falsely advertise the benefits of their product can face legal recourse or restrictions can be placed on advertisements affecting the ease of buying or selling a product. The alcoholic beverage industry, for example, faces excise taxation (a 'sin tax'), as well as limitations on the way it can advertise, who can purchase its products, and even where and when customers can purchase them.

Governments change expectations through purchasing power to set standards without promulgating laws. For example, in 2009, President Obama created an executive order demonstrating a preference for purchasing from minority-owned or veteran-owned organizations (Obama, 2009).

Governments also set expectations through their ability to convene multi-stakeholder forums (Allen, 2005). When private-sector organizations do not provide appropriate levels of goods or services, governments can convene panels of experts to give testimony, impose mandates, set standards, or prohibit production to establish thresholds of expected behavior. Regulations can address gaps in coverage and pricing inequities, codify expectations, ensure privacy, harmonize expectations, and create a minimal threshold of management.

Governments often set expectations by assuming certain types of risk. As risk tolerance changes, the expectations of businesses and governments also changes. Shifting tolerance for risk can be overlooked as risk is often under-socialized (Granovetter, 1973). That is, government regulation of markets assumes market efficiency, no information asymmetries, and no impulse purchasing. These assumptions don't hold true across the board as human behavior can thwart rationality and efficiency and be impulsive (Kahneman and Tversky, 1979). In addition, risk mitigation often assumes a linear, rational decision-making hierarchy with clearly prioritized needs/wants that are widely held and homogenous; these conditions are not always met.

Governments sometimes work to minimize information asymmetries between public and private sectors that might lead to information arbitrage (Patnaik, 2012). Information arbitrage is a form of inefficiency with risks and costs often assumed by governments but those risks can be passed onto the private sector or consumers. By setting explicit levels of information disclosure, governments set expectations of what information is shared, with whom, and when. Private-sector organizations, as first-movers, might pre-emptively address information asymmetries with the expectations that the firm might avoid future constraints (Tetrault-Sirsly and Lamertz, 2008). By pre-empting future constraints, voluntary behavior is in a firm's best interests, with spillover benefits by signaling good behavior (Bansal and Roth, 2000; Prakash and Potoski, 2014).

All in all, governments use a variety of mechanisms to set expectations including endorsing, facilitating, partnering, and mandating (United States, 2005). Governments have multiple roles that can encourage and enable businesses, in addition to their traditional role as a redistributor of profits.

Blurring boundaries between governments and civil society, organizations are challenging businesses long-held beliefs about the role of business, government, and society (Epstein, 1969; Preston and Post, 1975; Baron, 1995). The increasingly important role of civil society organizations in lieu of, or in addition to, governments as arbiters of information, service providers, or business partners has changed the landscape of a purely business–government relationship (Salamon et al., 2003). Non-profit organizations and the civil society sector more generally have swelled in number, scale, and scope over the past decades, shaping new expectations for businesses while also creating new business opportunities for modern managers (Austin, 2000; Salamon et al., 2003; Austin and Seitanidi, 2012a, 2012b).

In the next section we examine more closely non-profits and a variety of other civil society organizations as a frequently overlooked source of innovation and barometer of shifting attitudes. The analysis will focus on how technology has broadened our ideas of community, thus changing the face of civil society and consequently these organizations' expectations of businesses.

Civil society: changing expectations through public opinion

Nearly every civil social organization has different interests. As disparate groups without an authoritative voice, their demands can be wide-ranging, vague, and seemingly tangential to business concerns. While shifting civil society and community expectations can be lost in the cacophony of voices making demands of modern managers, understanding shifting civil society attitudes is more important than ever and can be considered a pre-emptive activity within this pre-political space.

Society is assumed to be groups of people bound by a similar culture with widely held beliefs. Similar behaviors and generally acceptable norms that don't vary too much are often presumed to coincide with a country's geographical boundaries. Yet, if you look at a map of Australia divided by indigenous cultures, each indigenous group has a distinct culture with its own customs, beliefs, and languages. 'One' country suddenly becomes a landmass composed of hundreds of local cultures. Numerous subcultures exist each with their own cultural heritage, language, and ways of working together. Treating Australia as one homogeneous country is misleading, at best, upsetting to numerous stakeholders, at a minimum, risking new business opportunities merely by assuming widespread common preferences.

The communities or civil society organizations arising based on specific issues, intentions (boycotts, sit-ins, protests, political assemblies), or identities (breast cancer survivors) are often motivated by outcomes other than financial success and may pursue a specific course of action well beyond what is considered financially prudent (Rowley and Moldoveanu, 2003).

Furthermore, while governments are often considered the sole, legitimate, and authoritative voice of citizens within their jurisdiction, no matter how large or how small, there are countless conflicting interests. It's impossible for governments to keep everyone happy or to represent everyone. During the Arab Spring of 2011, for example, numerous demonstrations across the Arab world toppled long-established authoritarian governments and renewed demands for representation in governments.

In this context, issues raised by civil society organizations are at times considered pre-political, as these germinating ideas may not have reached a critical mass nor attained a decibel level that commands the attention of governments. Alternatively, the inability of a government to create a unified voice can undermine the ability of the best-intentioned of governments to promulgate legislation. In addition there is a question of effectiveness of governments and the policymaking system as it is often easier to stall legislation rather than creating new laws addressing citizens' concerns.

In addition, mainstream technology such as social networks allows for the instantaneous and widespread distribution of information that significantly reduces the costs of organizing around common interests (Phillips and Freeman, 2008). Technology and its ability to facilitate the creation of communities based on common interests have broadened the definition of community beyond people in close geographic proximity.

Widely held attitudes of society are often reflected in international civil society organizations (CSOs). Yet, as the number, growth, scale, and scope of the civil society sector have grown extensively in the past few decades (Salamon et al., 2003), the breadth of organizations can be bewildering.

At the same time, the economic impact (e.g., procurement, employment, taxes) and professionalism, such as the ability to raise money, be a reliable partner, or convene multi-stakeholder conversations, has built legitimacy and extended CSOs' influence through sheer scale and scope (Salamon et al., 2003).

Without an explicit profit motive and often funded through private contributions, civil society organizations reflect a wide range of attitudes and are organized accordingly. Private and corporate foundations, relief and aid agencies, as well as religious-based organizations comprise the majority of civil society organizations. CSOs often desire worldwide scale and scope yet are constrained by demands for consistency, transparency, and accurate information.

Civil society organizations might choose the issue or community they wish to represent and target without consideration of consolidation or duplicative efforts. They take pride in connecting fragmented information, shaping attitudes, building consensus, and mobilizing disparate interests. By providing information that is not always readily available, they build credibility and connections. Civil society organizations include national and international trade, professional, and community associations such as the United Way. Or, single-issue organizations focused on consciousness rising include Earth First, Sierra Club, art organizations, volunteer fire departments, and professional associations such as the Corporate Responsibility Officers Association (CRO-A) and the Leukemia Society.

Civil society organizations might focus on a specific community, and may possess deep local knowledge and close relationships with influential leaders that complement private- and public-sector activities. National or international civil society organizations often work with local chapters or local communities in a semi-coordinated, federated, fashion. Boy Scouts of America, for example, have numerous chapters in nearly every community across the states dedicated to developing young men with character, integrity, and physical fitness (www. scouting.org).

The implications of CSOs for businesses are several: many CSO communities are voluntarily created not legally sanctioned. Virtual communities, dispersed communities, and CSO communities based on common interests often operate with different norms and expectations than traditional communities sharing specific geographical boundaries. Seemingly unorganized, the geographically dispersed communities can have many voices with many messages. These dispersed messages are easy to disregard.

For modern managers, treating all CSO communities similarly or treating all communities as if they are based on geographical boundaries is a missed opportunity. Different CSOs hold different attitudes towards business and expect different things from businesses in different ways. Attitudes shift broadly and swiftly with rather harsh judgment of both leaders and laggards. A business's response is often a scramble of numerous fragmented efforts and multiple projects, with companies addressing needs from isolated, individualized CSOs.

What is required of businesses in addressing the expectations of CSOs, however, is a focus on identifying initiatives that can be harmonized. Rather than focusing on numerous, dispersed impacts, a clear focus on solutions that materially affect the co-creation or destruction of financial alongside non-financial value is suggested even if only one individual is affected. Value creation does not just mean financial value. Unfortunately, what is often pursued is a one-size-fits-all 'solution' of paying more money that might be prohibitively expensive or managerially impractical in rural towns and villages far away from headquarters where the initiatives are often created (Barnett and Sunyoung, 2012).

Non-governmental organizations (NGOs) and quasi-autonomous non-governmental organizations (quangos) are a type of CSO facilitating the delivery of public goods and services. These organizations often play a critical role in linking local needs with the appropriate level of resources and skillsets from the private sector, thus filling an important gap in creating mutual benefits.

The civil society sector—especially religious, faith-based organizations—has a long history of shaping attitudes towards commerce in general and businesses more specifically. Religious groups, ministries, and missionaries work within local communities to spread beliefs as well as feed, clothe, and educate the poor, sick, or needy and are quite active in the US, filing shareholder resolutions to force businesses to address issues of social justice, for example (Rehbein et al., 2013).

The idea of fair trade dates back more than 50 years, when missionaries arranged to have Western churches sell African handicrafts and return the profits to the villages. In the late 1960s and 1970s, world shops sprang up all over Europe and the US to give sellers in developing countries access to world markets (Stecklow and White, 2004).

Religious-based missionaries can range in scope from international associations operating across many communities worldwide, such as Catholic charities, to local community groups such as Beacon House in Washington, DC.

Many US universities, originally funded by state governments, are increasingly funded by individual donations and endowments, which is blurring their identity as public entities or CSOs and is, in turn, raising questions such as access to education. Internationally, universities are government-funded yet are also increasingly taking private donations. Even in China, with its government-funded school system, there is a privately funded university in Shanghai. In the US, universities comprise a substantial portion of the non-profit sector (Salamon et al., 2003). Given their significant purchasing power, universities can affect private-sector business practices. For example, pressured by students and parents for more healthy and diverse food options, universities are negotiating contracts that limit sugary beverages or enhance the variety of ethnic offerings. As a result, Sodexo, a food service company generating a majority of its revenues from university cafeterias, is rethinking its food menus.

Overall, civil society organizations through scale, scope and voice are changing attitudes of what is expected of businesses as more and varied CSO communities are affected in the value creation process.

Convergence: blurring of boundaries

In this chapter we examined how expectations of value creation are changing through competition, regulations, and with changing attitudes within civil society. In short, these changed expectations are affecting and being affected by the value-creation process. The central point being straightforward: clarity is needed. Clarity is needed regarding how, with whom, and for whom value is created, since there are increasingly many different ways in which value can be created and destroyed.

Co-creating enduring value means being attentive to three multiplier effects of impacts. First, while the sheer number of impacts increases, the solutions to these impacts also increase. Second, non-financial considerations are inextricably intertwined with financial considerations (Baron, 1995). And third, co-creating enduring value requires navigating new territory with new players changing expectations about destroying value that is an externality borne by an unsuspecting third party.

In some regions of the world such as Africa and India, the informal sector comprises 80 percent of the entire population (Khavul, 2010; Vachani and Smith, 2008) suggesting that CSOs might be more important than formal governments for setting business expectations. The informal sector includes the black market, where governments might be unable or unwilling to enforce laws and organizations may be neither licensed nor registered to operate and do not pay taxes. Prices may not be standardized nor require cash payments. In-kind payments, bartering, or credit transactions may be the norm creating new risks and new opportunities for co-creating value.

Economies based on agriculture pose additional challenges: subsistence-style living, once-fertile soil being depleted without crop rotation, and limited opportunities for future generations to advance can amplify corporate impacts—especially if a corporation is providing seeds or fertilizer without additional education. Agrarian-based living can amplify labor issues such as family or child labor, while lack of educational opportunities, water use, and carbon footprint can increase the expectations of private enterprise.

Government-sponsored enterprises (GSEs) blur boundaries between public and private ownership, creating hybrid organizations that are neither profit maximizers nor public service providers yet are an integral aspect of supporting private-sector transactions as displayed in the 2008 global financial crises. In the US, GSEs such as Fannie Mae and Freddie Mac were created to securitize mortgages for increasing homeownership between 1980 and the 2000s (Koerber, 2011), yet contributed to the mortgage meltdown in 2008 and required a bailout of several billion dollars in the first decade of the century.

Converging pressures creates a multifaceted pachyderm: skeptics grouse that multilateral guidelines incur additional costs with no tangible benefit from the additional disclosure requirements. Without monitoring and enforcement, the self-reported nature of most information promotes self-description that is flattering to the company, while potentially diverting attention from real issues and providing the appearance of conformity. This allows the business to continue doing whatever it has always done without significant changes to mindsets or operations, effectively ignoring value-creating opportunities.

Optimists might argue multilateral guidelines, which promote a common, consistent threshold of acceptable behavior, create a level playing field, promote innovation, and allow firms to align society's and the business's goals through the core strategies of a firm. The voluntary nature of the guidelines allows for firms to experiment with different approaches prior to requirements being made compulsory via government regulation.

All in all, attitudes, preferences, beliefs, and perceptions are, by their nature, amorphous and fluid. The mechanisms by which affected communities voice their concerns through boycotts, protests, or political campaigns can crystallize public sentiment on significant issues and act as a catalyst for changing expectations (Bonardi and Keim, 2005). The question for business managers remains: are you aware of, and appropriately managing, corporate impacts as the expectations and risks are continuously changing?

Implications for co-creating value

One difficulty in assessing value across multiple stakeholder groups is the sheer volume of different definitions of value. To anticipate the demands of a seemingly fickle set of stakeholders that are simultaneously satisfied very rarely, in this chapter we examined how expectations of a firm are changing and how some firms are responding to this kaleidoscope of stakeholder demands. While some expectations are more visible thanks to social media, other expectations remain as entrenched as ever. Are customers willing to look the other way regarding their favorite brands' overseas labor practices if they are able to purchase a tank top for less than £2? And what are the odds that the people who made the tank top were paid a living wage?

In earlier chapters we focused on firm-centric value-creation processes by identifying impacts and multiplier effects radiating out from the firm's financial and production activities. In this chapter our focus is broadened to examine the value-creation process at a macro-level, emphasizing how the private, public, and socio-cultural pressures are changing expectations for tomorrow's businesses.

We purposely include all three sectors: business, government, and civil society, as the interplay among the three sectors is not just additive (1 + 1 + 1) but can have exponential effects that accelerate and amplify ever-changing expectations. In addition, different combinations of competition, regulations, and civil society pressures will likely prevail in different corners of the world.

The implications for co-creating value are three-fold. First, for businesses, achieving economies of scale with efficiencies while remaining effective by adapting to local customers and customs remains critical (Bartlett and Ghoshal, 1989). By making supply chains more efficient, competition continues unabated to secure loyal consumers. At the same time, ever-higher proportions of local content, customization of products to local preferences, and adaptation of the firm's processes for different workplace contexts are being demanded (e.g., minimum level of local suppliers and employees hired, reporting level of profits and taxes remaining local, customers demanding sourcing of materials, or creating new ways of serving existing or previously underserved markets) by an ever vociferous set of local, national and international CSOs.

Second, the number and type of regulations are increasingly complex. Regulations often involve multiple agencies (education, health, transportation, national security, and exchequer) at multiple levels (local, provincial, regional, state, federal or national, or pan-national) with plenty of opportunities for mission creep, lack of coordination, and limited sharing of pertinent data. As a result, businesses often focus on general regulations such as workplace safety or corporate taxes while working with industry-specific associations on common issues such as pricing, advertising restrictions, and export/import regulations. What often gets lost is the increased localization of municipal laws. That is, regulations are simultaneously becoming increasingly global and national while also becoming more localized, making the world of commerce a lot more complicated going forward. Regulation, when viewed as a failure of markets, is often vociferously fought at the local level regarding zoning permits, permits to serve alcohol, opening hours, and the like. Overall, the variety of regulations at multiple levels reflects a widening gap between what is expected of businesses and what is occurring.

Third, public attitudes towards commerce are changing. Widespread shifts in attitudes often precipitate legislative or regulatory activity. That is, widespread shifts in attitudes are often early indications of citizens' sentiments of acceptable business behaviors. As shifts in attitudes become generalized and gain momentum across populations, legislative activity often follows to codify norms. Recognizing early shifts in attitudes before rivals can create an advantage over competitors, as the firm can help shape the ideas. Understanding shifting attitudes is an opportunity to understand future actors, issues, ideas, and institutions during early phases of idea development and stakeholder mobilization. During the early phases of mobilization, managers can experiment with new products, new implementation schemes, and new ways of operating to meet unmet expectations before governmental mandates specify solutions and limit choice.

Looking ahead

This chapter explored how stakeholder groups are changing, which in turn changes the expectations of key players in the process of creating value. Three pressures shifting the processes of value creation were: fierce rivalry, changes in regulations/public policy, and shifting attitudes in civil society. As these pressures are morphing and affecting even more stakeholders in a variety of ways, the job of managers becomes exponentially trickier (Freeman, 1984).

Executives are increasingly asked to assume responsibility for activities that were once provided by others while also maintaining a focus on generating appropriate profits for their shareholders (Margolis and Walsh, 2003; Margolis, 2009). But should firms acquiesce to these increased demands? Most firms are ill-equipped to manage these additional responsibilities, and it's not in their interest to address every demand. Yet, the demands continue non-stop as firms are often best-positioned in terms of financial and personnel resources, networks, and expertise to address pressing issues.

Rather than treating the changed expectations as a trade-off between competing demands, we find that leading firms today are seeking convergence of common interests to create new opportunities for businesses and its stakeholders. That is, rather than a mindset focused on trade-offs, we call for a focus on win–win–win investments wherein value is created. The next chapter, Chapter 9, examines the convergence of issues and interests to create appropriate impacts. Chapter 9 is the first of a series of three chapters focused on the context of firms and how the context shapes the opportunities for corporate impacts. In Chapters 10 and 11, in addition to issues, we examine industries and nation-states respectively as important moderators of a firm's ability to co-create value.

9 | *Convergence: combining issues and interests to co-create value*

What's in a name?

Shakespeare

[A]ny business to be successful has to create value for customers, suppliers, employees, communities and financiers [shareholders, banks and others, people with the money] ... you can't look at any one of those stakes, or stakeholders if you like, in isolation.
Their interest has to go together.

R. Edward Freeman, 2008

Are impacts individual issues that must be managed?
Or, are impacts a part of discussions about how a firm creates value?

This book focuses on firms' impacts during the value-creation process. When a firm interacts with another stakeholder to exchange material, ideas, or impressions, an impact is made. At that point of impact, value may be created, destroyed, or remain in a latent state. It is simply in a manager's best interest to ensure value is created for mutual net gain. As explored in Chapters 1–6, four interactions between a firm and its stakeholders contribute to value being created or destroyed: through finances, with employees in the workplace, procuring and producing products and services, and/or via information-sharing.

At the point of impact, issues or gaps between expectations and reality are present. So questions arise of focusing attention on issues, the groups involved (the stakeholders), or the outcomes desired/anticipated (impacts).

Issues are often the focus. Issues are fungible ideas often with clear demarcations of interests on each side of an issue, making a relatively 'simple' cost–benefit analysis to identify winners and losers possible. But resolving an 'issue' may or may not create value. Resolving an issue might be a step towards value creation, but it is just one step. The ultimate outcome of value creation is all too frequently considered as a nebulous ideal that can be achieved in the future or as a responsibility for someone else to handle while managers are busy managing important issues. In addition, an issue-focus requires that an issue must exist before it receives management attention. By definition, an issue-focus places management in a defensive stance instead of in a more proactive position to pursue positive impacts to create value.

An impact-focused approach emphasizes convergence of mutual interests *and* the process of value creation with an explicit goal of value being co-created. A focus on impacts allows for bundling interests to create mutual benefits (net of harms) that endure over time. Convergence allows for new opportunities for new win–win–wins. The beauty of convergence is that each party can gain something of value to them: money or reputation or security, while the gains can be realized at different points in time (e.g., immediately versus a year from now). Convergence often requires innovation—ways to co-create value by finding mutual benefits where none previously existed. On the flip-side, value is destroyed when dissonance creates friction rather than an opportunity to innovate.

Finding point(s) of mutual benefit is neither easy nor straightforward. Yet, mutual benefit (net of costs) is a worthy goal since creating value is what businesses are best at doing and the threat of contributing to destroying value is in a business's best interest to avoid. In earlier chapters, finding points of mutual benefit required thinking about the many and varied ways in which a firm interacts with its stakeholders. Taking employees as an example: employees can be seen as labor that produces products and delivers services and who can be easily replaced in times of need. Typical employee issues might center on wages, workplace conditions, and productivity. Yet employees can be far more than just these issues.

For example, employees with stock-ownership options, board members, and institutional investors have long-term common interests as shareholders. Employees and governmental inspectors often team up with common interests in safe workplace conditions. Engaged and motivated employees can transfer their enthusiasm or belief in the firm to customers with positive impact on a firm's sales (Vock et al., 2014) or employees acting as customers could suggest new designs for new products. Treatment of employees has ripple effects on the potential hiring of new employees (Jones et al., 2014b). Employees as ambassadors of an organization can spread positive goodwill or counteract negative stories from the media. With this broader narrative of employees, employees become part of the solution when there are: shareholder disputes, a need to build a loyal customer base, design new products, retain and attract a motivated workforce, or a need for ambassadors for the company. In short, firms need to think creatively to find common interests among stakeholders. Rather than narratives of employees as a homogeneous group with singular interests, a more nuanced perspective is warranted.

Creating unique employee-based initiatives reinforcing employee pride might be a potential game-changer for the firm as it endeavors to attract even more top talent and remain competitive. Focusing on a few initiatives demonstrating a keen grasp of a firm's intended impacts (such as employee pride that builds a loyal customer base rather than generic responses to wage disputes) elevates an issue (employee satisfaction) to a conversation focused on impacts (pride and loyal customer base) and competitiveness rather than narrow demands from a single stakeholder group.

Since an issue-based focus is prevalent in businesses, the following sections examine the benefits and then the problems associated with creating value by using an issue-by-issue approach. Interestingly, an issue-by-issue approach to creating value was never intended by the original issues management scholars (Ansoff, 1975; Mahon, 1989; Wartick and Mahon, 1994). While issue-based approaches have been linked to creating value (e.g., Porter and Kramer, 2002, 2006, 2011), an issue approach has significant shortcomings (Crane et al., 2014a, 2014b). Namely, the chief criticism is the narrow focus on specific issues without including outcomes that are for the betterment of society including improved competitiveness (Crane et al., 2014a, 2014b). Solving complex societal problems through an issue-lens is both too narrow and too far removed from actual management practice (Crane et al., 2014a, 2014b) creating a preference for impact-based approaches. Impacts examine how value is co-created or co-destroyed and how the value-creation process endures over time despite externalities and in light of multiplier effects across a tangled web of stakeholders.

From a practical perspective, separating ESG (environmental, social, and governance) into discrete issue areas, for example, serves to reinforce a 'separate yet equal' treatment of these issues. Yet some firms might have significant governance impacts that a 'separate but equal' treatment doesn't address. The banking industry, as demonstrated by the global financial crises, has been under the spotlight for a variety of material governance issues. Governance issues are far more important than bank's disclosure of environmental efforts, for example. Yet extolling a bank's environmental efforts by using a 'separate but equal' approach may mask significant underlying risks regarding governance. As a result, a new focus on impacts including materiality (EU Commission, 2011) shows encouraging promise as management practice evolves beyond an issue-based approach.

An issue-by-issue approach

With an increased prevalence of ratings and ranking schemes comparing firms across economic, social, political, or ethical criterion, Porter and Kramer (2002, 2006) suggests prioritizing issues, which we will call: general issues, sourcing–producing–distributing issues, or game-changing issues. This simplifying typology in Figure 9.1 demonstrates how an issue (e.g., hunger) might be very important for some firms (such as grocery stores), yet not as important for other firms (such as car dealerships) by understanding connections between an issue (hunger) and a firm's competitiveness. Alleviating hunger by using the skills and expertise about food, nutrition, and sourcing in grocery stores might enhance competitiveness, while hunger and car dealerships may not enhance competitiveness: creating a sustained difference in alleviating hunger while sponsoring hunger alleviation may backfire for car dealers.

Overall, an advantage of an issue-by-issue approach is often in how issues are framed and communicated to others (Bartha, 1982; Mahon, 1989). By framing issues as general issues, sourcing–producing–distributing issues, or game-changers, stakeholders within the company are able to call management's attention to issues with the largest impacts on the company. Each type of issue is elaborated upon in the following text, with an explanation of the benefits gained by a firm addressing this type of issue.

General issues

General issues impacting by the firm include big, societal issues of the day: hunger, homelessness, poverty, education, and climate change,

General issues:

> Issues not significantly affecting the firm's ability to
> co-create enduring value.

Sourcing–producing–distributing issues:

> Issues significantly affecting the firm's ability to achieve
> its objectives through suppliers, distributors, or retail
> operations.

Game-changing issues:

> Issues significantly affecting the firm and its industry to
> survive or remain competitive if status quo is continued.

Figure 9.1 Issues and impacts

to name a few persistent general issues. These issues are widespread within the society that the firm wants to compete in or attract consumers in. As the relevant social issues are defined by the society at large, the firm may or may not have a specific expertise in addressing these issues. Further, the firm may or may not be directly contributing to the social problems, nor is the firm seen as having a potential 'solution' to 'solve' the issue. Yet firms may be considered as critical players to alleviate the problem.

General issues are collective, societal issues that are non-specific to the activities of the firm, yet reflect the demands of some part of society (Annan, 2001). Without a clear connection between general issues and the firm or the firm's value-creation process, the attention granted to these issues may ebb and flow as leadership changes, as issues shift in relative importance, or as political will fades and a new issue is prioritized as the most important issue *du jour*. Meanwhile, other general issues persist despite concerted efforts over long periods of time.

The benefits of addressing general issues without a clear tie to the business are generally minimal, with significant downside risks if the firm chooses to address general issues and later decides to reduce or eliminate its support altogether. Considered costs unrelated to the business of the business, these nice-to-have programs without a solid logic reinforcing the firm's commitment are generally the first to be axed when a recession occurs. Without a coherent story as to why the firm should be involved with the general issue—and often without evidence of the impact for the affected population or the potential benefits accruing to the firm—such programs are often carried over from year to year without a clear articulation to the purpose of the firm, or how the firm is uniquely capable of addressing the general issue. Without answering questions of why the firm should support this particular activity (and not that one) and how to best deliver on its promise (as well as what to avoid), support can be lost when new managers are assigned to oversee the project. If the benefits remain unclear, confounding the ability of the firm to articulate expected impacts and costs, support for general issues is likely to wane when competing priorities arise.

All too often, if general issues are addressed via arm's-length financial transactions, such as a product-based giveaway, without engaging employees, the general issue remains a general issue that any firm with slack resources can address. Porter and Kramer (2006) consider a firm addressing general social issues to be reactive rather than proactive. This back-foot, reactive stance towards addressing general issues, may not get the firm noticed and may indeed be a waste of shareholder's money (Friedman, 1970). Often considered little more than a 'me-too' symbolic response to society's demands, addressing these issues might waste scarce resources, cause more harm than net good, and set expectations that the firm is willing to help 'solve' an issue. There is also a business risk in setting expectations yet not delivering solutions that might create additional burdens in the future.

As questions are posed as to why this general issue is being addressed and how this 'investment' (which may indeed be a giveaway) benefits consumers, employees, or investors, perhaps the firm is indirectly exacerbating the issue by treating symptoms rather than addressing underlying issues. Overall, the issue remains unresolved yet the firm has made a claim (unmet as it is) to address a general issue. Indeed, the general issue might be spiraling out of control and getting worse.

Sourcing–producing–distributing issues

Issues related to sourcing, producing, and distributing products and services—that is, issues that extend the enterprise from originating materials to the final consumers—affect the ability of the firm to create value. As sourcing–producing–distributing decisions and indecisions come under tighter scrutiny, these issues often win the attention of management. As we talked about in greater length in Chapter 6 regarding multiplier effects along the value chain, these sourcing–producing–distributing issues often focus on procurement policies and marketing. Consequently, materiality of these issues and thus the management attention (top management verses line management, for example) and resources allocated (money, technology, human resources, etc.) are likely to differ based on the expected impacts—and risks from multiplier effects—on a firm.

If a firm is currently trying to staunch a procurement crisis, the attention and resources allocated to the issue are likely to be quite high as finances and reputation may be at risk. If, on the other hand, a crisis occurred sometime ago then fatigue may have set in with a commensurate lower level of resources and attention. For example, as talked about in Chapter 3, two years after Apple faced supplier disruptions at its Foxconn factory it was still experiencing challenges as product quality and expectations for safe workplace conditions were continually being ratcheted up (*China Daily*, 2012; *Bloomberg*, 2012).

Issues along the value chain from sourcing–producing–distributing might be aimed at mitigating harm. Alternatively, responding to these issues might be aimed at creating value that endures. In both cases (mitigating harm or creating future value), the value-creation process is affected. Issues aimed at mitigating harm often have an insurance-policy nature to them with the goal of getting to neutral rather than getting ahead of the issue (Godfrey, 2005; Godfrey et al., 2009). Mitigating harm is often an attempt to transfer attention from a negative activity to a more positive, or a neutral, image. Yet mitigating harm may not address the underlying sources of harm as it takes time, for example, to change sourcing policies to remove herbicides or genetically modified organisms from the food chain.

For example, in response to allegations of human trafficking, child labor, and unacceptable workplace conditions of suppliers, the company might provide statistics on the popularity of its products (an investor focus rather focusing on supplier-based issues) or the desirability of its stock to reframe the issue (e.g., Apple prior to the Foxconn incident). On the other hand, focusing on issues along the value chain that can co-create future value often involves stakeholder dialog to understand preferences and common outcomes (Henisz, 2014).

If a firm is portrayed as an egregious violator of environmental issues, for example, understanding why stakeholders have that perception and ways in which perceptions may be changed over time can begin through the stakeholder engagement process. While the portrayal of the firm might be justified and immediate efforts might be an attempt at mitigating harm, dialog may uncover ways the firm can innovate along its value chain to meet changing expectations. For example, a firm might be portrayed as a poor performer based on inaccurate or incomplete information unfairly depicting the firm's actions. In response, a firm might voluntarily provide more information and publish external, third-party verification reports on the firm's website or via social media to pre-empt inaccurate information being distributed (Price, 2000, 2002). Making sourcing guidelines or supplier criterion available online, such as Walmart currently does after considerable supply chain issues after the turn of the century, may encourage more suppliers to disclose their policies and practices to mitigate supply-chain risks.

Game-changing issues

A third type of issue, in addition to general issues and sourcing–producing–distributing issues depicted in Figure 9.1, is game-changing issues. Game-changing issues are issues that change the way an industry—or commerce more generally—operates. Game changing issues might gather steam due to the outcry from the media or the general public, or be codified in legislation changing business behavior. But they don't need to originate from external pressure. Businesses can create game-changers creating mutual win-win-wins changing the way in which the industry competes (e.g., tamper- and child-proof bottle caps on medicines). Game-changing issues by their very nature are both rare and strategic, as they affect the way a business or an industry competes (Ansoff, 1980).

These issues irrevocably change the way in which a business and its rivals compete. Addressing these issues signals that the firm is becoming part of a solution rather than a part of the problem. For example, competition might previously have been based on price alone but when prices don't account for externalities such as pollution or human trafficking, firms change the nature of competition by labeling their products as green, organic, or pesticide-free, for example, or signing up for certifications confirming the firm's labels are accurate.

De Beers, a diamond extraction and distribution company based in South Africa, for example, began promoting its diamonds as conflict-free diamonds to distinguish them from the conflict diamonds being extracted in conflict areas such as the Democratic Republic of the Congo. Conflict diamonds were being used to purchase arms for rebel groups supporting uprisings that De Beers wanted to separate itself from. In doing so, De Beers created a new market niche, retained its luxury brand by ensuring conflict-free and child-labor-free diamonds, and developed a new proprietary technology.

Alternatively, a small niche pocket of an industry might, over time, change the way in which an entire industry offers its products or delivers services. Ecotourism hotels a few decades ago, for example, might have been the only hotels that changed the sheets in a hotel room once every three days or changed towels only as needed as part of their eco-friendly offerings. Now, due to the significant cost savings in laundry services, water, and electricity, many hoteliers are adding signs in their hotel rooms asking for customers' preferences in changing sheets and towels. By making changes in how frequently hotels change sheets and towels, a new norm was established across a number of hotel chains.

Game-changing issues might occur due to external pressure from stakeholders or internal pressure from the business. External pressure from stakeholders is often in the form of changed expectations expressed by the media, the general public, or mandated by legislation of how businesses should or can behave. As groups coalesce around specific social issues, such as corruption or human trafficking, they are changing the expectations of how business is conducted. By moving from headline news that more often than not uses negative publicity that depicts poor behavior to new norms, businesses are responding to changed expectations.

Internal pressures resulting in game-changing behavior might be motivated by product innovations, new competitors, or both. For example, Tesla Motors, a high-end automobile manufacturer founded by Elon Musk, is experimenting with an electricity-based engine that could create a broad sweeping change to the way in which automobile manufacturers address pollution issues. The growth in electricity-based and hybrid engines using either fossil fuel and/or electricity comes after Toyota successfully created a niche market for its Prius automobile (Rothaermel, 2015).

New competitors in the hotel business such as Airbnb are challenging the traditional business model of hotel accommodations. Rather than booking accommodations in large hotel chains, Airbnb is encouraging homeowners with a spare bedroom and wanting an additional revenue stream to sign up for daily, weekly, or long-term boarders

(Ferenstein, 2014; MacMillan et al., 2014). By vetting the homeowners, their properties, and the potential boarders Airbnb offers lower costs with alternative venues for travelers opting to stay in private homes or rent rooms for a period of time. Overall, private housing reduces construction costs—which in turn may reduce demand for lumber and other natural resources—and saves consumers money, while providing a resale market for spare rooms.

All in all, the way in which businesses are addressing game-changing issues (e.g., fossil fuel/energy consumption, supply of hotel rooms, etc.) by combining so-called 'social' and business issues, are creating new norms. Rather than setting out to solve an 'issue', these innovative thought leaders are co-creating value. By thinking of business decisions as having social, economic, legal, and ethical impacts simultaneously, these thought leaders are reimagining the way in which businesses provide products and deliver services. Overall, the expectations of businesses and their industries are changing with some business models not adapting or not adapting fast enough to keep pace. By converging business and so-called social issues such as water and electricity savings from changing towels/sheets in hotel rooms, offering new products such as electricity-based automobiles, or new businesses such as private accommodations that reduce demand for new hotel construction, wide-scale change in some industries is occurring. At the end of the day, business issues have social implications and social issues have business implications. There's no separation.

Issues moving across categories

A general issue may become a sourcing-producing-distribution issue if the business enters new markets or produces new products. For example, if a firm expands its product offerings to a country that has known human-trafficking issues then the general issue of human trafficking might become a value-chain issue. If the firm continues to expand into countries with known human-trafficking issues, being recognized as a firm that is a leader in addressing human-trafficking issues can be a competitive advantage. As the reputation for addressing this complex issue spreads, and while governments or rivals come under pressure to address human trafficking, the firm leading in addressing human trafficking becomes uniquely qualified. It might become the preferred foreign direct investor or invited by a government to lead efforts in their country.

A pharmaceutical company looking to expand into a country with chronic diseases, for instance, might be able to manufacture (and sell at a profit) its pharmaceuticals but the firm might also be able to help the government address some underlying aspects of that chronic diseases. Perhaps education is lacking, or continued treatment in isolated areas, or some remote populations are underserved: issues that might be able to be addressed by the pharmaceutical company with its scientists, product knowledge and widespread logistics network. Firms that create game-changing responses by working with governments may create barriers to entry, for example, precluding competitors from taking market share. Partnering with governments to create solutions, however, may require reimagining a firm's traditional relationship with government to begin thinking about government as a supplier or as a consumer rather than just a regulator of the firm's operations. It could be important to understand how the firm's products—pharmaceuticals, for example—affect domestic competition if state-owned enterprises also offer pharmaceutical products, as well as how the products affect the nation's healthcare. Examining how nation-states affect co-creating value is discussed in more detail in Chapter 11.

Limits of an issue-by-issue approach

Focusing on individual, discrete issues can create unintended consequences that negatively impact value creation. Without a focus on the overall impacts sub-optimization can occur. That is the (issue) battle is won, but the (impact) war is lost. A narrow focus on the issue itself (treating the issue as a discrete issue) can overlook the more important aspects of how the issue connects to other issues (bundling and escalation of issues). Furthermore, a narrow focus on just a singular issue might obscure the symbolic and the substantive threats posed by the issue. Not recognizing the true impacts of an issue and how a seemingly 'simple' issue can affect the competitiveness of the firm has led to the downfall of numerous firms. We highlight three problems to an issue-by-issue approach of value creation in the text that follows.

Issues as discrete items

Using an issue-by-issue approach to creating value unnecessarily reduces value creation to a series of linked yet discrete initiatives.

A sense of how an issue relates to current or future value creation is relegated to the background, while the focus becomes crossing off an issue from a 'to do' list. By decoupling issues from their true impacts on a business, the issue can be isolated or, worse, ignored as 'not my job.'

This approach implies a focus on numerous issues, each issue making some type of impact in its own unique incremental manner, but each issue is neither tied to the overall direction nor the purpose of the business. How an issue helps the firm achieve its goals of value creation is often left unasked and unfortunately unanswered. In other words, solutions to issues when considered discrete items are vulnerable to being lopped off. A focus on solving discrete issues can encourage complacency within an organization that fails to understand how an emergent issue can morph over time with significant, wide-ranging impacts on the company. When did Blockbuster, a movie distributor, realize that Netflix was changing the business model of consumers gaining access to movies?

Focusing on a discrete issue rather than understanding the issue in light of the true impacts on a firm, early warning signals of a discrete, yet emergent, issue can be easily overlooked (Wartick and Mahon, 1994; Mahon et al., 2004). For example, grocery stores that ignore food products with genetically modified organisms (GMOs) will likely be left with a distinct competitive disadvantage if GMO discussions morph over time into demands for organic products, new sourcing labeling, and comprehensive tracking of food from farmer to the table (Griffin et al., 2005). Rather than engaging early with time to experiment with new products, healthy alternatives, or organic offerings while securing contracts with suppliers to fulfill these changed consumer expectations, many firms will be under considerable pressure to change and change quickly. Walmart, for example, was late to the organic foods movement with its 2001 public foray into organic foods. By 2013 the company announced it would expand the locally grown vegetable produce sold in its stores by 2015 (D'Innocenzio, 2013), slower than many of its competitors.

Similarly, tobacco firms in the US have been faced with a continuously hostile public reception for decades. Tobacco control groups collaborated in restricting cigarette access to youth and limiting advertising to minors, with frequent public demonstrations of the negative effects of smoking and second-hand smoke (Mahon and McGowan, 1996). As public pressure continually escalated, US manufacturers being asked to address the negative implications of cigarettes, cigars, and chewing tobacco sought relief from the barrage of negative public pressure by agreeing to sweeping legislation that limited liability and the number of lawsuits while ensuring public health. The 1997 Master Settlement Agreement (MSA) restricted manufacturers' prerogatives and resulted in a steady decrease in smokers a decade later (Jones and Silvestri, 2010). Under pressure in other markets, tobacco manufacturers are fighting the increased controls regarding the sale of tobacco in the EU, an important but declining market (Shubber, 2014), while India—an increasingly important market for tobacco manufacturers—is increasing the warning on tobacco products (Chilkoti, 2014). Global tobacco manufacturers focusing on only one province, region, or country will too narrowly focus on a discrete issue while bigger battles are shaping up elsewhere.

A portfolio of issues recognizes that issues are intertwined. Addressing just one tiny issue (pulling on one thread within a rope) often results in numerous related issues being brought to light. Bundling issues together can make it difficult to separate the individual issues. Alleviating poverty, for example, is often intertwined with education, access to markets, access to capital, infrastructure, and/or economic mobility issues, yet addressing one issue (access to education) may not make a noticeable difference on the overall goal of alleviating poverty.

Issues are also fluid, crossing political jurisdictions with ease, and are not easily categorized into convenient, measurable metrics. Issues, like diseases, can quickly move across political borders or countries, affecting multiple populations differently (Preston and Windsor, 1992; Mahon and McGowan, 1996; Windsor and Getz, 1999). The bubonic plague and the rapid spread of the 2014 Ebola virus, for example, indiscriminately affected populations of different geographies, socio-economic status, or regulatory regimes (Barry, 2005; Christensen and Liptak, 2014). The 2014 outbreak of the Ebola virus, has spread from Guinea, Liberia, and Sierra Leone, to Nigeria and Senegal, taking more than 2,400 lives and infecting thousands more (Christensen and Liptak, 2014). Medical issues such as Ebola, if not contained, can quickly become pandemics exacerbated by the global flows of people and products (Barry, 2005). Despite all that is known about Ebola, some of the most qualified medical professionals in the world have not been able to control the virus's contagion.

Issues that are not as easy to quantify and less visible can fall through the cracks even more easily. The downside of dismissing general issues out of hand, however, is that without a clear understanding of their true impact on the loss of talent, for example, supporting general issues might have created a halo effect contributing to the general perception of the business. Once a general issue such as HIV/AIDS in the 1980s escalated it negatively affected by stigmatizing many firms (Epstein, 1969; Ansoff, 1980; Mahon and McGowan, 1996).

Discrete issues can also be problematic for a firm's credibility. Too often, a policy or program directed at a single issue affecting one unit of the business is touted as a success for the entire company in sustainability reports. Without addressing how that specific success within a business unit positively affects the entire corporation, the sustainability report becomes a glossy marketing brochure that reflects only a tiny sliver of the firm.

Similarly, touting one issue, such as emissions reductions in office areas, while ignoring or downplaying more material but unchanged levels of emissions from heavy manufacturing units, can be (intentionally or unintentionally) misleading. A focus on materiality represents a shift towards thinking about the most important impacts (both positive and negative impacts) in the value-creation process. A firm's credibility is at stake when it highlights positive headline-generating impacts to appeal to the consumer-facing retail portion of the business without creating programs to address the true impacts of business's procurement, production, and distribution activities.

Legacy issues

Legacy issues reflect an issue that occurred in the past but continues to mask the firm's current efforts to portray its activities in a positive light. For example, the *Exxon Valdez* oil spill in Prince William Sound in Alaska continues to be a legacy issue for ExxonMobil nearly three decades after the spill occurred. Although the environmental effects of the spill have long since been addressed, the public still harbors a strong association between the company and this tragic event.

Similarly, Enron is still used as a pop culture reference for greed, even inspiring movies (*Enron: The Smartest Guys in the Room*) and musicals (*Enron*), which support the firm's legacy as a 'bad egg.' Yet before Enron's ultimate demise, the firm received numerous honors for community outreach, and was lauded for its risk mitigation skills

(Donaldson and Werhane, 1999). The perception, prior to Enron's fabled fall from grace, was of a well-managed, high-flying company that was well-regarded by many stakeholders. Yet these accolades were a thin veneer hiding the company's unsustainable business practices.

Microsoft, one of the largest companies in the world, has long tried to rework its reputation as a monopoly player, which reflects in large part the anti-trust allegations against the firm in the US and the EU. Interestingly, at the same time that Microsoft was undergoing anti-trust allegations from the Department of Justice in the late 1990s, another very large and well-known technology firm was facing similar allegations of anti-trust abuses at the US Federal Trade Commission. Many adults can recall Microsoft's battle in the Department of Justice in the late 1990s and still associate the company with anti-competitive practices, but few remember that Intel came under fire at the same time for similar offenses. The implications suggest that the way a company handles public, legacy issues is important to its ability to co-create value in the future.

Legacy issues can remain unresolved, popping up again and again in different forms like a nightmarish game of whack-a-mole. For example, changing the debate between tobacco manufacturers and tobacco control groups from 'a smoker's choice' to 'non-smokers' rights' to 'public health issue' has kept tobacco-related issues alive for decades.

Legacy issues can reflect philosophical differences in opinions and beliefs that cannot be resolved. With entrenched adversaries intent on putting the other side out of business, the rivals pursue well-worn, age-old patterns of engagement, hoping that their deep pockets are able to withstand the continued onslaught.

We often assume consumers are able to instantaneously, or at least quickly, absorb new information and replace old images with more current ones. Even if controversial legacy issues (such as the nuclear disasters at Three Mile Island, Chernobyl, or Fukushima) were to suddenly be erased from the planet's collective memory, the companies producing nuclear energy may or may not be creating value. For example, if a large conglomerate were to suddenly divest its nuclear power interests, would value be created? Or, does the public's focus on a controversial issue, in this case nuclear power, act as a lightning rod without a deeper understanding of the firm's value-creation process? Looking beyond legacy issues to examine underlying policies, processes, and practices that create enduring value, are the firms positioned to co-create value if legacy issues were suddenly reframed, from nuclear disaster to energy independence, for example?

Persistent issues

While legacy issues are tied to a specific firm or industry (e.g., the *Exxon Valdez* oil spill directly affected Exxon Mobil), persistent issues are widely prevalent issues often beyond the ability of any one organization to manage. Attempts to manage these issues often fail for lack of consistent accountability, transparency, and understanding of progress. Addressing persistent issues often requires multilateral, multi-organizational, and/or multi-sector approaches that can systematically address the complex issues involved.

Many societal issues are persistent issues: poverty, hunger, homelessness, child labor, disease, corruption, environmental destruction, discrimination, nepotism, infrastructure concerns, access to medical care, and the list goes on (Weick, 1979; Margolis and Walsh, 2003; Porter and Kramer, 2006). Without sufficient coordination, leadership, and consensus, progress on persistent issues can be slow or non-existent in the short term. As a result, many companies choose to address small aspects of a single persistent issue, resulting ostensibly in an eclectic array of issue-based activity, yet not making a noticeable difference on topics such as corruption, human trafficking, or environmental protection (Rowley and Berman, 2000).

In redefining persistent issues to be smaller, more manageable tasks, a firm takes action—a positive start. Yet another rational response is no response at all: 'it's not my job' or the issue 'is someone else's problem' with unintended consequences as discussed in Chapter 7. If the choice is to do something, the choices involve what aspect of the overarching issue to choose and how to address it by connecting the issue and the solution to the uniqueness of the firm.

Some firms might use their convening abilities to deveop forums for multi-stakeholder cooperation. While it is traditionally viewed as the responsibility of governments, especially democratically elected governments, to carry out the will of its citizens (Friedman, 1970; Jensen, 2002), governments might be unable or unwilling to provide a forum for discussion. If acting as a convening forum, one critical question for the private sector becomes prioritizing among many, intertwined, discrete issues.

One way to prioritize issues may be to focus on issues affecting multiple businesses but offer quick win–win–win scenarios. For example, a coordinated effort by operations, procurement, and perhaps marketing-oriented firms aimed at cutting consumption in carbon, water, and energy can save money and decrease dependence on electricity. With easy-to-measure decreases in consumption, the firms simultaneously support multiple goals. Pushing consumption initiatives throughout the supply chain, starting with exclusive or large suppliers, might be the second phase of creating win–win–wins.

And even more difficult is linking employee morale to customer satisfaction and customer service as new metrics to track success are required (Immelt, 2005). Finding the sweet spot that combines persistent issues that affect or are affected by the business creates a focus on impacts: issues must be discussed as impacting the business. Tying management responses back to the core purpose, value created by an organization is non-trivial yet often overlooked.

Having looked at the benefits and limitations of an issue-by-issue approach, we now turn our attention to the similar stakeholder-by-stakeholder approach that isolates and addresses each stakeholder group individually while the overarching goal of value creation can get lost. While a stakeholder-by-stakeholder approach was never intended by the original stakeholder theorists (Freeman, 1984; Freeman et al., 2007), in practice it occurs. Stakeholder researchers initially conceptualized a corporation's responsibilities in a stakeholder-by-stakeholder approach (see, for example, early editions of textbooks by Crane and Matten, 2003; Crane et al., 2013a, 2013b). The next section addresses the fallacies of focusing on isolating the needs and expectations of one stakeholder group from the value-creation process.

A stakeholder-by-stakeholder approach

Focusing on a single set of stakeholders is a common practice even if individualizing stakeholders was not the intention of a stakeholder approach to businesses (Freeman, 1984; Freeman et al., 2007). While many firms explicitly focus on specific stakeholders—being employee-focused, customer-focused, or investor-focused—four pitfalls of a narrow narrative focused on a singular stakeholder are highlighted in the text that follows.

Mixed messages

First, a stakeholder-by-stakeholder approach mischaracterizes stakeholders fulfilling multiple roles and wearing multiple 'hats' (Wood and Jones, 1995). For example, the government can be a regulator, customer, supplier, and overseer. Consumers can be employees, municipal officials, shareholders, and part of the general public. Employees can be investors in employee stock-ownership programs, customers, product ambassadors, and community members. The ways that a company views a stakeholder group will affect the way it addresses its perceived impacts on that group. The more thoroughly a firm understands stakeholders' different interests, the more likely that the firm will be able to positively impact its multiple stakeholders.

Misclassifying, or inappropriately responding to narrow signals stemming from a stakeholder group while not acknowledging the stakeholders' multiple and potentially conflicting interests can send mixed messages (Wood and Jones, 1995).

A message attuned to one stakeholder group such as employees might become muddied when directed towards parents, consumers, or municipal officials that are also employees. For example during the Ford Explorer tire recall in the early 2000s, Ford created a team of employees from operations, government relations, risk management, marketing, and human relations that met frequently with the CEO Jacques Nasser while the crisis was unfolding to create consistent messages that would resonate with multiple stakeholder groups simultaneously (Moll, 2003).

Muddied messages miss, in part, the reality that organizations and individuals are complex and multidimensional. Yet a relationship based on multiple points of mutual interest creates deeper, richer relationships expanding the solution sets for managers and creating even more options for finding mutual benefits.

Employees as whistleblowers, on the other hand, can effectively send a critical message. Companies are increasingly vulnerable when whistleblowers report news in real time with a message that goes viral and gathers a sympathetic social media and online following. Whistleblowers like Sherron Watkins, who reported accounting irregularities at Enron, can undermine the credibility of a corporate message.

Stifling innovation

Broadly classifying stakeholder groups such as consumers as a singular, homogeneous group with common preferences misses opportunities for nuanced product-market innovations. Broad classifications seemingly set in stone the role, interests, and relationship of a stakeholder with an organization, thereby stifling innovation. Thinking about communities solely in terms of adversarial local neighborhoods that make incessant demands, rather than as a locale housing current employees, potential employees, and consumers, unnecessarily limits the ability of the firm to anticipate problems or craft solutions.

Instead of thinking of the firm and its surrounding community as 'us versus them,' companies are re-imagining themselves as one of the many actors in the region, gathering strength by creating a coalition of like-minded businesses or citizen groups. Treating communities as gadflies or non-traditional stakeholders (Yaziji, 2004) renders the definition of 'community' too broad, too amorphous, and too vague for concrete action, as we discussed in Chapters 4 and 8.

Rather than broadly classifying stakeholders, developing fluidity when thinking about stakeholder relations allows for the same stakeholder to have different expectations in different contexts. As an important employer in town, for example, stakeholder groups such as community members, employees, and customers may expect a local company to be deeply involved in the community. The company may sponsor the local soccer team, donate land, or build a sports complex. In addition, the company may encourage employees to volunteer to build financial or computer literacy through schools, books, and libraries, which reinforces the commitment of the business to the community and vice versa.

Ostensible permanence

Similarly, over time, a monolithic categorization of a stakeholder suggests a permanence that just might not be accurate. Thinking of governments solely as regulators, for example, rather than allowing for governments to be suppliers or consumers limits the type of ways a firm may consider interacting and creating value with this stakeholder. Another problem with *a priori* categorization of stakeholder relationships are misleading perceptions of permanent 'friends' or permanent 'enemies.' Permanent friends (enemies) might be embedded, for example, in the country's political legacy and cultural traditions. For example, some companies might initially dread interacting with Greenpeace but eventually end up creating value for multiple stakeholders through effective partnerships. McDonald's and Greenpeace worked together with soybean traders based in Brazil to secure a moratorium on the purchase of soybeans from newly deforested areas in the Amazon. In doing so, McDonald's, Greenpeace, and the Brazilian government worked together with Cargill, one of the largest suppliers of Brazilian soy for chicken feed, which, in turn, was linked to McDonald's chicken nuggets. By partnering, these organizations linked together through their value chain activities and a common outcome were able to address deforestation, the interests of soy farmers, the unwitting contribution of large traders to social issues in the Amazon region, and requests from consumers for ethical sourcing (Kaufman, 2007).

As stakeholders' preferences change, which often happen rapidly, being able to track the willingness of consumers, governments, and societies to accommodate business behaviors that are codified into law in some locales (e.g., corruption, pollution, or workplace conditions) is becoming increasingly important. That is, while a country's law may remain silent or extant law is not enforced, consumers might express their preferences through their purchasing behavior. Alternatively after a crisis occurs, such as the fire at Rana Plaza in Bangladesh discussed in Chapter 7, it might be in a company's best interests to pay up-front costs for safety features rather than facing the wrath of worldwide scrutiny after a preventable crisis.

In some situations, stakeholders' interests remain steady ('permanent') for generations based on deeply entrenched religious, cultural, or political reasons. That is, some interests for some stakeholders are not negotiable. As Aboriginal people in the outback of Australia express preferences in terms of their children's children, for example, thinking 100 years out is not unheard of. As non-negotiable, long-standing interests, these century-long expectations expressed by certain groups become a minimal threshold of acceptable behavior rather than an interest that can be negotiated.

Seemingly permanent interests can have unintended consequences if one stakeholder is considered a gatekeeper for other stakeholders. That is, one stakeholder—a gatekeeper—might create a baseline of new expectations for other stakeholders. The US Food and Drug

Administration (FDA), for example, regulates pharmaceutical companies and has the authority to grant approval to proposed medicines. As a regulator, the FDA cannot be ignored as it is a permanent stakeholder with permanent authority to approve medicines. The FDA's recommendation signals the acceptable levels of pharmaceuticals for other countries and multiple non-pharma stakeholders. As such, the FDA is an important gatekeeper, setting a minimal threshold of acceptable behavior for pharmaceuticals; a company would be remiss if it treated the FDA as just another stakeholder before releasing certain medicines to the US market.

Foregoing multiplier effects and convergence opportunities

A fourth unintended consequence of taking a stakeholder-by-stakeholder approach is reinforcing a mindset that unnecessarily encourages a narrow, focused approach to corporate impacts (e.g., only financial impacts matter). For instance an employee-focused firm may pay considerable attention to their human relations department. Yet, employee-related impacts often permeate operations, marketing and sales, and finance-related decisions that can be unintentionally undermining incentives from the HR department. Expanding an employee focus to include these other functions requires elevating employee impacts to conversations at the most senior level about the company's future competitiveness. Employee-centric firms need to ask questions about how employees affect customers, how employees and their morale affect new product development, and how employees as owners are reflected in the governance of the company including membership of employees on the board of directors (Conley, 2007).

Thinking beyond specific dyadic relationships (e.g., employer–employee relations) requires thinking about stakeholder relationships more holistically. Rather than narrowly conceiving employee relationships as being centered on employees' identity as wage-earners, as depicted in Table 9.1, the firm needs to consider moving beyond generic employee-related issues to a more holistic relationship that examines employees, their families, and their relationships with customers, investors, and suppliers that create value. Focusing on the tacit knowledge gained by employees when working with customers on a daily basis can create new value for the firm, customers, and the employee (Vock et al., 2014). Some service-based industries such as hotel management are creating new business models by focusing first on employees and reaping

Table 9.1 *Narrow and broad approaches to thinking about impacts*

	Organization A (in isolation approach)	Organization B (convergence approach)
Financial investors	Returns on investment	Returns on investment, sustainable reputation, trust, credibility
Employees and workplace	Job creation, security, benefits, wages, child labor, stigma, plant closings, workplace conditions (EH&S), human dignity	Contractors and full-time equivalent employees, transfer of skills and expertise how you close a plant, nutrition, disease prevention
Suppliers, distributors, retailers	Delivery, quality, timeliness, convenience	Sourcing of raw materials, access to capital, access to markets, ability to grow
Neighbors, communities	Traffic, pollution, noise, dislocation	Disparities in haves and have-nots, self-sufficiency, self-governance, self-reliance, virtual communities, thought leaders, reputation
Governments	Taxes, political contributions, in-kind contributions, gifts, earmarks	Public health, transportation, education, housing, sewage, vulnerable or at-risk populations, national security

significant rewards with customers and investors that are sustained over time (Conley, 2007).

Firms typically approach employees as community members and neighbors leading to employee-oriented activities such as matching philanthropic contributions, employee-based volunteer programs, and employee-directed work teams as the ideal ways to engage with employees. Unintended consequences stemming from this myopic view are discussed in more detail as myths about impacts in Chapter 7.

Implications for co-creating value

This chapter looked at two traditional mindsets of how value is created or destroyed: an issue-by-issue approach and a stakeholder-by-stakeholder approach. More often than not, an issues or a stakeholder approach is adopted when a firm has a crisis and value is destroyed. More specifically, issues are bad and stakeholders are gadflies that want to bugger up the business. Both mindsets reinforce a back-foot, reactive, and defensive posture to issues and stakeholders as risks that need to be avoided rather than as opportunities to create value. An impacts perspectives examining how value is co-created *and* destroyed is in a business's interest as it seeks to build value as well as mitigate harms that destroy value.

An impacts perspective suggests that issues of high social significance directly under the control of a firm are opportunities for leadership. A company can lead by finding solutions rather than allowing a negotiated settlement through the public policy process, the industry to act at some later point in time, or through the court of public opinion. The risks involved in waiting for regulations to level the playing field include reputational risks of an issue lingering over time and permanently tainting a firm. Corporations, especially those with brand risk, are often quite keen to protect their brand, improve their competitiveness, and appeal to consumers by operating in a way that is in tune with expectations thus acting deliberately, and more rapidly than others.

The business risks of one brand tainting an entire portfolio of brands is very real, just ask General Motors, which recalled 13.8 million vehicles between 2009 and mid-2014 in the US —more than the 12.1 million vehicles it sold in the country during the same time period (Isidore, 2014). Similarly, the risks of one subsidiary tainting the entire portfolio of subsidiaries is very real, just ask Walmart Mexico, which secured construction permits by providing bribes of up to $24 million—when this was highlighted five years after the incident occurred it led to a change in senior leadership (Ackerman, 2012). Walmart's handling of the Rana Plaza fire in Bangladesh explored in Chapter 7 was attributed, in part, to the desire to reduce ongoing operating risks, as Walmart has been criticized for its labor practices and environmental footprint. In order to get ahead of these operational risks, in recent years Walmart has focused on reducing carbon, water, and energy consumption while closely examining its subsidiaries and suppliers in a detailed, systematic way to reduce operating risks (Greenhouse, 2005; Gumbel, 2005; *Environmental Leader*, 2012).

Rather than an impacts perspective based on opportunity and risks, as this chapter illustrates, firms traditionally focus on specific issues. Wisely choosing issues, rather than an issue being foisted upon a firm due to a crisis (BP and its newfound focus on safety as a result of the BP oil spill in the Gulf of Mexico, for example) is part of the implications for co-creating value. The opening question in Chapter 1 asking what community activity should a bank get involved with, for example, often results in banks choosing to create financial literacy programs or providing pro bono financial advisory help. The challenge then becomes one of credibility and uniqueness. Creating financial education activities dedicated to helping customers or the community as new sources of revenue for a bank is a way that might appear to be self-dealing and is important for authenticity.

The Charles Schwab Foundation's support of Operation HOPE—an initiative targeting inner-city youths, teens and adults—aligns the company's skills in financial advising with its desire to enhance lifelong financial literacy without the perception of self-dealing. If these outreach activities were creating unrealistic expectations with get-rich-quick schemes for at-risk populations or tapping a vulnerable population as an immediate source of additional clients then the perception of the Charles Schwab Foundation's intentions and outcomes would, rightly, be challenged.

Similarly, US-based Fannie Mae or Freddie Mac organizations have created financial literacy programs focused on promoting homeownership; built upon the organizations' area of expertise, they have the skills and experience to leverage to make a difference. While other firms might also be interested in expanding homeownership, possessing unique knowledge, specialized skills, and useful information about homeownership, budgeting, home repairs, or financial literacy can all be helpful for the community. Questions abound regarding realtors and financiers operating in their own best interests for short-term financial gains or providing appropriate information to potentially vulnerable populations in ways that are clear and understandable (Perry and Motley, 2009).

Similarly, insurance companies might become involved in after-school programs that support sports teams for middle-school students and at-risk teens. It makes sense for insurance companies to get at-risk teens off the streets, give them something productive to do with their time—build music programs, learn about web-design, digital technologies, virtual communities, create online games—and challenge the teens' creative energy to build career skills in productive ways rather than just hoping that drugs, robbery, rape, and defacing community property will go away. Lower crime rates are better for insurance companies, the local neighborhoods, and the teenagers.

Partnerships among the local municipality, local businesses affected by thefts, neighborhood schools, or community/religious organizations on teen engagement or community sports can create a win–win–win impact. A government with statistics on crime rates, incarcerated youths, at-risk youths, and neighborhood policing efforts also have a vested interest in making the community it serves a safer place, partnering with private enterprises interested in preventing crime, while non-profit neighborhood or religious organizations can assist with local insights, training programs, and other non-financial resources to ensure an ongoing viable program.

One implication of co-creating value through partnerships is credibility. Partnerships involving private companies to address issues of high social significance can create credibility risks as the perception of a firm's involvement might be based on nefarious motivations. Kroger, for example, wants to be considered a local grocery store, yet it sources produce from conflict zones with significant transportation costs. To counter this multinational perception, Kroger actively asks local schools and parent organizations (e.g., parent–teacher associations) what is needed locally in an effort to embed itself into the community.

For companies like Kroger and those in the fast-moving consumer goods (FMCG) industry, credibility can be a critical issue if they support numerous issues. Can one organization be an expert in education programs to boost pride and capacity in local villages, construction of transportation infrastructure to allow access to new markets, and development of a branded washing-up station in a Third World country to reinforce the importance of hygiene in disease prevention? While such projects may respond to community needs, enduring value may not be created when a school is built yet no qualified teachers can be found that are willing to teach students; a railroad is constructed but not maintained; or the sign above the washing-up station is faded and tattered after a few years, suggesting the firm's neglect of the project and the community.

Looking ahead

This chapter explored how myopic approaches to impacts using a traditional mindset entrenched in an issue-by-issue or a stakeholder-by-stakeholder approach can be counterproductive. A myopic view to corporate impacts can be detrimental, as the focus is too narrow on the specific issue or the specific stakeholder without addressing the underlying mechanisms that constrain value creation or destroy value.

There are no easy answers. Partnering, one response to addressing important business issues, can also be problematic. The next chapter, Chapter 10, examines partnerships as one of a number of mechanisms by which firms are creating win–win–wins, changing business models and responding to changed expectations. The next chapter looks beyond individual issues and individual stakeholder interests to examine how the industries in which a firm competes and shapes opportunities for companies to make an impact. By extending the view from individual firms to industries, mechanisms for co-creating value by collective efforts are explored in depth. We examine opportunities ranging from go-it-alone single-firm activities to more intensive, collaborative means for a firm to make an impact.

As competition heats up among firms, we look at cooperation alongside competition by expanding our focus from firms to include the role of industry associations, professional associations, and business associations to effectively shape expectations. These groups of businesses, often membership-oriented working on behalf of a range of organizations, can create a halo effect for the entire industry or draw unwanted attention by not appropriately addressing critical industry impacts. By working on common or collective goals, an industry or a group of firms within the same may interact more effectively with political leaders, civil society organizations, and multilateral actors or, at the broadest level, the general public.

In the penultimate chapter, Chapter 11, we expand further still our focus from firms and their industries to examine how a nation-state's expectations, regulations, and norms affect a business's competitiveness. By creatively, without exploitation, iterating between global and local impacts, Chapter 11 examines how multinational, and domestic firms are finding new ways to co-create value.

10 | *Aligning initiatives and mechanisms for impact*

Are corporate impacts a part of a larger conversation about the firm strategy? Is impact thinking integrated throughout an industry, especially in highly visible industries?

Corporate impacts viewed as:
charitable activities (philanthropy, volunteerism);
investment tools (SRI screening);
enhancing employee loyalty and pride;
new, green, sustainably and ethically sourced products;
a 'warts and all' idea;
reporting exercises (ESG reports);
tangible evidence of values, our beliefs, our purpose;
co-creating value.

In this chapter, we expand our focus from a singular firm to multiple firms, often from the same sector and often in highly visible industries. We explore how groups of firms collectively converge on common goals, such as poverty alleviation or drinking responsibility, and transform industries and their societies. By looking beyond single firms, we highlight particular sweet spots that for some industries (or firms within an industry) are uniquely qualified as forums for co-creating value.

Individual corporations often pick and choose from impacts on which to focus their attention—financial, personnel and facilities, products, and information—rather than looking for opportunities for convergence. Yet a firm's industry, as part of the competitive context, can undermine or reinforce the impacts of a business. Members of some industries can enhance their competitiveness by being a first mover in finding solutions to important impacts. The high-tech industry, for example, relies heavily on creative individuals with specific technical skills, so they are more likely to focus their efforts on impacts related to attracting top talent and retaining a productive workforce. Despite facing similar competitive, cultural, and regulatory pressures in a given market, some high tech firms are better at attracting and retaining top talent by embedding their beliefs throughout the organization.

The Information Technology Industry Council (ITIC), the premier policy and advocacy trade association for the high-tech industry, for example, helps ensure appropriate levels of behavior and share best practices across the industry. Yet the ITIC does not (yet) provide explicit guidelines on workplace conditions. Even in the absence of such industry guidelines, however, ITIC's members enjoy an extremely positive reputation for treatment of their employees. According to a *Forbes* report, ITIC member Microsoft continues to be recognized as one of the top companies for corporate social responsibility in North America, Latin America, and Asia Pacific. Google, another ITIC member, was highlighted in the same article specifically for workplace initiatives: 'Fifty-one percent of consumers across the 15 markets agree that Google is an appealing place to work and that it treats its employees well' (Smith, 2013).

Is it a coincidence that two firms within the same industry, facing similar competitive issues around the world, are voluntarily creating workplace programs to be differentiated and recognized as world leaders in their ability to attract and retain top talent? Workplace impacts, in this example, serve as an expression of corporate identity differentiating a firm from its competitors. Treating employees well is one mechanism by which a firm and its industry narrates, negotiates, and explains how it creates value with employees, investors, through products, and as thought leaders. By bringing workplace issues to the forefront of the high-tech industry, unintended consequences also arise such as questions of diversity in hiring minorities and few women in the top ranks of executives.

Corporations able to choose from a menu of initiatives focused on different impacts differentially benefit stakeholder groups. Given that resources are finite, how does a corporation choose which impacts to pursue, and why? Further, which impacts is it in the firm's best interests to pursue unilaterally and which impacts can it hand off to industry associations for collective action?

Traditionally, the choice among impacts might be based on selecting primary (direct) stakeholders over secondary stakeholders or those with indirect and complicit affects (Clarkson, 1995; Barnett and Salomon, 2006, 2012; McWilliams and Siegel, 2001; McWilliams et al., 2006). Yet, the most immediate, urgent requests of powerful stakeholders might perpetuate a short-term focus with a lot of fire-fighting as issues pop up time and again. Without prioritizing among issues (Porter and Kramer, 2006) or managing portfolios of issues (Mahon et al., 2004), the easiest, most convenient, yet least impactful response might be merely the next good cause (Smith, 2003).

This chapter focuses on making complex choices amid scarce resources under a cloud of uncertainty, requiring careful consideration when a firm should 'go-it-alone' or cooperate with others (Griffin and Prakash, 2014). One critical challenge becomes understanding the pressures stemming from the industry sector in which a firm competes, especially within highly visible industries. High-visibility industries generate the preponderance of jobs created in an area, have extensive externalities associated with their operations (e.g., extraction, deforestation, pollution), or can be thought leaders that influence policymakers. In short, these highly visible industries make significant impacts: have a disproportionate influence on people, such as employees and the potential for job creation; are able to transform industries and consumer demands through their products (e.g., Apple); can affect neighborhoods with local externalities; or affect broader communities as thought leaders able to shape regional, national, or international policy.

For analytic simplicity, we focus on initiatives (what to do) and mechanisms (how to implement). Initiatives (deciding what to do) are classified into functional and cross-functional categories. Functional initiatives emphasize a specific area within an organization, such as human relations, investor relations, marketing, or procurement—often with a (sub-optimal) stakeholder-by-stakeholder approach to issues and impacts as discussed in Chapter 9. That is, human-relations initiatives are likely to focus on hiring, firing, and retention policies while addressing workplace conditions. Investor relations initiatives, on the other hand, are likely to focus on the need and percentage of socially responsible investments and shareholder resolutions concerning governance or social issues. Similarly, consumer initiatives are likely to emphasize products, advertising and sales, distribution, and retailing with procurement practices addressing low-cost, convenient supplies continually over time.

Cross-functional initiatives, on the other hand, focus on leveraging interwoven, organization-wide resources that help define the firm. At a corporate or business-unit level, such as new product development or corporate governance, cross-functional initiatives integrate activities across an organization. New product development, for example, requires the marketing department to cooperate with operations and establish appropriate feedback loops to address concerns from consumers, designers, manufacturers, and retailers. Process changes can improve the purity, yield or consistency of the product, reduce emissions, and spur additional innovations (Griffin and Prakash, 2014). At an industry or multilateral level, cross-functional initiatives such as ISO 14000 involve numerous stakeholders in considering environmental regulations and appropriate environmental management systems.

Cross-functional initiatives might also draw insights from multiple geographies. That is, an initiative to improve governance of mining practices in Canada might examine practices elsewhere in the Americas, such as Mexico, Chile, and Colombia (Dashwood, 2014). Developing governance mechanisms to share practices and generate awareness is part of the process of successfully transferring practices across subsidiaries, firms, and nation-states (Barnett and Sunyoung, 2012).

On the other hand, the mechanisms (deciding how to achieve impacts) that firms create to achieve their desired impacts are classified into solo or collaborative categories. This categorization reflects the preference of a firm to work in isolation or in concert with others (e.g., trade associations or less formal multilateral efforts). By going it alone, a firm directs its resources and energies to achieve the impact it desires, often in a compressed timeframe with specific deliverables at the end of a project.

If a company prefers to work collaboratively, it might enlist a professional or industry association to assist in addressing stakeholder concerns. If, for example, the entire industry is perceived to be only as strong as the weakest link (e.g., the extraction industry with its industry associations EITI and ICMMA) keeping a vigilant eye on the worst performers is in everyone's best interest as the entire industry is tarred with the same bad behavior of the poorest performer. Alternatively, if the best performers can gradually pull away from the bottom performers and distinguish themselves as a specialized club without repercussions, the threshold of expected business behavior can shift permanently. Collaborating with international or local NGOs or creating public–private partnerships might enhance a firm's competitiveness by addressing a complex, entrenched issue. In the example of extraction industry, early efforts of individual firms to address HIV/ AIDS were a differentiator until industry norms shifted.

Assuming impacts reflect strategic choices made by firms, two sweet spots are highlighted. First, discovering synergies is one sweet spot that emerges when an industry association, for example, converges interests among a broad set of stakeholders. That is, as firms manage their portfolio of impacts across a range of stakeholders (investors, employees, consumers, suppliers, distributors and multiple communities), opportunities to converge interests emerge. Whereas a single firm may be able to devote limited resources to its diverse constellation of stakeholders, industry associations might be in a better position to help share best practices, understand trends, and create enduring outcomes.

A second sweet spot emerges by focusing on impacts instead of thinking about discrete initiatives (Wood and Jones, 1995). Looking beyond a discrete issue-by-issue approach makes sense for industry and professional associations because most issues, impacts and stakeholders, as discussed in Chapter 9, are neither isolated nor contained to a single firm. Impacts transcend traditional boundaries.

Figure 10.1 juxtaposes different ways to think about initiatives and mechanisms creating four different combinations. In the next section we examine the initiatives (what to do) and the mechanisms (how to implement) followed by four combinations aligning initiatives and mechanisms.

Initiatives (*what* to do)

Deciding among *what* activities a corporation should pursue and *how* a corporation manages its impact portfolio requires a company

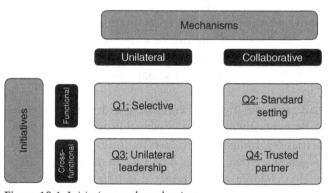

Figure 10.1 Initiatives and mechanisms

to choose from among numerous alternatives. The decision focuses on selecting initiatives that utilize unique corporate resources: skills, expertise, social capital, and stakeholder networks (Adler and Kwon, 2002; Dyer and Singh, 1998; Freeman et al., 2010).

Different firms in the beer industry, for example, facing similar competitive and political environments, often choose different portfolios of initiatives to pursue (Griffin and Weber, 2006). As a corporation formulates *what* it wants to accomplish, translating its resolve into concrete action requires a focus on the mechanisms of *how* decisions are implemented (Griffin and Prakash, 2014).

Functional initiatives: human resources, marketing, and corporate governance

Human resource (HR) initiatives, for example, might aim at inclusive policies increasing opportunities for all full-time employees, contract workers, and potential employees. These initiatives might emphasize specific issues such as women's representation, diversity, stigma, and ethnic or linguistic capabilities. These workplace/labor initiatives, as discussed in Chapters 3 and 9, are often championed by a single department (HR), appeal to current employees while signaling to prospective employees how they will be treated once hired (Jones et al., 2014b).

HR initiatives, as we talked about in Chapter 3 on employee impacts, might include the number of jobs created, safety, ensuring living wages, accident reduction, or lost time accidents. Other impacts might detail compliance with extant laws such as documents ensuring no child labor, forced labor, or human trafficking, while encouraging diversity, minority representation, religious tolerance, or stigma alleviation. Alternatively, employee impacts might be about healthcare (if not state-provided), well-being, benefits and pensions, or workplace initiatives such as ombudsman, training, and development.

Similarly, marketing initiatives and complying with voluntary codes co-create value by explicitly disclosing information and creating information assymetries regarding how products are sourced, used, or disbursed. That is, knowing that animals didn't die in the production of the product or that children are not targeted in beer ads might be of value to consumers.

Marketing initiatives often emphasize new product features, such as the introduction of seatbelts or the introduction of hybrid cars. Marketing-based initiatives can help emphasize the social and environmental features of products. Green marketing, pass-through philanthropy for consumers, improved product functionality (e.g., miniaturization), and designing new products are often the easiest changes to make initially, since savings are readily quantifiable to skeptical managers.

A firm may voluntarily create an advertising code of conduct, or work with an industry association implementing this type of voluntary standard. An advertising code of conduct, for example, addresses questions of products being advertised fairly without targeting vulnerable populations. Alternatively, a voluntarily code of advertising might encourage prohibiting behavior such as youth smoking or underage drinking.

A complicating factor is businesses selling products to intermediaries (e.g., clients, retail, or wholesalers) who in turn resell, repackage, or distribute to the consumers, the end users. Take the beer industry in the United States, for example. Beer manufacturers sell to retailers or wholesalers since tiered regulations restrict beer manufacturers from selling direct to consumers. Pharmaceuticals, on the other hand, are able to advertise direct to consumers (DTC). The proliferation of DTC advertising led to a large number of lawsuits against Merck in the early part of the twenty-first century after it recalled its cholesterol-lowering medicine Vioxx, which was linked to increased risk of heart attacks and death, eventually costing the company nearly $5 billion to settle lawsuits (Prakash and Valentine, 2007). The end users may also misuse or abuse the product, or use the product in ways that were never intended such as off-label use of prescription medications with deleterious multiplier effects as discussed in Chapters 3, 5 and 6.

Marketing initiatives often address perceived product risks, such as the consistency between the way in which the product is advertised and its brand's promise. For example, if a product is promoted as safe, high-quality, durable, and uncontaminated, but is subsequently recalled then employees, consumers, and regulators might question the consistency between the external messaging and the product itself. Understanding brand risk contagions could push firms to spend more time and resources on non-financial stakeholder strategies to strengthen their brands as we saw regarding GM at the beginning of the chapter.

Procurement initiatives are another example of functional initiatives. Procurement initiatives are directed at obtaining necessary inputs such as capital, raw materials, and technology. Procurement initiatives along the supply chain might include supplier codes of conduct or systems to monitor a firm's carbon, water, or energy footprints. Other initiatives such as securing permits to operate (e.g., extraction site licenses, fishing permits) as well as human rights, labor, and workplace issues are often handled within the supply chain (Swartz, 2010).

Starbucks, from the example in Chapter 1 created a strong supply chain of Fair Trade coffee growers in Colombia to ensure certain quality standards and prohibit child labor in exchange for guarantees from Starbucks to guarantee purchase of coffee beans. By working with the Colombian government, USAID, and Colombian farmers, Starbucks was able to strike a wide-ranging deal, with material impacts on its products, guaranteeing coffee bean supplies from one of the largest coffee-bean producing nations in the world.

While many procurement initiatives are enforced through contracts, the potential multiplier effects of these initiatives might transform an industry or an area. For example, trade or professional associations such as local Chambers of Commerce, the Carbon Disclosure Project (CDP), or the International Code of Conduct Association (ICOCA) purposely build alliances to create, monitor, and enforce common policies among members.

Cross-functional initiatives: development, environment, and corporate governance

Development initiatives are often directed at building infrastructure that in turn creates social capital in an area, which in turn creates future business opportunities. For example, building telecommunications infrastructure might enable a fisherman to call different wholesalers to find the best market price for fish caught that morning. Increasing access to information by removing information asymmetries regarding prices (and price gouging) can in theory strengthen commerce, stabilize households, and improve public health, education, or general welfare. A telecommunications infrastructure project, in this example, often combines efforts across a company—project management, procurement, grant-writing, and perhaps partnerships with public agencies. These projects are cross-functional requiring coordination and collaboration across the firm or across multiple firms.

Environmental initiatives, on the other hand, seek to generate positive environmental externalities or reduce negative externalities associated with producing goods and services. Environmental risks often require cross-functional initiatives as environmental impacts can include water, solid waste, emissions, or congestion externalities. To address these multifaceted environmental issues, procurement departments might need to coordinate with operations, which in turn might work with marketing, government, and community affairs to learn what is needed, to understand which changes are appropriate to implement, and to be transparent in the changes to operations. Environmental initiatives, highlighted in Chapters 5 and 6 as examples of spillover and multiplier effects, can create significant risks to some businesses.

Corporate governance initiatives are another set of cross-functional activities as they seek to improve corporate governance by creating rules and setting the tone at the top regarding appropriate business behavior. Reviewing the risks and vulnerabilities of the firm are key responsibilities of the board of directors with effects felt throughout the firm. Corporate governance initiatives could include authorizing reports on board diversity, responding to shareholder resolutions to unlock value by reorganizing the firm, or changing the board composition and disbursement of profit (Hillman et al., 2001).

These cross-functional initiatives often fall within a duty of care and a duty of oversight for fiscal health and the ongoing concern of the firm in the interests of the shareholders. During times of crises, such as when a takeover or acquisition proposal is being deliberated, the board's corporate governance initiative might seek investor protection, new financial disclosure requirements, limits of executive compensation, and in doing so reflect the priority of investors, executives, and public disclosure, respectively.

Mechanisms (*how* to implement)

A variety of mechanisms can be employed to achieve the desired corporate impacts, translating a firm's beliefs into concrete commitments, as a firm *implements* their activities to achieve the desired impact. Firms may have a favored mode of engagement, such as filing lawsuits or creating internal investigations. Or a firm may prefer to adapt the ways it works collectively based on the relationships, the information, and the resources available (Shaffer and Hillman, 2000). Increasingly, public–private partnerships (PPPs) and other types of collaborative arrangements are popular vehicles for corporations. We identify both firm-focused unilateral mechanisms and collaborative mechanisms to achieve desired impacts in the text that follows (Griffin and Prakash, 2014).

Solo mechanisms

Solo mechanisms are generally simple, practical ways of unilaterally changing how a firm manufactures a product, sells services, or conducts its business. A petrochemical company can change ingredients in automobile lubricants to reduce friction, increase the car's efficiency, and decrease wear of the engine while also reducing carbon emissions. Selling the new lubricant based on its carbon emission reductions may be attractive in new, niche markets with the profits pocketed by the firm.

Unilateral activities to reduce carbon, water, or energy consumption can have a significant effect on the bottom line for large MNCs. A multinational telecommunications company may install 'shower curtains' in its data warehousing units, isolating its heating and cooling areas, which in turn reduces electricity usage and saves the company money. The telecom company may then experiment with safe chilling temperatures to save even more money, while also ensuring the integrity of the data storage computers. And if the telecommunications company were to work with an governmental agency such as the US Underwriters Laboratory (UL) to ensure that data warehousing units can be chilled at a lower temperature (saving energy and money) for all data warehousing firms, a game-changer in industry standards can spread the electricity and cost savings across an entire industry.

Go-it-alone activities are often motivated by risks specific to the firm. The risks may stem from a current crisis or be anticipatory, as a form of insurance against future losses (Godfrey, 2005; Godfrey et al., 2009). As a firm develops its expertise in a few, selective, go-it-alone activities, it can coordinate relationships, build transparency, and decrease transaction costs in order to become the trusted intermediary.

As a trusted intermediary it influences the type of information shared, creating information asymmetries and the potential for information arbitrage. By setting expectations of the expected risks and corresponding impacts, these risk management techniques, however, are predicated on the belief that risks are known and accurately measured. When systemic shifts (e.g., the global financial crisis) or rapid changes (e.g., technology and social media trends) prompt modifications in risk calculation, existing methods can become rapidly outdated resulting in a firm or industry facing intense public scrutiny.

Another example of unilateral initiatives is cash and in-kind donations by the firm or an independent (private) charitable foundation associated with the firm. These product donations or cash giveaways are often considered a waste of shareholder's resources if not tied to the core purpose of the firm (see Chapter 7). Citizens dependent upon daily dosages of medicines to treat chronic diseases such as diabetes, heart disease, or HIV/AIDs, for example, can be acutely impacted by fluctuations in corporate donations (Annan, 2001). Similarly, seasonal contributions of food products during holidays, for example, might create unintended consequences of spoiled foods or highlight insufficient distribution, hampering the largess from alleviating hunger. Thus, unilateral initiatives are often enhanced by collaborative partnering to ensure an ongoing, sustainable supply of goods and services. We talk about collaborative partnering in the next section.

Collaborative partnering

Ranging in formality, duration, and complexity, collaborative mechanisms include different arrangements of public–private partnerships (PPPs), tripartite partnerships (public–private–civil society), or public sector–NGO relations. Public–private partnerships are often the most prevalent. Formal contracts between corporations and non-for-profit, quasi-governmental, or non-governmental organizations (Austin and Seitanidi, 2012a, 2012b), PPPs also include less formal, more ad hoc arrangements combining the resources and capabilities of both sectors.

Collaborative mechanisms often focus on complex issues difficult to solve via one sector. For example, housing, social welfare, or infrastructure projects to build airports or create Wi-Fi networks across a state often require funding, construction, and maintenance coordination among the public, private, and civil society sectors. Collaborative mechanisms might be formal long-term contracts with numerous signatures from all parties specifying job descriptions, expected timelines and deliverables. Formal collaborations designed around functional activities such as abolishing human trafficking may set standards specifying minimal thresholds of expectations.

Industry and trade associations often create collaborative agreements to create value by sharing information (see Chapter 8). Agreements such as Fair Trade for coffee and cocoa growers share information on growing conditions, fertilizing, and harvesting to improve product yields, enhance price, and guarantee demand. Firms working with Fair Trade and its partners such as Rainforest Alliance Network coordinate the application of limited resources, educate members, focus their efforts, and leverage knowledge. When collaboration results in a change from hierarchical command and control to one in which firms become interdependent upon the behavior of others, industry standards are often voluntarily adopted to ensure efficiency and avoid the loss of control (Thauer, 2014).

Alternatively PPPs may be informal agreements to build trusted partners and improve coordination in the unlikely event of specific crises. For example, it is in the interests of communities, firms, and local officials to voluntarily practice emergency management drills using mock mass casualty exercises if these business risks exist at a local manufacturing plant. A mock exercise can improve coordination among law enforcement, a firm's security detail, and local emergency management personnel to benefit the local communities with improved information, creating an advantage if a real-life event occurred.

As organizations become more interdependent with other organizations through social networking or crowdfunding platforms, new business and partnering models that co-create value are emerging based on information sharing and built upon trust. A relatively new company, Nation Builder (www.nationbuilder.com), connects like-minded people via blogs, Wikipedia entries, tweets, and search engines with databases to monitor and customize engagement strategies. Sharing a common affinity to a university or a brand, for example, these networks are changing the ways in which collaboration and value creation can occur spontaneously in a rapidly changing milieu.

Collaborative agreements to develop financial literacy skills are creating unique partnerships between businesses, community organizations, and university students that teach more students about personal finance than many organizations can reach on their own. University students work over a period of six months to help elementary students develop the business skills to open and operate a lemonade stand (www.lemonadeday.org) creating a win-win-win. As a coordinated effort, numerous lemonade stands are opened on the same day across multiple neighborhoods in a public school district generating excitement, developing business skills, and forging partnerships that a single organization couldn't accomplish alone. Transferring management skills, confidence, and expertise, such as advertising or project management, can inspire value creation in individuals, households, and small businesses.

Implications for co-creating value

In the ordinary course of doing business, corporations have the potential to create mutual benefits through financial, employee, product, and information-based impacts (Chapters 3, 4, and 5). Deciding what to do and how to achieve the desired outcome (e.g., for the firm to forge ahead by itself or build a network with others) requires clear objectives, commitment of resources, and coordination with internal and/or external stakeholders to achieve consistency and build credibility that endures over time. Yet, the firm, embedded in a network of relations, doesn't operate in isolation. The context of value creation is important: issues, industries and nation-states. This chapter examined industry-level collaborative mechanisms to create value.

When looking at groups of firms within an industry, comparing and contrasting impacts can be quite complicated. For example, consider Table 10.1 listing five different companies within the same industry along several material impacts deemed important by the entire industry. Evaluating the firms along these impacts can lead to perverse results. Since all companies perform poorly in governance, does that mean that the entire industry should take up governance issues? Since all companies are relatively good at addressing environmental issues, does that mean this industry can be used as a benchmark for extraction industries having significant, longstanding material environmental issues, rendering all firms approximately equal in managing material

Table 10.1 *Comparing five companies in one industry on six material impacts*

	Co. 1	Co. 2	Co. 3	Co. 4	Co. 5
	(scale: 1-low; 6-high)				
Education	5	6	1	5	4
Employees	3	3	3	4	4
Environment	5	6	5	6	5
Governance	2	2	2	2	1
Supply Chain	2	2	6	2	5
Community	6	3	3	2	2
Average	3.83	3.67	3.33	3.5	3.5

impacts? Or, does an average of all six categories make sense? Or, do the companies differentiate themselves on individualized impacts based on what they do relatively better than their rivals, thus creating specialties for each firm without improving the overall industry impacts?

Looking ahead

For many companies, a significant challenge is creating a coherent and consistent strategy to co-create value that effectively addresses critical business impacts. We have examined impacts, spillover and multiplier effects, and the context in which decisions are made as issues, industries, and nation-states moderate the process of co-creating value. As many businesses operate among multiple countries, the next chapter introduces some nuances of co-creating value in a global economy.

Assessing how country-level pressures affect the value creation process is difficult due to the sheer number of countries involved for each company. And translating global initiatives for local contexts is made even more difficult by the lack of consistency and accessibility of country-specific information (Barnett and Sunyoung, 2012). Conglomerates face a similar challenge. Conglomerates with unrelated, diversified units have, by design, a very high level of complexity that makes addressing corporate impacts more difficult. Industry-level benchmarking and best practices often don't apply when examining several subsidiaries within a conglomerate.

In the next chapter, Chapter 11, we examine positive and negative multiplier effects of operating across multiple countries. One of the key challenges is appropriately leveraging a standard global strategy while retaining culturally sensitive products and value-creation processes. This global–local tension is explored in more detail, with the complicating factor of more institutions such as multilaterals crowding out individual corporations' messages in a global economy.

11 | *Integrating global and local impacts in a global economy*

At present, a common understanding of acceptable worldwide management practices that creates (without destroying) value does not exist.
A common understanding may, indeed, never exist. Yet demands for
universal standards ensuring minimal safeguards, with accountability
and verification, are accelerating at an accelerating rate (Donaldson,
1996; Donaldson and Dunfee, 1999; Gilbert and Rasche, 2008; Hess,
2008; Waddock, 2008b; Webb, 2008). Global governance standards
bridge the gap by building universal trust with consistency and credibility based on verification while being sensitive to local needs with
flexibility and customization (Gilbert and Rasche, 2008; Zammuto,
2008). Implications for achieving these dual objectives—unified
global governance standards alongside flexibility for voluntary, local
adaptation—are examined in this chapter.

Creating value, especially in large MNCs, often raises concomitant
questions about human trafficking, poverty, and disaster management while remaining sensitive to relevant local issues such homelessness, workplace conditions, or living wages (Scherer et al., 2013). Yet,
global issues are often perceived as too demanding, too large, and/or
too complex for a single corporation to make a meaningful impact
(Weick, 1984).

All too often, a firm's response to global mandates is tied to the
firm's ability to create value and its standing in their local neighborhoods (Rasche and Kell, 2010). Alternatively, numerous prior, ultimately unsuccessful attempts by well-meaning and/or well-funded
governments, individuals, worship houses, or community groups
that the potential positive impact of a private business is obscured
at best.

With seemingly extensive rules-based oversight from boards of
directors as well as local, provincial, and federal governments, a gap
persists between voluntary corporate initiatives and formal policies
that provide oversight and guidance for corporations, often referred

244

to as a firm's corporate governance (Griffin and Prakash 2014; Gilbert and Rasche, 2008; Goranova and Ryan, 2014). Yet, why, with layers of corporate oversight do negative spillovers stemming from corporate (in)actions persist? And, what is a company to do in its quest to continually create value while addressing its potential for destroying value, too? In short, why should a firm bother trying to address its global impacts at all? The quick answer is: it is often in the firm's best interests to do something—however small or seemingly insignificant initially. The longer answer is explored in this chapter.

Two underlying assumptions at the interface of corporate impacts and corporate governance (CG) are addressed: first, a focus on corporate impacts with its values- or market-based emphasis is, potentially, one means to voluntarily, yet imperfectly, address the mandated, rules-based governance gaps. Second, rules-based global standards often underestimate the complexity inherent in creating adaptable, long-term solutions to entrenched, local issues. That is, firms are often navigating in a multilevel game (e.g., a 3D chess game) on a day-to-day basis, creating numerous accountability and execution problems that extend well beyond the reach of a boardroom.

Corporate impacts and global governance: an introduction

Certainly, if corporations can prevent something bad from happening, they should do so, regardless of the location where the harm is occurring. And, if corporations are directly involved in the creation of a product known to harm consumers or create unsafe workplaces then they should stop. Beyond these dictums reflecting a minimalistic human rights norm of 'do no harm,' the lack of clear global accountability can obfuscate the externalities directly or indirectly stemming from the activities of corporations. While the home country might have explicit laws outlawing certain behaviors, the host country may be chosen precisely because they do not. So what is a firm to do? The minimum required by local, extant law or voluntarily take actions beyond compliance with extant law that address the corporation's impacts?

Traditionally, a firm's response was predicated on its competitive, product-market context: the twin pressures of globalization and localization (Bartlett and Ghoshal, 1989). While multinational corporations (MNCs) are viewed as agents of global economic integration, large organizations are impacted by pressures, often in ways they cannot adequately control. With globalization, MNCs must manage different expectations of more and varied stakeholders. Consequently, MNCs negotiate with an array of global stakeholders in a variety of arenas: global activist groups who oppose them, international regimes that govern them, and 24/7 media that scrutinizes them. MNCs often need to respond to active investigations from employees, suppliers, consumers, political actors, and institutions in their home and host countries, yet they may choose to remain quiet. It is within this multi-national context, with blurred and bright lines that might change from day to day, that we critically examine a firm's impacts with imperfect rules-based corporate governance in the process of co-creating value.

Focusing on an MNC's portfolio of impacts looks beyond short-term profits to appropriately address expectations stemming from multiple stakeholders: suppliers, consumers, communities, and governments in addition to investors (Griffin and Prakash, 2014). A firm's traditional responsibilities are depicted as pursuing profits while simultaneously complying with extant law 'without fraud or deception' (Friedman, 1970). Functioning honestly, demonstrating environmental steward-ship, treating labor with dignity, providing safe products/services, and enhancing the welfare of their communities are actions that go above and beyond compliance with extant law are voluntary actions (McWilliams and Siegel, 2001). While voluntary activities may also be in the best interests of the firm they are voluntary (Prakash and Griffin, 2012) and not often directly aligned with a firm's desired impacts. That is, *if* firms can earn the trust of critical stakeholders; differentiate themselves from competitors; use information from stakeholders to improve operations, products, and delivery systems; create product/service innovations; and signal their credibility to a range of stakeholders, then voluntary, beyond-compliance initiatives are in the best interest of the firm and the stakeholders it depends upon. Trust is assumed to exist. Interdependency means making the firm stronger requires strengthening stakeholder relations too.

Some companies, such as Coca-Cola, have learned to thrive in such a challenging socio-political environment by creating a web of global relationships premised on voluntary initiatives. Coca-Cola, operating in more than 200 countries and partnering with more than 300 bottlers, prides itself on its ability to maintain a local 'feel' in the communities in which it operates, such as its global 5 by 20 initiative to empower five million women along its value chain by 2020

(Jenkins et al., 2013). Effective voluntary programs can potentially correct a failure in the market for virtue (Vogel, 2005) thereby allowing firms to enjoy a de facto 'social license to operate' (Gunningham et al., 2003).

Critics, however, offer a narrower, less sanguine view of a corporation inappropriately addressing negative spillover and multiplier effects through philanthropic giveaways or compliance-driven initiatives. Echoing the theme espoused by Friedman (1970), a Heritage Foundation paper notes the following:

> Like a vitamin regimen that exceeds recommended daily amounts, corporate social responsibility (CSR)—once seen as a healthy thing in small doses—now poses a toxic threat to American business ... However, if the latest and most radical wave of supposedly 'voluntary' CSR standards, principles, and strategies is fully embraced by the corporate world, it will unleash additional efforts by CSR proponents (special-interest NGOs and intrusive government bureaucrats) to redefine the very purpose of business and lash private companies to ever greater burdens and constraints. (Roberts and Markley, 2012)

Being distracted by voluntary responses to the sometimes conflicting and sometimes cohering expectations of a milieu of domestic and global stakeholders, political actors, and home and host country institutions (Prakash and Griffin, 2012), it is difficult, if not impossible, for a firm to remain competitive (McWilliams and Siegel, 2001). Further, being compliant with extant local laws is sufficient as provincial or federal municipalities are the appropriate actors to define minimally acceptable terms of exchange and externalities (Friedman, 1970).

Yet, increasingly, multilateral organizations are leading conversations on adopting minimal governance standards of worldwide business practices. Global governance standards, ideally, overcome limits of nation-state oversight (Baron, 1995; Waddock, 2008b) and bridge the gap between achieving a firm's goals while ensuring firms operate in tune with expectations of local communities (Gates, 2008; Waddock, 2008b; Zadek, 2003, 2004). Bridging the gap requires genuineness and good governance (Donaldson, 1996; Donaldson and Dunfee, 1999; KPMG, 2008; Williams, 2004; Windsor, 2004, 2006) with significant managerial implications for co-creating enduring value.

This chapter proposes an MNC's successful adoption of global governance standards is conditioned by the firm's ability to achieve a unified global focus while simultaneously developing its ability to respond meaningfully to local constituencies (Arthaud-Day, 2005; Baron, 1995; Boddewyn, 2003; Gilbert and Rasche, 2008; Porter and Kramer, 2006; Webb, 2008). Enduring commitments to global governance standards can create positive tensions that unleash innovations within MNCs (Bies et al., 2007) to enhance efficiency while simultaneously encouraging innovations and cultural sensitivity to promote effectiveness within local communities. Rather than being caught in the middle between local/federal government mandates requiring new jobs in local areas, for example, and competitive demands to create scale of economies for cost savings, MNCs are encouraged to innovate in products and process to set new standards.

The chapter proceeds as follows: first, we examine two rationales for global governance standards: legitimacy (leading to global consistency) and information disclosure (encouraging local adaptation). Second, we examine traditional MNCs' competitive strategies based on product-market strategies (Bartlett and Ghoshal, 1991, 1998). These product market strategies are incomplete for modern managers without awareness of socio-political and cultural pressures requiring local sensitivity towards firms' impacts: finances, employees in the workplace, products along the value chain, and information-sharing. Spillover and multiplier effects from mismanaging firms impacts in a global economy can be quite significant. Yet solutions are generally not scalable. Finally, we discuss the implications of increased legitimacy and information disclosure by focusing on firms 'stuck in the middle': firms failing to address local sensitivities and not exhibiting minimal levels of acceptable behavior worldwide.

Global governance

Global governance standards highlighting accountability and engagement have become increasingly *global* as well as more commonplace in the twenty-first century (Gilbert and Rasche, 2008; Hess, 2001, 2007, 2008). Ranging from multilateral-led collaborations on guidelines for management, codes of conduct, and assurance verification (e.g., Global Reporting Initiative GRI-G3, ISO 26000, Carbon Disclosure Project, AccountAbility 1000 Framework, Social Accountability 8000, OECD MNE Guidelines); industry-led initiatives (e.g., Responsible Care, Sullivan and Caux Principles, Equator Principles, Extraction Industry Transparency Initiative); firm-led voluntary reporting (Kolk and van

Tulder, 2002; KPMG, 2008; Zadek, 2003); as well as nation-states with mandatory financial and ethical disclosures (e.g., the UK's Companies Act of 2006; the American Sarbanes-Oxley Act of 2002), these rating, ranking, and evaluation systems exist and are likely to continue to persist (Gilbert and Rasche, 2008; Kell, 2005; Porter and Kramer, 2006; Waddock, 2008b).

Global governance standards serve two primary purposes. First, they build legitimacy. And second, they provide valuable information to firms and stakeholders through disclosure and verification processes (Hess, 2001, 2007; Hess et al., 2008; Tetrault-Sirsly and Lamertz, 2008; Waddock, 2008b; Webb, 2008; Zadek, 2003, 2004).

The benefits of legitimacy-building and education of myriad stakeholders, however, are weighed against their perception as unnecessary hurdles creating unfair cost burdens with extensive time commitments for multinationals (Friedman, 1970; Gilbert and Rasche, 2008; Jensen, 2002; Porter and Kramer, 2006; Rasche and Esser, 2006). To wit, disclosure can be perceived as 'nothing more than public relations gestures meant to ward off grassroots attacks by social activists' (Fry and Hock, 1976, cited by Ullmann, 1985, p. 542) or as a means to divert public attention away from negative externalities (Laufer, 2003).

While one purpose of global standards is to build legitimacy, implementation of global standards can undermine (or reinforce) the intentions of the governance policy. Decoupling the firm's formal structure and disclosure policies from its core operations can enable local activities to vary in response to practical and cultural considerations (Meyer and Rowan, 1983; Tolbert and Zucker, 1983). However, an easily decoupled structure or disclosure policy can provide the appearance of conformity to external expectations while insulating much of the organization from those expectations (Weaver et al., 1999, p. 541).

It's the inherent tension while implementing global standards—the shortcoming of standards as unfair cost burdens and empty gestures while enhancing legitimacy with appropriate information disclosure—that highlights the need for innovative management and governance in the coming decades.

Legitimacy

One rationale for global governance standards is obtaining or maintaining organizational legitimacy (Aerts et al., 2006; Deegan, 2002; Deegan at al., 2002; Milne and Patten, 2002; O'Donovan, 2002;

Wilmshurst and Frost, 2000). Global standards build the legitimacy of MNCs by institutionalizing consistent hypernorms, policies, or structures across nation-states and across business units for the entire corporation (DiMaggio and Powell, 1983; Donaldson and Dunfee, 1999; Gilbert and Rasche, 2008; Webb, 2008). MNEs face unique challenges because they operate in multiple institutional contexts (Kostova and Zaheer, 1999). An MNC headquartered in Copenhagen, for example, with subsidiaries in China, Brazil, and Australia must obtain and maintain legitimacy in each of these disparate arenas. Global governance standards are one tactic for organizations to obtain and maintain legitimacy (Driscoll, 2006).

Institutionalizing accountability hypernorms and policies throughout an MNC requires a corporate commitment to identifying acceptable and penalizing unacceptable behavior (Donaldson and Dunfee, 1999; Gilbert and Rasche, 2008). Using an integrated stakeholder approach (Clarkson, 1995; Freeman et al., 2007; Waddock, 2008b; Wood et al., 2006), firm's socio-economic-political and ethical priorities are made explicit, internalized, verified, and communicated (Clarkson, 1995; Donaldson and Dunfee, 1999; Hess, 2008). Management systems, infrastructure, incentives, and communication flows, by design, reinforce management's commitment to global accountability. In lieu of management commitment to global standards being a 'nice-to-do,' discretionary, or window-dressing exercise (Carroll, 1979; Porter and Kramer, 2006; Weaver et al., 1999), verification, accountability, and adoption of acceptable behaviors and norms can be assured (Gilbert and Rasche, 2008). In assuring its various constituencies, legitimacy is conferred upon the MNC (DiMaggio and Powell, 1983; Hess, 2008).

Multilateral-led global standards support institutionalizing minimal thresholds of acceptable behavior across nation-states and across issues (DiMaggio and Powell, 1983; Donaldson and Dunfee, 1999; Donaldson and Preston, 1995; Galaskiewicz, 1991; Mahon et al., 2004; Waddock, 2008b; Windsor, 2004). Bundling socio-political-ethical concerns (e.g., simultaneously considering carbon, water, and energy footprints) encourages integration of discrete activities. Integration can create innovation through efficiencies, effectiveness, and/or efficacy. Effective integration is neither trivial nor straightforward as it requires managing across multiple and often conflicting arenas of resolution: employee attitudes and behaviors, local neighbors, provincial governments, federal agencies, stock market analysts as well as the court of public opinion (Mahon et al., 2004; Windsor, 2004).

Under increased pressure to build worldwide legitimacy and bundle related concerns (Porter and Kramer, 2006; Rasche and Esser, 2006), MNCs have adopted process-oriented systems to prioritize, professionalize, and more comprehensively respond to governance demands (e.g., GRI). At times voluntarily and at other times through mandates, these process-oriented systems encourage holistic thinking about a firm's inputs (e.g., natural resources, raw materials, and energy), throughputs (e.g., waste discharged into air), and/or outcomes (e.g., access to medicines or hospitals). Professionalized, systematic processes embedded within accountability standards verify if, when, and the extent to which MNCs consistently do what it says it will do with myriad stakeholders around the world (Hess, 2007; Zadek, 1998, 2004).

Information disclosure

A second—and increasingly important—rationale for global standards is information disclosure. Standardized disclosure from widely accepted accountability norms increases the depth and breadth of information available to all stakeholders (e.g., potential and current financiers, employees, regulators, etc.). A benefit of mandated disclosure is standardized reporting formats with similar information reported across issue areas allowing for ease of comparison across companies and across subsidiaries (Gilbert and Rasche, 2008). Widespread and standardized information disclosure allows stakeholders to identify best practices and learn from the experiences among many corporations. Disclosure ensures access to information allowing 'interested stakeholders to act upon the information as they see fit' (Hess, 2008, p. 457).

Voluntary firm-led and industry-led accountability initiatives have sought to gain information advantages and retain managers' autonomy by voluntarily reporting socio-political activities (Epstein, 1969; Kolk and van Tulder, 2002). As one form of voluntary self-regulation, integrated reports can assist in gaining competitive advantages (Logsdon and Wood, 2002, 2005; Tetrault-Sirsly and Lamertz, 2008). By understanding their own strengths and weaknesses, identifying potential opportunities for improvement, and benchmarking themselves against competition, global governance standards enhance organizational learning (Zadek, 1998). This, in turn, can lead to continuous improvement in efficiency and management, resulting in lower costs, potentially increased access to capital, and enhanced local responsiveness.

Information disclosure provides advantages with specific stakeholders (Gilbert and Rasche, 2008) such as prospective and current employees (Greening and Turban, 2000) and shareholders (Margolis and Walsh, 2001). Readily available information, in turn, engages broader stakeholder networks such as creditors evaluating investments and suppliers of suppliers trying to remain on an MNC's accepted suppliers list (Dunham et al., 2006; Phillips and Caldwell, 2005; Waddock, 2008b). Tapping into broad stakeholder networks can lead to better scanning of consumer/regulatory demands, anticipating issues and responding appropriate to current issues before they become crises (Freeman, 1984; Mahon, 1989; Mitroff et al., 1987; Pfeffer and Salancik, 1978; Wartick and Mahon, 1994).

Global governance standards also enhance trust by creating safeguards with information verification systems (Friedman, 1970; Gilbert and Rasche, 2008; Jensen, 2002; Jones, 1995; Wicks et al., 1999; Williamson, 1985). By influence and mandate, global standards enhance information disclosure in conjunction with third-party verification systems (Frooman, 1999; Jones, 1995; Rasche and Esser, 2006). Verification alongside disclosure affects perceptions of the organization (Daft and Weick, 1984; Jones, 1995; Rindova et al., 2005) as well as the ability to secure resources (Post et al., 2002) and to engage stakeholders (Hart and Sharma, 2004; Harting et al., 2006)— enhancing local responsiveness.

Overall, verification enhances reputation (Fombrun and Shanley, 1990; Rindova et al., 2005; Zammuto, 2008) and satisfices stakeholders (Tetrault-Sirsly and Lamertz, 2008) while providing for the common good (Margolis and Walsh, 2003) in local neighborhoods, across nation-states and across issues (Gilbert and Rasche, 2008).

Examples

Accountability standards to enhance governance are not new (Hess, 2001, 2007) yet are increasingly *global* (Hess, 2008). We highlight several government-led, industry-led, and multilateral-led accountability standards to illustrate how each set of initiatives differ in balancing the dual objectives of: legitimacy via consistency across nation-states and information disclosure via sensitivity to local responses. For a more comprehensive listing of global standards see Waddock (2008b) and Hess (2008).

Formal, government-led governance standards have existed since governments were chartered (e.g., Magna Carta in the UK). Focused on specific nation-states, these standards serve to reinforce an understanding of legitimate ethical, legal, and social behavior of citizens (subjects) and corporations (Baron, 1995, 1997; Epstein, 1969) embedded within national business systems (Matten and Moon, 2008). Government regulations are coercive mechanisms to ensure minimally acceptable levels of legitimate corporate behavior (DiMaggio and Powell, 1983). Information disclosure is increasingly part of government-led regulations but information requirements differ from nation-state to nation-state. Government-led accountability standards range from: regulations on accounting practices (e.g., GAAP) and materially significant disclosures (UK Management Act of 2006); to listing requirements for stock exchanges (e.g., the Johannesburg has explicit human rights requirements); to specific operating conditions and security oversights (e.g., the US Securities and Exchange Commission).

Industry-led standards often advance corporate responsibility by promoting voluntary information disclosure and self-regulation to preserve management autonomy (Epstein, 1969). Industry-led standards generally stipulate minimal thresholds of legitimate behavior on specific issues with widely varying levels of disclosure requirements, oversight, and enforcement. Often originated as 'soft' laws to address unintended consequences of specific regulations or policies, industry-led standards are often voluntary and promoted by non-governmental and multilateral organizations (Kolk, 2005; Williams and Conley, 2008). At times 'stuck in the middle' with neither sufficient incentives nor punitive punishments, industry-led accountability standards are frequently hailed as first attempts at coalition building to identify and prioritize common issues, albeit initially the lowest common denominator, while publicly sharing acceptable responses. Examples of industry-led accountability standards include: Responsible Care from chemical manufacturers in the 1980s; Fair Trade from coffee growers, certified organic initiatives, and genetically modified labeling in the 1990s; and more recently the Extraction Industry Transparency Initiative from the extraction industry, the Kimberley Process from the diamond industry, and the Equator Principles from the banking sector (Kolk, 2005; Williams and Conley, 2008).

More recently, multilateral-led non-governmental organizations (NGOs) and civil society organizations (CSOs) such as the United Nations, World Bank Group, and the International Finance Corporation (IFC), and the International Organization for Standardization (ISO) have led global discussions on hypernorms such as corruption, human rights, working conditions, and climate change (Donaldson and Dunfee, 1999; Gilbert and Rasche, 2008; Webb, 2008). These multilateral-led consortia work to identify widely held beliefs and articulate shared values applicable across multiple nation-states while being open to widely varying local operationalization (Gilbert and Rasche, 2008). Pre-existing standards are often bundled into comprehensive approaches (e.g., the United Nations Global Compact) focused on hypernorms (Donaldson and Dunfee, 1999; Kell, 2005) such as treating humans with dignity and fair operating practices. Often voluntary but increasingly with widespread adoption, many multilateral initiatives focus initially on information disclosure (Zadek, 2003) or self-report (Williams and Conley, 2008) reflecting how hypernorms are adopted and, with help from local NGOs, implemented at the local levels (Gilbert and Rasche, 2008).

Overall, the past decade has seen a marked growth in the number and complexity of global standards with even more standards likely in the coming decades. Managing the tension between over-specification that tries to satisfy all contingencies or a grand compromise that satisfies none, global standards have differed in their emphasis of (a) ensuring uniform thresholds of behavior across nation-states while (b) encouraging flexibility to local sensitivities (Gilbert and Rasche, 2008).

The dual objectives of global standards—universal worldwide consistency alongside local responsiveness—reflect the dual objectives identified in Bartlett and Ghoshal's (1991, 1998) MNC competitive framework. In the next section, we examine Bartlett and Ghoshal's traditional MNC competitive strategies, highlighting implications for managing corporate impacts and co-creating enduring value with myriad stakeholders.

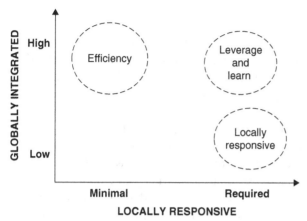

Figure 11.1 Globalization and local responsiveness

Twin pressures: globalization and local responsiveness

In the 1980s, Barlett and Ghoshal argued competitive pressures were driving businesses towards global integration to achieve low costs and scale of economies while simultaneously increasing demands for differentiated products and services adapted to local preferences. Homogenization of tastes, standardization of products, and rationalization of supply chains, delivery systems, and manufacturing processes are driving costs lower to improve efficiency and reduce prices. At the same time, demands for culturally sensitive local responsiveness requires differentiated products and services customized to local tastes, while meeting legal thresholds of various nation-states and municipalities.

These dual-acting forces—demands for global consistency juxtaposed with local product responsiveness—are the primary pressures identified in Bartlett and Ghoshal's (1991, 1998) model of competitive dynamics for multinationals. Bartlett and Ghoshal (see Figure 11.1) identify three product strategies based on economic rationales: global based on efficiency, multi-domestic based on local responsiveness, and transnational strategies based on leveraging and learning across contexts. In this section we highlight the benefits and limits of these MNC strategies. Each competitive strategy is described in the following text with implications for enhancing corporate legitimacy leading to global consistency in policies, execution and values, not just products, while information sharing, encouraging adaptation to local constituencies.

Global strategy

A global product strategy focuses on global efficiencies, economies of scale, and satisfying consumers' demands with low-cost products that are identical, or very similar, in multiple markets. Foreign-based operations in a global corporation are often seen as distribution conduits for headquarters.

A firm with a global product strategy generally has a centralized operational hub deploying essentially the same product around the world. Investing in central manufacturing, it builds a service base that serves an entire region. Negotiating market entry and investments with governments is easier with a larger scale that increases the respect and bargaining power of these multinationals. These firms have strong global brands, global distribution chains, and high-volume, low-cost manufacturing with widely available products having little or no customization. Extraction and natural resource firms such as Alcoa, BP, BHP Billiton, and Weyerhaeuser as well as consumer-oriented firms responding to converging consumer tastes (e.g., Toyota's Corolla, Nokia's cell phones, Apple's iPod, Coca-Cola's Coke) exhibit global competitive strategies. Manufacturing firms such as United Technologies' Otis elevators, Pirelli and Bridgestone tires as well as high-tech or branded companies such as Infosys, Intel, Microsoft, Quicksilver's surfboards, and Google's search engine exhibit global product strategies.

From a corporate legitimacy perspective to ensure co-created value endures, global strategies are consistent with adaptation of global standards. Global strategies advance socio-political and economic legitimacy by adopting uniform thresholds of acceptable standards worldwide (Arthaud-Day, 2005; Gilbert and Rasche, 2008). Partnering with multilateral organizations (e.g., World Health Organization, International Finance Corporation, World Bank Group), global MNCs pursuing global strategies actively promote their desire for legitimate and universal standards. Traditionally, these firms focus on product impacts or financial impacts rather than employee or information-sharing impacts across multiple communities. Fierce competition for becoming the accepted worldwide standard can stem from product or technical superiority (e.g., Toyota's Prius, Google, Intel), low-cost processing capabilities (e.g., BP, Citigroup), political preferences and standards (e.g., VCR versus Beta; Microsoft versus Linux), or widespread consumer demand (e.g., Apple's iPhone or RIM's Blackberry). Only more recently, with the growth of industry-led and multilateral-led accountability initiatives focused on information-sharing, employee and workplace conditions, are global companies addressing multiple impacts simultaneously while acknowledging spillovers and multiplier effects. Global accountability standards demonstrate the desire for universal thresholds defining legitimate behavior—whether through hard law, soft law, or self-regulatory initiatives (Gilbert and Rasche, 2008; Waddock, 2008b).

Multi-domestic strategy

A multi-domestic product strategy stems from strong pressures driving businesses towards nuanced, local responsiveness with differentiated products and services. Local traditions, customized preferences, and mandates for locally sourced products accelerate demands for local responsiveness. Firms with multi-domestic strategies are adept at responding to demands for customized products and services. Responding to multiple expectations and multiple local communities, a firm creates products market-by-market, region-by-region, or neighborhood-by-neighborhood. Socio-political mandates from local or national governments increase demands for local responsiveness by limiting imports, assessing duties, raising tariffs, or requiring local sourcing. Often European-based MNCs initially invested in foreign countries with multi-domestic product strategies until scale of economies were created (Bartlett and Ghoshal, 1991, 1998; Ghoshal and Bartlett, 1990).

Unilever and its administrative heritage of decentralized, highly autonomous country managers created consumer products adapted to local conditions. Consumer-based companies such as Philips consumer electronics, Kroger grocery stores, and ecotourism organizations operate with multi-domestic product strategies. Conglomerates with unrelated business units, such as Australian-based Wesfarmers, and companies that grew via acquisitions tend to have multi-domestic product strategies. Royal Dutch Shell, for example, operated primarily with a multi-domestic strategy having decentralized, nationally self-sufficient country managers that encouraged and exploited local opportunities until the mid-1990s (Post et al., 2002).

Accountability standards rely heavily on local information disclosure for manufacturing, knowledge-based, and service industries.

Locally responsive product strategies and accountability standards focus on local oversight with verification to enhance information sharing. Moving beyond accountability exercises that enhance MNCs' public image via mere lip service (Fry and Hock, 1976; Ullmann, 1985) or in easily decoupled policies and practices (Weaver et al., 1999), verification processes begin alleviating concerns that accountability reports are primarily a communications ploy. Transparency and local accountability within and across nation-states is prized (Gilbert and Rasche, 2008). Verification is conducted by independent consultancies with additional oversight provided by non-governmental (NGOs) and local civil society organizations (CSOs). While specific activities differ across operating sites, corporate activities outside of—although in conjunction with—market activities are made explicit with public disclosure of relevant information.

Transnational strategy

Bartlett and Ghoshal's third product strategy combines demands for global integration via efficient, low-cost economies of scale alongside adaptations to local tastes (Bartlett and Ghoshal, 1991, 1998). A transnational product strategy optimally satisfices demands for customized products while offering the same high quality and low cost as standardized global products. Responding to local demands, the transnational company learns how to continually innovate as tastes, technologies, regulations, exchange rates, and suppliers change (Bartlett and Ghoshal, 1998). Juxtaposing local responsiveness with demands for widespread standards, transnational executives build in flexibility and resilience in sourcing, product design and service delivery.

Subsidiaries are encouraged to differentiate based on local consumer preferences, technology advantages, or low-cost inputs. Depending on subsidiaries' regulatory environment, the inherent tensions between combination decentralized governance with local autonomy versus semi-standardized products is mutually adjusted. Learning among subsidiaries is encouraged. And, innovation with knowledge transfer shared across the entire organization is encouraged.

Examples of transnational strategies exist in consulting businesses (e.g., IBM and PricewaterhouseCoopers), investment banks, and the financial services industry with intertwined credit markets around the world. Manufacturing companies such as Sony and GE are encouraging 'glocalization' to combine global legitimacy and local responsiveness.

Focused explicitly on integrating management systems and improving management processes, accountability standards to leverage the learnings across a firm extending to its suppliers of suppliers and its entire distribution network (Freeman et al., 2007). Emphasizing the importance of intra-organizational sharing of information, these accountability standards focus on product and process innovations leading to scale of economies, low-cost production systems, differentiated products, and information-sharing while learning best practices across subsidiaries. The process of collecting and analyzing local impacts on employees in the workplace alongside product and financial data across many subsidiaries can prompt managers to ask questions about current activities. Answering questions about negative impacts, for instance, prompted from an internal investigation is often preferred to answering similar questions posed by an angry mob of neighbors.Having to commit information to paper, spreadsheets, intranets, or publicly available reports can encourage learning first-hand how tasks are accomplished and how they might be improved (Wagner and Dittmar, 2006).

Limitations of traditional product-market strategies in global economies

Four implications for managers using traditional product-market strategies yet trying to co-create value dependent upon myriad stakeholders are identified: (a) competitive (global) strategies working at odds with firms' (multi-domestic) employee and information-sharing initiatives; (b) the rise of global civil society organizations changing the dynamics of information disclosure; (c) implicit assumption of socio-political stability in emerging economies; and (d) increased demand for global governance standards.

First, many *global* product strategies have been effectively implemented across nation-states (Bartlett and Ghoshal, 1991). Co-creating value with employees in the workplace and localized information-sharing initiatives, on the other hand, are perceived as *multi-domestic*, with severe limitations from nation-state influences (Baron, 1995, 1997). Baron argues:

A comprehensive *global* or *international* [socio-political] nonmarket strategy seems unlikely to be successful, however, because ... [m]any nonmarket issues have a strong domestic orientation and are more likely than market strategies to require *multidomestic* strategies. (Baron, 1995, pp. 62–63, emphasis added)

A bias towards local responsiveness has contributed to a proliferation of local, community-based stakeholder activities (Griffin and Mahon, 1997; Margolis and Walsh, 2003) that are often not tightly tied to an MNC's value-creation process (Freeman et al., 2007; Porter and Kramer, 2006) reinforcing a heritage of *multi-domestic* stakeholder initiatives.

Global standards that are truly applicable worldwide have an additional hurdle of creating legitimate specifications not tied to specific nation-states while remaining meaningful across countries (Gilbert and Rasche, 2008). Foreign subsidiary managers can be frustrated with requests from headquarters for implementing 'yet another new program' (Kostova, 1999). Having different socio-political, employee and community concerns and goals than headquarters (Ghoshal and Bartlett, 1990), subsidiaries may ceremonially adopt global disclosure initiatives (Kostova and Roth, 2002). Ceremonial adoption is the 'formal adoption of a practice on the part of a recipient unit's employees for legitimacy reasons without their believing in its real value for the organization' (Kostova and Roth, 2002, p. 220). Ceremonial adoption is likely when a subsidiary's managers and employees feel that the mandated practice is not valuable together with strong pressure from the MNC to adopt the practice. In the case of global governance standards, subsidiaries might ceremonially adopt such an effort without believing in it—destroying or attenuating value creation.

Second, the rise of *global* civil society organizations is rivaling the rise of the nation-state (Salamon et al., 2003) and changing the dynamics of information disclosure as discussed in more detail in Chapter 8. Many corporations, when creating product strategies, consider nation-state governments as the sole official and legitimate representative of a country's citizens. Legal mandates, officially sanctioned through regulations, create the acceptable threshold of legitimate corporate behavior. Global and local citizen groups, civil society organizations, and multi-stakeholder initiatives are often considered special interest groups advocating for behaviors beyond the legal requirement (McWilliams and Siegel, 2001; McWilliams et al., 2006). Global standards, on the other hand, explicitly embrace global multilateral consortia, with a focus on hypernorms (Donaldson and Dunfee, 1999) and nuanced adjustments at the local levels (Donaldson, 1996; Gilbert and Rasche, 2008). Local and national governments, in this scenario, are encouraged to be enforcers having third-party oversight (Webb, 2008; Williams and Conley, 2008) not necessarily the initiators of global policy.

Third, emerging markets are generally treated *implicitly* in competitive product strategies while global governance standards treat emerging markets *explicitly*. Many competitive strategies have been defined, tested, and focused on firms headquartered in developed economies with stable or predictable socio-political dynamics including strong, democratically elected governments as assumed by Friedman (1970). Emerging markets are often treated as an opportunity for producing goods using low labor costs (Bartlett and Ghoshal, 1998; Porter and Kramer, 2006). These market-based initiatives underexamine or undervalue socio-political risks and the multi-faceted financial, employee, product and information-based impacts inherent in any business. In developing or war-torn countries, for example, businesses must actively be mindful of socio-political or economic activities that could undermine their legitimacy and standing with government officials. Actively integrating socio-political and economic considerations is neither an underlying assumption of Bartlett and Ghoshal (1991, 1998) nor of many firms (Margolis and Walsh, 2003).

Global governance standards, on the other hand, focus on emerging markets to safeguard vulnerable populations, mitigate externalities, and encourage development. Focused on global concerns such as pollution degradation, human rights, and governance, global standards encourage explicit consideration of socio-political risks and opportunities with transparent information disclosure protocols.

Fourth, many business issues are *increasingly global*, with concomitant expectations of coordinated, consistent global responses. Widespread, entrenched, and persistent issues that have traditionally been considered government issues often cross borders and affect business operations. Global issues such as population growth, extreme poverty, global climate change, water scarcity, and eradication of disease increasingly affect how businesses reliably conduct their operations. Regularity of suppliers, training costs of employees, absenteeism, ensuring security in distribution chains, or being the employer of choice in tight labor markets is increasingly contingent upon businesses clearly focusing on global public health issues such as hygiene, water quality, polio, SARS, avian bird flu, malaria, or HIV/AIDS.

Business interests are increasingly intertwined with global interests for commodity and branded companies. Commodity-based corporations continuously seeking legitimacy with worldwide supply chains (e.g., extraction industries, petrochemical industries, coffee growers, tobacco producers) can differentiate their products based on ethical sourcing alongside low cost (Kolk, 2005). Similarly, consumer-based companies seeking global brand opportunities promote and cultivate legitimacy. Well-respected global brands can attract employees in tight labor markets, enhance pride in employees, build respect with governments, increase trust among stakeholders and lower transaction costs (Jones, 1995). Operating in increasingly unstable markets, well-respected globally branded companies can build stability and access to global markets. At the same time, branded corporations are establishing in-house thresholds of acceptable behaviors to enhance their future investments (e.g., testing for pet food contamination, removing tainted milk powder, or identifying lead in children's toys).

NGOs, CSOs, and businesses are accelerating their ability to leverage and link global information. Ubiquitous access to information on the internet with web-based podcasts from BBC International, CNN Worldwide, *Financial Times*, and *China Daily* are encouraging a consistent, professional approach to responding to stakeholder concerns, encouraging global consistency.

At the same time, a 24/7 news cycle with web-based information among a social networked Facebook generation encourages each citizen with a camera phone to be a news reporter. New stories are often reported first by local citizens via iReport or YouTube. The 2005 UK bus bombing outside the Tavistock Square tube station was first reported by local citizens. Access to vital information encourages firms to actively engage in local activities—especially if their products, employees, brand, or supply chain are susceptible to being out of tune with the way the world works (Gates, 2008). The rapid dispersion of information from multiple sources pressures MNCs to be 'ahead of the information curve,' to understand the business's socio-political and economic impacts, and be readily prepared for (mis)information onslaughts that reflects the MNC's global norms as well as being sensitive to local needs.

And finally, businesses are learning how to collaborate, selectively, with multilateral institutions to reduce operating uncertainty. Alongside the growth in multilateral organizations (e.g., UN Global Compact, GRI, ILO, World Bank, IMF, IFC, missionaries) businesses are actively seeking multi-stakeholder partnerships to build organizational legitimacy and enhance collective action. Two examples from climate change include: the 2005 Australian Conservation Foundation (ACF) multi-stakeholder report advocating early action on climate change. Similarly, the 2007 US Climate Action Partnership built relations among domestic businesses, MNCs, and NGOs to create a common set of shared values to mitigate uncertainty, build coalitions, and urge widespread policy action.

Overall, an increase in global issues, networked interests, rapid dispersion of information, and a complex array of institutions are encouraging *global* standards with information-sharing and verification across nation-state borders. Promoting legitimacy, enhancing information disclosure, and rewarding organizational learning, rules-based and principles-based global governance tools are increasingly important in the efforts of organizations to build credible commitments worldwide. We conclude with several implications for MNCs 'stuck in the middle': without consistent corporate governance standards, not participating in voluntary global governance discussions and those not operating in tune with the expectations of their local communities.

Stuck betwixt and between global and local pressures

When combining the dual tensions of global governance standards—uniform consistency with information-sharing and verification across nation-states alongside flexibility for local responsiveness—innovative opportunities are unleashed. Companies with *transnational* strategies requiring local responsiveness and global consistency are best positioned to innovate and leverage increased demands for co-creating value by managing a corporation's myriad impacts. We focus on four innovation opportunities: performance-based learning (measuring firm performance against the firm's goals and stakeholder expectations response-based learning (hearing stakeholder concerns—usually in the wake of catastrophes); assurance-based learning (engaging in an external reporting process); and engagement-based learning (reviewing firm performance against stakeholders' expectations) (Wood et al., 2006).

First, performance standards within *global* standards are continuously evolving. MNCs without clarity of focus on their firm's worldwide multi-faceted impacts will increasingly be playing catch up to lower costs and improve efficiencies while expectations are continuously ratcheted up. Innovations in accountability standards are extending beyond physical, easier-to-count, measurable items such as water usage and carbon consumption to ensure non-tangible items such as human dignity, trust, goodwill, and legitimacy. A focus on tacit hypernorms is bundling previously discrete issues. For example, a focus on human dignity now might extend beyond contractual agreements with internal employees to all customers, and suppliers. MNCs compliant with home-country or host-country standards may not be able to sufficiently respond to worldwide scrutiny—putting future investments at risk. While local enforcements may vary, a 24/7 news cycle continuously updates information on newsworthy activities affecting firm's perception as operating in tune with the world today.

Second, rapid responses are increasingly the norm, yet governance standards increasingly emphasize bundled issues that cross borders. Organizations are expected to rapidly respond to all stakeholders when these complex issues unravel. Understanding 'whole of company' corporate responses requires active and early coordination across global audiences. Systematically collecting, disclosing, and learning/sharing best practices across the organization on impacts alongside economic impacts can pre-empt—or buy precious time before—unwanted disclosures in the news media from watchdog CSOs or NGOs. In addition to counting the number of jobs created, taxes paid, and wages of employees, MNCs are increasingly asked to respond to questions about: promoting peace and prosperity; alleviating homeless and poverty; and contributions to social repair.

Third, assurance-based learning requires integrated management systems. Accountability standards demand public disclosure with verification of information across subsidiaries, across issues, and across stakeholder groups. After aggregating subsidiaries, verified responses to 'whole of company' questions are expected: how are all employees being treated, including full-time equivalent employees, suppliers, and contract workers? What safety, health, and environmental workplace practices are consistent across all operation sites? Measurable metrics that convincingly convey year-over-year improvements, future goals, and benchmarks against rivals are built into new integrated management systems. While many environmental metrics focus on physical evidence (i.e., toxicity, tons of waste transferred or burned), universally accepted metrics on fairness, discourse, satisfaction, and compliance require adaptation to local sensitivities (Gilbert and Rasche, 2008).

Fourth, meaningfully engaging stakeholders can lead to process and product innovations. Multi-stakeholder forums engage relevant stakeholders to address complex issues. Building trust, cooperation, and coordination among industry associations, multilateral organizations, the media, CSOs, and NGOs can increase dependencies and identify mutual needs leading to innovative public–private partnering. Alternatively, easily decoupling communications and corporate activities (Weaver et al., 1999) can create corporate scapegoats rather than addressing fundamental concerns underlying global governance standards (Hess, 2008). Credibly connecting the ideas, activities and reporting of what a MNC says it does with what others perceive it is doing requires concerted engagement among relevant stakeholders. Credible engagement can enhance corporate reputations, which, in turn, can contribute to attracting and retaining customers and employees and can build greater support among key stakeholders—a mutually beneficial virtuous cycle.

Overall, global governance standards are likely to create innovations among companies that learn across borders and across issues. Transnational product strategies are uniquely positioned to successfully adopt an impact-oriented mindset to co-creating value. Transnational strategies can achieve a unified and uniform global focus on hypernorms while simultaneously creating flexible responses to local sensitivities (Arthaud-Day, 2005; Baron, 1995; Boddewyn, 2003; Gilbert and Rasche, 2008; Porter and Kramer, 2006; Webb, 2008). On the other hand, commitment to global governance standards is likely to create tensions amongst multi-domestic firms with highly decentralized management structures and especially those MNCs with dispersed business units. These firms' innovations will likely remain captured by localized interests.

An opportunity exists for creating net positive impacts with mutual benefits shared between the firm and its stakeholders. By recognizing that today's friend might be tomorrow's foe, and vice versa, a focus on mutual benefits and expected impacts allows for an outcomes approach rather than a friend/foe dynamic that has, by definition, two opposing forces.

Scalability

Making a net positive impact can be particularly productive, or potentially problematic, for large businesses. Large businesses tend to supply more products and/or services and have more stakeholders than small businesses. Large businesses, however, can be slow to respond and send muddied or infrequent signals that cloud the messages and blunt the intended impact of the firm. While any business can become complacent, large businesses without continual oversight could easily overlook subtle signals of inertia. Over time, inertia can require significant shifts (such as a threat to the firm's survival) to shake up existing norms (Ansoff, 1975).

Small businesses are often more nimble in their response to changing expectations. Small companies can explore and experiment, at lower investment costs and higher rewards, with investment and implementation decisions. Decision criterion for investment and implementation is (a) coupled and (b) set at a higher rate for large corporations. By design, large companies might be doubly hampered in linking the investment (identifying the issue) to the firm's response (implementing change). The need for higher hurdle rates and the desire for scale might hamper the ability to experiment, invest, and change in meaningful ways. Larger businesses are also more vulnerable to destroying value and are more likely to miss opportunities that create value due to their desire for large, scalable projects with appropriate returns. That being said, when a large multinational decides to make an impact, their decisions can have immediate impacts on stakeholders directly and indirectly connected to the firm.

Even seemingly small, discrete efforts can have significant impacts when applied across a large business. Replacing light bulbs with LED bulbs, for example, can have enormous direct impacts on electricity bills. The city of Detroit is undertaking a project to replace 55,000 street lights with LED bulbs with significant expected savings (Katz and Bradley, 2014). Walmart has numerous green initiatives to reduce packaging, including shelf-ready initiatives and encouraging suppliers to use less packaging materials or to manufacture concentrated forms of popular, everyday consumer goods such as laundry detergent. Efficiencies in energy, carbon, water, and waste reduces consumption, creating cost savings that can quickly add up (Gunther, 2011).

A critical difference between exploratory programs of large and small businesses is scalability. Quite often the expectations of scale within a large business can dwarf the program's actual impact. A large investment bank, for example, might create an exploratory microfinance program with a budget of roughly $50–100 million. That's a lot of money dedicated to microfinance. Yet from a metrics perspective, within a $300 billion bank, this program on microfinance is less than half of 1 percent of revenues. As a relatively small proportion of the entire bank's revenues, the manager running the microfinance program is not likely to have a seat at the top table reporting to senior leadership. And the manager may or may not be in line to be promoted to a program that accounts for 10 percent of bank's revenues. All too often the significance of an initiative such as this microfinance initiative is understood as a response when pressed by regulators, the media, or concerned organizations about the investment bank's contributions to stakeholders other than shareholders to buff the image or as an insurance against past, present, or future crises.

Which in turn increases the probability of microfinance stories in a large investment bank becoming a bolted-on program. Alternatively, re-imagining microfinance units as an opportunity to creatively think about how to spin-off or integrate the insights as a loss leader in emerging markets, or how to learn more about the unbanked, or how to benefit small businesses as a goal in and of itself rather than encouraging small businesses to expand and then become a client.

Some global energy companies, for example, create exploratory renewables programs. While these are sizable investments of billions of dollars, the requirement of a renewables market of sufficient *size*, *scale*, and *returns* for a large, global multinational continues to remain under development. Shale gas, coal seam gas, solar power, wind turbines, and hydroelectric power might be profitable but at a lower return than a global energy company's requirements. Or these projects might be profitable only for small-scale projects and thus be overlooked as a commercially viable option. The investment can be quite large but when considered in relation to the size of the corporation itself, the percentage and the priority of renewables or alternative energy sources might be a paltry percentage of the overall business.

The size of the firm creates multiplier effects yet expectations might multiply more rapidly for firms controlling their entire value chain as discussed in Chapters 5 and 6. Large, vertically integrated firms dependent upon natural resources, for example, controlling the extraction of materials as well as retail operations, have unique opportunities for creating value. As vertically integrated firms they control the value chain and conceivably have access to information about operations, workplace conditions, human trafficking, child labor, and other employee-related issues. By coordinating information they can contractually ensure the hiring, firing, training, and workplace conditions of employees. Alternatively, vertically integrated firms can be vilified for inappropriate use of natural resources, exploitation of cheap labor, or extracting rents from resource rich countries that benefit wars, corruption, or are due to bribery.

Governments often assist with scalability in specific cases of natural monopolies and protecting nascent industries (Baron, 2012). Telephone companies are often granted natural monopolies to build landline-based communications network that would otherwise be prohibitively expensive in a competitive market. A competitive market, for example, might encourage multiple telephone poles each with multiple telephone wires strung alongside Main Street. Similarly, electrical companies would have additional poles and wires, making for an unsightly amalgamation of poles and wires. Instead, governments grant natural monopolies with one caveat, which might be that the companies must ensure universal service (universal service meaning all citizens have access to the utility rather than just those in say, urban areas that might be more cost-effective than rural customers). In a similar manner, governments fund the sunk costs necessary to build large-scale infrastructure projects such as roads, sewage, and trash collection that might not otherwise be advantageous to small-scale private operators.

Governments, when it comes to scaling projects, may protect new markets or new products and act as an incubator of important industries. Thinking of governments as an incubator of new products can be counterintuitive. Using government funding to develop material science on fabrics and miniaturize technology for defense purposes has commercial opportunities, too. For example, embedding sensors into fabrics that change color in the presence of deadly carbon monoxide can be important for emergency workers when fighting a fire. If a sensor can be developed to emit light under low light conditions, that could be important for commercial use for runners or bikers traveling along poorly lit trails at night. Or having sensors tied to GPS systems to locate a runner and guide him/her home might be useful for hikers, backpackers, or other commercial applications. Embedding sensors into fabrics could become a commercially viable plan, yet these products are not likely to supplant established corporations because of the requirements of scale and scope of athletic wear companies, for example. By creating incentives for nascent ideas and enabling experimentation, a firm may encourage new ways to address entrenched issues (e.g., safer nuclear energy or commercially viable shale gas and fracturing).

Small businesses and small countries

Integrating impacts, by design, into a business from its initial stages can be quite powerful in ways that older firms bolting on impacts cannot (Grayson and Hodges, 2004). Designing for impact-thinking from the get-go opens up unique opportunities for reimagining relationships with employees, clients, and consumers. Purposely integrating interests to embed incentives to create value is likely to result in different contracts, different metrics, and varied ways that motivate and account for relationships.

Family-based businesses, for example, often focus on long-term health, even though they have small volumes because their name is their reputation. By working with stakeholders and intensely focusing on nurturing transactions with an eye towards enduring relationships that evolve over time, family businesses often can take a long-term view. Going beyond short-term financial focus, a family owned restaurant, for example, can incorporate convenience, availability, and quality assurances without concern for shareholders. It can expand with complementary services to build awareness and build market share before focusing on profits similar to Jeff Bezos's firm, Amazon.

Entrepreneurs are often uniquely facile at looking at problems as sources of opportunities. Entrepreneurs quite often combine economic outcomes with employee, product, or information outcomes to create a win–win–win opportunity (Martin and Osberg, 2007). By incorporating corporate impacts from the onset, the goal is a sustainable advantage that can pivot at the margins by experimenting with new ways of conducting business. Being nimble and flexible allows a level of freedom within small businesses to experiment with small initiatives to grow into something larger across the entire organization.

Small countries, by focusing on specific impacts, are often innovators in specific areas that can be built upon by others. The Swedish government, for example, has built a website with information about where it spends its aid money and the impact its spending has had. Singapore, one of the smallest countries when measured by land mass, is a world leader in promoting public cleanliness for all its citizens and visitors. Similarly, Switzerland is well-known for being a safe haven for bank accounts due to the security and unrelenting stability of its banking system. While Denmark has aggressive energy-neutral targets that have led to innovations in public transport, bicycles, wind turbines, and other energy-related industries.

Implications for co-creating value

A holistic view of a company's impacts, especially for multinational companies, even small or family-owned multinationals, examines how firms effectively navigate the twin pressures of globalization and localization. With increased pressures for global standards in the workplace (e.g., corruption, fraud, and child labor), while local stakeholders are increasingly vociferous, navigating the twin pressures is more important, yet more difficult than ever before. Consistency with a principles-based approach while allowing ensuring a minimum threshold through a rules-based approach is increasingly common. In addition, the need for rapid responses, even in multibillion-dollar enterprises, is creating new communications headaches and new strategies for addressing local concerns. Implications for both consistency and rapid, localized responses are changing mindsets about co-creating value and are examined in the text that follows.

First, consistency is increasingly prized in order to address product-market and socio-cultural demands efficiently. The irony: addressing local demands may create seemingly incompatible strategies—customizing responses to local socio-cultural needs while striving for worldwide product-market efficiencies—yet be appropriate for addressing global standards while meeting local needs. If MNCs strive for efficiencies with a one-size-fits-all response to socio-cultural needs in the same way they respond to product-market efficiency demands, they risk facing accusations of insensitivity to local community with a headline that might proclaim: 'Profits before people.' When a local crisis hits, this perception is downright dangerous!

MNCs seeking to adopt global product-market strategies might unthinkingly also adopt global socio-cultural strategies using a one-size-fits all mentality. Yet, if political boundaries and social customs are powerful enough to constrain growth, harm the firm's reputation, or alter its competitiveness, a global one-size-fits-all strategy may be less useful and potentially very harmful. On the other hand, if rapid responsiveness to local needs is required, multi-domestic strategies that require adapting to local markets by customizing parents' expertise may be preferable. Customizing parents' expertise, an effective response, might be overlooked as it may require reallocating scarce resources and be counterintuitive with the efficiency-focused (not effectiveness-focused) commodity production processes.

In effect, MNCs face 'two-level games' (Putnam, 2000) in both product-market and socially-sensitive contexts where what they do in one sphere impacts the other and vice versa (Prakash and Griffin, 2012). When the multiple local–global tensions are added into the product-market and socio-cultural stakeholder milieu, co-creating value becomes a 3D chess set with multiple players, layers, and sets of rules (den Hond et al., 2014) with plenty of room for new winners and losers.

Second, learning is needed to rapidly respond with a nuanced sensitivity towards local needs. The premise is that corporations' activities need to cohere across their multi-faceted impacts. Yet corporations need to be globally competitive and locally aware. Community groups are increasingly throwing wrenches into the monolithic responses of corporations deploying the same activities, unilaterally (often dictated by headquarters staff), around the globe in every neighborhood. Community groups are able to mobilize quickly, effectively use social media (YouTube, Twitter, blogs, Instagram, flash mobs) to get their message out whereby local events are quickly transformed into world news.

Incorporating lessons learned at the local level across subsidiaries is neither easy nor straightforward. However, successfully leveraging lessons about corporate impacts across communities, markets, and countries can lead to differentiation of the firm and new innovations in products and processes.

Understanding local nuances requires awareness of a firm's impacts. Given the assumption that efficient markets have perfect information that seamlessly adjusts without lag time, remaining vigilant of financials *should* be relatively simple. Firms, as the efficient capital market theory goes, adjust rapidly to financial signals. If, however, signals stem from non-financial sources, such a surge of nationalism from economic fluctuations, inflation, natural disaster, or war, then firms need to focus on impacts to improve their response time.

Looking ahead

At its heart, effectively managing corporate impacts is about a new narrative about co-creating value with mutual benefits (net of externalities) for many stakeholders. A focus on impacts requires clarity of focus to zero in on the most material aspects of modern businesses affecting a wide range of stakeholders. Focusing solely on financial impacts is too myopic in today's world. By focusing on the direct, indirect, and multiplier effects stemming from finances, employees in the workplace, products through the value chain, and information creates a more holistic and realistic picture of a firm's true impacts. As firms affect and are affected by other stakeholders, how firms impact others, with multiplier effects that spill over, are increasingly in a firm's best interest to pay attention to.

Clarity of focus on impacts that create and destroy value needed since boundaries between public, private, and civil society sectors are blurring, meaning that expectations of businesses are growing at an accelerating rate. As boundaries blur, managers are continually being asked to address new problems (Margolis, 2009), crafting solutions based on a broader, more holistic view of management: corporate impacts.

Amid blurring boundaries, more organizations with varied motivations are vying for the hearts, minds, and pocketbooks of the world's consumer and opinion leaders. Corporate impacts are being scrutinized by many more organizations, individuals, and agencies with ever-changing motivations and mechanisms for making their view heard (e.g., blogs, YouTube, tweets, etc.). Given limited resources, choices need to be made. With the goal of creating value, deciding how to choose and how to manage is important. The great challenge lies in sorting through the corporation's impacts in light of their ability affecting the co-creation of value. In the next chapter we summarize the lessons being learned about the art and science of co-creating value.

12 | *The art and science of managing impacts*

Managing corporate impacts to co-create enduring value requires continuous cooperation and commitment amongst numerous stakeholders. Focusing solely on one stakeholder group to the exclusion of all others, without understanding the interplay among stakeholders or the multiplier effects of the business misses opportunities for creating value. Even worse, a myopic view of the value-creation process can unwittingly destroy value or severely limit the ability to co-create value going forward. A focus on the impacts of a business, the points of interaction between the business and its stakeholders, creates an opportunity to shape stakeholders' expectations and anticipate the salient opportunities and concerns of tomorrow. Taking a more comprehensive view of impacts to include financial, employee and the workplace, products and services, as well as information-based impacts, this book builds out a more robust narrative of the firm. By talking about the actual impacts, in light of the true costs, this book begins a conversation about the multifaceted ways in which firms purposely and meaningfully impact others—for good and at times with harmful effects. Designing business interactions to build upon positive impacts while being mindful of, and mitigating, the value lost and the costs imposed makes for a business that is more likely to endure over time.

A focus on impacts heightens the sensitivity to the context in which businesses operate. Being aware of and appropriately addressing salient issues across a myriad of stakeholders in different jurisdictions is increasingly important yet even more difficult. The growth of businesses to even more neighborhoods, with different voices from myriad stakeholders suggesting an ever shifting set of priorities, is confusing at best and destroys value, for all, at worst. Businesses can be a force for good or harm. Mindfully designing impacts to build out the good while purposely mitigating harm is in everyone's best interests. More firms are more likely to be asked by even more stakeholders 'what have you done for me lately?' Responding in corporate speak with only a return to the investor viewpoint is likely to result in a brief con-versation with limited buy-in for the business's future growth, appeal to a limited set of new applicants, or pride within existing employees that are not shareholders.

This book makes three contributions. First, it focuses explicitly on impacts expanding the traditional perspective of financial-only impact to include a corporation's impacts with employees in the workplace, impacts with customers via products and services delivered, as well as impacts on local communities and the broader communities through information-based impacts that shape perceptions of the firm's actions and intentions.

Second, by juxtaposing multiple impacts simultaneously, new com-binations of creating value emerge. For example, as the links between the perceptions of employees, customers, and regulators are more closely examined, does a consistent (positive or consistent negative) perception across all three stakeholders enable growth or does one stakeholder have the ability to trump all others in different contexts? It is just as likely, however, that new avenues for destroying value will come to light as the spotlight shifts to encompass the negative implica-tions of poor treatment of employees, unsafe workplace conditions, products that harm human health or the environment, or information is released that questions the veracity of the firm's claims.

And third, this book heightens the scrutiny of the context in which businesses operate: issues, industries, and nation-states with ever-changing expectations stemming from rivalry, regulations, and civil society. Treating the firm as an open system that affects and is affected by its stakeholders, this book begins to tease out the conditions under which different firms are more likely to (erroneously) focus on one type of impact over another. By exploring the materiality of issues, expectations of different industries and regulatory thresholds of vari-ous nation-states, the context in which business operates shapes the behavior and the attitudes of the local operations, which in turn ena-bles value to be created that is in a business's own self-interest yet also, and unfortunately, allows for lives to be exploited.

Co-creating value

Co-creating value is a process that includes multiple stakeholders—investors, sure, as well as employees, suppliers, suppliers of suppliers, government officials, customers and a variety of other stakeholders. Assuming that profits are the purpose of a firm to exist and the sole reason and measuring stick for creating value is risky. The pursuit of profits at the exclusion of all else is simply not in the firm's best interest given the multifaceted demands—growing at an increasing pace—of businesses today. Examining the value created in terms of only financial impacts is risky as more and more stakeholders make demands on businesses that simply cannot be satiated with monetary contributions. For example, perceptions of neighbors or regulators might be enhanced by thoughtful investments but often can't be bought with money. And if money can buy a permit, for example, the next year when a new organization offers something even better, the ante goes up and up and up. Monetary contributions in these cases aren't a differentiator, rather they are just an ante. Time, effort, and credible commitments are needed to sustain the value created.

Money is not always the currency of value: stable employment, creating jobs, the prestige or status of a company, security, or being a part of something larger might be of value too (Godfrey, 2014). By emphasizing one outcome (e.g., financial earnings) with one pre-eminent stakeholder (the shareholder) other opportunities for value creation with employees, customers, suppliers, neighborhoods, and distributors are unfortunately overlooked—or worse, put asunder. This book argues that long-term, enduring success requires a focus on a variety of impacts, their interactions, and their potential to create or destroy value in the value-creation process.

Companies can survive and even thrive focused solely on financial impacts, as profits can be used to ameliorate ways in which value is destroyed. A financially focused approach to management allows for specialization, localization, and measurement, and can be implemented across partners, enforced in contracts, and result in a single-minded workforce.

Yet in today's ever-changing business world, focusing narrowly and solely on just one stakeholder is simply risky. One piece of the impact puzzle is a clear understanding of a company's financial impact, but the mosaic of considerations necessary to create enduring value demand more than just financial information. When attention is hyper-focused on financial exchanges, *how* value is created and the types of value that firms co-create is often overlooked, unwittingly leading to value being destroyed. This book suggests it is in a manager's best interest, with unexpected payoffs, to understand the points of impact between a firm and its stakeholders, where value is created rather than destroyed.

Evaluating projects and assessing satisfaction is often based on multiple dimensions: the reliability of a firm to deliver products and services as contracted might be more important than—and significantly affect—the negotiated price. Products that require just-in-time delivery, saving inventory and warehousing costs, as well as the exponential growth in firms able to deliver an internet-ordered item the next day, have demonstrated the opportunity for new business models based on convenience and availability.

The importance of information-sharing—to be known and welcomed by the local municipalities, to attract top talent, to build a quality of life for the local region, to encourage other businesses to co-locate nearby—is an intangible asset that enhances firm performance and, in turn, reinforces a culture that, in turn, enhances firm performance (Surroca et al., 2010). In a mutually reinforcing virtuous cycle, firms that have figured out how to systematically address impacts by interweaving solutions throughout the firm and the value chain, and enable others to address these complex issues are able to differentiate themselves (Russo, 2009; Russo and Fouts, 1997). Spillover effects might include improved reputation among financial analysts, increased access to capital, satisfaction with stakeholders and the ability to weather a lengthy crisis, if and when it occurs (Cheng et al., 2014; Crane et al., 2014a, 2014b; Ioannou and Serafeim, 2012; Henisz et al., 2014; Henisz, 2014) as the BP oil spill in Chapter 1 tested BP's relationships with key stakeholders.

Imagine a company centered on enhancing financial returns to investors. Now, imagine a similar-sized, equally profitable company in the same industry focused on creating products that consumers continuously rave about with strong sales. And now, imagine a third company of similar size, in the same industry, with the same profit profile operating predominantly online encouraging consumers to publicly comment on their satisfaction and encouraging suppliers to be transparent regarding workplace conditions and recent violations. Assuming all three companies are equally profitable, which company would you want to invest in or own? To work for? To buy from? To partner with?

As an investor, owner, employee, client, or partner, would you have enough information to assess the ability of these three firms to continuously create value based on these descriptions? What additional information would you need in order to determine if each firm could weather a recession, provide tomorrow's product at a competitive price, and be a worthwhile employer? Information on relationships, processes, and multiplier effects, for example, are also important to address. If you are a prospective employee, how might you be treated (Henisz et al., 2014)?

If you are a supplier, are contracts based on volume and price alone or is there an opportunity to deepen the transactions based on convenience, quality, flexibility, or responsiveness? If you are a policymaker or opinion leader, what ripple effects might you expect if the firm becomes a new neighbor? If you are a local neighbor, how will local employment, congestion, pollution, education opportunities, and knock-off effects be addressed? If you are an entrepreneur, will other companies be attracted to the community?

Presumably, more information is needed to evaluate the firms, as you might want to rank them against one another or within their industry, against their neighbors, or as the thought leaders on best practices. Perhaps additional information beyond today's positive financial returns to investors, evidence of potential lawsuits, composition of the board of directors, or pending contracts is also needed. When choosing among firms that are equally profitable today, evaluating tomorrow's prospects to own, to work for, to buy from, or to partner with often requires more than just financial returns.

Unfortunately, considering a firm's impacts often targets individualized, discrete activities. That is, procurement strategies focus on purchasing decisions, human resource strategies focus on attracting and retaining key employees, while marketing strategies focus on the next big social cause that the products can be linked to. Meanwhile, the company's foundation is making an impact by donating money, encouraging employees to volunteer, or providing in-kind products. The net impact of these individualized activities spread across a firm does make a significant difference to the individuals involved by building comradery, creating a culture that motivates even more engagement. An engaged workforce is more likely to be a satisfied, productive, workforce (Greening and Turban, 2000; Turban and Greening, 1997). But all too often, once the individuals championing a specific activity, volunteer program, or outreach endeavor move to a new position, get additional responsibility, or leave the firm, the activity stops. The effort, goodwill, and energy for initiating a project that makes a difference are, unfortunately, not sustained over time.

The challenge becomes building the ability for sharing, learning, and leveraging the insights from one impact to the next, from one neighborhood to the next, from one plant site to another factory, or from one silo (purchasing) to another (retailing or distribution). This requires oversight, coordination, and continuous commitment. Localized activities that creatively address the needs and concerns of individual stakeholders while linking to the purpose of the firm creates a 'sweet spot' of win–win–wins. Or, alternatively, it embeds the firm in a messy middle that satisfies no one and wastes resources.

Understanding how a firm continuously creates value requires continual vigilance. Multiple impacts (with spillovers and multipliers) open up a broader set of issues, yet require a broader set of solutions. The sheer number of stakeholders can be paralyzing for managers. Managers mapping the firm's financial, personnel, products, and information impacts along the value chain and across geographies requires a *science*-like attention towards interests, issues, and information, as well as the *art* of negotiation and communications to converge interests.

Systematically examining a corporation's impacts and its multiplier effects can uncover opportunities in the value-creation process. More broadly, thinking about a firm embedded within its varied social, political, and economic communities expands the number and scope of the ways in which value can be created or destroyed. Understanding why, what, how, and with whom value is co-created, and the type of value created, firms are more likely to create enduring value over time and changing contexts.

Creating value, rather than capturing it

Creating value, traditionally, has meant creating financial returns for the owners of the firm. End of story. In this traditional storyline, creating value is reduced to a simple heuristic: maximize profits for shareholders. Yet, the heuristic unfortunately overlooks the process by which value is created or destroyed. What if employees work in unsafe conditions, products can harm consumers, and the reputation of the firm is spiraling downwards? Would you invest, and invest for the long term, if profits remain positive? Holding steady to the status quo misses opportunities to shape expectations, make desired impacts, and create new value.

Interestingly, many firms might capture value and try to hold onto value rather than continuously co-create value. As we know from psychology: losses loom larger than gains (Kahneman and Tversky, 1979). Individuals remember negative events that destroy value while more easily shrugging off positive gains. This aversion to losing financial value, for instance, has numerous manifestations for capturing value. First, being satisfied with capturing or redistributing value rather than creating value suggests an orientation towards the status quo that retains financial value. In lieu of building or creating value, capturing value might engender defensive moves that inhibit mobility or create barriers, inhibiting the ability to create future value.

Second, capturing value might focus on staving off losses or losing profits (more) slowly. While losing profits more slowly might be one ploy to delay the eventual demise of a product or organization, it can work for only a limited time period. Alternatively, changing perceptions about the product through communication channels can capture value—again, with a limited time frame.

Third, capturing value might mean getting to neutral ground. That is, if a firm is perceived to be destroying value, such as inappropriately extracting resources from the earth, then moving to neutral net impacts might be a 'win' for the industry. Yet, neutral net impacts don't mean that the firm is creating value. It just might be transferring the value from one stakeholder group (local communities) to another stakeholder group (investors). Stakeholders that bear the burdens of the business might be different than the stakeholders that receive the benefits of the business (Wood and Jones, 1995).

Fourth, capturing value might be having an 'insurance policy' when a crisis emerges. When a crisis threatens the livelihood of the entire industry, an insurance policy might mitigate the harm of value being destroyed. That is, if a firm is perceived to be a trusted partner with a stellar reputation, then it might use reputation chits to stave off damage once a crisis hits. For example, during the 2012 *Deepwater Horizon* oil spill, BP lost shareholder value more slowly than other companies did after other large-scale oil spills.

Creating value, rather than merely capturing value, occurs when net positive impacts align business investments with the unmet needs of its stakeholders. For example, anticipating consumers' unmet needs might begin with integrating geographical information systems (GIS) with the location of an ATM kiosk the consumer just used. A jeans store located around the corner might use this information to prompt a pop-up ad to appear on the consumer's cell phone.

Corporate impacts and co-creating enduring value

In Chapter 2, we examined a narrow view of corporate impact by thinking about value creation in terms of financial impacts. Financial impacts, when all risks are monetized, are generally easier to measure and compare and can simplify managerial decisions to a single criterion for decision-making. Yet not all risks can be accounted for or monetized using a financial yardstick. Separating financial impacts into four different ways to think about shareholders' relationships with other stakeholders creates: win–wins, parade of horribles, investments, and pernicious behaviors. The most desirable mindset is for firms to create win–wins with shareholders and other stakeholders. Yet, one of the most prominent mindsets is thinking about impacts as part of a risk mitigation strategy with an aim to prevent a parade of horribles or limit its negative impacts once started rather than seeking investments in co-creating win-win-wins.

Another way to think about financial impacts is through investments that may one day have financial payoffs for the investors in the future. And finally, firms engaging in pernicious behaviors think of harms to non-financial stakeholders as necessary to do business. Understanding how different firms think about financial impacts, and position their portfolio vis-à-vis competitors leads to integrating financial and non-financial impacts more holistically.

Chapter 3 suggests thinking about corporate impacts more broadly than merely financial impacts to interweave employee and product impacts. Since firms can create or destroy value through interactions with stakeholders, examining the points of impact between a firm and its employees in the workplace or with consumers through sourcing, production and delivery decisions, we look for opportunities that build or destroy value. Creating value for employees goes beyond paying a fair wage—beyond-compliance human resources policies and programs designed for a firm's specific needs can help attract and retain the most qualified staff and improve the company's image. Creating value for consumers requires an understanding of what consumers want and need. Today's customers want safe, high-quality products, but they are also starting to ask where their products came from, so successful firms know their audience, as well as their supply chain.

Chapter 4 addressed value creation through information-sharing. Information-based value, and how information shapes (or is perceived to shape) attitudes, beliefs, and customs, is all too often an afterthought in a company's impact strategies. As the internet has made the quantity of information greater and more dispersed, effectively managing relationships beyond a firm's geography-based or local interests-based communities are becoming more important to survival. Local, geographically constrained communities are too restrictive when thinking about a corporation's impacts through information. By enabling others to create value that they wouldn't otherwise be able to create, corporate impacts on communities of users, virtual communities, thought leaders, the financial analyst community, public policy officials, and the media, as well as informal communities such as potential suppliers are important, yet are often overlooked or misunderstood. Addressing community concerns via philanthropy, while noble with lofty goals, is often not enough and more often than not misses the mark entirely. Successful firms are redefining community while engaging and partnering with myriad community organizations to co-create value for shareholders and other stakeholders.

Chapters 5 and 6 combine and integrate the four types of corporate impacts (financial, employees in the workplace, products, and information-based) to examine a firm's spillover and multiplier effects. Firms are beginning to consider how financial, product, employee, and information impacts are intricately and inextricably linked to the creation of value. The new challenge is examining net impacts, impacts net of spillover effects which includes considering groups indirectly able to affect the firm's ability to create value. Co-creating enduring value will be related to a firm's ability to understand its multiplier effects: along the value chain, over time, and across multiple geographies.

Chapter 7 addresses some of the longstanding assumptions about how firms think about, act on, and talk about their non-financial impacts. For example, attempting to offset negative impacts with philanthropic donations could have positive effects, but it is not necessarily the most efficient or effective way for a firm to address its externalities. While all firms are uniquely qualified to make a net positive impact, small firms can respond more nimbly to issues and co-create value with stakeholders to remain competitive. Alternatively, conceiving of corporate impacts as equivalent to managing community risk creates a myopic view of impacts.

Chapter 8 examines the changing landscape of businesses embedded within public policy and civil society. Ever-evolving expectations from competitors, regulators, and civil society are creating new opportunities for new value to be created. These dynamic, and sometimes dueling, pressures can be a bane or a benefit in the firm's value-creation process. Amid uncertainty with scarce resources, choices need to be made: choose and choose wisely else the choice will be made for firms.

Chapter 9 focuses attention on the context in which firms make decisions about impacts. Using a short-sided issues-by-issues approach or a stakeholder-by-stakeholder approach rather than a holistic, integrative impacts approach is discussed. Issue-by-issue approaches break down stakeholder interests into bite-sized pieces, making them more digestible for management, yet creating a myopic and often defensive strategy that is not always linked to how a firm creates value.

Chapter 10 focuses on how industry pressures affect firms' decisions when choosing among initiatives and mechanisms to address negative impacts. Initiatives are choices about what a firm should or can do while mechanisms are decisions about how to implement the choice. Juxtaposing what to do (which initiatives to pursue) and how to implement (which mechanisms are appropriately aligned for the initiatives selected), highlights the importance of a firm's competitive context. Some firms will choose 'signature' initiatives focused on a narrow impact (employee volunteering for instance) while other firms choose a more collaborative approach. Co-creating value unilaterally, which is generally the simpler and more practical option, or multilaterally, in collaboration with any number and variety of public, private, or civil society organizations, is an important choice.

Chapter 11 examines the unique challenges multinational corporations face as they simultaneously address global and local pressures akin to a 3D chess match. On the one hand, multinational corporations desire economies of scale in order to remain efficient and competitive. On the other hand, ignoring the disparate local needs could mean overlooking opportunities or risks that later prove fatal to the firm. In some cases, global standards help firms resolve the global versus local tensions, but in most cases the firm needs to consider how it delegates authority, gathers and discloses information, responds to rapidly changing local contexts, and learns from experiences in other markets—prioritizing information-based impacts simultaneously alongside financial, employee and product concerns.

Finding the sweet spot by design

Taking a 'whole of company' approach towards creating value balances consistency with nuanced local responses. Thought leaders create value among multiple stakeholders simultaneously to build resilience and times of uncertainty; build pride within a worldwide workforce; become a respected partner of choice with NGOs and governments; enhance worldwide reputation; address global issues where they can make a significant difference; and brand their companies as more than just product or service providers.

Forward-thinking business executives are interweaving impacts into everyday corporate strategy decisions to co-create innovative, mutually beneficial value. By meeting the needs of core constituents and using unique resources and capabilities, the sweet spot of how value can be co-created is expanding. Some grocery stores and consumer product companies, for example, are co-creating value with consumer and community constituents. Pharmaceuticals, agriculture-based organizations, and beverage companies are building upon their unique resources and capabilities to co-create value by leveraging their convening power and access to information on public health, hydrology, and water quality/access, respectively. Similarly, petrochemical and energy firms have the potential to lead in understanding carbon footprints and building locally sensitive renewable energy strategies.

Opportunities for more value creation are evolving. Businesses are too. Those businesses once considered 'too big to fail' are failing while 'operating business as usual' is creating headline news, pressuring businesses to articulate the value created.

Competition will impose clarity of focus on value created as firms are under intense levels of scrutiny with more requests for disclosure.

Competing solely on financial impacts is often not enough: information on employee treatment in the workplace, how products are sourced along the value chain, and the information disclosure is opening up new opportunities for creating value in the eyes of stakeholders. Impact activities as philanthropic gestures or as a communications tool will likely be cut back without a strong connection tied back to how the firm co-creates value.

Benchmarking will continue unabated as managers seek to retain their autonomy by increasing transparency and decreasing information asymmetries. Disclosure has unexpected payoffs for business groups, professional associations, trade associations, or local chambers of commerce that use their convening power to promote positive impacts, share best practices, or engage in information arbitrage. As a testament to multi-stakeholder initiatives, the groups who collaborated to create the ISO 26000, the UN Global Compact, the International Code of Conduct Association (ICOCA), and the International Declaration of Human Rights are examples of emerging governance mechanisms. Much room for improvement still exists, as voluntary global governance schemes often lack appropriate oversight or enforcement mechanisms and may be too broad to reflect local contexts, factors that render them less effective.

While an ongoing debate focuses on what is being measured, the real impact will be the discussions examining underlying logics of why, if, how, and when to commit to co-creating value. These discussions in the boardroom and neighborhood community centers will lead to businesses delineating their activities and how they align with their own interests and the interests of neighbors, regulators, employees, investors, and other stakeholders.

Asking better questions

A firm's ability to co-create enduring value is shaped by others. Stakeholders in the form of employees, customers, suppliers, communities and governments explicitly (or implicitly) shape customs, traditions, and expectations (e.g., government agencies as legitimate representatives within democratic countries). Yet, more and varied communities affect the ability of a firm to create value. Consider virtual communities heavily dependent upon online/web-based interactions (e.g., World of Warcraft) or single interests (e.g., the Royal

Society for the Protection of Birds, breast cancer survivors, master gardeners, firefighters' unions, the local PTA, etc.). A focus on a firm's multi-faceted impacts on ever-evolving communities of stakeholders, is shifting expectations of businesses. Businesses are responding.

Firms focus on outcomes (e.g., 'this is how we make a difference to these stakeholders by alleviating poverty') alongside their inputs (e.g., 'we source from sustainable suppliers') and outputs (e.g., 'we produce millions of at-cost medicines or xyz products for this underserved community each year') in order to gain a more robust understanding of the value co-created by business with its stakeholders. As businesses move beyond a narrow focus on financial flows, to assess their true, multifaceted impacts new mindsets are emerging, new risks are being evaluated, new opportunities arise and new value is being created. Assessing investment opportunities in light of their true impacts will require rethinking the costs and benefits of projects to include different dimensions such as retaining inspired employees or building healthy neighborhoods with individuals able to regularly show up to work rather than being afflicted by preventable diseases. Persistent problems such as healthcare might be reframed to address underlying conditions such as irrigation, sewage, water quality and availability, education, etc., creating new opportunities for new businesses.

Unlike traditional business thinking which considers almost exclusively financial impacts, corporate impacts emphasize a holistic understanding incorporating financial, employee, product, and information-based material impacts.

Firms create value. At the same time, and often unwittingly, firms also destroy value. This book suggests that it is in a business's self-interest to create value in light of the true impacts of the firm on others. Co-creating value simply and explicitly acknowledges the many and varied stakeholders that contribute to the value-creation process: employees, suppliers of suppliers, communities, regulators, investors, customers, and myriad others. Co-creating value also means purposefully mitigating the destruction of value, which in turn reduces risks, decreases costs, builds trust, enhances reputation, and creates a more satisfied, engaged workforce that in turn attracts top talent to the firm.

Thinking about value creation only in terms of financial impacts, which are easier to measure and often readily available to compare one firm to another, creates an incomplete and oftentimes skewed view of the beneficiaries of a firm's activities. Accounting for the impacts of other stakeholders, the value created, and the value destroyed across a myriad group is hard yet important for a firm's continued competitiveness. As more and varied stakeholders—and stakeholders of stakeholders—ask more questions about how value is created and the types of value, the risks of not addressing these concerns is expanding. Rather than waiting for significant crises to expose the shallow veneer of being a good neighbor, threaten the survival of firms, or irreparably damage reputations, firms are learning to juggle the many impacts a firm can and does have. Firms are innovating rather than balancing, learning and adapting from stakeholders and crafting new paths to create even more value. They are doing this voluntarily, without onerous governmental mandates, simply because it is in their best interest to co-create value. Articulating the value co-created with and for customers, employees, suppliers, communities and governments alongside investors is new. Co-creating enduring value requires these new narratives. Rather than just capturing value, creating new value that includes acknowledging all those who shared in the value-creation process is simply in the business's self-interest.

References

Abrams, F.W. (1951). Management's responsibilities in a complex world. *Harvard Business Review*, 29(3): 29–34.

Ackerman, J.M. (2012). Walmart scandal in Mexico points to US hypocrisy. *The Daily Beast*, April 23. www.thedailybeast.com/articles/2012/04/23/wal-mart-scandal-in-mexico-points-to-u-s-hypocrisy.html.

Adler, P.S. and Kwon, S.W. (2002). Social capital: prospects for a new concept. *Academy of Management Review*, 27(1): 17–40.

Aerts, W., Cormier, D., and Magnan, M. (2006). Intra-industry imitation in corporate environmental reporting: an international perspective. *Journal of Accounting and Public Policy*, 25: 299–331.

Ahrens, F. (2010). Toyota's shares slide as its reputation loses steam. *Washington Post*, February 4. www.washingtonpost.com/wp-dyn/content/article/2010/02/03/AR2010020302109.html.

Allen, G. (2005). An integrated model: the evolution of public affairs down under. In P. Harris and C. Fleisher (eds.), *The Handbook of Public Affairs*. London: Sage Publications.

(2007). *Corporate Community Investment in Australia*. Melbourne: Centre for Corporate Public Affairs.

Alperson, M. (1995). *Corporate Giving Strategies that Create Business Value: A Research Report*. New York: The Conference Board.

Anderson, R.C. and White, R. (2009). *Confessions of a Radical Industrialist: Profits, People, Purpose: Doing Business by Respecting the Earth*. New York: St. Martin's Press.

Andriof, J. and McIntosh, M. (eds.) (2001). *Perspectives on Corporate Citizenship*. Sheffield: Greenleaf Publishing.

Annan, K. (2001). *The 'Unparalleled Nightmare' of AIDS*. Speech to the US Chamber of Commerce, June 1.

Ansoff, H.I. (1975). Managing strategic surprise by response to weak signals. *California Management Review*, 18: 21–34

(1980). Strategic issue management. *Strategic Management Journal*, 1: 131–148.

Apple (2011). *Apple Suppliers Responsibility—2011 Progress Report*. www.apple.com/supplier-responsibility/pdf/Apple_SR_2011_Progress_Report.pdf.

Apple (2012). *Apple Supplier Responsibility—2012 Progress Report.* www.images.apple.com/supplierresponsibility/pdf/Apple_SR_2012_Progress_Report.

Armstrong, M. and Boseley, S. (2003). Corporate giving on the increase. *The Guardian,* November 17. www.theguardian.com/business/2003/nov/17/northernrock.ftse.

Arthaud-Day, M.L. (2005). Transnational corporate social responsibility: a tri-dimensional approach to international CSR research. *Business Ethics Quarterly,* 15(1): 1–22.

Associated Press (2013). Brands risk image in varying Bangladesh responses. *USA Today,* May 6. www.usatoday.com/story/news/world/2013/05/06/brands-risk-image-in-varying-bangladesh-responses/2138299.

Austin, J.E. (2000). Strategic alliances between nonprofits and businesses. *Nonprofit & Voluntary Sector Quarterly,* 29(1): 69–97.

Austin, J.E. and Seitanidi, M.M. (2012a). Collaborative value creation: a review of partnering between nonprofits and businesses: part I, value creation spectrum and collaboration stages. *Nonprofit & Voluntary Sector Quarterly,* 41(5): 726–758.

(2012b). Collaborative value creation: a review of partnering between nonprofits and businesses: part 2, partnership processes and outcomes. *Nonprofit & Voluntary Sector Quarterly,* 41(6): 829–868.

Bansal, P. and Roth, K. (2000). Why companies go green: a model of ecological responsiveness. *Academy of Management Journal,* 43: 717–736.

Barboza, D. (2010). Another death at electronics supplier in China. *New York Times,* May 21. www.nytimes.com/2010/05/22/technology/22suicide.html.

Barnett, M.L. and Salomon, R.M. (2006). Beyond dichotomy: the curvilinear relationship between corporate social performance and corporate financial performance. *Strategic Management Journal,* 21: 1101–1122.

Barnett, M.L. and Salomon R.M. (2012). Does it pay to be really good? Addressing the shape of the relationship between social and financial performance. *Strategic Management Journal,* 33(11): 1304–1320.

Barnett, M.L. and Sunyoung, L. (2012). Business as usual? An exploration of the determinants of success in the multinational transfer of corporate responsibility initiatives. *Business & Politics,* 14(3): 1–27.

Baron, D.P. (1995). Integrated strategy: market and nonmarket components. *California Management Review,* 37(2): 47–65

(1997). Integrated strategy and international trade disputes: the Kodak-Fujifilm case. *Journal of Economics & Management Strategy,* 6(2): 291–346.

(2012). *Business and its Environment,* 7th edn. Upper Saddle River, NJ: Prentice-Hall.

Barry, J.M. (2005). *The Great Influenza: The Story of the Deadliest Pandemic in History.* New York: Penguin Books.

Bartha, P.F. (1982). Managing corporate external issues: an analytical framework. *Business Quarterly*, Fall, 78–90.

Bartlett, C.A. and Ghoshal, S. (1989). *Managing Across Borders: The Transnational Solution*. Cambridge, MA: Harvard Business School Press.

(1991). *Managing Across Borders: The Transnational Solution*, 2nd edn, Cambridge, MA: Harvard Business School Press.

(1998). *Managing Across Borders: The Transnational Solution*, 2nd edn. Cambridge, MA: Harvard Business School Press.

Bies, R.J., Bartunek, J., Fort, T.L., and Zald, M. (2007). Corporations as social change agents: individual, interpersonal, institutional, and environmental dynamics. *Academy of Management Review*, 32(3): 788–793.

Blinder, A.S. (2006). Offshoring: the next industrial revolution? *Foreign Affairs*, 85(2): 113–128.

Bloomberg. (2012). Foxconn labor disputes disrupt iPhone output for 2nd time, *Bloomberg*, October 8. www.bloomberg.com/news/2012-10-07/foxconn-labor-disputes-disrupt-iphone-output-for-2nd-time.html.

Boddewyn, J.J. (2003). Understanding and advancing the concept of 'nonmarket.' *Business & Society*, 42(3): 297–327.

Bonardi, J.-P. and Keim, G.D. (2005). Corporate political strategies for widely salient issues. *Academy of Management Review*, 30(3): 555–576.

Börzel, T.A. and Risse, T. (2009). *The Effect of International Institutions: From the Recognition of Norms to the Compliance with Them*. SSRN Working Paper Series (01). www.search.proquest.com/docview/189902152?accountid=11243.

Bosworth, M. (2014). The upside of being let go by Nokia. *BBC News Magazine*, January 31. www.bbc.co.uk/news/magazine-25965140.

Bradley, J. (2008). *Cadbury's Purple Reign: The Story Behind Chocolate's Best-Loved Brand*. Hoboken, NY: John Wiley & Sons.

Brammer, S. and Millington, A. (2003). The evolution of corporate charitable contributions in the UK between 1989 and 1999: industry structure and stakeholder influence. *Business Ethics: A European Review*, 12(3): 216–228.

(2004). Stakeholder pressure, organizational size, and the allocation of departmental responsibility for the management of corporate charitable giving. *Business & Society*, 43(3): 268–295.

Brammer, S. and Pavelin, S. (2005). Corporate community contributions in the United Kingdom and the United States. *Journal of Business Ethics*, 56: 15–26.

Broder, J.M. (2013). With 2 ships damaged, Shell suspends Artic drilling. *The New York Times*, February 27. www.nytimes.com/2013/02/28/business/energy-environment/shell-suspends-arctic-drilling-for-2013.html?_r=2&.

Brown, B. and Perry, S. (1994). Removing the financial performance halo for Fortune's most admired companies. *Academy of Management Journal.* 37(4): 1346–1359.

Bryant, B. (2011). *Deepwater Horizon* and the Gulf oil spill—the key questions answered. *The Guardian*, April 20. www.theguardian.com/environment/2011/apr/20/deepwater-horizon-key-questions-answered.

Buchholtz, A.K., Amason, A.C., and Rutherford, M.A. (1999). Beyond resources: the mediating effect of top management discretion and values on corporate philanthropy. *Business & Society*, 38(2): 167–187.

Campbell, D., Moore, G., and Metzger, M. (2002). Corporate philanthropy in the UK 1985–2000: some empirical findings. *Journal of Business Ethics*, 39 (1/2): 29–41.

Carroll, A.B. (1979). A three dimensional conceptual model of corporate social performance. *Academy of Management Review*, 4: 497–506.

(1999). Corporate social responsibility: evolution of a definitional construct. *Business & Society*, 38(3): 268–295.

Chang, J., Goldberg, J.I., and Schrag, N.J. (1996). *Topics in Philanthropy: Cross-border Charitable Giving.* New York: New York University School of Law. www1.law.nyu.edu/ncpl/pdfs/Monograph/Monograph 1996CrossBorder.pdf.

Cheng, B., Ioannou, I., and Serafeim, G. (2014). Corporate social responsibility and access to finance. *Strategic Management Journal*, 35: 1–23.

Chilkoti, A. (2014). India steps up tobacco warnings to combat nearly 1M deaths. *Financial Times*, October 23. www.blogs.ft.com/beyond-brics/2014/10/23/india-steps-up-tobacco-warnings-to-combat-nearly-1m-deaths.

China Daily (2012). Foxconn denies workers went on strike at plant. *China Daily*, October 7. www.china.org.cn/business/2012-10/07/content_26714079.htm.

Christensen, J. and Liptak, K. (2014). Obama: US ready to take the lead in Ebola fight. *CNN*, September 16. www.cnn.com/2014/09/16/health/obama-ebola.

CIA (2013). *The World Factbook 2013–14.* Washington, DC: Central Intelligence Agency.

Clarkson, M.B.E. (1995). A stakeholder framework for analyzing and evaluating corporate social performance. *Academy of Management Review*, 20(1): 92–117.

Clay, J. (2005). *Exploring the Links Between International Business and Poverty Reduction: A Case Study of Unilever in Indonesia.* Eynsham: Information Press.

Clifford, S. (2010). Wal-Mart plans to buy more local produce. *NYTimes.com.* www.nytimes.com/2010/10/15/business/15walmart.html?_r=0.

Cochran, P.L and Wood, A.R. (1984). Corporate social responsibility and financial performance. *Academy of Management Journal*, 27: 42–56.

Conley, C. (2007). *Peak: How Great Companies Get Their Mojo from Maslow*. San Francisco, CA: Jossey-Bass.

Connell, J.O. (2011). Wal-Mart package for DC includes job-training program, $21 million in donations. *The Washington Post*. www.washingtonpost.com/local/wal-mart-package-for-dc-includes-job-training-program-21-million-in-donations/2011/11/22/gIQAQx1bmN_story.html.

Corporate Responsibility Officer Association (2011). *Structuring & Staffing Corporate Responsibility: A Guidebook*. Washington, DC: CROA. www.croassociation.org/files/structuring%20and%20staffing%20 cr%202011.pdf.

Crane, A. and Matten, D. (2003). *Business Ethics*. Oxford: Oxford University Press.

Crane, A., Matten, D., and Spence, L. (2013a). *Corporate Social Responsibility: Readings and Cases in a Global Context*. Oxford: Oxford University Press.

    (2013b). *Corporate Social Responsibility*. London and New York: Routledge Press.

Crane, A., Palazzo, G., Spence, L., and Matten, D. (2014a). Contesting the value of 'creating shared value.' *California Management Review*, 56(2): 130–149.

    (2014b). A reply to 'A response to Andrew Crane et al.'s article by Michael E. Porter and Mark R. Kramer.' *California Management Review*, 56(2): 151–153.

Daft, R. and Weick, K. (1984). Toward a model of organizations as interpretation systems. *Academy of Management Review*, 9(2): 284–295.

Dalheim, S., Lombardo, M., Mohapatra, A., Barre, A., and Gladman, K. (2010). *Board Oversight of Environmental and Social Issues: An Analysis of Current North American Practice*. Bethesda, MD: Calvert Asset Management Company, Inc. and the Corporate Library.

Daniels, A. (2014). Charities try new strategies as fundraising rebounds. *The Chronicle of Philanthropy*, June 17. www.philanthropy.com/article/ Charities-Try-New-Strategies/147167.

Dashwood, H. (2014). Sustainable development and industry self-regulation: developments in the global mining sector. *Business & Society*, 53(4): 551–582.

de Bakker, F.G.A., Groenewegen, P., and den Hond, F. (2005). A bibliometric analysis of 30 years of research and theory on corporate social responsibility and corporate social performance. *Business & Society*, 44(3): 283–317.

de Bakker, F.G.A., Groenewegen, P., and den Hond, F. (2006). A research note on the use of bibliometrics to review the corporate social responsibility and corporate social performance literature. *Business & Society*, 45(1): 7–19.

Deegan, C. (2002). The legitimising effect of social and environmental disclosures—a theoretical foundation. *Accounting, Auditing & Accountability Journal*, 15(3): 282.

Deegan, C., Rankin, M., and Tobin, J. (2002). An examination of the corporate social and environmental disclosures of BHP from 1983–1997: a test of legitimacy theory. *Accounting, Auditing & Accountability Journal*, 15(3): 312.

Delmas, M., Hoffmann, V.H., and Kuss. M. (2011). Strategy, and competitive advantage under the tip of the iceberg: absorptive capacity, environmental. *Business & Society*, 50(1): 116–154

den Hond, F., Rehbein, K.A., de Bakker, F.G.A., and Kooijmans-van Lankveld, H. (2014). Playing on two chessboards: reputation effects between corporate social responsibility and corporate political activity. *Journal of Management Studies*, 51: 790–813.

Dess, G.G. and Beard, D.W. (1984). Dimensions of organizational task environments. *Administrative Science Quarterly*, 29, 52–74.

DiMaggio, P.J. and Powell, W.W. (1983). The iron cage revisited: institutional isomorphism and collective rationality in organizational fields. *American Sociological Review*, 48: 147–160. Reprinted in P.J. DiMaggio and W.W. Powell (eds.) (1991). *The New Institutionalism in Organizational Analysis*. Chicago, IL: University of Chicago Press.

D'Innocenzio, A. (2013). Walmart to purchase produce directly from local growers. *The Huffington Post*, June 3. www.huffingtonpost.com/2013/06/03/walmart-produce-fruit-vegetables_n_3378575.html.

Donaldson, T. (1996). Values in tension: ethics away from home. *Harvard Business Review*, 4–12.

Donaldson, T. and Dunfee, T. (1999). *Ties that Bind: A Social Contracts Approach to Business Ethics*. Cambridge, MA: Harvard Business School Press.

Donaldson, T. and Preston, L.E. (1995). The stakeholder theory of the corporation: concepts, evidence, and implications. *Academy of Management Review*, 20: 65–91.

Donaldson, T. and Werhane, P. (1999). *Ethical Issues in Business: A Philosophical Approach*. London: Pearson.

Driscoll, C. (2006) The not so clear-cut nature of organizational legitimating mechanisms in the Canadian forest sector. *Business & Society*, 45(3): 322–353.

Dunham, L., Freeman, R.E., and Liedtka, J. (2006). Enhancing stakeholder practice: a particularized exploration of community. *Business Ethics Quarterly*, 16(1): 23–42.

Dye, J. and Stempel, J. (2014). GM hit with $10 billion lawsuit. *Reuters*, June 18. www.reuters.com/article/2014/06/18/us-gm-reca ll-lawsuit-idUSKBN0ET1SR20140618.

Dyer, J.H. and Singh, H. (1998). The relational view: cooperative strategy and sources of interorganizational competitive advantage. *Academy of Management Review*, 23(4): 660–679.

Easterly, W. (2006). *The White Man's Burden: Why the West's Efforts to Aid the Rest Have Done So Much Ill and So Little Good*. New York: Penguin Press.

Economia (2010). Colombia es un Mercado nacionalista. *Elespectador. com*, December 10. www.elespectador.com/impreso/negocios/ articuloimpreso-240013-colombia-un-mercado-nacionalista.

The Economist (2005). The good company: companies today are exhorted to be socially responsible. What, exactly, does this mean? *The Economist*, January 20. www.economist.com/node/3577141.

The Economist (2008). Just good business. Special report: corporate social responsibility. *The Economist*, January 17. www.economist.com/ node/10491077.

The Economist (2015). Corporate social responsibility: do-gooding policies help firms when they can prosecuted. *The Economist*, June 27. www. economist.com/node/21656218.

Edelman, R. (2014). *Leading a Jewish Family Business, Presented at the Jewish Federation of Greater Atlanta* [Video file]. www.youtube.com/ watch?v=lUN2rd56a8&feature=youtu.be.

Edmondson, B. (2014). *Ice Cream Social: The Struggle for the Soul of Ben & Jerry's*. San Francisco, CA: Berret-Koehler Publishers.

Elankumaran, S., Seal, R., and Hashmi, A. (2005). Transcending transformation: enlightening endeavours at Tata Steel. *Journal of Business Ethics*, 56: 109–119.

Environmental Leader (2012). Walmart rockets from 15th to Third in EPA Green power rankings. *Environmental Leader*, February 1. www.environmentalleader.com/2012/02/01/walmart-rockets-from-15th-to-third-on-epa-green-power-rankings/#ixzz3I1gKg3v8.

Epstein, E. (1969). *The Corporation in American Politics*. Englewood Cliffs, NJ: Prentice Hall.

Epstein, M.J., Yuthas, K., and Sanghavi, D. (2013). *CSR and the Companies Act, 2013: Be Bold, Take Action*. Mumbai: Dasra. www.dasra.org/ csr-guide.pdf.

EU Commission (2003). *Corporate Social Responsibility: A Business Contribution to Sustainable Development.* Brussels: EU Commission. www.community-wealth.org/content/corporate-social-responsibility- business-contribution- sustainable-development-white-paper.

EU Commission (2011). *A Renewed EU Strategy 2011–2014 for Corporate Social Responsibility.* Brussels: EU Commission. www.eur-lex.europa.eu/LexUriServ/LexUriServ.do?uri=COM:2011:0681:FIN:EN:PDF.

Evan, W.M. (1965). The organization set: toward a theory of inter-organizational relations. In J.D. Thompson (ed.), *Approaches to Organizational Design.* Pittsburgh, PA: University of Pittsburgh Press, pp. 173–191.

Fahrenthold, D.A. and Kindy, K. (2010). Six months after the spill, BP's money is changing the gulf as much as its oil. *Washington Post,* October 20. www.washingtonpost.com/wp-dyn/content/article/2010/10/19/AR2010101907468.html.

Ferenstein, G. (2014). Uber and Airbnb's incredible growth in 4 charts. *Venture Beat,* June 19. www.venturebeat.com/2014/06/19/uber-and-airbnbs-incredible-growth-in-4-charts.

Flanigan, J. (1990). Why do they admire Philip Morris? *LA Times.* www.articles.latimes.com/1990-01-14/business/fi-395_1_philip-morris.

Fombrun, C. (1996). *Reputation: Realizing Value from the Corporate Image.* Boston, MA: Harvard Business School Press.

Fombrun, C. and Shanley, M. (1990). What's in a name? Reputation building and corporate strategy. *Academy of Management Journal,* 33(2): 233–258.

Fort, T.L. and Schipani, C. A. (2004). *The Role of Business in Fostering Peaceful Societies.* Cambridge: Cambridge University Press.

Freeman, R.E. (1984). *Strategic Management: A Stakeholder Approach.* Marshfield, MA: Pitman Publishing.

Freeman, R.E. and Gilbert, D.R. (1988). *Corporate Strategy and the Search for Ethics.* Englewood Cliffs, NJ: Prentice Hall.

Freeman, R.E., Harrison, J.S., and Wicks, A.C. (2007). *Managing for Stakeholders: Survival, Reputation, and Success.* New Haven: Yale University Press.

Freeman, R.E., Harrison, J.S., Wicks, A.C., Parmar, B.L., and Colle, D.E. (2010). *Stakeholder Theory: The State of the Art.* Cambridge: Cambridge University Press.

Friedman, M. (1970). Social responsibility of business. *The New York Times Magazine,* 33, 122–126.

Frooman, J. (1999). Stakeholder influence strategies. *Academy of Management Review,* 24(2): 191–205.

Fry, F.L. and Hock, R.J. (1976). Who claims corporate responsibility? The biggest and the worst. *Business and Society Review*, 18: 62–65.

Galaskiewicz, J. (1991). Making corporate actors accountable: institution-building in Minneapolis-St. Paul. In W.W. Powell and P.J. DiMaggio (eds.), *The New Institutionalism in Organizational Analysis*. Chicago, IL: University of Chicago Press, pp. 293–310.

Gates, W.H. (2008). *A New Approach to Capitalism in the 21st Century*. www.weforum.org/pdf.php?download=59533.

Gayathri, A. (2013). Wal-Mart audit, following Rana Plaza accident, finds safety issues at Bangladesh factories. *International Business Times*, November 18. www.ibtimes.com/wal-mart-audit-following-rana-pl aza-accident-finds-safety-issues-bangladesh-factories-1473640.

Gerde, V.W. and White, C.G. (2003). Auditor independence, accounting firms, and the Securities and Exchange Commission. *Business & Society*, 42(1): 83–114.

Ghoshal, S. and Bartlett, C. (1990). The multinational corporation as an interorganizational network. *Academy of Management Review*, 15(4): 584–602.

Gilbert, D.U. and Rasche, A. (2008). Opportunities and problems of standardized ethics initiatives—a stakeholder theory perspective. *Journal of Business Ethics*, 85: 755–773.

Godfrey, P.C. (2005). The relationship between corporate philanthropy and shareholder wealth: a risk management perspective. *Academy of Management Review*, 30(4): 777–798.

   (2014). *More Than Money: Five Forms of Capital to Create Wealth and Eliminate Poverty*. Stanford, CA: Stanford University Press.

Godfrey, P.C., Merrill, C.B., and Hansen, J.M. (2009). The relationship between corporate social responsibility and shareholder value: an empirical test of the risk management hypothesis. *Strategic Management Journal*, 30(4): 425–445.

Goldenberg, S. (2010a). Obama: 'No more offshore drilling in Gulf of Mexico until 2017.' *The Guardian*, December 3. www.theguardian. com/environment/2010/dec/02/obama-offshore-drilling.

   (2010b). United States sues BP over Gulf oil disaster. *The Guardian*, December 15. www.theguardian.com/business/2010/dec/16/united-states-sues-bp-gulf-oil?INTCMP=SRCH.

Goldman, D. (2015). Zuckerberg has his Tim Cook moment. *CNN Money*, January 28. http://money.cnn.com/2015/01/28/technology/social/zuckerberg-internet-cook.

Goranova, M. and Ryan, L.V. (2014). Shareholder activism: a multidisciplinary review. *Journal of Management*, 40(5): 1230–1268.

Granovetter, M. (1973). The strength of weak ties. *American Journal of Sociology*, 78(6): 1360–1380.

(1985). Economic action and social structure: the problem of embeddedness. *American Journal of Sociology*, 91(3): 481–510.

Grayson, D. and Hodges, A. (2004). *Corporate Social Opportunity! Seven Steps to Make Corporate Social Responsibility Work for Your Business*. Sheffield: Greenleaf Publishing.

Greenhouse, S. (2005). Suit says Wal-Mart is lax on labor abuses overseas. *New York Times Business*, September 14. www.nytimes.com/2005/09/14/business/14walmart.html?_r=0.

(2013). As firms line up on factories, Wal-Mart plans solo effort. *The New York Times*, May 14. www.nytimes.com/2013/05/15/business/six-retailers-join-bangladesh-factory-pact.html?pagewanted=all&_r=0.

Greening, D.W. and Turban, D.B. (2000). Corporate social performance as a competitive advantage in attracting a quality workforce. *Business & Society*, 39(3): 254–280.

Griffin, J.J. (2000). Corporate social performance: research directions for the 21st century. *Business & Society*, 39(4): 479–491.

(2008). Re-examining corporate community investment: Allen's Australian Centre for Corporate Public Affairs (ACCPA) corporate community involvement report. *Journal of Public Affairs*, 8: 219–227.

Griffin, J.J. and Dunn, P. (2004). Corporate public affairs: commitment, resources, and structure. *Business & Society*, 43(2): 196–220.

Griffin, J.J. and Mahon, J.F. (1997). The corporate social performance and corporate financial performance debate twenty-five years of incomparable research. *Business & Society*, 36(1): 5–31.

Griffin, J.J. and Prakash, A. (2014). Corporate responsibility: initiatives and mechanisms. *Business & Society*, 53: 465–482.

Griffin, J.J. and Weber, J. (2006). Industry social analysis examining the beer industry. *Business & Society*, 45(4): 413–440.

Griffin, J.J., McNulty, M., and Schoeffler, W. (2005). Shaping Brazil's emerging GMO policy: opportunities for leadership. *Journal of Public Affairs*, 5(3–4): 287–298.

Griffin, J.J., Bryant, A., and Koerber, C.P. (2015). Corporate responsibility and employee relations: from external pressure to action. *Group & Organization Management*, 40(3): 378–404.

Griffin, R.P. (2010). *Characteristics of the National Capital Region Homeland Security Network: A Case Study of the Practice of Coordination at the Regional Metropolitan Level*. Doctoral dissertation. Blacksburg, VA: Virginia Polytechnic Institute and State University.

Grimsey, D. and Lewis, M.K. (2007). *Public Private Partnerships: The Worldwide Revolution in Infrastructure Provision and Project Finance.* Cheltenham: Edward Elgar.

Gumbel, A. (2005). Wal-Mart: is this the worst company in the world? *The Independent*, November 2. www.independent.co.uk/news/world/americas/walmart-is-this-the-worst-company-in-the-world-324050.html.

Gunningham, N., Kagan, R.A., and Thornton, D. (2003). *Shades of Green: Business, Regulation, and Environment.* Stanford, CA: Stanford University Press.

Gunther, M. (2011). Have I fallen in love with Walmart? *Grist*, December 4. www.marcgunther.com/have-i-fallen-in-love-with-walmart.

Gutierrez, C. (2010). Moody's cuts BP credit rating. *Forbes*, June 18. www.forbes.com/2010/06/18/moodys-cuts-bp-rating-markets-equities-spill.html.

Harrison, J.S. and Freeman, R.E. (1999). Stakeholders, social responsibility, and performance: empirical evidence and theoretical perspectives. *Academy of Management Journal*, 42(5): 479–485.

Harrison, J.S. and Wicks, A.C. (2012). Stakeholder theory, value, and firm performance. *Business Ethics Quarterly*, 23(1): 97–124.

Hart, S.L. and Sharma, S. (2004). Engaging fringe stakeholders for competitive imagination. *Academy of Management Executive*, 18(1): 7–18.

Harting, T.R., Harmeling, S.S., and Venkataraman, S. (2006). Innovative stakeholder relations: when 'ethics pays' (and when it doesn't). *Business Ethics Quarterly*, 16(1): 43–68.

Healy, R. (2014). *Corporate Political Strategy: Why Firms Do What They Do.* London and New York: Routledge Press.

Healy, R. and Griffin, J.J. (2004). Building BP's reputation: tooting your own horn, 2001–2002, *Public Relations Quarterly*, 49(4).

Heineman, B.W. (2008). *High Performance with High Integrity.* Boston, MA: Harvard Business Press.

Henisz, W.J. (2014). *Corporate Diplomacy: Building Reputations and Relationships with External Stakeholders.* Sheffield: Greenleaf Publishing.

Henisz, W.J., Dorobantu, S., and Nartey, L. (2014). Spinning gold: the financial returns to stakeholder engagement. *Strategic Management Journal*, 35: 1727–1748.

Hess, D. (2001). Regulating corporate social performance: a new look at social accounting, auditing, and reporting. *Business Ethics Quarterly*, 11(2): 307–330.

  (2007). Social reporting and new governance regulation: the prospects of achieving corporate accountability through transparency. *Business Ethics Quarterly*, 17(3): 453–476.

(2008). The three pillars of corporate social reporting as new governance regulation: disclosure, dialogue, and development. *Business Ethics Quarterly*, 18(4): 447–482.

Hess, D., Rogovsky, N., and Dunfee, T. (2008). The next wave of corporate community involvement: Corporate social initiatives. In A. Crane, D. Matten, and L. Spence (eds.), *Corporate Social Responsibility: Readings and Cases in a Global Context*. Oxford: Oxford University Press.

Hillman, A.J., Keim, G.D., and Luce, R.A. (2001). Board composition and stakeholder performance: do stakeholder directors make a difference? *Business & Society*, 40(3): 295–314.

Hoffman, A.J. (1999). Institutional evolution and change: environmentalism and the US chemical industry. *Academy of Management Journal*, 42: 351–371.

Hoffman, A.J. and Jennings, P.D. (2011). The BP oil spill as cultural anomaly? Institutional context, conflict and change. *Journal of Management Inquiry*, 20(2): 100–112.

Hoffman, A.J. and Ocasio, W. (2001). Not all events are attended equally: toward a middle-range theory of industry attention to external events. *Organization Science*, 12(4): 414–434.

Hull, D. (2012). 13 things to know about California's cap-and-trade program. *Mercury News*, November. www.mercurynews.com/ci_2209253 3/13-things-know-about-california-cap-trade-program.

Husted, B.W. and de Jesus Salazar, J. (2006). Taking Friedman seriously: maximizing profits and social performance. *Journal of Management Studies*, 43(1): 75–91.

Ikenson, D.J. (2009). *Hard Lessons from the Auto Bailouts*. Cato Policy Report, Cato Institute. www.cato.org/policy-report/novemberdecember-2009/hard-lessons-auto-bailouts.

Immelt, J. (2005). *Eco-Imagination, Opening Remarks*. Washington, DC: The George Washington University. www.ge.com/about-us/ecomagination.

Ioannou, I. and Serafeim, G. (2012). What drives corporate social performance? The role of nation-level institutions. *Journal of International Business Studies*, 43(9): 834–864.

Isidore, C. (2014). GM cars sold: 12 million. Recalled: 13.8 million. *CNN Money*, May 22. www.money.cnn.com/2014/05/21/news/companies/gm-recall-nightmare/index.html.

Jenkins, B., Valikai, K., and Baptista, P. (2013). *The Coca-Cola Company's 5by20 Initiative: Empowering Women Entrepreneurs Along the Value Chain*. Cambridge, MA: Harvard Kennedy School CSR Initiative.

Jensen, M.C. (2002). Value maximization, stakeholder theory, and the corporate objective function. *Business Ethics Quarterly*, 12(2): 235–256.

Jones, B., Wright, T., Shapiro, J., and Keane, R (2014a). *The State of the International Order.* Washington, DC: Brookings Institute Foreign Policy Paper. www.brookings.edu/~/media/research/files/reports/2014/02/state %20of%20the%20international%20order/intlorder_report.

Jones, D.A., Willness, C.R., and Madey, S. (2014b). Why are job seekers attracted by corporate social performance? Experimental and field tests of three signal-based mechanisms. *Academy of Management Journal,* 57: 383–404.

Jones, T.M. (1991). Ethical decision making by individuals in organizations: an issue-contingent model. *Academy of Management Review,* 16(2): 366–395.

(1995). Instrumental stakeholder theory: a synthesis of ethics and economics. *Academy of Management Review,* 20(2): 404–437.

Jones, W.J. and Silvestri, G.A. (2010). The Master Settlement Agreement and its impact on tobacco use 10 years later: lessons for physicians about health policy making. *Chest,* 137(3): 692–700.

Kageyama, Y. (2014). After Fukushima, Japan gets green boom and glut. www.news.yahoo.com/fukushima-japan-gets-green-boom-070439530.html.

Kahneman, D. and Tversky, A. (1979). Prospect theory: an analysis of decision under risk. *Econometrica,* 47: 263–291.

Kapner, S., Mukerji, B., and Banjo, S. (2013). Before Dhaka collapse, some firms fled risk: Wal-Mart and Levi Strauss were among retailers that backed away from Bangladesh's multistory garment factories. *The Wall Street Journal,* May 8. www.wsj.com/news/articles/SB1000142412788 7324766604578458802423873488.

Katz, B. and Bradley, J. (2014). A year later, what cities can learn from Detroit's bankruptcy. *Fortune,* July 23. www.brookings.edu/research/opinions/2014/07/22-detroit-bankruptcy-year-later-katz-bradley.

Kaufman, M. (2007). New allies on the Amazon. *Washington Post,* April 23. www.washingtonpost.com/wp-dyn/content/article/2007/04/23/AR2007042301903.htm.

Kedia, B. and Kuntz, E.C. (1981). The context of social performance: an empirical study of Texas banks. In L.E. Preston (ed.), *Research in Corporate Social Performance and Policy,* 3rd edn. Greenwich, CT: JAI Press, pp. 133–154.

Kell, G. (2005). The Global Compact: selected experiences and reflections. *Journal of Business Ethics,* 59: 69–79.

Khavul, S. (2010). Microfinance: creating opportunities for the poor? *Academy of Management Perspectives,* 24(3): 58–72.

Kiron, D., Shockley, R., Kruschwitz, N., Finch, G., and Haydock, M. (2011). Analytics: the widening divide. *MIT Sloan Management Review,* 53(2): 1–22.

Kish-Gephart, J.J., Harrison, D.A., and Treviño, L.K. (2010). Bad apples, bad cases, and bad barrels: meta-analytic evidence about sources of unethical decisions at work. *Journal of Applied Psychology*, 95(1): 1–31.

Koerber, C.P. (2011). *Lending to Low and Moderate Income Borrowers: Board Composition, Stakeholder Outreach and Regulatory Environment.* Doctoral dissertation. Washington, DC: George Washington University. www.pqdtopen.proquest.com/pqdtopen/doc/858608348.html?FMT=AI.

Kolk, A. (2005). Corporate social responsibility in the coffee sector: the dynamics of MNC responses and code development. *European Management Journal*, 23(2): 228–236.

Kolk, A. and van Tulder, R. (2002). The effectiveness of self-regulation: corporate codes of conduct and child labour. *European Management Journal*, 20(3): 260–271.

Korn, M. (2014). High beef prices force the return of 'pink slime.' *Yahoo! Finance*, August, 24. http://finance.yahoo.com/news/high-beef-prices-fo rce-the-return-of–pink-slime-133522348.html.

Kostova, T. (1999). Transnational transfer of strategic organizational practices: A contextual perspective. *Academy of Management Review*, 24(2): 308–324.

Kostova, T. and Roth, K. (2002). Adoption of an organizational practice by subsidiaries of multinational corporations: institutional and relational effects. *Academy of Management Journal*, 45(1): 215–233.

Kostova, T. and Zaheer, S. (1999) Organizational legitimacy under conditions of complexity: the case of the multinational enterprise. *Academy of Management Review*, 24(1): 64–81.

Kotler, P. (2007). *On Corporate Social Responsibility.* Presented as the Robert P. Maxon lecture, April, Washington, DC: George Washington University. www.business.gwu.edu/wp-content/uploads/2014/09/ICR_ Maxon_Kotler_Lecture.pdf.

KPMG (2005). *International Survey of Corporate Responsibility Reporting.* New York: KPMG Global Sustainability Services. www.gppi.net/fileadmin/gppi/kpmg2005.pdf.

KPMG (2008). *International Survey of Corporate Responsibility Reporting.* New York: KPMG Global Sustainability Services. www.kpmg.com/EU/ en/Documents/KPMG_International_survey_Corporate_responsibility_Survey_Reporting_2008.pdf.

KPMG (2011). *International Survey of Corporate Responsibility Reporting.* New York: KPMG Global Sustainability Services. www.kpmg.com/EU/ en/Documents/KPMG_International_survey_Corporate_responsibility_Survey_Reporting_2011.pdf.

Krauss, C. and Schwartz, J. (2012). BP will plead guilty and pay over $4 billion, *The New York Times*, November 15. www.nytimes.com/2012/11/16/business/global/16iht-bp16.html?pagewanted=all&_r=0.

Krugman, P. (2009). How did economists get it so wrong? *The New York Times Magazine*, September 6, 36–43.

Lala, R.M. (1984). *The Heartbeat of a Trust: Fifty Years of the Sir Dorabji Tata Trust*. New Delhi: Tata McGraw-Hill.

(2007). *The Romance of Tata Steel*. New Delhi: Penguin, Viking.

Lane, P. (2012). A sense of place: geography matters as much as ever, despite the digital revolution. *The Economist*, October 27.

Larino, J. (2015). BP oil spill trial wraps up nearly 2 years after historic litigation began. *The Times-Picayune*, February 2.

Laufer, W.S. (2003). Social accountability and corporate greenwashing. *Journal of Business Ethics*, 43(3): 253.

Lawrence, A.T. (2002). The drivers of stakeholder engagement: reflections on the case of Royal Dutch Shell. *Journal of Corporate Citizenship*, 6: 71–85.

Leipziger, D. (2009). *SA8000, the First Decade: Implementation, Influence, and Impact*. Sheffield: Greenleaf Publishing Limited.

Long, H. (2014). GM recalls reach 30 million for year. *CNN Money*, October 4. www.money.cnn.com/2014/10/04/news/companies/gm-recalls-30-million-vehicles.

Logsdon, J.M. and Wood, D.J. (2002). Business citizenship: from domestic to global level of analysis. *Business Ethics Quarterly*, 12(2): 155–187.

(2005). Global business citizenship and voluntary codes of ethical conduct. *Journal of Business Ethics*, 59: 55–67.

Lucea, R. and Doh, J. (2012). International strategy for the non-market context: stakeholders, issues, networks, and geography. *Business & Politics*, 14(3): 1–30.

Macalaster, T. (2010). BP frozen out of Arctic oil drilling race, *The Guardian*, August 25. www.theguardian.com/environment/2010/aug/25/bp-arctic-greenland-oil-drilling.

Mackey, J. and Sisodia, R. (2013). *Conscious Capitalism: Liberating the Heroic Spirit of Business*. Cambridge, MA: Harvard Business Review Press.

Mackey, M. (2010). Oil spill: 90 days out, a bold look at the big numbers. *The Fiscal Times*, July 20. www.thefiscaltimes.com/Articles/2010/07/20/Oil-Spill-Bold-Look-Bare-Economic-Numbers.

MacMillan, D., Specter, M., and Rusli, E.M. (2014). Airbnb weighs employee stock sale at 13 billion valuation. *The Wall Street Journal*, October 23. www.wsj.com/articles/airbnb-mulls-employee-stock-sale-at-13-billion-valuation-1414100930.

Mahon J.F. (1989). Corporate political strategy. *Business in the Contemporary World*, 2(1): 50–62.

Mahon, J.F. and Griffin, J.J. (1999). Painting a portrait: a reply. *Business & Society*, 38(1): 126–133.

Mahon, J.F. and McGowan, R.A. (1996). *Industry as a Player in the Political and Social Arena: Defining the Competitive Environment.* Greenwich, CT: Quorum Books.

Mahon, J.F., Heugens, P.M.A.R., and Lamertz, K. (2004). Social networks and nonmarket strategy, *Journal of Public Affairs*, 4(2): 170–189.

Marcus, A.A. and Goodman, R.S. (1986). Compliance and performance: toward a contingency theory. In L.E. Preston and J.E. Post (eds.), *Research in Corporate Social Performance and Policy*, 8th edn. Greenwich, CT: JAI Press, Inc., pp. 193–221.

Margolis, J.D. (2009). The responsibility gap. *Hedgehog Review*, 11(2): 41–53.

Margolis, J.D. and Walsh, J.P. (2001). *People and Profits? The Search for a Link between a Company's Social and Financial Performance.* Mahwah, NJ: Lawrence Erlbaum Associates.

(2003). Misery loves companies: rethinking social initiatives by business. *Administrative Science Quarterly*, 48: 268–305.

Martin, R.L. and Osberg, S. (2007). Social entrepreneurship: the case for definition. *Stanford Social Innovation Review*, spring: 29–39. www.ssireview. org/articles/entry/social_entrepreneurship_the_case_for_definition.

Matten, D. and Moon, J. (2008). 'Implicit' and 'explicit' CSR: a conceptual framework for a comparative understanding of corporate social responsibility. *Academy of Management Review*, 33(2): 404–424.

Maxfield, J. (2014). Amazon.com is 20 years old, but still an infant. *The Motley Fool*, September 29. www.fool.com/investing/general/2014/09/29/amazoncom-is-20-years-old-but-still-an-infant.aspx.

McCain Foods Limited (2009). *McCain Foods' Global Social Responsibility Report 2009.* www.mccain.com/newsroom/Pages/McCainReleasesitsFirstGlobalCSRReport.aspx.

McGuire, J.B., Sundgren, A., and Schneeweis, T. (1988). Corporate social responsibility and firm financial performance. *Academy of Management Journal*, 31(4): 854–872.

McKinsey (2014). *Sustainability's Strategic Worth: McKinsey Global Survey Results.* New York: McKinsey & Company, Insights & Publications. www.mckinsey.com/insights/sustainability/sustainabilitys_strategic_worth_mckinsey_global_survey_results.

McWilliams, A. and Siegel, D. (2001). Corporate social responsibility: a theory of the firm perspective. *Academy of Management Review*, 26(1): 117–127.

McWilliams, A., Siegel, D.S., and Wright, P.M. (2006). Corporate social responsibility: strategic implications. *Journal of Management Studies*, 43(1): 1–18.

Meyer, J. and Rowan, B. (1983). Institutionalized organizations: formal structure as myth and ceremony. In P.J. DiMaggio and W.W. Powell (eds.), *The New Institutionalism in Organizational Analysis*. Chicago, IL: University of Chicago Press, pp. 41–62.

Miles, R.H. (1987). *Managing the Corporate Social Environment: A Grounded Theory*. Englewood Cliffs, NJ: Prentice-Hall.

Milne, M.J. and Patten, D.M. (2002). Securing organizational legitimacy: an experimental decision case examining the impact of environmental disclosures. *Accounting, Auditing & Accountability Journal*, 15(3): 372.

Mitnick, B.M. (1995). Systematics and CSR: the theory and processes of normative referencing. *Business & Society*, 34(1): 5–33.

Mitnick, B.M. and Mahon, J.F. (2007). The concept of reputational bliss. *Journal of Business Ethics*, 72(4): 323–333.

Mitroff, I. (1994). Crisis management and environmentalism: a natural fit. *California Management Review*, 36(2): 101–113.

Mitroff, I., Shrivastava, P., and Udwadia, F.E. (1987). Effective crisis management. *Academy of Management Executive*, 1(3): 283–292.

Moll, R. (2003). Ford Motor Company and the Firestone tyre recall. *Journal of Public Affairs*, 3(3): 200–211.

Muirhead, S.A. and Tillman, A. (2000). *The Impact of Mergers and Acquisitions on Corporate Citizenship*. www.conference-board.org/publications/publicationdetail.cfm?publicationid=448.

Murphy, P. (2001). Top companies leave charities in the cold. *Society Guardian*, November 5. www.theguardian.com/society/2001/nov/05/charities.

Murray, T. and Kapur, N. (2014). In new report, KKR deepens commitment to tackling ESG concerns. *Environmental Defense Fund + Business*, July 14. www.business.edf.org/blog/tag/private-equity-2.

Obama, B. (2009). *President Obama Signs an Executive Order Focused on Federal Leadership in Environmental, Energy, and Economic Performance*, October 5. www.whitehouse.gov/the_press_office/President-Obama-signs-an-Executive-Order-Focused-on-Federal-Leadership-in-Environmental-Energy-and-Economic-Performance.

O'Donovan, G. (2002). Environmental disclosures in the annual report: extending the applicability and predictive power of legitimacy theory. *Accounting, Auditing & Accountability Journal*, 15(3): 344–372.

Orlitzky, M., Schmidt, F.L., and Rynes, S.L. (2003). Corporate social and financial performance: a meta-analysis. *Organization Studies*, 24(3): 403–411.

Pasternak, K. (2014). How branding is helping GM survive recall disaster. *Marshall*, September 24. www.marshallstrategy.com/blog/consumer/how-branding-is-helping-gm-survive-recall-disaster.

Patnaik, S. (2012). *Essays in International Non-market Strategy and the Political Economy of Environmental Regulation*. Doctoral dissertation. Boston, MA: Harvard University.

Perry, V.G. and Blumenthal, P.M. (2012). Understanding the fine print: the need for effective testing of mandatory mortgage loan disclosure. *Journal of Public Policy & Marketing*, 31(2): 305–312.

Perry, V.G. and Motley, C.M. (2009). Where's the fine print? Marketing and the mortgage market crisis. *California Management Review*, 52(1): 29–44.

Pfeffer, J. and Salancik, G. (1978). *The External Control of Organizations: A Resource Dependence Perspective*. New York: Harper & Row.

Phillips, R. and Caldwell, C.B. (2005). Value chain responsibility: a farewell to arm's length. *Business and Society Review*, 110(4): 345–370.

Phillips, R.A. and Freeman, R.E. (2008). Corporate citizenship and community stakeholders. In A.G. Scherer and G. Palazzo (eds.), *Handbook of Research on Global Corporate Citizenship*. Cheltenham: Edward Elgar Publishing, pp. 99–115.

Porter, M.E. (1985). *Competitive Advantage: Creating and Sustaining Superior Performance*. New York: The Free Press.

Porter, M.E. and Kramer, M.R. (2002). The competitive advantage of corporate philanthropy. *Harvard Business Review*, 80(12): 56–68.

(2006). Strategy and society: the link between competitive strategy and corporate social responsibility. *Harvard Business Review*, 84(12): 78–92.

(2011). Creating shared value. *Harvard Business Review*, 89(1): 2–17. www.hbr.org/2011/01/the-big-idea-creating-shared-value.

Porter, M.E. and van der Linde, C. (1995). Toward a new conception of the environment-competitiveness relationship. *Journal of Economic Perspectives*, 9(4): 97–118.

Post, J.E., Preston, L.E., and Sachs, S. (2002). *Redefining the Corporation: Stakeholder Management and Organizational Wealth*. Stanford, CA: Stanford University Press.

Prakash, A. and Griffin, J.J. (2012). Corporate responsibility, multinationals, and nation-states. *Business & Politics*, 14(3): 1–10.

Prakash, A. and Gugerty, M.K. (2010). *Advocacy Organizations and Collective Action*. Cambridge: Cambridge University Press.

Prakash, A. and Potoski. M. (2006). Racing to the bottom? Globalization, environmental governance, and ISO 14001. *American Journal of Political Science*, 50: 347–361.

Prakash, A. and Potoski, M. (2014). Global private regimes, domestic public law: ISO 14001 and pollution reduction. *Comparative Political Studies*, 47(3): 369–394.

Prakash, S. and Valentine, V. (2007). *Timeline: The Rise and Fall of Vioxx*. www.npr.org/templates/story/story.php?storyId=5470430.

Preston, L.E. and Post, J.E. (1975). *Private Management and Public Policy: The Principle of Public Responsibility*. Englewood Cliffs, NJ: Prentice-Hall, Inc.

Preston, L.E. and Windsor, D. (1992). *The Rules of the Game in the Global Economy: Policy Regimes for International Business*. Boston, MA: Kluwer Academic Publishers.

Price, T. (2000). *Cyber Activism: Advocacy Groups and the Internet*. Washington, DC: Foundation for Public Affairs. www.thepriceswrite.com/cyberactivism.pdf.

(2002). *Public Affairs Strategies in the Internet Age*. Washington, DC: Foundation for Public Affairs. www.thepriceswrite.com/strategies.pdf.

Putnam, R.D. (2000). *Bowling Alone: The Collapse and Revival of American Community*. New York: Simon & Schuster.

Rana Plaza (2014). www.ranaplaza-arrangement.org.

Rasche, A. and Esser, D.E. (2006). From stakeholder management to stakeholder accountability: applying Habermasian discourse ethics to accountability research. *Journal of Business Ethics*, 65(3): 251–267.

Rasche, A. and Kell, G. (eds.) (2010). *The United Nations Global Compact: Achievement, Trends and Challenges*. Cambridge and New York: Cambridge University Press.

Raufflet, E.B. and Mills, A.J. (2009). *The Dark Side: Critical Cases on the Downside of Business*. Sheffield: Greenleaf Publishing Limited.

Raynolds, L.T., Long, M.A., and Murray, D.L. (2014). Regulating corporate responsibility in the American market: a comparative analysis of voluntary certifications. *Competition and Change*, 18(2): 91–110.

Rehbein, K., Logsdon, J.M., and Van Buren, H.J. (2013). Corporate responses to shareholder activists: considering the dialogue alternative. *Journal of Business Ethics*, 112(1): 137–154.

Renz, L. (2001). *Giving in the Aftermath of 9/11: Foundations and Corporations Respond*. Washington, DC: The Foundation Center.

(2002). *Giving in the Aftermath of 9/11: An Update on the Foundations and Corporations Response*. Washington, DC: The Foundation Center.

Rindova, V.P., Williamson, I.O., Petkova, A., and Sever, J.M. (2005). Being good or being known: an empirical examination of the dimensions, antecedents, and consequences of organizational reputation. *Academy of Management Journal*, 48(6): 1033–1049.

Rivoli, P. (2005). *Travels of a T-Shirt in a Global Economy: An Economist Examines the Markets, Power, and Politics of World Trade*. Hoboken, NY: John Wiley & Sons.

Roberts, J.M. and Markley, A.W. (2012). *US Should Oppose International Corporate Social Responsibility Mandates*. The Heritage Foundation. www.heritage.org/research/reports/2012/05/why-the-us-should-op pose-international-corporate-social-responsibility-csr-mandates.

Rothaermel, F.T. (2015). *Strategic Management: Concepts*, 2nd edn. Burr Ridge, IL: McGraw-Hill.

Rowley, T. (1997). Moving beyond dyadic ties: a network theory of stakeholder influences. *Academy of Management Review*, 22(4): 887–910.

Rowley, T. and Berman, S.L. (2000). A brand new brand of CSP. *Business & Society*, 39(4): 397–418.

Rowley, T. and Moldoveanu, M. (2003). When will stakeholder groups act? An interest- and identity-based model of stakeholder group mobilization. *Academy of Management Review*, 28(2): 204–219.

Russo, M.V. (2009). Explaining the impact of ISO 14001 on emission performance: a dynamic capabilities perspective on process and learning. *Business Strategy and the Environment*, 18: 307–319.

Russo, M.V. and Fouts, P.A. (1997). A resource-based perspective on corporate environmental performance and profitability. *Academy of Management Journal*, 40: 534–559.

Salamon, L.M., Sokowoski, S.W., and List, R. (2003). *Global Civil Society: An Overview*. Baltimore, MD: Johns Hopkins University Center for Civil Society Study.

Salkin, A. (2013). *From Scratch: Inside the Food Network*. New York: Putnam Adult.

Santoro, M.A. and Strauss, R.J. (2012). *Wall Street Values: Business Ethics and the Global Financial Crisis*. Cambridge: Cambridge University Press.

Scherer, A.G., Palazzo, G., and Seidl, D. (2013). Managing legitimacy in complex and heterogeneous environments: sustainable development in a globalized world. *Journal of Management Studies*, 50(2): 259–284.

Selznick, P. (1957). *Leadership in Administration: A Sociological Interpretation*. Berkeley, CA: University of California Press.

Shaffer, B. and Hillman, A.J. (2000). The development of business-government strategies by diversified firms. *Strategic Management Journal*, 21: 175–190.

Shubber, K. (2014). Tobacco groups win right to challenge EU health rules. *Financial Times*, November 3. www.ft.com/intl/cms/s/0/a5f15bf4-6 37e-11e4-8216-00144feabdc0.html#axzz3I2FpJLJo.

Smith, C., Child, J., and Rowlinson, M. (1990). *Reshaping Work: The Cadbury Experience*. Cambridge: Cambridge University Press.

Smith, J. (2013). The companies with the best CSR reputations. *Forbes*. www.forbes.com/sites/jacquelynsmith/2013/10/02/the-companies-with-the-best-csr-reputations-2.

Smith, N.C. (1994). The new corporate philanthropy. *Harvard Business Review*, May/June, 105–116.

  (2003). Corporate social responsibility: whether or how? *California Management Review*, 45(4): 52–76.

Social Media (2014). 1800 Enterprises, LLC [Video file]. www.youtube.com/watch?v=1pahLo5TTy4.

Stecklow, S. and White, E. (2004). What price virtue? At some retailers, 'fair trade' carries a very high cost. *Wall Street Journal*, June 8. www.online.wsj.com/articles/SB108664921254731069.

Stempel, J. (2014). US judge upholds BP 'gross negligence' Gulf spill ruling. *Reuters*, November 13. www.reuters.com/article/2014/11/14/us-bp-spill-idUSKCN0IY01320141114.

Stern, G.M. (1976). *The Buffalo Creek Disaster*. New York: Vintage Books.

Stout, L. (2012). *The Shareholder Value Myth: How Putting Shareholders First Harms Investors, Corporations, and the Public*. San Francisco, CA: Berrett-Koehler Publishers.

Strasser, M. (2014). A year after Bangladesh's deadly factory collapse, western companies slow to compensate victims. *Newsweek*, April 24. www.newsweek.com/year-after-bangladeshs-deadly-factory-collapse-western-companies-slow-compensate-248506.

Surroca, J., Tribo, J.A., and Waddock, S.A. (2010). Corporate responsibility and financial performance: the role of intangible resources. *Strategic Management Journal*, 31: 463–490.

Swartz, J. (2010). Timberland's CEO on standing up to 65,000 angry activists. *Harvard Business Review*, September, 39–43.

Sweney, M. (2010). BP falls out of index of top 100 brands after *Deepwater Horizon* oil spill. *The Guardian*, September 16. www.theguardian.com/media/2010/sep/16/apple-iphone-interbrand.

Tetrault-Sirsly, C.A. and Lamertz, K. (2008). When does a corporate social responsibility initiative provide a first-mover advantage? *Business & Society*, 47(3): 343–369.

Thauer, C. (2014). Goodness comes from within: inter-organizational dynamics of corporate social responsibility. *Business & Society*, 53(4): 483–516.

Thomas, K. and Foster, M. (2010). Toyota boasted saving $100m on recall, documents show. *The Washington Times*, February 22.

www.washingtontimes.com/news/2010/feb/22/toyota-boasted-saving-100m-recall/?page=all.

Timberg, C. and Birnbaum, M. (2014). In Google case, EU court says people are entitled to control their own online histories. *The Washington Post*, May 13. www.washingtonpost.com/business/technology/eu-court-people-entitled-to-control-own-online-histories/2014/05/13/8e4495d6-dabf-11e3-8009-71de85b9c527_story.html.

Tolbert, P.S. and Zucker, L.G. (1983). Institutional sources of change in the formal structure of organizations: the diffusion of civil service reform. *Administrative Science Quarterly*, 28(1): 22–39.

Tseng, N-H. (2010). BP after the spill: bankrupt, bought or business as usual? *Fortune*, June 7. http://archive.fortune.com/2010/06/04/news/companies/gulf_coast_BP_bankruptcy_odds.fortune/index.htm.

Turban, D.B. and Greening, D.W. (1997). Corporate social performance and organizational attractiveness to prospective employees. *Academy of Management Journal*, 40: 658–672.

Ullmann, A.A. (1985). Data in search of a theory: a critical examination of the relationships among social performance, social disclosure, and economic performance of US firms. *Academy of Management Review*, 10(3): 540–557.

United States (2005). *Globalization: Numerous Federal Activities Complement US Business's Global Corporate Social Responsibility Efforts*. Government Accountability Organization Report #GAO-05-744 Global CR. Washington, DC: US Government Accountability Office.

USAID (2013). USAID & Starbucks support Colombian small-coffee farmers to improve their livelihoods. *USAID*, August 26. www.usaid.gov/news-information/press-releases/usaid-starbucks-support-colombian-small-coffee-farmers-improve-livelihoods.

Vachani, S. and Smith, N.C. (2008). Socially responsible distribution: strategies for reaching the bottom of the pyramid. *California Management Review*, 50: 52–84.

Vock, V., Dolen, W.V., and Kolk, A. (2014). Micro-level interactions in business-nonprofit partnerships. *Business & Society*, 53(4): 517–550.

Vogel, D. (2005). *The Market for Virtue: The Potential and Limits of Corporate Social Responsibility*. Washington, DC: Brookings Institution Press.

Waddock, S.A. (2008a). *The Difference Makers: How Social and Institutional Entrepreneurs Created the Corporate Responsibility Movement*. Sheffield: Greenleaf Publishing Ltd.

(2008b). Building a new institutional infrastructure for corporate responsibility. *Academy of Management Perspectives*, 22(3): 87–108.

Waddock, S.A. and Graves, S.B. (1997). The corporate social performance-financial performance link. *Strategic Management Journal*, 18(4): 303–319.

Wagner, S. and Dittmar, L. (2006). The unexpected benefits of Sarbanes-Oxley. *Harvard Business Review*, 84(4): 133–140.

Waldmeir, P. (2014). China food scandal hits Yum! brand sales. *Financial Times*, October 8. www.ft.com/intl/cms/s/0/04a188f8-4ec7-11e4-b205-00144feab7de.html?siteedition=intl#axzz3I2FpJLJo.

Wartick, S.L. and Mahon, J.H. (1994). Toward a substantive definition of the corporate issue construct: a review and synthesis of the literature. *Business & Society*, 33(3): 293–311.

Wearden, G. (2010). BP credit rating slashed as oil spill costs mount. *The Guardian*, June 15. www.theguardian.com/business/2010/jun/15/bp-credit-rating-slashed-oil-spill-costs.

Weaver, G.R., Trevino, L.K., and Cochran, P.L. (1999). Integrated and decoupled corporate social performance: management commitments, external pressures, and corporate ethics practices. *Academy of Management Review*, 24(1): 539–552.

Webb, K. (2008). *The ISO 26000 Social Responsibility Standard: A Progress Report from the Front*. Presented at Georgetown University Seminar on Corporate Social Responsibility: Law, Operations and Strategy.

Webb, T. (2010a). BP oil spill: failed safety device on *Deepwater Horizon* rig was modified in China. *The Guardian*, July 18. www.theguardian.com/environment/2010/jul/18/deepwater-horizon-blow-out-preventer-china.

(2010b). Shell could pursue BP for Gulf damages. *The Guardian*, July 29. www.theguardian.com/business/2010/jul/29/shell-bp-damages-claim.

(2010c). BP charges well partner Anadarko $1bn for its share of oil spill clean up. *The Guardian*, August 3. www.theguardian.com/business/2010/aug/03/bp-gulf-oil-spill-costs.

(2011). BP to cut production amid impact of *Deepwater Horizon* spill. *The Guardian*, January 30. www.theguardian.com/business/2011/jan/30/bp-production-targets-deepwater-horizon-spill.

Webb, T. and Bawden, T. (2011). Court order halts BP talks with Rosneft. *The Guardian*, February 1. www.theguardian.com/business/2011/feb/01/bp-loss-gulf-oil-spill-resumes-dividend.

Webb, T. and Pilkington, E. (2010). Gulf oil spill: BP could face ban as US launches criminal investigation. *The Guardian*, June 1. www.theguardian.com/environment/2010/jun/01/gulf-oil-spill-bp-future.

Weick, K.E. (1979). *The Social Psychology of Organizing*. Reading, MA: Addison-Wesley Publishing Company, Inc.

(1984). Small wins: redefining the scale of social problems. *American Psychologist*, 39(1): 40–49.

Wicks, A.C., Berman, S.L., and Jones, T.M. (1999). The structure of optimal trust: moral and strategic implications. *Academy of Management Review*, 24(1): 99–116.

Williams, C. and Conley, X. (2008). *Equator Principles*. Presented at the Georgetown University Law Center workshop on Corporate Social Responsibility: Law, Operations & Strategy.

Williams, O.F. (2004). The UN Global Compact: the challenge and the promise. *Business Ethics Quarterly*, 14(4): 755–774.

Williamson, O.E. (1985). *The Economic Institution of Capitalism*. New York: Free Press.

Wilmshurst, T.D. and Frost, G.R. (2000). Corporate environmental reporting: a test of legitimacy theory. *Accounting, Auditing & Accountability Journal*, 13(1): 10.

Windsor, D. (2004). The development of international business norms. *Business Ethics Quarterly*, 14(4): 729–754.

(2006). Corporate social responsibility: three key approaches. *Journal of Management Studies*, 43(1): 93–114.

Windsor, D. and Getz, K.A. (1999). Regional market integration and the development of global norms for enterprise conduct: the case of international bribery. *Business & Society*, 38(4): 415–449.

Wood, D.J. (1991). Corporate social performance revisited. *Academy of Management Review*, 16(4): 691–718.

Wood, D.J. and Jones, R.E. (1995). Stakeholder mismatching: a theoretical problem in empirical research on corporate social performance. *International Journal of Organizational Analysis*, 3: 229–267.

Wood, D.J., Logsdon, J.M., Lewellyn, P.G., and Davenport, K. (2006) *Global Business Citizenship: A Transformative Framework for Ethics and Sustainable Capitalism*. Armonk, NY: M.E. Sharpe.

World Bank (2001). *Access to Safe Water*. www.worldbank.org/depweb/english/modules/environm/water.

Yaziji, M. (2004). Turning gadflies into allies. *Harvard Business Review*, 82(2): 110–115.

Yunus, M. (2007). *Creating a World without Poverty: Social Business and the Future of Capitalism*. New York: Perseus Books Group.

Yunus, M. and Weber, K. (2007). *Creating a World without Poverty: Social Business and the Future of Capitalism*. New York: Public Affairs.

Zadek, S. (1998). Balancing performance, ethics, and accountability. *Journal of Business Ethics*, 17(13): 1421–1442.

(2003). *The Civil Corporation: The New Economy of Corporate Citizenship*. London: Earthscan.

(2004). The path to corporate responsibility. *Harvard Business Review*, 82(12): 125–132.

Zammuto, R.F. (2008). Accreditation and the globalization of business. *Academy of Management Learning & Education*, 7(2): 256–268.

Zoellick, R.B. (2011). *Beyond Aid*. Speech by World Bank Group President Presented at George Washington University. http://web.worldbank.org/WBSITE/EXTERNAL/NEWS/0,contentMDK:23000133~pagePK:34370~piPK:42770~theSitePK:4607,00.html.

Examples of web-based resources

I. Impacts via core business practices
   a. Financing: SR investors, stock indexes, research and investment firms, organizations with SR investments, microfinance organizations
   b. Governance, employees: diversity, governance, employee relations
   c. Working conditions: employees/human rights—regulations
   d. Social entrepreneurship
II. Impacts through the value chain and industry coalitions
   a. Regional/national business principles, ratings, verification, and standards setting
III. Impacts shaping global expectations:
   a. Global business principles/industry coalitions
   b. Global policy, standards
   c. Reports, ratings, rankings, surveys
   d. Ratings and rankings
   e. Activists
IV. Press, magazines, newsletters, online
V. Academic centers, institutes, journals, think tanks

I. Impacts via core business practices

a. Financing: SR investors, stock indexes, research and investment firms, organizations with SR investments, microfinance organizations

SR investors	
CalPERS	www.calpers.ca.gov
Calvert	www.calvert.comwww.globalsolutions.org
Citizens Global	www.globalsolutions.org

313

Domini Social Funds	www.domini.com
Dreyfus	www.dreyfus.com
Green Century	www.greencentury.com
Parnassus	www.parnassus.com
Pax World	www.paxworld.com
Smith Barney	www.smithbarney.com
Trillium	www.trilliuminvest.com
Walden Asset Management	www.waldenassetmanagement.com

Stock indexes with sustainability orientation

Domini 400 Social Index	www.kld.com/indexes/ds400index/index.html
Dow Jones Sustainability Index	www.sustainability-index.com
FTSE4Good	www.ftse4good.com

Research and investment-oriented firms

Analistas Internationales en Sostenibildad SA, Spain	www.ais.com.es
Avanzi SRI Research s.r.l., Italy	www.avanzi-sri.org
Centre Info SA, Switzerland	www.centerinfo.ch
Dutch Sustainability Research BV, Netherlands	www.dsresearch.nl
GES Investment Services, AB, Sweden	www.ges-invest.com
Jantzi Research, Inc. (publishes Canadian Social Investment Database)	www.jantziresearch.com/index. asp?section=2&level_2=3
KAYEMA Investment Research & Analysis, Israel	www.kayema.com
KLD Research and Analytics (publishes Socrates database)	www.kld.com
Pensions & Investment Research Consultants Ltd., UK	www.pirc.co.uk
Scoris GmbH, Germany	www.scoris.de
SIRI Group (Sustainability Investment Research International)	www.siricompany.com
SIRIS—Sustainable Investment Research Institute P/L, Australia	www.siris.com.au

Social investment, other organizations

Coop America	www.coopamerica.org
Council for Responsible Public Investment	www.publicinvestment.org
Fair Pension (United Kingdom)	www.fairpensions.org.uk/index.htm
GoodMoney	www.goodmoney.com
Institutional Shareholder Services (Environmental, Social, Governance)	www.issproxy.com/institutional/esg/ index.jsp
Institute for Responsible Investing	www.bcccc.net/ responsibleinvestment
Interfaith Center on Corporate Responsibility (ICCR)	www.iccr.org
Investor Responsibility Research Center (IRRC)	www.iisd.org/standards/csr.asp
Responsible Wealth	www.responsiblewealth.org
Social Venture Network	www.svn.org
SocialFunds.com	www.socialfunds.com

Microfinance organizations

ABCUL Credit Unions	www.abcul.org/page/index.cfm
ACCION International	www.accion.org
ACCION USA	www.accionusa.org
Al Amana	www.alamana.org
African Development Banks Group	www.afdb.org/home.htm
Africa Microfinance Network (AFMIN)	www.afmin-ci.org
African Rural and Agricultural Credit Association (AFRACA)	www.gdrc.org/icm/afraca/afraca.html
Association Pour Le Droit a l'Initiative Economique (ADIE)	www.adie.org
ASA	www.asabd.org
BRAC	www.brac.net
Bank Rakyat Indonesia (BRI)	www.bri.co.id/english/mikrobanking/ aboutmikrobanking.aspx
Consultative Group to Assist the Poor (CGAP)	www.cgap.org
Enda Inter-Arabe	www.endarabe.org.tn
FinMark Trust	www.finmarktrust.org.za
Freedom from Hunger	www.freefromhunger.org

Foundation Zakoura	www.zakourafondation.org
Grameen Bank	www.grameen-info.org
Grameen Foundation USA	www.omidyar.net/corp/p_gf.shtml
Imp-Act	www.ids.ac.uk/impact
Microcredit European Conference	www.europa.eu.int/comm/enterprise/ events/microcredit
Microcredit Summit Campaign	www.microcreditsummit.org
Microfinance Centre for CEE & NIS	www.mfc.org.pl
Microfinance Regulatory Council	www.mfrc.co.za/index.php
Microfinance Securities	www.omidyar.net/corp/p_mf.shtml
MicroSave Africa	www.microsave-africa.com
MicroVest	www.omidyar.net/corp/p_microvest. shtml
Opportunity International	www.opportunity.org
PlaNet Finance	www.planetfinance.org/ PlaNetFinance/PagePortail/index. htm
Programme de renforcement des capacities des institutions de microfinance en Afrique francophone (CAPAF)	www.capaf.org
Sanabel Microfinance Network of the Arab Countries	www.sanabelnetwork.org
ShoreCap International Ltd	www.shorecap.net
Social Fund for Development-Yemen	www.sfd-yemen.org/SMED_Unit.htm
Unitus	www.unitus.com

Social investment professional organizations/associations

European Social Investment Forum (EuropSIF, Addressing Sustainability Through Financial Markets)	www.eurosif.org
Social Investment Forum	www.socialinvest.org
Social Investment Forum, UK	www.uksif.org/uksif
Social Investment Research Analysts Network (SIRAN)	www.siran.org
SRI in the Rockies (conference)	www.sriintherockies.com

b. Governance, employees: diversity, governance, employee relations

Business for Social Responsibility	www.bsr.org/jobs/csr/index.cfm
CSRwire	www.csrwire.com
Ethical Performance weekly job postings	www.ethicalperformance.com/recruitment/index.php
Microfinance job postings	www.microfinancegateway.org
Graduation Pledge	www.graduationpledge.org/jobs.html
Development Executive Group	developmentex.com/oppsummary.jsp
Net Impact	www.netimpact.org
International Labour Organization (ILO)	www.ilo.org
Lifeworth	www.lifeworth.com
Q-RES Project, Italy	www.qres.it
Global Business Coalition on HIV/AIDS, TB, and Malaria	www.businessfightsmalaria.org
Global Leadership Campaign	www.usglc.org

Governance

Business & Human Rights Resource Centre	www.business-humanrights.org
Business in the Community	www.bitc.org.uk
Business for Social Responsibility	www.bsr.org/
Business Partners for Development	www.bpdweb.org
Business and Human Rights Resource Center	www.business-humanrights.org/Home
Corporation 2020	www.corporation2020.org
Ethical Trading Initiative	www.ethicaltrade.org
Development Executive Group	www.developmentex.com/index.jsp
GAN-NET (Global Action Network Net)	www.gan-net.net
Making Waves: The Centre for Community Enterprise(Canada)	www.cedworks.com/waves.html
Responsible Business Initiative	www.rbipk.org
UN Millennium Development Goals	www.un.org/millenniumgoals
World Economic Forum	www.weforum.org
World Social Forum	www.forumsocialmundial.org.br/index.php?cd_language=2
CSR in the Americas	www.csramericas.org

Ethical Trading Initiative	www.ethicaltrade.org
Global Reporting Initiative (GRI)	www.globalreporting.org
Global Sullivan Principles	www.globalsullivanprinciples.org/principles.htm
Inter-American Development Bank (IDB)	www.iadb.org
International Chamber of Commerce	www.iccwbo.org
International Organization for Standardization (ISO)	www.iso.org
National Policy Association	www.npa1.org/default.asp
Organisation for Economic Co-Operation and Development (OECD)	www.oecd.org
OECD Guidelines for Multinational Enterprises	www.oecd.org/document/58/0,2340,en_2649_201185_2349370_1_1_1_1,00.html
Transparency International	www.transparency.org
United Nations Global Compact	www.unglobalcompact.org
Values Management System, Germany	www.dnwe.de
Business Council on Global Development	www.bcgdevelop.com/
Global Leadership Campaign	www.usglc.org/
Global Reporting Imitative	www.globalreporting.org
International Business Leaders Forum	www.iblf.org

Thought leaders: business principles, governance, employees

Caux Roundtable Principles for Business	www.cauxroundtable.org/principles.html
CEREX Principles	www.ceres.org
Equator Principles (financial industry)	www.equator-principles.com
Global Sustainability Index	www.global100.org/2005/index.asp
Global Sullivan Principles	www.thesullivanfoundation.org/gsp
OECD Guidelines for Multinational Enterprises	www.oecd.org/department/0,2688,en_2649_34889_1_1_1_1_1,00.html
Principles for Responsible Investing (launched April 2006)	www.unpri.org
Private Voluntary Organization (PVO) Standards (2006)	www.interaction.org/pvostandards/index.html

Tripartite Declaration of Principles Concerning Multinational Enterprises	www.ilo.org/public/english/standards/norm/sources/mne.htm
UN Global Compact Principles (launched 2000)	www.unglobalcompact.org
USS LTD report *Enhanced Analytics for a new Generation of Investor: How the Investment Industry Can Use Extra-Financial Factors in Investing*	http://usshq.co.uk/enhancedanalytics.php
SustainAbility	www.sustainability.com

c. Working conditions: employees/human rights—regulations

End Human Trafficking Now	www.humantrafficking.org
Ambedkar Principles	www.indianet.nl/ambedkarpinciples.html
American Rights at Work Report	www.americanrightsatwork.org
International Alert	www.international-alert.org

d. Social entrepreneurship

Ashoka	www.ashoka.org
Social Investment Forum	www.socialinvest.org
Enterprise and Social Policy Instituto Ethos (Ethos Institute for Business and Social Responsibility)	www.ethos.org.br
GAN-NET (Global Action Network Net)	www.gan-net.net
Responsible Business Initiative	www.rbipk.org
UN Millennium Development Goals	www.un.org/millenniumgoals
World Economic Forum	www.weforum.org
World Social Forum	www.forumsocialmundial.org.br/index.php?cd_language=2
Tamarack: The Social Economy (Canada)	http://tamarackcommunity.ca/g3s10_M4C2.html
CSR in the Americas	www.csramericas.org
Ethical Trading Initiative	www.ethicaltrade.org

Amnesty International	www.amnesty.org
Global Reporting Initiative (GRI)	www.globalreporting.org
Global Sullivan Principles	www.globalsullivanprinciples.org/ principles.htm
Social Investment Forum	www.socialinvest.org/areas/research/ trends/sri_trends_report_2005.pdf
International Organization for Standardization (ISO)	www.iso.org
National Policy Association	www.npa1.org/default.asp
Transparency International	www.transparency.org
United Nations Global Compact	www.unglobalcompact.org
Values Management System, Germany	www.dnwe.de
Center for Global Development	www.cgdev.org
Center for International Private Enterprise	www.cipe.org
Global Business Coalition on HIV/ AIDS, TB, and Malaria	www.businessfightsmalaria.org
Millennium Challenge Corporation	www.mca.gov

II. Impacts through the value chain and industry coalitions

a. Regional/national business principles, ratings, verification, and standards setting

World Economic Forum	www.weforum.org
WBCSD report *From Challenge to Opportunity*	www.wbcsd.org
Business for Social Responsibility online magazine	www.bsr.org/CSRresources/Leading Perspectives
ISO Working Group on Social Responsibility's 3rd Plenary International Business Leaders Forum	www.iso.org www.iblf.org

China	www.csrchina.com
European Union	www.acceleratingcsr.eu/en/about/140
New Voice of Business Launch in US	www.newvoiceofbusiness.org
Hawkamah, Dubai	www.hawkamah.org

Responsibilities Sociala launch in Romania	www.responsabilitasociala.ro
Dubai Centre for Corporate Values	www.dccv.ae/about-dccv.html
Business in the Community's *DRAFT*	www.bitc.org.uk/resources/ publications/princip_consult.html
The Business Civic Leadership Center of the US Chamber of Commerce	www.uschamber.com/bclc
ORSE and CSR Europe release CSR in China	www.respact.at/content/repact.news. article/2348.html
US Aid Global Development Alliance Report	www.usaid.gov/our_work/global_ partnerships/gda/report2006.html
German Council for Sustainable Development	www.nachhaltigkeitsrat.de/projects/ csr/index.html
German GTZ sponsors *Roundtable for Social Standards and CSR*	www.csr-roundtable.com
Canada's National Roundtable on Corporate Social Responsibility in the Extractive Sector in Developing Countries	www.international.gc.ca/ cip-pic/current_discussions/ csr-roundtables-en.asp
EU Shareholder's rights directive	europa.eu.int/comm/ internal_market/company/ shareholders
EU CSR Website	www.csr-vaderegio.net
Inter-American Development Bank	www.iabd.org
Inter-American Development Banks first Sustainability Review	www.iadb.org/sustainability
IFC's Policy and Performance Standards for Social and Environment	www.ifc.org/policyreview
EU Commission launches European Alliances for CSR	http://europea.eu.int/comm/ enmterprise/csr/policy.htm
IFC launches: *Guide to Biodiversity for the private sector*	www.ifc.org/biodiversityguide
UN Global Impact launches consultation for new Academic Network	www.unglobalcompact.org
UN Global Compact Report *Business Against Corruption*	www.unglobalcompact. org/newsandevents/ recent_publications

UN Finance Initiative and Global Compact launch *Principles for Responsible Investment*	www.unpri.org
OECD launches guidance for companies doing business in countries with weak governance zones	www.oecd.org/daf/investment/ guidelines
UN Draft Declaration on the Rights of Indigenous People	www.ochchr.org/english/issues/ indigeous/groups
UNEP Finance Initiative launches *Show Me the Money: Linking Environmental, Social and Governance Issues to Company Value*	www.unepfi.org
IFC and ILO collaborate on Better Work Program	www.ifc.org/ifcext/media.nsf
UN Secretary General's Special Representative for Business and Human Rights report: *Human Rights and Management Practices of Fortune Global 500 Firms: Results of a Survey*	www.business-humanrights. org/gettingsrated/ unspecialrepresentative www.bsr.org/meta/FG500_Report
World Bank/IFC report *Doing Business: How to Reform*	www.doingbusiness.org
UNEP Finance Initiative's *Sustainability Credit Risk Management Guidelines for Africa*	www.unepfi.org
The Association for Sustainable and Responsible Investment in Asia	www.asria.org/publications
Tokyo Stock Exchange announces plan for CSR Index	www.tse.or.jp/english/ news/2006/200604/060425
SASIX the South Africa Social Investment Exchange	www.sasix.co.za
Bursa Malaysia's CSR Framework	www.klse.com.ny.my/website/bm/ abouy_us/investor_relations/csr
Eurosif's 2006 European SRI Study	www.eurosif.org/publications/ sri_studies
China CSR Map launched by GTZ, CSR Asia, SynTao, others	www.chinacsrmap.org/E_index.asp

III. Impacts shaping global expectations

a. *Global business principles/industry coalitions*

Business and Human Rights Resource Center	www.business-humanrights.org/ Home
Corporation 2020	www.corporation2020.org
Enterprise and Social Policy Instituto Ethos	www.ethos.org.br
Ethical Trading Initiative	www.ethicaltrade.org
European Partners for the Environment	www.epe.be
GAN-NET (Global Action Network Net)	www.gan-net.net
Making Waves: The Centre for Community Enterprise (Canada)	www.cedworks.com/waves.html
Responsible Business Initiative	www.rbipk.org
Tamarack: The Social Economy (Canada)	tamarackcommunity.ca/g3s10_M4C2.html
UN Millennium Development Goals	www.un.org/millenniumgoals
World Economic Forum	www.weforum.org
World Social Forum	www.forumsocialmundial.org.br/index.php?cd_language=2
Covalence	www.eurekalert.org/pub_releases/2006-01/ra-pct010506.php

b. *Global policy, standards*

Covalence	www.eurekalert.org/pub_releases/2006-01/ra-pct010506.php
The Global Sustainability Index	www.global100.org/what.asp
S&P's Stakeholder Relations in Corporate Governance	http://eng.sibirtelecom.ru/r-sp
Fortunes Global 500	http://money.cnn.com/magazines/fortune/global500/2008
Burson-Marstellar and Roper ASW Research	www.csrwire.com/PressRelease.php?id=2262
St. James Ethics Centre	www.socialfunds.com/news/article.cgi/1366.html

Corporate Responsibility Index	www.corporate-responsibility.com. au/PDFs/feedback_example.pdf
Multinational Monitor	http://multinationalmonitor.org
WTO	www.wto.org
Global CSR Reporting Awards	www.standardsusers.org/ files/Global%20CSR%20 Reporting%20Awards%202008. pdf
Conference Board	www.conference-board.org
Business Roundtable	www.roundtable.org
Corporate Citizens Report	www.business-ethics.com

c. Reports, ratings, rankings, surveys

AccountAbility	www.accountability.org.uk
Corporate Citizenship Company, The	www.corporate-citizenship.co.uk
CSRhub	www.csrhub.com
Fair Labor Organization	www.fairlabor.org
Fair Trade Labeling Organizations	www.fairtrade.net
Forest Stewardship Council	www.fscus.org
Global Reporting Initiative (GRI)	www.globalreporting.org
Good Guide app	www.goodguide.org
Innovest Strategic Value Advisors	www.innovestgroup.com
Institute for Global Ethics	www.globalethics.org
ISO Strategic Advisory Group on Corporate Social Responsibility of ISO 26000	www.iso.org
PwC (PriceWaterhouseCoopers)	www.pwc.com/sustainability
Rugmark International	www.rugmark.net
Smith O'Brien	www.smithobrien.com
Social Accountability International (SAI)	www.sa-intl.org
SustainAbility	www.sustainability.com
Sustainable Value Partners	www.sustainablevaluepartners.com

Transfair	www.transfairusa.org
Transparency International	www.transparency.org
Utopies (1993, sustainable development)	www.utopies.com
Verite	www.verite.org

d. Ratings and rankings

50 Best Companies for Minorities (Fortune)	http://money.cnn.com/magazines/ fortune/fortune_archive
100 Best Companies to Work For (Fortune)	http://money.cnn.com/magazines/ fortune/bestcompanies/2008/ full_list/
100 Best Companies for Working Mothers	www.workingmother.com
Best 100 Corporate Citizens (Business Ethics)	www.business-ethics.com
America's Most Admired Companies (Fortune)	www.money.cnn.com/magazines/ fortune
Global Most Admired Companies (Fortune)	www.money.cnn.com/magazines/ fortune
Hispanic Corporate 100	www.hispaniconline.com/buss&finn/ corp100-2005.html
Inner City 100	www.theinnercity100.org
Most Valuable Brands (InTerbrand)	www.interbrand.com/surveys.asp
Corporate Responsibility Index, Top 100 Companies that Count (London Times)	http://news.ft.com
Top 30 Companies for Executive Women	www.nafe.com/index.php
World's Most Respected Companies (PwC and Financial Times)	www.news.ft.com
SustainAbility and the Skoll Foundation launch partnership on social enterprise	www.skollfoundation.org/media/ press_releases/internal/032106.asp http://sustainabilityratings.com/

e. Activists

Corporate Accountability Project	www.corporations.org
Corporate Accountability International	www.stopcorporateabuse.org/cms/ index.cfm?group_id=1000
Corporate Predators	www.corporatepredators.org
Corporate Watch	www.corpwatch.org
Global Exchange	www.globalexchange.org
Human Rights Watch	www.hrw.org
Human Rights Advocates	www.humanrightsadvocates.org
The Multinational Monitor	www.multinationalmonitor.org
Sweatshop Watch	www.corpwatch.org

IV. Press, magazines, newsletters, online

The Guardian	www.guardian.co.uk/environment/2007/aug/15/ ethicalliving1
The Times	http://women.timesonline.co.uk/tol/life_and_style/ women/fashion/article2963696.ece
Le Temps	www.letemps.ch/template/recherche.asp?page=recher cher&contenupage=identification&types=search& artID=220564
Green Biz	www.greenbiz.com/news/2007/11/08/wal-mart-ma rks-spencer-fuel-retail-industrys-green-strategy
Rapaport News	www.diamonds.net/News/NewsItem. aspx?ArticleID=19834
BBC	www.bbc.co.uk

Stanford Social Innovation Review	www.ssireview.org
Business Ethics Magazine launches *Good Company* Radio	http://lime.com/ radio_program_guide
Sierra Club Chronicles	www.sierraclubtv.org/
Value: Tomorrow's Markets, Enterprise & Investment	valuenewsnetwork.com/index.cfm
UNEP's Green TV	www.green.tv
Amnesty International Business & Human Rights	www.amnestyusa.org/business/ index.do
Corporate Governance Asia web site	www.corporategovernance-asia.com

PBS documentary *design* *e2: the economies of being environmentally conscious*	www.pbs.org/designe2
The CRO (Corporate Responsibility Officer Association	www.thecro.com

V. Academic centers, institutes, journals, think tanks

Academic-affiliated organizations and units

Ashridge Center for Business and Society, England	www.ashridge.org.uk/www/ ACBAS.nsf/Web/Ashridge+Centr e+for+Business+and+Society
Aspen Institute Business in Society Program	www.caseplace.org
Bainbridge Graduate Institute	www.bgiedu.rog
Centre for Corporate Citizenship, University of South Africa (UNISA)	www.unisa.ac.za/Default.asp?Cmd= ViewContent&Content=18145
Corporate Citizenship Research Unit at Deakin University (Australia)	www.deakin.edu.au/arts/ccr
Corporate Citizenship Unit at Warwick University (United Kingdom)	www2.warwick.ac.uk/fac/soc/wbs/ research/ccu
Corporate Social Responsibility Initiative, Kennedy School of Government, Harvard University	www.ksg.harvard.edu/cbg/CSRI/ about.htm
CSR Academy	www.csraacademy.org.uk
European Academy for Business in Society	www.eabis.org
European Business Ethics Network	www.eben.org
International Association for Business and Society	www.iabs.net
NetImpact (student organization, founded 1993)	www.netimpact.org
Social Issues in Management, Division, Academy of Management	sim.aomonline.org
Society for Business Ethics	www.societyforbusinessethics.org
Sustainable Enterprise Academy (SEA), York University	www.sustainableenterpriseacademy. com/SSB-Extra/sea.nsf/docs/SEA

Global Network Initiative	www.globalnetworkinitiative.org/faq/index.php#45

Selective academic journals related to business in society

Business and Society	www.bas.sagepub.com
Business and Society Review	www.blackwellpublishing.com/journal.asp?ref=0045-3609
Business Ethics Quarterly	www.pdcnet.org/beq.html
Greener Management International	www.greenleaf-publishing.com/default.asp?ContentID=8
Journal of Business Ethics	www.springer.com/philosophy/ethics/journal/10551
Journal of Corporate Citizenship	www.greenleaf-publishing.com/default.asp?ContentID=7
Organization and Environment	www.coba.usf.edu/jermier/journal.htm
Eurosif and Le Monde begin SRI/CSR series (first article March 14, 2006)	www.lemonde.fr
The New York Times Special Section *The Business of Green* (May 17, 2006)	www.eurosif.org/pub2/lib/2006/03/newsl/sect01.shtml#e0101
Fortune China Magazine's special CSR edition	www.nytimes.com/pages/business/businessspecial2/index.html
(login required; Mandarin)	www.fortunechina.com/topic/m_cover.asp

Selective business membership organizations

Association of Sustainability Practitioners	www.asp-online.org
US Chamber of Commerce Business Civic Leadership Center	www.uschamber.com/bclc/default.htm?n=tb
Business for Social Responsibility (BSR)	www.bsr.org
Business in the Community	www.bitcs.org.uk/index.html
Canadian Business for Social Responsibility	www.cbsr.bc.ca
Caux Round Table	www.cauxroundtable.org
CERES	www.ceres.org
CSR Europe (1995)	www.csreurope.org

Fondacion Empressa y Sociedad	www.empresaysociedad.rog/feys/es
Ethics Resource Center	www.ethics.org
GEMI (Global Environmental Management Initiative)	www.gemi.rog
International Business Leaders Forum	www.iblf.net
New Economics Foundation	www.instituteforphilanthropy.org.uk/re5.html
Utopies World Economics Forum	www.weforum.org
World Business Council for Sustainable Development	www.wbcsd.org
World Council for Corporate Governance	www.wcfcg.net/index.htm

Other institutions

Dubai Code of Conduct	www.dubaifaqs.com/dubai-code-of-conduct.php
Global Ethic Foundation	www.weltethos.org
Green Reporting Forum (Japan, awards)	no website available
International Center for Trade and Sustainable Development	www.ictsd.org
US Department of Commerce, Good Governance Program	www.ita.doc.gov/goodgovernance/
Turkish Ethics Values Foundation	www.ethics.org/l_turkey.html

Alternative ways of measuring quality of life/progress

Calvert-Henderson Quality of Life Indicators	www.calvert-henderson.com
Redefining Progress Genuine Progress Indicator	www.rprogress.org
UN Millennium Goals	www.un.org/millnniumgoals
Committee for Economic Development report	www.ced.org/projects/corporategov.shtml#2006corpgov

Index

Printed in the United States
By Bookmasters